A Doubtful and Perilous Experiment

A DOUBTFUL AND PERILOUS EXPERIMENT

ADVISORY OPINIONS, STATE CONSTITUTIONS, AND JUDICIAL SUPREMACY

Mel A. Topf

OXFORD
UNIVERSITY PRESS

OXFORD
UNIVERSITY PRESS

Oxford University Press, Inc., publishes works that further Oxford University's objective of excellence in research, scholarship, and education.

Oxford New York
Auckland Cape Town Dar es Salaam Hong Kong Karachi Kuala Lumpur Madrid Melbourne Mexico City Nairobi New Delhi Shanghai Taipei Toronto

With offices in
Argentina Austria Brazil Chile Czech Republic France Greece Guatemala Hungary Italy Japan Poland Portugal Singapore South Korea Switzerland Thailand Turkey Ukraine Vietnam

Published by Oxford University Press, Inc.
198 Madison Avenue, New York, New York 10016

Library of Congress Cataloging-in-Publication Data

Topf, Mel A.
A doubtful and perilous experiment : advisory opinions, state constitutions, and judicial supremacy / Mel A. Topf.
p. cm.
Includes bibliographical references and index.
ISBN 978-0-19-975676-6 (hardback : alk. paper)
1. Advisory opinions–United States–States. 2. Judicial review–United States–States.
3. Constitutional law–United States–States. I. Title.
KF4579.A38T67 2011
347.73'12–dc22 2011007838

---

1 3 5 7 9 8 6 4 2

Printed in the United States of America on acid-free paper

Note to Readers
This publication is designed to provide accurate and authoritative information in regard to the subject matter covered. It is based upon sources believed to be accurate and reliable and is intended to be current as of the time it was written. It is sold with the understanding that the publisher is not engaged in rendering legal, accounting, or other professional services. If legal advice or other expert assistance is required, the services of a competent professional person should be sought. Also, to confirm that the information has not been affected or changed by recent developments, traditional legal research techniques should be used, including checking primary sources where appropriate.

(Based on the Declaration of Principles jointly adopted by a Committee of the American Bar Association and a Committee of Publishers and Associations.)

CONTENTS

ACKNOWLEDGMENTS

The idea for a study of state supreme court advisory opinions came, by chance, out of my six years as a member of a state ethics commission. The commission in Rhode Island has the unusual constitutional power to create its own code of ethics. It is also authorized by the state constitution to investigate public officials for violations of the code, and to impose fines and even to remove from office officials found in violation. During my tenure, the governor on occasion challenged our rules and policies in the state supreme court, whose opinions contributed greatly to defining the extent of the commission's powers. I thought little of it at the time, but the governor's challenges were usually in the form of requests to the justices of the supreme court for advisory opinions. Only later did I come to realize that this apparently innocuous activity of advice-giving raised such serious questions that it was worth writing about.

But neither the realizing nor the writing would have happened without the help and, especially, the encouragement of friends and colleagues.

"Anyone who ever gave you confidence, you owe them a lot," says Holly Golightly in *Breakfast at Tiffany's*. Indeed. It is a pleasure to have this opportunity to acknowledge those who helped me complete this book. I want also, though, to acknowledge those who gave me the confidence to embark on this book in the first place. I owe them a lot.

They include two good friends, always there to support, to guide, and to correct and admonish, in matters legal and otherwise: Rae B. Condon, Esq., and Prof. Robert H. Whorf. Rae and Bob also read and commented on portions of drafts, and Rae assisted me in crucial early stages of research, my sole research assistant. Prof. Robert F. Williams took a phone call in 2008 from someone he never met, and he spent nearly an hour patiently encouraging his caller to begin this book. Prof. Williams also, much later, read and commented on portions of the draft. Prof. Carl Bogus offered the advice and encouragement he freely gives to his students and former students, as the first person I approached about writing a book (and who instructed me to call Prof. Williams). Keith Hawkins first guided me onto the long road of things legal when I met him at Oxford University in the summer of 1985. He gave unselfishly of his time and his astonishing expertise and wisdom. That long road would lead, over the following quarter century, to the world of the law and legal scholarship, to a law degree (thirty-five years after my Ph.D.), to a license to practice law, and to this book. Alyssa Boss, as a student law review editor, first planted the idea of my writing articles on the law. She pressed me to write my first article on advisory opinions, kept me at it, and expertly edited my drafts. She managed to do this and still graduate at the top of her law school class.

I am grateful also to Prof. Edward Eberle, who read a complete draft, and to W.O. Farber, who provided information and insights about a South Dakota constitutional convention to which he was a delegate. It may not be considered proper to claim that any group of people is superior to others. But librarians, in their dedicated, unassuming and expert way, have been without fail and without exception so immensely helpful that I make that claim. Emilie Benoit, of the law library at the Roger Williams University School of Law, patiently and promptly answered many questions. Also at that library, Thelma Dzialo aided me in searching for congressional documents from the New Deal era and Nan Balliot helped me find many sources. Ann Eichenger of the South Dakota State Library sought out documents for me. My thanks also go to the library staff at Harvard Law School, especially Deanna Barmakian for her help and initiative in finding obscure (and in one instance, missing) records; to the staff of the John Hay Library at Brown University; to Steven Grimes of the Rhode Island State Archives; and to the Massachusetts Archives, the Massachusetts Historical Society, the Rhode Island Historical Society, and the law libraries of New York University and Stanford University.

My thanks to President Roy Nirschel and Provost Laura de Abruna of Roger Williams University for their approval of releases from teaching duties during fall 2010, which permitted this book to be completed in reasonable time, and to former President Anthony Santoro, who granted me a special sabbatical in 2001–2002, allowing me to attend New York University School of Law that year. My thanks also to my book team at Oxford University Press, who subjected my book to excellent editorial supervision and were a pleasure to work with. They Include Chris Collins, Michelle Lipinski, Emily Perry, Jessica Picone, Maureen Cirnitski and Viswanath Prasanna.

* * * * *

Portions of this book were adapted from the following articles.

Communicating Legitimacy in U.S. Supreme Court Decision, 12 LANGUAGE AND COMMUNICATION 17 (1992).

The Jurisprudence of the Advisory Opinion Process in Rhode Island, 2 ROGER WILLIAMS L. REV. 207 (1997).

The Advisory Opinion on Separation of Powers: The Uncertain Contours of Advisory Opinion Jurisprudence in Rhode Island, 5 ROGER WILLIAMS L. REV. 385 (2000).

State Supreme Court Advisory Opinions as Illegitimate Judicial Review, 2001 L. REV. MICH. ST. U.–DET. COLL. OF LAW 101.

The Origins and Early History of Supreme Judicial Court Advisory Opinions in Massachusetts, 7 MASS. LEGAL HIST. 21 (2001).

INTRODUCTION

It was Colorado Chief Justice Helm who, over a century ago, called his court's constitutional duty to advise the governor and legislature "a doubtful and perilous experiment."[1] We think of giving advice as relatively innocuous. The advisees are entirely free to ask for the advice when and if they choose, and to follow the advice or not as they please. And when the justices' advice is a fully nonjudicial service to the other branches to assist them in their duties, the advice having no force of precedent, entirely nonbinding on those seeking advice or on anyone else (as most advising justices claim), it seems rather harmless. Further, such advice has its advantages. It permits judges to advise on, say, whether a pending bill is constitutional, well before the bill becomes law, takes effect, then perhaps is challenged in litigation, and after that, at considerable expense and delay, found unconstitutional on appeal. Hence in the ten states with statutory or constitutional provisions providing for their supreme courts' advising the legislature or executive, the advising would seem to be unobjectionable. What could seem doubtful, much less perilous, about this?

This book attempts to answer the question by way of offering a narrative about state supreme court advisory opinions. I want to show that such opinions are more significant and more problematic, and indeed more doubtful and perilous, than they may at first seem. "For each provision in a state constitution," writes Robert F. Williams, "no matter how seemingly trivial, there is a story to be told."[2] This is a story about the way advisory opinions have triggered controversies over separation of powers, due process, and other fundamental doctrines, and over judicial independence. It is about the advising justices' own, remarkably open uneasiness, even hostility, toward what the advisory justices in one state called "this peculiar obligation," and it is the story of how they and others responded, often uneasily and defensively.[3] It is a story as well about the role of advisory opinions in Progressive and New Deal thinking about the nature and goals of government, and it is about judicial review and, ultimately, about advisory opinions' relation to judicial supremacy. It is about advice itself as an instrument in the exercise of political power and as a check on that exercise, and about the inherent tension between the two and the contributions of that tension to constitutionalism. And since advisory opinions have long been rejected outright in the federal judiciary, it is a story of an instance of

---

[1] *In re Senate Resolution Relating to Senate Bill No. 65*, 21 P. 478, 479 (Colo. 1889).

[2] Robert F. Williams, *Introduction: The Stories of State Constitutional Law*, 18 Nova L. Rev. 715, 716 (1994).

[3] The quote is from *Opinion to the Governor*, 191 A.2d 611, 614 (R.I. 1963).

"pure" state constitutionalism, one that will, I hope, contribute to the larger narrative about state constitutionalism.

Once we look around for advisory opinions in American judicial history and jurisprudence, like the pigeons of St. Marks they seem to be everywhere, in and about virtually all of justiciability doctrine, in the origin and through the jurisprudence of declaratory judgments, flitting in and out of the enduring debates over separation of powers and due process, especially in the modern, administrative state, and—warily, uneasily—around judicial review and judicial independence, and in eighteenth-century anger about plural office holding and in twenty-first-century debates about the power of the judiciary.[4]

I want to recover from its obscurity the story of state supreme court advisory opinions and its relation to American constitutionalism. I will argue that the responses to advisory opinions reveal a remarkably consistent group of concerns over two centuries, not only about the role of the judiciary in a constitutional republic, but about the extent to which advisory opinion authority and jurisprudence developed along with the stature and power of the judiciary. In particular as the U.S. Supreme Court "embraced an expansive role for the federal judiciary,"[5] state supreme courts have followed, with, as I will show, the ten advisory opinion states using their advisory jurisdiction to legitimize assertion of judicial supremacy or at least to allow themselves to be subject to pressures from the political branches into doing so. Finally, as a story of "governmental power, separated and shared," this book tells about advisory opinions as a remarkable but ultimately failed experiment in state constitutionalism.[6]

This narrative has little in the way of Whig history, that is history here as steady and purposeful progress in the development of advisory opinion jurisprudence, or as progress toward the acceptance of its practice, or as neat rationales for why some states came to adopt state supreme court advisory jurisdiction—some in the eighteenth century, some in the nineteenth, some in the twentieth—or for why other states did not. What Simon Schama proposes applies here, that "in the end we must be satisfied with nothing more than broken lines of communication with the past."[7] Yet we can manage to construct a narrative about different states responding differently to a provision unique to state constitutions, originating in an unremarkable English and colonial practice. Advisory opinions serve as an example of how state constitution making has "served as forums for confronting . . . principles and institutions of governance that have gone uncontested at the national level."[8] What unifies the story of state supreme court advisory opinions, despite its "abrasions, agonisms, drift, and tensions," is a constitutional discourse centering over two centuries and more on the question of how

---

[4] The St. Marks image is adapted from EVELYN WAUGH, BRIDESHEAD REVISITED 197 (1945).

[5] Thomas Healey, *The Rise of Unnecessary Constitutional Rulings*, 83 N.C. L. REV. 847, 871 (2005).

[6] The quoted phrase is from Robert F. Williams, *Foreword: A Research Agenda in State Constitutional Law*, 66 TEMP. L. REV. 1145, 1147 (1993).

[7] SIMON SCHAMA, DEAD CERTAINTIES (UNWARRANTED SPECULATIONS) 325 (1991).

[8] John J. Dinan, *Framing a "People's Government": State Constitution-Making in the Progressive Era*, 30 RUTGERS L. J. 933, 937 (1999).

power in a republic should be apportioned in order to check its otherwise inevitable abuse.[9]

A Brief Definition

A state supreme court advisory opinion is the response by the court's justices, rendered at the request of either the governor or a house of the legislature, on legal or constitutional questions pending before the requesting authority.[10] While the nominal purpose is to provide legal advice to the requesting authority, in reality the primary purpose of advisory opinions "seems to be to avoid the enactment of unconstitutional statutes."[11] Advisory opinions may cover many types of requests on a wide variety of legal or constitutional issues, and no attempt at classifying them seems to capture any quality to the questions sent to the justices. Here is a fairly typical grouping of subjects of advisory opinions:

- Constitutional rights
- Elections and reapportionment
- Governmental powers
- Fiscal issues
- General governmental mechanics
- Miscellaneous[12]

Different advisory opinion states may focus on different subjects. In New Hampshire, for example, taxes were for a while addressed incessantly in advisory opinions. Between 1913 and 1959, of ninety advisory opinions rendered, thirty-three covered taxes of all kinds, with at least one each on property, cigarettes, gasoline, income, inheritance, sales, airplane fuel, franchise, stock in trade, and dividend and interest.

---

[9] The quote is from KEN I. KERSCH, CONSTRUCTING CIVIL LIBERTIES 11 (2004) (discussing "Whiggish narratives of constitutional development").

[10] Definitions have always been largely similar. Ellingwood in 1918, for example, called it "the advice of the judges who compose the court of last resort in a given jurisdiction, rendered at the request of certain executive or legislative organs." ALBERT R. ELLINGWOOD, DEPARTMENTAL COOPERATION IN STATE GOVERNMENT vii–viii (1918).

[11] Note, *Advisory Opinions on the Constitutionality of Statutes*, 69 HARVARD L. REV. 1302, 1304 (1956).

[12] Charles M. Carberry, *The State Advisory Opinion in Perspective*, 14 FORDHAM L. REV. 81, 108–09 (1975). Farina, in her study of Massachusetts advisory opinions, offers these groups: appointment or removal of executive officials, finances, scope of legislative powers, electoral process, and procedural. Cynthia R. Farina, *Supreme Judicial Court Advisory Opinions: Two Centuries of Interbranch Dialogue*, *in* THE HISTORY OF THE LAW IN MASSACHUSETTS: THE SUPREME JUDICIAL COURT 1692–1992, at 353, 367–69 (Russell K. Osgood ed., 1993). Persky offers the following: revenue and expenditures, intergovernmental disputes, criminal law, individual rights, and remedial legislation. Jonathan D. Persky, *Ghosts That Slay: A Contemporary Look at State Advisory Opinions*, 37 CONN. L. REV. 1155, 1195–1205 (2005). Other classifications are in ELLINGWOOD, DEPARTMENTAL COOPERATION 99–146; Oliver P. Field, *The Advisory Opinion—An Analysis*, 24 INDIANA L.J. 203, 210 (1949); Hugo A. Dubuque, *The Duty of Judges as Constitutional Advisors*, 24 AMERICAN L. REV. 369, 378–82 (1890).

It is sometimes difficult to tell what underlying issues were behind requests for advice since there is usually no record from courts below, no adversarial proceeding to bring out clashes of opinions that might have sparked the request. Often the request is simply a letter of a few sentences from the requesting authority presenting the question. Many advisory opinions appear, at any rate, to be mundane, on details of legislative procedure for example, or salaries for a commission.[13] Many, however, arise out of major controversies and crises of the time, on segregation-related violence in Alabama in the early 1960s, for example, or fluoridation of drinking water, or the firings of teachers in the 1950s for refusing to testify about membership in the Communist Party, or Prohibition, or discrimination against Chinese under the Fourteenth Amendment's Equal Protection Clause, or voting rights of soldiers away during the Civil War or of African Americans after the *Dred Scott* decision.[14]

Important Elements of Advisory Opinion Jurisdiction

The ten advisory opinion clauses now in effect are generally alike, probably owing to their common origin in the Massachusetts advisory opinion clause. (All current advisory opinion provisions are collected in Appendix A.) Several of the clauses' elements have

---

[13] *E.g.*, *In re Opinion of the Justices*, 99 Mass. 636 (1868) (advising that a bill is not presented to the governor unless "laid before the governor personally" and not merely sent from the legislature to the secretary of state); *In re Opinion of the Justices*, 203 N.W. 462 (S.D. 1925) (advising on the validity of appropriations of salaries for members of an auditing commission, advising that they are valid if the amounts in question are specified and limited).

[14] *Opinion of the Justices*, 156 So.2d 639 (Ala. 1963) (advising that governor has authority to send police to places "where, in process of school desegregation, civil insurrection and sabotage are threatened"); *Opinion of the Justices of the Supreme Court in Response to Questions Propounded by the Governor of Delaware*, 243 A.2d 716 (Del. 1968) (advising that fluoridation of water a reasonable exercise of the police power); *Opinion of the Justices to the House of Representatives*, 126 N.E.2d 100 (Mass. 1955) (advising that statute requiring discharge of college teachers refusing to waive Fifth Amendment rights and to testify on Communist Party membership is unconstitutional); *Opinion of the Justices to the House of Representatives*, 127 N.E.2d 663 (Mass. 1955) (advising that statute requiring discharge of public school teachers refusing to waive Fifth Amendment rights and to testify on Communist Party membership is constitutional); *Opinion of the Justices, Relative to the Eighteenth Amendment of the Constitution of the United States*, 160 N.E. 439 (Mass. 1928) (advising that statute permitting a ballot initiative on public opinion about the repeal of the Eighteenth Amendment is unconstitutional, as mere statement of popular opinion without effective force of law, but rather "something in substance vain and inoperative"); *In re Opinion of the Justices*, 94 N.E. 558 (Mass. 1911) (advising that it is unconstitutional to make it a criminal offense for women under twenty-one to enter a Chinese restaurant or hotel, or for a Chinese restaurant or hotel to serve such women); *Opinion of the Justices of the Supreme Judicial Court on the Constitutionality of the Soldiers' Voting Bill*, 45 N.H. 595 (1864) (advising that bill to permit New Hampshire soldiers to vote "at the places where the voters may be," held constitutional); compare *In re The Right of Electors in the Military Service of the United States*, 102 A. 913 (R.I. 1918), and *Opinion to the House of Representatives*, 25 A.2d 360 (R.I. 1942) (advising that state constitution does not permit voting outside the state, including those in military service); *Opinion of the Justices of the Supreme Judicial Court, on Question Propounded by the Senate*, 44 Me. 505 (1857) (advising that "free colored persons of African descent . . . are entitled to vote" in Maine).

played significant roles in the development of advisory opinion jurisprudence and in the controversies that are addressed later in this book.

Mandatory or discretionary. Six of the ten advisory opinion provisions command the justices to render advisory opinions whenever requested, typically stating that the requesting authority "may require" or has "the authority to require" the opinions of the justices, or that the justices "shall" advise or, a bit redundantly, "shall be obliged" to advise.[15] The justices in these states frequently affirm their obligation, sometimes owing to their manifest uneasiness about their advising duties. The Rhode Island justices, for example, in 1961 were expressly reluctant to render an advisory opinion "academically" on a question whose answer could have no effect. They answered anyway "[w]ith some misgivings," since, they said, "we are obliged to respond."[16] Similarly, the Colorado supreme court, soon after it was given advisory duties, opined that a question to them from the governor pertained exclusively to the legislature, and for the justices to render an advisory opinion would conflict with the state constitution's separation of powers provision. But, they said, "we do not feel at liberty to decline answering; we feel constrained by the imperative command of the constitution to give our opinion."[17]

A former Maine chief justice opposed the idea that the Maine justices under their constitution could refuse to advise. Like it or not the "justices have no discretion in the matter," he said. Their opinion is not "requested" under the advisory opinion provision; it is "required." "There is no suggestion that [the justices] may choose whether or not to give it."[18] In light of the mandatory language, one of the most significant changes in advisory opinion practice—"a most startling development"—occurred in the latter half of the nineteenth century, when advising justices began to assert their authority over when to advise and when not.[19]

In Alabama the requesting authority may "request" an advisory opinion of the justices, which the justices have explicitly ruled means that they may not be required to advise.[20] The remaining three states (Delaware, Florida, and Michigan) join Alabama in holding that advising is discretionary, despite some ambiguous language in their provisions. In Florida and Michigan the requesting authority may only "request" an opinion, as in Alabama. Delaware's advisory opinion provision provides that the justices "may

---

[15] Colorado, Maine, Massachusetts, New Hampshire, Rhode Island, and South Dakota. Missouri's advisory opinion provision, rescinded in 1875, was also mandatory.

[16] *Opinion to the Governor*, 174 A.2d 553, 554 (R.I. 1961).

[17] *In re Speakership of the House of Representatives*, 25 P. 707, 708 (Colo. 1890). The state's advisory opinion clause was introduced in its 1886 constitution.

[18] Lucilius A. Emery, *Opinion of the Justices*, 11 Maine L. Rev. 15, 16 (1917). While sitting as chief justice a decade earlier, Emery wrote to oppose advisory opinions. This is discussed in Chapter 2, which studies attacks on advisory opinions. *See* Lucilius A. Emery, *Advisory Opinions from Justices*, 2 Maine L. Rev. 1 (1908).

[19] This is the focus of Chapter 3. The quote is from R. K. Hoffman, *Why Not Advisory Opinions for Illinois?*, 31 Chi.-Kent L. Rev. 141, 149 (1952).

[20] *See, e.g.*, *Opinion of the Justices*, 394 So.2d 957, 959 (Ala. 1981) (The Alabama advisory opinion provision, "[u]nder a long prevailing view, . . . [has] been considered as privileging—but not requiring—the individual justices of the Supreme Court to give advisory opinions.").

give" their opinion, which is discretionary enough, though it adds that they do so "whenever the Governor of this State or a majority of the members elected to each House may by resolution require [an advisory opinion] for public information, or to enable them to discharge their duties." The term "require" here seems to connote "need" of the opinion rather than a demand on the justices. The justices themselves have not ruled specifically on this.

The distinction between mandatory and discretionary advisory opinion provisions has largely, though not entirely, diminished, since all advisory justices, as we will see in Chapter 3, have set standards for deciding when to render advisory opinions, regardless of the authorizing language.

The requesting authority. The requesting authority—the branch authorized to request advisory opinions—is either the executive or either house of the legislature. The advisory opinion provisions of eight states permit all three to seek advice.[21] Requests from either legislative house must usually be a "formal and collective action" of the house, and not merely a request by some members, even a majority, or by the house's leaders alone.[22] Delaware's advisory opinion statute uniquely permits the legislature to request opinions only jointly, by "a majority of the members elected to each house," prohibiting each house from seeking advice independently of the other. Two states, Florida and South Dakota, permit the governor but not the legislature to seek an advisory opinion.[23]

"Justices" or "the court" as advice-giver. This apparently minor distinction has triggered major discussions and rulings about the nature of advisory opinion authority, as we will see. Advisory opinion provisions in seven of the ten states refer to the advice-giver as "the justices of the supreme court" or the like.[24] In three states—Colorado, Michigan, and South Dakota—the advisory opinion provisions refer only to the "supreme court" as the advice-giver. On that apparently slight difference has arguably

---

[21] Massachusetts and New Hampshire originally specified that requests must be made by "the governor and the council," apparently jointly. (Originating in the colonial and early state governments, "governor and council" signifies the "government" in the European sense—the executive). New Hampshire's advisory opinion provision still includes the phrase, but in Massachusetts the constitution was amended in 1964 to "the Governor *or* the Council." Mass. const. amend. lxxxv (emphasis added). The issue was first raised in 1913 when the justices refused to answer a request from the governor alone, requiring a joint request, despite earlier advisory opinions granted to the governor or the council alone. *See Answer of the Justices*, 102 N.E. 644 (Mass. 1913); *see also* Farina, *Supreme Judicial Court Advisory Opinions*, 364–65.

[22] *Reply of the Supreme Court to a Communication from Certain Members of the House of Representatives in the General Assembly*, 191 A. 269 (R.I. 1937) (refusing to advise since a request from a majority of the members of the House is not a formal action of the House); *In re Advisory Opinion (Chief Justice)*, 507 A.2d 1316, 1318 (R.I. 1986) (refusing to advise in part because request was from House and Senate leaders only, and "[n]o formal action was taken in a collective fashion" by either house).

[23] *See* J. F. Hagemann, *The Advisory Opinion in South Dakota*, 16 S.D. L. Rev. 291, 300 (1971), on attempts by the South Dakota legislature to have the governor in effect transfer requests for advice on the constitutionality of pending legislation to the court, with some success.

[24] The Alabama, Delaware, Florida, and New Hampshire provisions refer to the "justices of the supreme court." Maine and Massachusetts refer to the "justices of the supreme judicial court," the high courts' name in those states. Rhode Island's advisory opinion provision refers to the "judges of the supreme court."

rested a major doctrinal distinction regarding the important issue of whether advisory opinions are binding or whether they are mere advice, binding on no one. The general standard is that if the advice-givers are designated as "justices" or "judges," then the advice comes from each member of the court, not from the court, and so represents their individual, personal opinions. In the three states where the provisions refer to the "supreme court," interpretations of that phrase conflict. In Colorado, the supreme court called it one of the "peculiar features" of the state's advisory opinions clause that it refers to the "supreme court" as advice-giver, and this early on led the court to assert a nonbinding doctrine. Since "it is the court, not the justices, that must answer, . . . our responses . . . have all the force and effect of judicial precedents."[25]

South Dakota's advisory opinion provision originally referred to "the judges of the supreme court" as advice-giver, but they nonetheless held that their advisory opinions are binding. Without explanation, the court in 1897 mentioned the governor's authority "to obtain from the judges ex parte legal opinions having the force and effect of judicial precedents." It may have been in order to justify their refusal to advise in one instance since the advice there would infringe on the rights of individuals, which of course would not be the case were the advice nonbinding.[26] In 1972 the South Dakota constitution's advisory opinion clause was amended by removing the words "judges of the" so that the provision refers only to the court, reinforcing the court's advisory opinions as binding.[27] In Michigan the supreme court simply held that their advisory opinions are not binding. In a long footnote in the court's fifth advisory opinion, the court set forth a jurisprudence of advisory opinions, beginning with stating that "[i]t is important to emphasize that an advisory opinion does not constitute an opinion of the Court and is not precedentially binding."[28]

Limits on types of requests. The advisory opinion provisions with one exception have one or both of two broad limitations on the type of questions that are permitted. These have become both the foundation and the rationale for the development of a jurisprudence of advisory opinions. First, four states limit requests to constitutional questions (Alabama, Delaware, Florida, and Michigan). Six states require that the requesting authority seek advice only "upon important questions of law" and "upon solemn occasions," phrases in the original Massachusetts advisory opinion clause and adopted by Colorado, Maine, Michigan, New Hampshire, and South Dakota. (Michigan is the only state whose advisory opinion provision refers both to these two phrases and to constitutional questions.) Rhode Island is the exception, the only state

---

[25] *In re Resolution Relating to Senate Bill No. 65*, 21 P. at 479. The Colorado court has also ruled that since its advisory opinions are binding opinions of the court, a majority of the justices must agree to the advice rendered. *In re Interrogatories Propounded by McNichols*, 350 P.2d 811 (Colo. 1960).

[26] *In re Resolution No. 30*, 72 N.W. 892 (S.D. 1897).

[27] S.D. const. am. Art. 5, sec. 5.

[28] *In the Matter of the Requests of the Governor and the Senate on the Constitutionality of Act No. 294 of the Public Acts of 1972*, 208 N.W.2d 469, 471 (Mich. 1973). The court cited a concurring opinion to its first advisory opinion asserting this point. *Advisory Opinion re Constitutionality of P.A. 1966, No. 261*, 149 N.W.2d 443 (Mich. 1967) (Black, J., concurring).

whose provision includes neither the two phrases nor limiting advice to constitutional questions. The provision requires only that the justices give their opinions "upon any question of law."

Permitting briefs and oral argument. Although briefs and arguments have increasingly become part of advisory opinion proceedings (a subject discussed below), seven states' advisory opinion provisions are silent on this. In these states the justices have discretion to permit briefs and argument, either from interested parties or amici curiae, and they generally permit them on an irregular basis, apparently depending on the perceived degree of public interest or importance. After receiving a request for advice, the justices may issue an order requesting or inviting briefs or argument, or both, either from specific organizations, departments, or persons such as the attorney general, or, as an open call, to any organization or person interested in the question.[29]

Three advisory opinion states, however, expressly provide for briefs and argument, though in two of them, Alabama and Delaware, they are at the discretion of the justices, so that it does not seem to be much different from the seven advisory opinion provisions that are silent on this. In Alabama the advisory opinion statute provides that the justices "may" receive briefs "from other attorneys as amici curiae," and, similarly, Delaware's advisory opinion statute provides that the justices "may" appoint a member of the state bar to brief or argue the legal issues.[30] Florida is the only advisory opinion state where the justices, since 1968, must permit "interested persons to be heard on the questions presented." Tied to this is the requirement that the justices not render their opinion "earlier than ten days from the filing and docketing of the request [for briefs], unless in their judgment the delay would cause public injury"[31] This presumably is to permit sufficient time to those wishing to argue or submit briefs.

Time constraints. Michigan's advisory opinion provision is the only one that specifies a narrow period in which advisory opinions may be requested, which makes the provision "uniquely constraining."[32] The requesting authority may seek an opinion on the constitutionality of legislation "only after it has been enacted into law but before its effective date." The court has several times refused to render an opinion on this ground.[33]

---

[29] *E.g.*, *In re Request for Advisory Opinion Regarding Constitutionality of 2005 PA 71*, 712 N.W.2d 450 (Mich. 2006) (Order, requesting attorney general to submit brief, and inviting submissions from the state Bureau of Elections, the state's Democratic and Republican parties, and "[o]ther persons or groups interested in the determination of the question presented in this matter," all of whom "may move the Court for permission to file briefs amicus curiae on either or both sides of the submitted question.").

[30] Ala. Code sec. 12-2-11, and Del. Code Ann. Tit. 10, sec. 141(b). Both are included in Appendix A.

[31] Fla. const. art. 14, sec. 1(c). *See* T. A. Smiljanich, *Advisory Opinions in Florida: An Experiment in Intergovernmental Cooperation*, 24 U. Fla. L. Rev. 328, 332 (1972).

[32] Persky, *Ghosts That Slay*, 1194.

[33] *E.g.*, *Request for Advisory Opinion on Constitutionality of 1975 PA 222*, 235 N.W.2d 745 (Mich. 1975) (Advice refused because statute already in effect.); *Request for Advisory Opinion on the Constitutionality of 1975 PA 195 and 196*, 236 N.W.2d 62 (Mich. 1975) (Statute already in effect.); *Request for Advisory Opinion on the Constitutionality of 1979 PA 57*, 281 N.W.2d 322 (Mich. 1979) ("A bill which does not become a law

* * *

Advising those in power, a little-studied but ubiquitous activity, is fraught with political tensions and questions of legitimacy. Chapter 1 presents a theory of the relation of advising to the exercise of power. I want to throw light on what this book argues is the untenable position that advising duties compel a purportedly independent judiciary to maintain. The chapter then addresses the question of why and how advisory opinions ended up in some state constitutions. For decades after their creation beginning in 1780, the advisory opinions provisions were rarely used and drew little attention and no controversy. Then, suddenly, at the 1820 Massachusetts constitutional convention, Joseph Story attacked with striking virulence the Massachusetts advisory opinion provision, and the debate has not ended. Chapter 2 recounts the progress of these attacks, and explains it in part by the rising stature of the judiciary together with the increasingly sharply defined conception of separation of powers. The chapter also reviews the rejection of advisory opinions in the judiciaries of the other forty states and the federal government, that is, wherever they were not specifically authorized. In these jurisdictions there developed a distinct jurisprudence of rejection, applied in such doctrines as standing or adequate and independent state grounds.

Chapters 3, 4, and 5 look into the responses to the attacks on the legitimacy of advisory opinions. First is the story of the reluctance, often the downright hostility, of the advising justices. Chief Justice Helm's comment, made in an advisory opinion, that the judicial duty of advising was a "doubtful and perilous experiment" was not extreme or unusual. Very likely no other state or federal constitutional provision has sparked such judicial animosity as have the advisory opinion provisions. Out of this animosity there arose a fully developed jurisprudence of advisory opinions. This was in large part a set of restrictions depicting when the justices will refuse to advise, often put forth assertively if not defiantly in the face of advisory opinion provisions that were, for the most part, mandatory and giving the justices no express authority to refuse, as one justice or another would occasionally point out.

Chapter 4 considers the arguments offered in defense of advisory opinions, appearing relatively late in their history and, surprisingly, doctrinally weak. The defenses rarely confronted the doctrinal attacks—separation of powers, due process, judicial independence, and so on—relying instead on the "soft" arguments about the practical advantages of advisory opinions in avoiding the delay and expense of appellate review, and in increasing cooperation and harmony among the governmental departments. Soft as they may have been, the defenses carried considerable force during the Progressive and New Deal eras, and indeed proposals to amend the U.S. Constitution to require the Supreme Court to render advisory opinions to Congress were put forth as a remedy to staunch the federal courts' invalidating New Deal legislation.

---

unless this Court takes some action has not 'been enacted into law' within the meaning of this Constitutional provision.").

One often and strongly asserted defense of advisory opinions is a passive one. Advisory opinions are nonbinding. They are not judicial decisions, and, advising justices have said for nearly two centuries, these opinions carry no precedential weight. This nonbinding doctrine is therefore a sort of cure-all for the doctrinal attacks on advisory opinions. They cannot, it is argued, offend separation of powers or violate due process rights, or do other harm, since they are not binding anyway. Chapter 5 looks at the nonbinding doctrine and its challenges, and concludes that it is questionable both in theory and in fact. Some contend, but few believe, that when the justices of the state's highest court offer advice, it may be safely ignored. The nonbinding doctrine is in the curious position within advisory opinion jurisprudence of being firmly established in theory and almost entirely ignored in practice.

A recent development in some advisory opinion states is the waiving by the justices of their restrictions on advising when they believe that the question propounded is of sufficient public important to warrant the waiver. Chapter 6 argues that this waiver, together with the weaknesses of the nonbinding doctrine and the enduring doctrinal challenges to the legitimacy of the advisory jurisdiction, result in a disturbingly unchecked capacity for the advising justices to affect the political process. Further, this expanded advisory power reinforces judicial supremacy in the advisory states. The chapter, and the book, conclude that "this peculiar obligation" is an interesting but failed experiment of state constitutionalism.

The book has several appendices. Appendix A collects all advisory opinions provisions now in effect. Advisory opinions outside the United States, both in other countries and in the international courts, is a subject necessarily beyond the scope of this book, but Appendix B offers a note on it. Appendix C is an annotated bibliography of all articles (and the two books) devoted wholly or mainly to advisory opinions that were published from the 1880s through 2010. For readers interested in advisory opinions in a particular state, Appendix D offers a checklist of articles devoted to advisory opinions in a single state, organized by state.

There are no current comprehensive listings of advisory opinions. Several sources offer extensive lists. Albert R. Ellingwood, Departmental Cooperation in State Government, 269–300, includes what was intended to be a complete list of all advisory opinions to 1917. A list of advisory opinions in five states (Colorado, Maine, Massachusetts, New Hampshire, and South Dakota), complete to 1937, is in Oliver P. Field, "The Advisory Opinion—An Analysis," 24 IND. L.J. 203, 223–229 (1949). South Dakota's advisory opinions to 1971 are listed in John F. Hagemann, "The Advisory Opinion in South Dakota," 16 S.D. L. REV. 291, 306 (1971). Florida's advisory opinions to 1971 are in T. A. Smiljanich, "Advisory Opinions in Florida: An Experiment in Intergovernmental Cooperation," 24 U. FLA. L. REV. 328, 340–345 (1972). Alabama's advisory opinions to 1951 are in C. Dallas Sands, "Government by Judiciary—Advisory Opinions in Alabama," 4 ALA. L. REV. 1. 40–43 (1951).

1 }

This Peculiar Obligation

THE PROBLEM OF STATE SUPREME COURTS AS ADVISORS

Advising and Political Power

Advising within the corridors of power is typically understood essentially in functionalist terms, as an accommodation to assist those in power. From that viewpoint judges advising the legislature or executive on matters legal or constitutional seems neither to carry much peril nor to be an especially peculiar obligation. I want to show, however, that advising carries inherent political tensions and asserts a kind of balance of power. It is inescapably an instrument in the exercise of power and, at the same time, a check on that power. This creates the tension and the balance, which has been institutionalized in many ways, and which, for purposes of this book, is integral to the constitutionalism that underlies the role of judges as advisors, and which ultimately explains how advisory opinions must be judged a failure.

This problem of advising's relation to the dynamics of power has been little studied, despite the importance and ubiquity of advising in government in general and in executive decision-making in particular. Advising has not held any prominent place in political theory. Despite its frequent mention in political narratives from earliest times, there appears to be no comprehensive analysis devoted to the theory and practice of advising in the exercise of political power. That a ruler must receive wise counsel has been so frequently noted without credible opposing views that it seems to amount to little more than proverbial, literally so in the Bible, where among many other places the Book of Proverbs reminds us that wisdom is "with those who take advice" and that "without counsel plans go wrong," and even that "by wise guidance" one may successfully wage war.[1]

There are risks. The advice may be rejected, for example, and the advisor may suffer the often serious consequences of loss of face. In the Second Book of Samuel one advisor, Ahithophel, usually gave counsel so good that to consult him "was as if one consulted the word of God: so was all the counsel of Ahithophel esteemed." During Absalom's rebellion against his father King David, Ahithophel gave advice that "pleased

---

[1] Proverbs 13:10, 15:22, and 24:6. Biblical passages are from the Revised Standard Version, in *The New Oxford Annotated Bible* (1977).

Absalom and all the elders of Israel." Absalom, however, sought another advisor, heard him, and then rejected Ahithophel's advice in favor of the other's. "When Ahithophel saw that his counsel was not followed, he saddled his ass, and went home to his own city. And he set his house in order, and hanged himself."[2] There may of course be consequences for the ruler as well. The chronicler of the First Book of Kings attributes the tragic and permanent split of the northern tribes of Judah from the southern tribes of Israel to Rehoboam, King Solomon's son and successor, who rejected the advice of "the old men" in favor of advice from "the young men who had grown up with him."[3] Machiavelli was wary about advisors but nonetheless wrote that rulers "should always take counsel," even if with great care, "because men will always turn out bad for you unless they are forced to be good." Further, rulers must "choose their advisors very carefully" because the "plague of flattery is hard to escape."[4]

While advice has always been perceived as important in governance, discussion of its roles has usually been limited to its three functions. Assistance is the most common and plausible function of advice-giving, especially with modern government's dependence on experts, and the one usually attributed to the duty of judges to advise. A second and equally important function of advising is legitimization. "From an advisory body . . . the Government obtains . . . political legitimacy with respect to its policy decisions."[5] This, we will see, is an important if unacknowledged purpose of state supreme court advisory opinions. The legitimacy that advising lends to executive decision-making stems in great part from the implicit consent of advisors who have taken part in influencing the decision. "Men often oppose a thing, merely because they have had no agency in planning it," wrote Hamilton.[6] For example, a major cause of the failure of Franklin Roosevelt's "court packing" bill, one modern commentator believes, was his "decision to eschew the counsel" of congressional leaders, which "left many Democrats feeling disgruntled at having been excluded from the process of making a decision of such import."[7]

A third, more controversial, rationale is shielding the executive. Rulers and their defenders have forever attributed bad decisions to poor advice, deflecting attacks away from the ruler. Imperial China, however alien its governance is to us, is entirely typical in this respect. "However pointed the criticism [of government], it was always sheathed in implications that the emperor, though wise and good, had been misled and deceived

---

[2] 2 Sam. 16:23–17:23.

[3] 1 Kings 12:1–12:20.

[4] NICCOLO MACHIAVELLI, THE PRINCE, Ch. 23, at 67, 68 (1513; Norton Critical Edition 1977).

[5] Cummock v. Gore, 180 F.3d 282, 292 (D.C. Cir. 1999). *See also* Jay S. Bybee, *Advising the President: Separation of Powers and the Federal Advisory Committee Act*, 104 YALE L.J. 51, 58–59 (1994). Stuart Jay notes that while judges advising the British King was long accepted, it was still controversial in part because seeking the advice "from the judges often appeared to be a thinly disguised means of legitimizing the King's plans. Early commentators understood this pretext." STUART JAY, MOST HUMBLE SERVANTS: THE ADVISING ROLE OF EARLY JUDGES, 14 (1997).

[6] ALEXANDER HAMILTON, FEDERALIST No. 70, 454 (1788; Benjamin F. Wright ed., 1996).

[7] BARRY CUSHMAN, RETHINKING THE NEW DEAL COURT: THE STRUCTURE OF A CONSTITUTIONAL REVOLUTION, 14 (1998).

by unscrupulous attendants and advisors."[8] The notion that advisors make good "cover" for a ruler that is always "wise and good" does not of course find easy acceptance in a republic. One reason the Federal Convention rejected proposals to create an advisory council to "assist the President in conducting the Public Affairs"[9] was, two modern observers note, that it would "serve to shield the President from responsibility for the actions he might take."[10] At the Convention, James Wilson, joining in opposition to the advisory council, asserted that such a council "oftener serves to cover, than prevent malpractice."[11] James Iredell, addressing the North Carolina ratifying convention, opposed the council in part because the president "might easily combine with his Council, and it might be impossible to fix a fact upon him. It would be difficult to know, whether the President or Counsellors were most to blame."[12]

Looking at advising in this functionalist way tends to downplay the extent to which advising has been integral to the dynamic of governing. What is often not attended to is the tension inherent in advising between executive and advisors as the latter become imbued with separate and competing interests, in fact become institutionalized to guarantee the power to affirm those interests. This gives rise to a distinct duality. On the one hand is advising's accommodationist mode, serving to assist or shield or legitimize the executive. On the other is the less noted but inescapable mode of advising as agonal, acting to assert the advisors' interests against the executive and, more importantly, to check the power of the executive. When, in signing the Magna Carta, King John agreed, in the presence of a hostile barony, not to assess aids (specific payments to the king) unless he first obtained "the common counsel of the realm," he specified who will advise ("archbishops, bishops, abbots, earls, and greater barons"), how he will secure the advice (through their meeting "at a fixed place" and "for a fixed date"), and by means of formal notice and summons that "will state the reason for the summons."[13] These attributes of the advising process are "fixed"—guaranteed—both in the sense of being institutionalized and in the sense of firmly documented checks on the monarch's power. Both testify to the potential for conflict—the inherent tension—between monarch and magnates, and to the constant need to control a recalcitrant king, and to assert, when needed, legitimate resistance to the king. The centrality of this advice-giving and -receiving process is evident in the extent to which one modern (though indirect)

---

[8] Charles O. Hucker, The Traditional Chinese State in Ming Times (1368–1644) 41 (1961). While Hucker describes imperial rule in the Ming Dynasty, the observation serves generally.

[9] 2 Records of the Federal Convention of 1787 at 342 (Max Farrand ed., 1937).

[10] Steven G. Calabresi & Saikrishna B. Prakesh, *The President's Power to Execute the Laws*, 104 Yale L.J. 541, 628 (1994).

[11] 1 Records of the Federal Convention, 97.

[12] 2 Debates on the Constitution 874 (Library of America 1993). The U.S. Constitution's Opinions Clause (U.S. Const. art. ii, sec. 2, cl. 1), to be discussed later in this chapter, was apparently the result of the rejection of the advisory council provision, intending to preserve some kind of formal advising activity for the president. *See* Saikrishna B. Prakesh, *Hail to the Chief Administrator: The Framers and the President's Administrative Powers*, 102 Yale L.J. 991, 1004–7 (1993) (on the history of the Opinions Clause at the Federal Convention).

[13] Magna Carta, Cap. 14, in J. C. Holt, Magna Carta 455 (2d ed. 1992).

descendant of this advising process—Parliament—embodies the same attributes, even if nowadays only as formalities, however much the relation of British monarch and Parliament has changed over time. When the Queen dissolves Parliament and calls for a new one, it is by "Our Royal Will and Pleasure" but also, as her 2010 Proclamation stated in its first sentence, "by and with the advice of Our Privy Council," and her calling of another Parliament was specifically in order "to meet Our People, and to have their Advice in Parliament." And, in accord with Magna Carta, the Proclamation further stated that the members of Parliament are to be called by summons, with the time and place specified.[14]

The tension and the balance inherent in advice-giving create a crucial political space for government action. Advising contributes centrally to what Hannah Arendt called "the reality of the public realm" which "relies on the simultaneous presence of innumerable perspectives and aspects in which the common world presents itself and for which no common measurement or denominator can ever be devised."[15] Multiple perspectives are not just a rationale for advice. It is only through them that, as Arendt puts it, "can worldly reality truly appear."[16] Hence the virtue of multiple advisors. When James Madison wrote that in "a multitude of counselors there is the best choice for honesty, if not wisdom," he was echoing sources as diverse as the Bible and Thomas Hobbes, echoing, that is, traditional wisdom.[17]

It could reasonably be argued that in government, in the beginning was advising, and it is by and through advising's tension and balance that government became institutionalized. Early on, the English kings' ministers acted as advisors, chosen by the king at his pleasure.[18] While the advising was at first likely informal, it gradually institutionalized itself in various ways—Ordinary Council, Privy Council, Cabinet Council, Great Council, King's Council, Commons, Lords—such that the advising became what George O. Sayles called "an essential element in the fabric of government."[19] From the

---

[14] *A Proclamation for Dissolving the Present Parliament, and Declaring the Calling of Another*, April 12, 2010. Retrieved from the website of the LONDON GAZETTE on August 4, 2010.

[15] HANNAH ARENDT, THE HUMAN CONDITION 57 (Anchor ed. 1958).

[16] *Id.*

[17] James Madison, Letter to Edmund Randolph, May 1, 1781, *in* 1 THE WRITINGS OF JAMES MADISON 19 (1999; Gaillard Hund ed.,). *See, e.g.*, Proverbs 15:22 ("With many advisors [plans] succeed."); Proverbs 24:6 ("[I]n abundance of counselors there is victory."); THOMAS HOBBES, LEVIATHAN, Part II, Ch. 25, 109 (1651; Everyman's Library 1914) ("A man that doth his business by the help of many prudent Counsellors . . . does it best.").

[18] SYDNEY W. BAILEY, BRITISH PARLIAMENTARY DEMOCRACY 166 (2d ed. 1962).

[19] GEORGE O. SAYLES, THE KING'S PARLIAMENT OF ENGLAND 127 (1974). Sayles traces the institutionalization and bureaucratization of British governmental bodies, an early stage of which is "the place in the administration occupied by the body whose right and duty it was to advise and, according to one view, control the king—the baronage." SAYLES, 21. Sayles points to the example of the Provisions of Oxford (1258), which reintroduced the position of justiciar, now as head of the judiciary. Under the Provisions, the king (then Henry III) "must act by the advice of the baronage," Sayles says. "Elaborate and intricate arrangements were made for the council that was to advise, and in effect, to control the king." *Id.* at 52. Despite the apparent similarity, "council" and "counsel" are not related, the former deriving from the Latin (*concilium*) for an assembly or meeting, the latter from the Latin (*consiliare*) for advising. In English, however, "the two words were, from the beginning, completely confused." OXFORD ENGLISH DICTIONARY, at "Council."

beginning the advising function was perceived as a "reciprocal duty of the barons to give counsel and the king to receive it."[20] As the advising became institutionalized, the tension between being the king's advisors and asserting their own rights and powers was, and would remain, central to the reification and development of British government. The Lords, for example, were thus part of His Majesty's Government on the one hand, and a check on it on the other, a "dual function of the Lords" that "was always well recognized."[21] From the tension inherent in this duality "there evolved the written and unwritten contracts of the [English] constitution."[22] In other words, this tension and duality constituted the political space in which much of English constitutional government would develop.[23]

The judges as other advisors would act within this duality, between their role as advisors serving their monarch and judges asserting the law that both ruler and ruled must obey, a duality all the stronger as the judiciary became institutionally distinct and independent. Before the later eighteenth century there was little distinction between judges and others in the king's service in that they represented the person of the king or the king-in-Parliament. "In the earliest formulation of the English courts, judges were the king's surrogates—his servants—for dispensing justice. . . . Over time, even though the Lords and the Crown evolved into independent institutions, the judges continued to have ties with both the executive and the upper house of Parliament. Calling on judges

---

[20] *Id.* at 26. The relation is only a formal one now, modern governance and power completely in the hands of Parliament, but it is a formality that is carefully maintained. The Duke of Windsor set out the modern relation directly enough. "Whenever the Prime Minister 'advises' the King he is using a respectful form of words to express the will and decision of the Government. The King is virtually bound to accept such 'advice.' Furthermore, he cannot seek such 'advice' elsewhere. However, in the exercise of his undoubted powers, if he chooses not to accept the 'advice' thus formally tendered, then his Ministers resign." THE DUKE OF WINDSOR, A KING'S STORY 343 (1951). Quoted in BAILEY, BRITISH PARLIAMENT, 21. The Duke of Windsor (the former Edward VIII, who abdicated in 1936) was of course writing from the viewpoint of a former king, but his description is accurate enough.

[21] *Id.* at 127. For a full treatment of the subject, including the growing institutionalization of advising, see generally Bryce Lyon, *A Constitutional and Legal History of Medieval England* (2d ed. 1980).

[22] WALTER LIPPMANN, THE PUBLIC PHILOSOPHY 31 (1955; Mentor edition 1966) (describing the relation between king and lords as "the tension and the balance of the two powers—that of the ruler and the ruled"). Lippmann was studying the development of what he called "the malady of democratic states as a derangement in the relation between the mass of the people and the government." *Id.* at 30.

[23] Or, likely, the space in which any government's constitution developed. The notion that at some early stage of government rulers governed purely through personal advisors is likely a kind of fiction or myth, akin to a Lockean state of nature (which David Hume called "a mere philosophical fiction"), since there appears to be no historical evidence for such a stage of government. In the historical record the advising is institutionalized in some form of assembly, the althing or witenagemot, tribal elders, war councils, synods, and so on. The assembly was reified by the ruler's nominal call for advice, so that governance was, so to speak, conceived as a formal process of advising. Bryce Lyon, in his account of the Anglo-Saxon witenagemot, describes it as "an arbitrarily organized assembly completely undefined in composition. When any number, great or small, of the aristocrats were asked by the king to give him counsel and consent or to witness and license a royal act, this seemed to constitute a witenagemot. It is certain that on all important matters the king consulted with the witenagemot to secure its advice and consent." LYON, CONSTITUTIONAL AND LEGAL HISTORY 46. Hume's comment is in DAVID HUME, A TREATISE OF HUMAN NATURE 493 (1739; ed. L. A. Selby-Bigge, 1888, 1967).

for counsel was thus by long tradition a prerogative of monarchs and Lords."[24] Well into the eighteenth century, and so in the judiciaries of the American colonies, judges were routinely and unremarkably among the king's (or his royal governors') advisors. This duty certainly applied to their judicial activity itself. "The court is the King's court."[25] It was not until after 1700 that the judges, until then "in theory and practice servants to the Crown," achieved some "formal independence by way of statutorily mandated life tenure."[26] Through the eighteenth century, though, "the legality of extrajudicial opinions was accepted even by those who criticized the practice."[27]

Despite occasional reluctance to advise, indeed sometimes a "general aversion" to it,[28] the judges never expressed doubt about the legality or constitutionality of their duty to advise. Certainly no claims were made that the judiciary was some sort of separate branch of government, independent of the king or the Lords.[29] In the colonies as well, while the eighteenth century witnessed and increasingly recognized the distinction between legislative and judicial functions, "there never came a point at which the colonies operated under the theory of separated branches that would have called into question the practice of judges providing advice to the executive and legislature."[30] The reluctance, though, is significant as the inevitable result of this group of advisors becoming institutionalized and so gaining both its own identity and a sense of its own power and legitimacy on the one hand and the duty to exercise that power in the interests of justice on the other. It is at this point that the judges'—or any advisory bodies'—duties put it into a condition of uneasy duality, both subject to the ruler's demand for advice and asserting its own positions, positions often intended to check the power of the ruler.

The councils created by the early state constitutions paralleled the judges in that they were also entirely typical in the irreconcilable tension between their nominal purposes of advising the executive and their acting as a check on legislative or executive power. The Massachusetts constitution of 1780 established "a Council for advising the Governor," whose advice must be recorded and the record made available to the legislature.[31] The provisions regarding the council say little about its purpose or rationale, but

---

[24] JAY, MOST HUMBLE SERVANTS, 6.

[25] SAYLES, KING'S PARLIAMENT OF ENGLAND, 28.

[26] JAY, MOST HUMBLE SERVANTS, 48. On the development of judicial independence in eighteenth-century England and the colonies, and the controversies surrounding judicial independence, see Joseph H. Smith, *An Independent Judiciary: The Colonial Background*, 124 U. PA. L. REV. 1104 (1976). A study of early judicial independence in each of the original thirteen states is in Scott Douglas Gerber's forthcoming A DISTINCT JUDICIAL POWER: THE ORIGINS OF AN INDEPENDENT JUDICIARY, 1606–1787 (2011).

[27] Jay, Most Humble Servants, 19.

[28] P. C. McKeever & B. O. Perry, *The Case for an Advisory Function in the Federal Judiciary*, 50 GEORGETOWN L.J. 787 (1962) (noting that the judges' aversion to advising can be traced back at least to 1485 in England).

[29] *See* JAY, MOST HUMBLE SERVANTS, 22 ("[D]espite reservations of some prominent judges and notwithstanding occasional resistance to providing . . . counsel to the executive, there was overall acceptance of its lawfulness prior to the nineteenth century."). On the reluctance of the English judges to advise, see also Note, *Comment: Advisory Opinions*, 21 YALE L.J. 83 (1911).

[30] Jay, Most Humble Servants, 52.

[31] Mass. const. of 1780, Ch. II, sec. iii. All seven articles in section iii are devoted mainly to the council.

that is asserted very directly in the "Address" of the convention when it sent the proposed constitution to the people for ratification. The paragraph discussing the council begins: "To prevent the Governor from abusing the Power which is necessary to be put in his hands, we have provided that he shall have a Council to advise him at all Times and upon all important Occasions."[32]

Various proposals for a council of revision were presented at the Federal Convention, but the councils would have direct veto power over legislation and no advisory duties. A leading opponent of the proposed constitution, George Mason, opposed it in part because there would be no advisory council, creating, he believed, the danger of the department heads becoming the president's council, "the worst and most dangerous of all ingredients for such a council," apparently because in that case the advice would not be truly independent and so could not act as a check on the president.[33] Proposals were made for a purely advisory executive council similar to the British king's Privy Council, and Pinckney proposed an advisory opinion provision similar to that of Massachusetts, but none of these passed.[34]

The only residue of the Federal Convention's proposals regarding advising the president is the Opinions Clause, which provides that the president "may require the Opinion, in writing, of the principal Officer in each of the executive Departments, upon any Subject relating to the Duties of their respective Office."[35] Innocuous as it is, it suggests the anxiety of the framers about retaining at least a modicum of the ancient advisory procedures. "The history of the [Opinions] Clause reveals that it was meant to assuage those who felt that the President would be lacking advice about how to exercise his constitutional powers."[36] The clause had been tied to the last of the proposals to give the president an advisory council from whose members (which included the Chief Justice) the president could seek written opinions, though the president was not

---

[32] Oscar Handlin & Mary Handlin, eds., Popular Sources of Political Authority: Documents on the Massachusetts Convention of 1780 at 438 (1966). The council is also cited in the constitution's section on the executive, where the focus is on the executive's right to demand advice. The section provides that the governor has authority to convene the council "at his discretion."

[33] 2 Records of the Federal Convention, 637–640. *See also* M. J. C. Vile, Constitutionalism and the Separation of Powers 155 (1967).

[34] At the Convention proposals for executive councils were debated on June 4, July 21, August 15, and August 20. Pinckney's proposal for an advisory opinion provision came up on August 20. *See* 1 Records of the Federal Convention, 107–14; 2 Records of the Federal Convention, 73–83, 294–302, 334–44. *See also* Jay, Most Humble Servants, 66–74, for a full account of the Convention's proposals for a council of revision and a privy council. All the states' original constitutions, except those of New Hampshire and New York, provided for an executive council to the governor with an official advisory duty. It was the task of these councils, as one constitution simply put it, "to advise the Governor in the execution of his office." North Carolina const. of 1776, Art. XVI, *in* The Federal and State Constitutions (1909; F. N. Thorpe ed.). Retrieved December 11, 2007, from the website of the Avalon Project, Yale Law School. *See also* Willi P. Adams, The First American Constitutions 266–71 (1980).

[35] U.S. Const., art. 2, sec. 2.

[36] Steven G. Calabresi & Saikrishna B. Prakesh, *The President's Power to Execute the Laws*, 104 Yale L.J. 541, 627 (1994).

required to accept the advice.[37] The proposal, in which the advisory body was called the "Privy Council," was sent to committee, which returned only the Opinions Clause. The Convention was apparently concerned that the council would become a shield. "The Convention rejected the Council because it wanted to leave no room for doubt: The President was accountable for decisions."[38]

Advising, then, whatever its place in constitutional structures never escapes its essential duality in the exercise of power. Advisors to the executive inevitably assert a restraint on the executive's exercise of power, assert their own rights, powers, and privileges, and reaffirm their constitutional place, even as they nominally assist or guide the executive. The executive receiving advice may be seeking legitimacy or protection or an affirmation of its authority, or have other intentions and purposes. This is the tension inherent in the advisory authority of the state supreme court justices in the states requiring or permitting the justices to advise the executive or legislature. It may help explain the puzzling question of why the judges' advising duty, for centuries common and unremarkable in England and colonial America, needed to be constitutionalized.

Everlasting Disgrace: Advisory Opinions, Constitutions, and the Evils of Plural Office Holding

THE MASSACHUSETTS CONVENTION OF 1779–1780

Why were advisory opinions constitutionalized? The first state constitutional advisory opinion provision appeared in the Massachusetts constitution of 1780, still in force today: "Each branch of the legislature, as well as the governor or the council, shall have the authority to require the opinions of the justices of the supreme judicial court, upon important questions of law, and upon solemn occasions."[39] Most if not all subsequent advisory opinions provisions were modeled on this one.[40] It is not clear why it was entrenched in the constitution at all. The centuries-old practice of judges advising the legislature and executive had been accepted, even if with some reluctance, in England,

---

[37] 2 Records of the Federal Convention, 342. This account of the "Privy Council" proposal and the Opinions Clause relies chiefly on Calabresi & Prakash, *The President's Power*, 627–29.

[38] Calabrasi & Prakesh, *The President's Power*, 628. The authors argue that the Opinions Clause was intended to limit presidential authority "by implicitly forbidding the President from demanding opinions on subjects not related to the statutory duties of an [executive branch] officer." This was "in sharp contrast" to the British king, whose Privy Council was obliged to advise on any question the king chose to put. *Id.* 634. For a critique of the view of Calabresi and Prakash on the Opinions Clause, *see* Martin S. Flaherty, *The Most Dangerous Branch*, 105 Yale L.J. 1725, 1795–98 (1996). Calabresi and Prakash wrote largely in response to Lawrence Lessig & Cass Sunstein, *The President and the Administration*, 94 Col. L. Rev. 1 (1994), in particular their view of the Opinions Clause regarding the relation of the president to the executive branch department heads.

[39] Mass. Const. pt. II, ch. 3, art. 2.

[40] *See, e.g.*, James B. Thayer, *Advisory Opinions*, *in* Legal Essays 42, 45 (1908; 1st ed. 1885). The creation of the advisory opinions provisions in the other advisory states are reviewed later in this chapter.

where it remained "unremarkable"[41] and carried over to the colonies with no recorded opposition or controversy. No eighteenth-century theory of government in England or America "regarded advisory practices of government as threatening to constitutional safeguards of the judiciary."[42] Further, the advisory opinion clause is the only one of the constitution's five provisions in the chapter on the judiciary that identifies a duty of the judges, and the only one that so much as mentions Supreme Judicial Court.[43]

Before the convention that created the advisory opinion clause in the 1780 Massachusetts constitution, there seemed to be no interest anywhere in the new states in constitutionalizing this generally accepted practice. From May 1776, when the Second Continental Congress proposed that the states adopt written constitutions, until the Massachusetts convention that would adopt the state's 1780 constitution met in 1779, the years were dense with debate on the nature and purpose of constitutions for the states, but surviving records reveal no interest anywhere in an advisory opinion provision. In Massachusetts the subject did not arise in the 1776 and 1777 debates and resolutions calling for the new state's general assembly and council to convene to create a constitution, nor did it arise at that convention.[44] Nothing like an advisory opinion clause appeared in the proposed constitution sent to the people in 1778.[45] The towns decisively defeated it, in many cases stating reasons and commenting on constitutional principles in their results; some, including the towns of Sutton, Lenox, and Essex, at length.[46] Amid the many complaints about defects, and amidst the dozens of proposals for changes, there is no mention of a need for a provision regarding advice from the judiciary to the executive or legislature.

Notwithstanding this silence, the 1780 convention constitutionalized advisory opinions. The reason usually offered for the adoption of the advisory provision is its reception from England. "We may fairly conclude that . . . the advisory opinion in the Massachusetts constitution . . . was a deliberate formulation of the existing English practice."[47] The writer was asserting common knowledge. The Massachusetts justices themselves observed in 1878 that the advisory opinion clause, "as reported in the convention that framed the [1780] Constitution, . . . evidently had in view the usage of the

---

[41] JAY, MOST HUMBLE SERVANTS, 31. *See also* ELLINGWOOD, DEPARTMENTAL COOPERATION, 33; Persky, *Ghosts That Slay*, 1166 ("The advisory opinion itself was a direct adoption of the English practice.").

[42] JAY, MOST HUMBLE SERVANTS, 31.

[43] Of the four other provisions, one establishes a good behavior standard for judicial tenure (art. I); another sets a seven-year term for justices of the peace (art. III); a third is on the "times and places" that the probate judges sit (art. IV); and the fourth requires that appeals of cases relating to probate and to marriage be heard by the governor and council unless the legislature provides otherwise (art. V).

[44] *Journal of the Convention*, *in* Handlin & Handlin, POPULAR SOURCES, 177–89. The convention was held June 1777 to March 1778.

[45] The text of the proposed constitution of 1778 is in Handlin & Handlin, POPULAR SOURCES, 190–201.

[46] *Id.* at 202–365. The Sutton result is at 235–28, Lenox result at 253–58, and Essex result at 324–65. On the Essex result, see GORDON S. WOOD, THE CREATION OF THE AMERICAN REPUBLIC 217–19 (1969); and Alexander J. Cella, *The People of Massachusetts, a New Republic, and the Constitution of 1780: The Evolution of Principles of Popular Control of Political Authority 1774–1780*, 14 SUFFOLK U. L. REV. 974, 992–96 (1980).

[47] ELLINGWOOD, DEPARTMENTAL COOPERATION, 33. *See also* Thayer, *Advisory Opinions*, 45.

English Constitution."[48] This may explain the origins of advisory opinions, but it fails to explain the constitutionalizing of the practice, expressly guaranteeing the authority of the executive and legislature to secure the justices' advice. One writer, one of the few to address this question, suggests that the framers in 1780 "aimed merely at securing coordination between the government, and promoting a uniformity of interpretation that would make for greater justice and efficiency."[49] He offers, however, no evidence to show that the framers had such interests, and the virtues of coordination and efficiency reflect the writer's twentieth century, Progressive biases more than eighteenth-century concerns.[50]

Another writer suggests that the "original purpose [of the 1780 advisory opinion provision] was probably to secure sound advice from experts in the law" since at the time Massachusetts had no attorney general to give such advice. The provision was intended for advice "to solve the initial problems of setting up a new government."[51] However plausible, these reasons do not explain why the practice of judges advising needed to be constitutionalized. One explanation might be that constitutionalizing advisory opinion authority overcomes separation of powers. The 1780 Massachusetts constitution indeed included an explicit separation clause, barring each of the three branches from exercising the powers of the other two, "[t]o the end it may be a government of laws and not of men."[52] The advisory opinion duty does have the effect of requiring the justices, at the demand of either of the other branches, to involve themselves in legislative or judicial decision-making. A constitutional provision would be needed, in this view, to overcome the strictures of an explicit separation of powers provision that requires, in part, that the "judicial shall never exercise the legislative and executive powers, or either of them."[53] This would seem to indicate that the founders of the 1780 constitution were so sensitive to the demands of separation doctrine that they included a specific advisory opinion clause as counterbalance.

This, however, imposes modern thinking about separation of powers on an era when "functional separation of powers as we have come to know it . . . was more apparent than real."[54] The separation clauses in the early constitutions typically gave strong "verbal recognition" to the doctrine, but the doctrine in fact "was vague and permissive" and "easily exploited by different persons for different purposes." In general state government in practice bore little resemblance to the doctrine. "For what more than anything makes the use of Montesquieu's maxim in 1776 perplexing is the great disparity between the affirmation of the need to separate the several governmental departments and the actual political practice the state governments followed. . . . Americans . . . were

[48] *Opinion of the Justices*, 126 Mass. 557, 561 (1878).

[49] Ellingwood, Departmental Cooperation, 33.

[50] Chapter 4 discusses Progressive views of the advisory opinion authority.

[51] Note, *Advisory Opinions on the Constitutionality of Statutes*, 1304.

[52] Mass. Const. 1780, Part I, art. xxx.

[53] *Id.*

[54] Theodore Y. Blumoff, *Separation of Powers and the Origin of the Appointment Clause*, 37 Syracuse L. Rev. 1037, 1052 (1987).

apparently not concerned with a real division of departmental functions."[55] And, relevant to our concerns here, eighteenth-century views of separation of powers often involved only separation of legislative and executive powers, without regard to the judiciary, typically seen as an arm of the executive branch in the colonies.[56] For John Adams himself, author of the draft of the 1780 constitution, separation of powers "chiefly meant . . . the exclusion of the legislature from interference with the executive; otherwise he gave little consideration to the subject."[57]

Why, then, if not substantially concerned about separation of powers, did the convention framing the 1780 constitution think it necessary to sound advisory opinions in the constitution? The contemporary record offers little help. After the proposed constitution of 1778 was defeated at the polls, the Massachusetts House of Representatives called for a convention in September 1779. At its first session, held September 1–7, the convention formed a thirty-member committee to develop a draft constitution. The committee in turn appointed John Adams, Samuel Adams, and convention president James Bowdoin to be a subcommittee charged with producing the draft. This subcommittee left the actual writing to John Adams. His draft included an advisory opinion provision, which remained substantially unchanged through the convention's deliberations and the public debate afterwards, and it retains its place in the Massachusetts constitution today.[58]

The extant records relating to the 1780 convention reveal nothing on the need for a constitutional provision guaranteeing advisory opinions. Neither the original of John Adams's draft, not the records of the subcommittee of three, nor of the committee of thirty, survive.[59] No official record of debate in convention is preserved. None of

---

[55] WOOD, CREATION OF THE AMERICAN REPUBLIC, 153–54. Wood is writing of the original 1776 generation of state constitutions, but the point holds for constitutions developed during the next ten years at least. *See* Gerhard Caspar, *An Essay in Separation of Powers: Some Early Versions and Practices*," 30 WM. AND MARY L. REV. 211, 216 (1989) ("As one reviews the state constitutions adopted between 1776 and 1787 for the ways in which they implemented separation of powers notions, one is struck by the fact that the particulars display an exceedingly weak version of separation of powers."). The "maxim" of Montesquieu is that "[w]hen the legislative and executive powers are united in the same person, or in the same body of magistrates, there can be no liberty." SPIRIT OF THE LAWS, Bk. XI, Sec. 6. Quoted in WOOD, CREATION OF THE AMERICAN REPUBLIC, 152.

[56] *See, e.g.*, JAY, MOST HUMBLE SERVANTS, 49 ("Typical accounts of the judicial power placed it as part of the executive."); Robert F. Williams, *The State Constitutions of the Founding Decade: Pennsylvania's Radical 1776 Constitution and Its Influences on American Constitutionalism*, 62 TEMPLE L. REV. 541, 572 (1989) ("In the early years of the Revolution, the judiciary had almost been forgotten. If anything, it was considered part of the executive power.").

[57] ZOLTAN HARASZTI, JOHN ADAMS AND THE PROPHETS OF PROGRESS, 28 (1952).

[58] This account relies on JOHN ADAMS, 3 DIARY AND AUTOBIOGRAPHY 324 (1961) ("I had drawn up at his [Samuel Adams's] and Mr. Bowdoins [*sic*] request a Constitution for Massachusetts."). The account is confirmed in Samuel E. Morison, *The Struggle over the Adoption of the Constitution of Massachusetts, 1780*, 50 MASS. HIST. SOC'Y PROC. 353 (1917); Handlin & Handlin, POPULAR SOURCES, 25–25; Robert J. Taylor, *Construction of the Massachusetts Constitution*, 90 PROC. OF THE AM. ANTIQUARIAN SOC'Y 317 (1980); RONALD M. PETERS, JR., THE MASSACHUSETTS CONSTITUTION OF 1780: A SOCIAL COMPACT 20–21 (1978); *Editorial Note*, 8 PAPERS OF JOHN ADAMS 228–36 (1989).

[59] *See* 8 PAPERS OF JOHN ADAMS, 235 (1989).

Adams's published writings made reference to the advisory opinion provision.[60] The convention journal cited the passage of the advisory opinion clause with a few changes in wording but without comment or explanation.[61] The *Address of the Convention . . . to Their Constituents*, which accompanied the publication of the convention's final draft in March 1780, discussed the provisions on the judiciary in some detail but made no mention of the advisory opinion clause.[62]

The record of returns of the towns reporting their votes are full of comments on the proposed constitution but reveals virtually nothing on the advisory opinion clause. Here is an account of all the references to the clause. Of the 222 towns reporting their results, twenty-four recorded votes on the clause, but twenty-one of them recorded nothing but the votes.[63] The other three referred to the clause, but the references are brief and obscure. The town of Bellingham simply reported without explanation that the clause was "Rejected."[64] Shelburne reported that it opposed the clause, eleven to none, because the voters opposed a three-branch government.[65] Apparently the advisory opinion clause was viewed as inconsistent with this. Medfield favored the clause but recommended without explanation that the reference to the governor and council be deleted.[66]

Other than these few remarks, there are no substantive references to the Massachusetts advisory opinion provision in all the contemporary records.

PLURAL OFFICE HOLDING

We have nothing in the record, then, that explains the first appearance of an advisory opinion clause in state constitutions. We may, however, be able to draw out a rationale by looking at a minor change from an early version of the clause, and by considering what constitutionalizing such a provision might have signified to the framers.

---

[60] *See* 2 Diary and Autobiography of John Adams 401 (1964; L. H. Butterfield ed.). The convention began consideration of Adams's draft in its second session, which met October 28 to November 12. Adams's diary entries stop the previous July 31, just before he arrived from Europe, and they start again on November 13, as he embarked for the return to Europe. He attended no other sessions of the convention, which dissolved after the constitution was ratified in June 1780. *See also* John R. Howe Jr., The Changing Political Thought of John Adams 82 (1966).

[61] Journal of the Convention, 81–86. The changes were: "Senate" deleted and replaced with "each branch of the legislature"; "judges" deleted and replaced with "Justices of the said Court," which in turn was changed to "Justices of the Supreme Judicial Court" in the final version sent to the people. *Id.* at 242.

[62] The complete text of the "Address" is in Handlin & Handlin, Popular Sources, 434–40.

[63] Analysis of the returns relies on *id.* at 473–930.

[64] *Id.* at 746.

[65] *Id.* at 594, 596 ("Article 2d [the advisory opinion clause]. Objections: why we Don't Except this article is we Don't alow of three Branches."). Separating branches of government was still the focus of some controversy. The danger perceived was that under separation of powers the "branches of government served to divide and become rival spheres of authority." For many, the best check on power was frequent popular elections. *See* John Philip Reid, Legislating the Courts: Judicial Dependence in Early National New Hampshire 7 (2009).

[66] *Id.* at 783 ("[Article] 2d. Expunge the words Governour and Counsel.").

By 1780 it was generally accepted in the new nation that a provision placed in a written constitution separated it from government and protected it from political forces. A constitution was seen as "superior to the entire government"[67] because it is "antecedent to, more fundamental than, and controlling the operation of institutions of government."[68] We should not confuse this distinction with later, almost mystical ideas of American constitutionalism. In the 1780s, Robert Williams observes, there had as yet "developed no special aura around the notion of a constitution. . . . Veneration of constitutions did not figure prominently in public discourse."[69] James Willard Hurst noted that it was only after 1880 "that the constitutional idea fully enters the catalog of basic American beliefs." The first framers of constitutions were writing "in a very practical atmosphere." They "saw their work in terms of contests for power and advantage, or the security of power and advantage already won."[70] One purpose served by an explicit grant of constitutional authority was to distinguish and protect an exception to some general constitutional prohibition.[71] The advisory opinion clause was likely put forth as such an exception. Despite lack of documentary evidence, a visible marker lies in the earliest extant draft of the 1780 Massachusetts constitution, that which the committee of thirty reported to the convention. Here is the advisory opinion clause as it appeared in that draft, together with the immediately preceding clause:

> [Art.] II.—No Justice of the Superior Court of Judicature, Court of Assize, and General Gaol Delivery, shall have a seat in the Senate, or House of Representatives.
>
> [Art.] III.—The Senate, nevertheless, as well as the Governor and Council, shall have the authority to require the opinions of the judges upon important questions of law, and upon solemn occasions.[72]

The "nevertheless," later removed when the convention transposed Article II to another place,[73] may be a key to the problem. The word signifies that that the judges' advisory duty shall stand, notwithstanding the previous clause's general prohibition against judges sitting in the legislature. The advisory opinion clause was apparently intended as an enumerated exception to a ban on the justices of the Supreme Judicial Court holding another public office, that is, a ban on plural office holding.

---

[67] Wood, Creation of the American Republic, 266.

[68] Bernard Bailyn, The Ideological Origins of the American Revolution 176 (1967). *See also* Adams, The First American Constitutions 63–66 (1980) (reviewing the development of distinctions between legislation and constitution making in the Revolutionary era); Wood, Creation, 273–82; Daniel J. Hulsebosch, Imperia in Imperio: *The Multiple Constitutions of Empire in New York, 1750–1777*, 16 Law & Hist. Rev. 319, 320–26 (1998) (discussing the seventeenth and eighteenth century meanings of "constitution," and noting the development of the distinction between government and a "transcendent constitution").

[69] Williams, *The State Constitutions of the Founding Decade*, 541.

[70] James Willard Hurst, The Growth of American Law: The Law Makers 199–204 (1950). Quoted in Robert F. Williams, State Constitutional Law: Cases and Materials 1080 (1999; 3d ed.).

[71] G. Alan Tarr, Understanding State Constitutions 8 (1998).

[72] Committee of Thirty Draft, Chapter IV, Arts. II and III, *in* Journal of the Convention, 211.

[73] *See* John Adams, 4 The Works of John Adams 255 (1856).

What is the connection? Why would a clause banning an instance of plural office holding be seen as an impediment to the executive or legislature seeking judges' advice, an impediment to be overcome by a constitutional provision securing the authority to seek the advice? The problem seems to have been that the justices appeared to have two offices. First was their position as impartial and independent interpreters of law and administrators of justice. The 1780 constitution provided strong protections, as would the federal Constitution later, by establishing the judiciary as a structurally independent branch and by guaranteeing that the judges' salaries were irreducible and (unique among all officers appointed by governor and council) that they held their office during good behavior.[74] The second office came effectively from the advisory opinion provision, under which the justices held the extrajudicial position of advisors to the executive and legislature. The duty to advise was mandatory, under which the justices left their independent position in a separate branch of government and became subject to the command of the political branches.

Holding two such positions may not be holding two distinct, formal offices, though it does involve two separate sets of duties, one judicial, the other nonjudicial.[75] At any rate it would likely appear to be something like plural office holding as understood then and as widely practiced in England and the colonies.[76] And that was an appearance that struck an extraordinarily sensitive nerve. The reaction to plural office holding in the Revolutionary era was intense, often extreme, and the origin of a constitutionalized power to seek advice from the judges was very likely situated in this heated issue. Plural office holding, though it might appear to us to be at bottom a question of separation of powers, was for that time a different, more concrete and more sinister matter. Separation of powers, as a doctrine anyway, was of course prominent and influential among the founders, about which they wrote and spoke at length, but as we have seen, while by 1787 half the state constitutions had three-branch separation clauses, "[s]eparation dogma loomed larger in the rhetoric of . . . early state constitutions than in the reality of state politics."[77]

---

[74] Mass. Const. of 1780, Part the First, art. xxx (establishing executive, legislative, and judicial branches and prohibiting each from exercising the powers of the others; *id.* at Part the Second, Ch. II, sec. I, art. Xiii ("Permanent and honorable salaries shall be established by law for the Justices of the supreme judicial court"); *id.* at Ch. III, art. I ("All judicial officers . . . shall hold their offices during good behavior."). Anger over plural office holding may have been as much a motive for creating constitutional separation of powers as Montesquieu's theories, especially in the street, where suspicions of such abuses of power as "corruption" (the sale of offices to placemen) may have been more important than the theories of a French intellectual.

[75] On the question the distinction between multiplicity of offices and multiplicity of duties, see Note, *Extrajudicial Duties of Judges*, 47 Iowa L. Rev. 1026, 1031 (1962) (reviewing state and federal law restricting judges' extrajudicial activities).

[76] *See* Scott D. Gerber, A Distinct Judicial Power: The Origins of an Independent Judiciary, 1606–1787, manuscript at 140 (forthcoming 2011).

[77] Blumoff, *Separation of Powers and the Origins of the Appointments Clause*, 1051–52.

While Americans "were apparently not concerned with a real division of departmental functions,"[78] plural office holding was something else altogether. It was the target of intense hostility during a period when constitutionally "[w]hat was at stake was how the new state governments would be structured and which groups in society would have the dominant policy-making role under the new governments. . . . Quite literally, control over the new governments, which would exercise plenary power without any higher authority, was up for grabs."[79] If half the states' constitutions had separation clauses by 1787, *all of them* had plural office holding prohibitions from the start in 1776. Americans' resentment of plural officeholders was "translated . . . into their constitutions in 1776, striking out against those oligarchies of office holding by which men had so long selfishly fed their own interests and fattened themselves at the expense of the public."[80] All the 1776 constitutions (except South Carolina's) were clear especially on prohibiting persons holding public office from profiting by being members of the legislative assemblies.[81] Samuel Adams wrote in 1775 of "our patriots [who] have loudly and very justly complained [about] a plurality of places incompatible with each other being vested in the same person," a practice which, he said, if allowed to continue under the new governments "will be an everlasting disgrace."[82] In that same year the town of Worcester gave instructions to its representative to the state legislature warning of the danger of the legislature's appointing "each other into the most lucrative executive offices."[83] As early as 1766 it had been a major point of controversy in Massachusetts. Thomas Hutchinson, last royal governor in the state, was sharply attacked for holding plural offices. While lieutenant governor in 1766 he was also chief justice, an office, the speaker of the house wrote, "most certainly incompatible with that of a politician. . . . The integrity of the judge may sometimes embarrass the politician but there is infinitely more danger in the long run of the politician's spoiling the good and upright judge."[84]

The hostility was rooted in the era's deep-seated suspicion of concentrations of power. The suspicion was reflected in bicameralism, separation of powers, checks and balances, and federalism, measures the framers, in their "hatred of plural office holding," took in part "to prevent particular individuals from amassing absolute power by jointly holding office in more than one institution of government at the same time."[85] Separation of powers itself was often as not justified as a means to this end: the "violation of separation of powers that they [the early state constitutions] most guarded against

---

[78] Wood, Creation, 153

[79] Williams, *The State Constitutions of the Founding Decade*, 545, 549–50.

[80] Wood, Creation, 156.

[81] *Id.* at 158.

[82] Letter from Samuel Adams to Elbridge Gerry, Oct. 29, 1775, quoted in Ellen E. Brennan, Plural Office-Holding in Massachusetts, 1760–1780, 114 (1945).

[83] Brennan, Plural Office-Holding in Massachusetts, 111.

[84] Bernard Bailyn, The Ordeal of Thomas Hutchinson 112, 117–18 (1974). *See also* Brennan, Plural Office-Holding in Massachusetts, Chapter 1, on the controversy over Hutchinson's office holding.

[85] Steven G. Calabresi & Joan L. Larson, *One Person, One Office: Separation of Powers or Separation of Personnel?*, 79 Cornell L. Rev. 1045, 1053 and 1047 (1994).

was dual office-holding,"[86] because separation, in limiting plural office holding, "was initially a means for preventing political corruption rather than a principle describing fundamental institutional relationships."[87]

The despised "corruption" of the British Parliament by the monarch and his ministers was a negative model for the framers of the new state constitutions. The incompatibility principles embodied in the state and federal constitutions "seemed to have been grounded less in separation-of-powers theory than in the Framers' vivid memory of the British Kings' practice of 'bribing' members of Parliament . . . and judges with joint appointments to lucrative executive posts."[88]

Plural office holding received extensive attention at the Massachusetts convention. The separation of powers clause was to be "made concrete by the provision of Chapter VI, art. II," the plural office holding clause.[89] Independence of department was to be "attained primarily by a separation in office-holding, and not by a separation of abstract powers of government."[90] When the convention took up the draft's Article II on plural office holding, it considered it much too restrictive. "[A]fter very extensive debates" it was sent to a committee with instructions to "ascertain what offices, to be held under the Commonwealth, shall be declared incompatible with each other; what offices shall disqualify the possessor from holding a seat in either House of Assembly; and also what number and kind of offices, it may be inconsistent with the public good should be held by any one person."[91] The committee reported back with a proposed revision containing a lengthy, detailed list of executive and judicial offices the holders of which would be barred from sitting in the legislature, including "every state office of any significance."[92] The convention accepted most of the committee's list of offices and even added others.[93]

Debate on this continued to the convention's very end. The final version of the clause, now entitled "Incompatibility of and Exclusion from Office," was agreed to and passed only on the last day of the convention and was the last article voted on.[94] When the proposed constitution was sent to the towns, several responded that even this provision

---

[86] G. Alan Tarr, Book Review, 28 Rutgers L. J. 865, 868–69 (1997) (reviewing Marc W. Kruman, Between Authority and Liberty: State Constitution Making in Revolutionary America (1997)).

[87] Donald Lutz, Popular Consent and Popular Control 97 (1980). Bernard Bailyn notes the prohibitions against plural office holding deriving from dangers of corruption and "influence" in The Origins of American Politics 79 (1969).

[88] Calabresi & Larson, *One Person, One Office*, 1050–51 and 1053. *See also* Neal Kumar Katyal, *Judges as Advicegivers*, 50 Stanford L. Rev. 1709, 1727 (1998) (on the proposals at the Federal Convention of 1787 to address plural office holding, and referring to "the Framers' hatred of plural office holding").

[89] Brennan, Plural Office-Holding in Massachusetts, viii.

[90] *Id.* at 5.

[91] Journal of the Constitutional Convention, 65, 211.

[92] Brennan, Plural Office-Holding in Massachusetts, 144–45. *See* Journal of the Constitutional Convention, 81.

[93] Journal of the Constitutional Convention, 138.

[94] *Id.* at 163–66.

was not sufficient, demanding that most if not all judges be barred outright from sitting in the legislature.[95]

Plural office holding was so deeply distrusted and so much in the foreground of public debate as to render suspect those justices comprising a purportedly independent judiciary while holding the second, extrajudicial "office" of advisors at the call of both legislature and executive. An advisory opinion clause constitutionally guaranteed the preservation of a long-accepted practice while protecting the justices from damage to their authority and prestige by the taint of accusation of plural office holding.

Creating Advisory Opinion Jurisdictions

An account of the creation of advisory opinion provisions after that of Massachusetts may be told relatively quickly, in part because the record in most instances is sparse and in part because advisory opinions raised little—often no—debate or even extended discussion at constitutional conventions or in legislatures.

NEW HAMPSHIRE (1784)

In this respect New Hampshire confirms the observation that when states revise their constitutions, one factor in deciding whether simply to borrow a provision from another state "is the salience of the constitutional issue being addressed. If the issue is not salient or controversial, then the tendency is to borrow with little examination readily available constitutional language."[96] New Hampshire's 1784 constitution included an advisory opinion provision modeled closely on the Massachusetts clause.[97] As with Massachusetts, no contemporary records account for the inclusion of the clause. Plural office holding, though, was every bit a live controversy as in Massachusetts.[98] Hatred of plural office holding played a major role in the state's attempts to adopt a new constitution. Soon after the adoption of the constitution of 1776, "[o]ne of the most prevalent complaints was that the legislature was run by a small clique of leaders who held all the responsible offices as well as their seats in the legislature."[99] Some towns went so far as to pass "resolutions condemning the practice of plural office-holding, and the legislature felt compelled in 1778 to call a convention to replace the constitution of 1776."[100] (The 1778

---

[95] Handlin & Handlin, POPULAR SOURCES, 524 (Town of Norton), 528 (Rehoboth), 621 (West Springfield), 715 (Barnstable), 827 (Grafton), 845 (Northborough).

[96] TARR, UNDERSTANDING STATE CONSTITUTIONS, 54–55.

[97] N.H. const. Part 2 (1784). (No article or section number. Now Part 2, art. 74.) The texts of all advisory opinion provisions are in Appendix A.

[98] GERBER, A DISTINCT JUDICIAL POWER, manuscript at 186 (forthcoming 2011).

[99] RICHARD F. UPTON, SEPARATION OF POWERS IN NEW HAMPSHIRE, 46–47 (1938) (unpublished thesis, Harvard Law School), quoted in GERBER, A DISTINCT JUDICIAL POWER, manuscript at 186. My account of the role of controversies about plural office holding in the development of New Hampshire's early proposed constitutions relies on *id.* at 181–94. Gerber's account does not discuss advisory opinions.

[100] *Id.* at 186.

convention was "the first time in the history of the world that a convention was elected and met for the sole purpose of drafting a constitution that was to be submitted to the people for ratification or rejection.")[101] The convention sent three proposed constitutions to the people. The proposals of 1779 and 1781 were rejected. The journals of the sessions are lost. Both of these proposed constitutions were sent to the people accompanied by addresses explaining the respective constitutions, which survive. Neither address refers to the advisory opinion clause. The third proposed constitution, sent out with no address, was accepted in 1783, including the advisory opinion provision which remains today.[102] In all three proposed constitutions the respective sections on the judiciary, including the advisory opinion clause, were nearly identical to the corresponding section of the 1780 Massachusetts Constitution, from which they were clearly derived.

At the state's 1791 constitutional convention, the 1784 constitution's judiciary section was heavily revised, but the advisory opinion clause was left unchanged. This convention journal survives. The report of the convention's Committee on Alterations and Amendments, which proposed revisions to the judiciary section, included no reference to the advisory opinion clause, nor was there any reference to it when the proposed revisions were sent to the people.[103] In short, the records on New Hampshire's constitution-making during this period contain no debate, comment, or explanation regarding the advisory opinion clause.

MAINE (1820)

Maine exemplifies the new states' tendency to model their constitutions on other states, seeking "to avoid controversy."[104] One reason that may have been a consideration for the Maine delegates, is that the creation of the state (by separating from Massachusetts) was the other half of the Missouri Compromise and its attempt to resolve the growing controversy over slavery in the territories.[105] The Maine delegates in 1820 "largely ignored the Massachusetts constitution under which they lived," and looked to several

---

[101] *Id.*

[102] *See* 8 Town Papers of New Hampshire, 834–914 (1875). My thanks to Deanna Barmakian of the Harvard Law School library for her help seeking out obscure materials on the New Hampshire conventions. The earlier conventions in New Hampshire may not have kept journals. *See* Eugene M. Van Loan III, *Judicial Review and Its Limits: Part I (Legitimacy), New Hampshire Bar J.*, 52, 60 (Autumn 2006) (on the history of judicial review in New Hampshire, and noting that "no journal was kept of the debate in the several conventions which crafted the document eventually ratified as [New Hampshire's] Constitution of 1784"). *See also* Susan E. Marshall, New Hampshire State Constitution—A Reference Guide 29 (2004).

[103] Journal of the Proceedings of the Convention of New Hampshire for Revising the Constitution of Said State, 10 N.H. Provincial and State Papers, 63–71 (1875). The convention took up the committee's proposed changes paragraph by paragraph. *Id.* at. 91–112; on the judiciary section, *id.* at 97–100. As to the advisory opinion clause the sole reference is this: "The next [paragraph] respecting the Legislature requiring the opinions of the Supreme Court, etc., was accepted." *Id.* at 100. The revisions to the constitution as it was submitted to the people included no reference to the advisory opinion clause. *Id.* 113–26.

[104] G. Alan Tarr, *Models and Fashions in State Constitutionalism*, 1998 Wisc. L. Rev. 729, 731.

[105] "In February 1820 the U. S. Senate voted to couple the admission of Missouri as a slave state with the admission of Maine as a free state. A further amendment was also passed prohibiting slavery in the rest of the

other states.[106] Nevertheless the delegates did adopt in whole the Massachusetts constitution's judiciary section, including the advisory opinion clause. Ironically, the year Maine adopted the clause, 1820, was the year a Massachusetts convention proposed (unsuccessfully) to delete it from that state's constitution, the earliest instance of advisory opinions becoming a controversy.[107] At any rate, the New Hampshire convention simply adopted the whole of the Massachusetts constitution's article on the judiciary, including its advisory opinion provision, "unanimously," the convention journal records, "without debate."[108] The Maine clause differs from that of Massachusetts only in allowing the council to seek advice independently of the governor.[109] The reference to the council was later removed.

RHODE ISLAND (1842)

Rhode Island was one of the two of the original states (with Connecticut) that held to its royal charter after independence, creating its own constitution only in 1842. The judiciary committee at the state's 1841 constitutional convention proposed an advisory opinion provision similar to that of Massachusetts.[110] But the draft submitted to the convention had no advisory opinion provision. The record is silent on why. The convention was at any rate unsuccessful, and another one convened the following year.[111] The 1842 convention, using a draft from the previous convention, made revisions which included inserting the advisory opinion clause that remains in the constitution today. The Journal of the Convention records simply that the article on the judiciary "was taken up, read, and adopted to stand part of the Constitution."[112]

DELAWARE (1852)

Delaware is one of the two states (with Alabama) that provide for supreme court advisory opinions by statute alone rather than constitutionally.[113] The original statute was enacted in 1852, but advisory opinions seem rarely to have been used over the

---

Louisiana purchase north of the southern border of Missouri." ROBERT A. DEVINE, ET AL., 1 AMERICA PAST AND PRESENT 280 (1995).

[106] Tarr, *Models and Fashions*, 734.

[107] The Massachusetts convention's proposal is discussed in Chapter 2.

[108] DEBATES AND JOURNAL OF THE CONSTITUTIONAL CONVENTION OF THE STATE OF MAINE 1819–'20 [*sic*] (1894), "Article VI. Judicial Power." ("The six sections in this article passed unanimously without debate.").

[109] *See* ELLINGWOOD, DEPARTMENTAL COOPERATION, 40–41.

[110] *Rhode Island Constitutional Convention* (1841), Report of the Judiciary Committee, section 7.

[111] On the unsuccessful 1841 constitutional convention, *see* WILLIAM C. MCLOUGHLIN, RHODE ISLAND: A HISTORY 130 (1978).

[112] JOURNAL OF THE CONVENTION, September 28, 1842 and September 29, 1842. The printed, published version of the adopted constitution changed without comment "any matter of law" to "any question of law."

[113] Del. Code 1852, sec. 482, as amended by 64 Del. Laws, c. 214 (1983). The 1983 amendment allows the legislature as well as the governor to request advisory opinions. Now encoded as Del. Code Ann. Ch. 10, sec. 141.

next century.[114] In 1952 the governor sought an advisory opinion, and for the first time the high court addressed the question of the constitutionality of advisory opinion jurisdiction based on mere statutory authority, given the obvious separation of powers issues that this raises. The court ruled the advisory opinion statute constitutional, in part because advising is a nonjudicial function, and in Delaware "from early time the General Assembly has frequently imposed upon the members of the State judiciary duties of a non-judicial nature," so that "an advisory opinion of the kind required by our statute is not a judicial act; it is more the performance of an advisory function."[115] Further, the Delaware constitution "contains no provision expressly declaring that the three departments of government shall be kept separate," so that separation of powers concerns do not apply.[116]

MISSOURI (1865; repealed 1875)

Missouri's short-lived advisory opinion constitutional provision was introduced in the state's 1865 Reconstruction constitution, and removed from its constitution of 1875, the only instance of the repeal of such a provision.[117] The journal of the convention that framed the 1865 constitution does not explain the inclusion of the advisory opinion provision, but records only two items regarding it. One was to strike "and upon solemn occasions," the other to strike the whole provision. The journal notes simply that both were rejected.[118] The provision, the first in a constitution outside New England, was similar to that of Massachusetts but was the first to limit advisory opinions to questions of constitutional law, and the first to require that the opinions be published along with the court's regular decisions.[119] The record throws no light on the reasons for these innovations,

---

[114] Ellingwood comments in 1918 that "the governor does not seem to have made any attempt to avail himself" of the advisory opinion provision. Ellingwood, Departmental Cooperation, 69. A litigated case in 1930 mentions that advisory opinions "in this state, are usually not reported." State *ex rel.* Satterthwaite v. Highfield, 152 A. 45, 52 (Del. 1930).

[115] *In re Opinions of the Justices*, 88 A.2d 128, 135–36 (Del. 1952).

[116] *Id.* at 137–38. The absence of a separation of powers provision in Delaware's constitution has been balanced by development of a judicial doctrine of implied separation, though this has not had impact on advisory opinions in the state. *See* Elyse H. Wallach, *Constitutional Law—Judicial Branch—Separation of Powers and the Need for an Independent Judiciary to Defend Against a Direct Legislative Encroachment on Its Authority*, 37 Rutgers L.J. 1529, 1538 (2006) (noting that the Delaware constitution "contains no explicit separation of powers provision. Instead separation of powers is implied by the division of authority among three distinct branches."). The court has not addressed the extent to which this implied separation of powers may affect the constitutionality of advisory opinions in Delaware.

[117] *See* Gerald T. Dunne, The Missouri Supreme Court: From *Dred Scott* to *Nancy Cruzan*, 61–65, 75–79 (1993) (on the constitutions of 1865 and 1875). Dunne comments that the "1865 constitution generally resembled those imposed on the states of the defeated South by intrusive, unassimilable, unrepresentative, and alien elements, and the 1875 successor similarly reflected the general return of those areas to consensus control." *Id.* at 64.

[118] Journal of the Missouri State Convention, January 6–April 10, 1865, 169 (March 21, 1865) (1865).

[119] "The judges of the Supreme Court shall give their opinion upon important questions of constitutional law, and upon solemn occasions, when required by the governor, the senate, or the house of representatives;

which would eventually become the practice for all the advisory opinion states. Regarding the provision's removal in 1875, Dunne observes that it was owing to the supreme court's "increasingly swollen docket," but, as we will see in Chapter 2, its removal very likely had much more to do with the Missouri justices' striking animosity toward their advisory duties, and perhaps because the clause was associated with the impositions of the 1865 Reconstruction constitution.[120] The journal of the 1875 convention records no debate on removal of the clause.[121]

FLORIDA (1868)

Florida like Missouri introduced an advisory opinion clause in its Reconstruction-era constitution, though unlike Missouri it retains the clause, much modified, today. The original 1868 provision allowed questions on interpretation of the state constitution "or on any point of law."[122] This broad language was sharply narrowed by an 1875 amendment which deleted "any point of law" and limited the governor to questions on the constitutionality of his executive acts. The governor may seek opinions only "as to the interpretation of any portion of this Constitution upon any question affecting his Executive powers and duties."[123] This had the effect, perhaps intended, of reducing significantly the number of advisory opinion requests and increasing the number of the justices' refusals to answer requests.[124] The constitution of 1968 retained the limiting language but added the requirement, unique among advisory opinion provisions, that the justices must "permit interested parties to be heard on the questions presented." It also apparently made the governor's requests discretionary upon the justices rather than mandatory.[125]

COLORADO (1886)

The reason Colorado adopted an advisory opinion provision ten years after becoming a state is clear enough. Apparently having less to do with noble experiments in state constitutional governance and more to do with simple politics, advisory opinions were a response to "the problem of unconstitutional legislation which then plagued the state."[126] As soon as the advisory opinion clause was adopted, the supreme court was inundated

---

and all such opinions shall be published in connection with the reported decisions of said court." Mo. const. (1865), Art. VI, sec. 11.

[120] DUNNE, THE MISSOURI SUPREME COURT, 78. Dunne cites no sources in support of his view about the court being overloaded.

[121] JOURNAL OF THE MISSOURI CONSTITUTIONAL CONVENTION OF 1875 (1920).

[122] Fla. Const. (1868), art. V, sec. 16.

[123] The amendment to the 1868 constitution was included in the 1885 constitution. Fla. const. (1885), art. 4, sec. 13.

[124] *See* ELLINGWOOD, DEPARTMENTAL COOPERATION, 47–48.

[125] Fla. const. (1968), art. IV, sec. 1(c).

[126] R. K. Hoffman, *Why Not Advisory Opinions for Illinois?*, 31 CHI.-KENT L. REV. 141, 145 (1952).

with requests.[127] It rendered seventeen advisory opinions in 1886 alone, even though the clause took effect only in November of that year. By early 1889, by which time the court imposed a full set of restrictions on advising, the court had rendered thirty-three advisory opinions, a number equal to the total of those rendered by all the other advisory opinion states from the beginning to 1889.

The court seemed troubled from the start. Its first advisory opinion quoted the advisory opinion clause and then proclaimed, somewhat desperately, that "[i]t is obvious" that it "will become the medium of great abuses, unless the purpose be clearly comprehended and its spirit be strictly obeyed by both the general assembly and the court."[128] The question dealt with water rights, certainly among the most politically sensitive and conflict-ridden issues of the time and place, one which the opinion described as "a subject second to none in its importance and intricacy." The court refused to answer, noting that the questions affect "vast property rights," public policy questions, and currently litigated cases.[129] It was not until 1889 that the court put forth a set of standards for when it will answer questions and when it will refuse.[130] The 1889 opinion explained why the new state, after ten years' experience, adopted an advisory opinion provision, a response to the detailed and restriction-filled nature of state constitutions. It was, the court said, mainly because of the "great difficulty in the enactment of laws" owing to the many constitutional limits and their consequent "[p]erplexity and confusion" resulting in the court holding much legislation unconstitutional. To avoid further such "injurious consequences," the legislature was given the opportunity to seek advice on the constitutionality of legislation "in advance."[131] Though the opinion imposed restrictions on advising, a large number of requests came to the court in the following decade—fifty-one from 1890 to 1899 (though it refused to answer fourteen). After that, however, the numbers declined sharply, and of these the court refused to answer a sizable proportion.[132]

SOUTH DAKOTA (1889)

As part of one of its several attempts to achieve statehood, the future state of South Dakota held a convention in 1885 which framed a proposed constitution that included an advisory opinion provision.[133] Congress rejected statehood, but in another try in

---

[127] The Colorado clause was the first to designate the "supreme court" rather than "the justices" as the advice-giver. This may have been inadvertent (a point discussed later), but the court interpreted this to mean that in Colorado advisory opinions are binding and carry the force of precedent. *See In re Senate Resolution Relating to Senate Bill No. 65*, 21 at 478, 479 (Colo. 1889).

[128] *In the Matter of Senate Resolution on the Subject of Irrigation*, 21 P. 470, 470 (Colo. 1886).

[129] *Id.* at 470–71.

[130] This subject is covered in Chapter 3.

[131] *In re Senate Resolution Relating to Senate Bill No. 65*, 21 P. 479–80.

[132] The court received eighty-four advisory opinion requests from 1886 to 1889. Over the following half-century it averaged only one advisory opinion request every two years, and refused to answer 40 percent of those.

[133] Proceedings of the Dakota Constitutional Convention, 15 (1885). ("Mr. Ryan offered the following resolution: Resolved, That the Judges of the Supreme Court may be at any time required by the

1889, the future state was successful, and North and South Dakota were formed out of much of the Dakota Territory. South Dakota's first state constitution included an advisory opinion provision similar to that of 1885 and which is substantially the provision it has today, making advising mandatory and limiting the requesting authority to the governor.[134] Neither the 1885 nor the 1889 convention saw much discussion on advisory opinions. The delegate at the 1885 convention who put the question to a vote remarked only that he "did not care to present any views . . . to the Convention," noting only that the convention's judiciary committee unanimously agreed on the provision. The record states simply that the judiciary committee's "report is adopted."[135]

ALABAMA (1922)

Alabama is the other of the two states (with Delaware) where advisory opinions are provided for by statute rather than by constitution. The Alabama justices attempted to accord the statute and the state's constitution, much as the Delaware justices would do, but in Alabama the issue arose immediately and the justices were in sharp dissent. The state's advisory opinion statute, enacted in 1923, included a statement that the opinions are not binding but "shall be advisory only," reviews the purposes of the act, and permits the justices to receive briefs from the attorney general and from amici curiae.[136] A week after the advisory opinion bill became law, the governor sent to the justices several questions on state indebtedness.[137] The justices replied, but only after ruling that the advisory opinion statute was constitutional. They did not explain why they thought it necessary to do so, since the record shows no challenges sent to the court. The strong dissents by two justices attacking the constitutionality of the statute, however, indicate that the sharp disagreement among the justices themselves sparked the opinion's ruling on constitutionality.

The majority justices' opinion is careful and extensive, even labored, in its defense of the statute's constitutionality. They reviewed advisory opinions practices in the advisory states, and reviewed as well the rejection of advisory opinions in other states. Then they inquired "whether the act is offensive to the Constitution of Alabama," and they concluded that the only provisions that may be offended are those on separation of powers.[138] They concluded that rendering advisory opinions is not a judicial function. Hence it "is manifest" that the advisory opinion statute does not impose a judicial duty

---

Governor to render their opinion upon any legal or constitutional question which he may submit to them.")

[134] JOURNAL OF THE CONVENTION [of 1889] 80. North Dakota also considered—but rejected—an advisory opinion provision (discussed in Chapter 2).

[135] PROCEEDINGS OF THE DAKOTA CONSTITUTIONAL CONVENTION [of 1885], 391.

[136] Ala. Code 1923, sec. 10290 (now Ala. Code, sec. 12-2-10 to 12-2-12).

[137] The statute went into effect February 13, 1923. The governor's letter requesting advice is dated February 20, 1923. *See In re Opinions of the Justices*, 96 So. 487, 488 (Ala. 1923).

[138] *In re Opinion of the Justices*, 96 So. at 489–90. Recall that the Delaware justices found that state's advisory opinion clause constitutional in part because the state's constitution contained no separation of powers clause.

and is no encroachment on the judiciary. The Alabama legislature "is not restrained from imposing or conferring upon a judicial officer, in his individual capacity as such, non-judicial duties or functions." Though advisory opinions may be on legal or constitutional questions, they are "advisory merely," nonbinding opinions of individual justices, and as such cannot offend separation of powers.[139] One observer called this a "rather unique solution."[140] It is remarkable, at any rate, for the justices to argue that a duty may be imposed on them, as long as it is nonjudicial, when, we will see, other jurisdictions rejected advisory duties on just that ground. Since the duty is nonjudicial, the justices acting in their individual capacities, by this reasoning the justices may, constitutionally, "go fishing, play golf, or advise the governor and legislature on matters of constitutional law."[141]

The two dissenting justices rejected this argument completely. The advisory opinion statute, they wrote, offends the state constitution because "the legislature is wholly without power to impose its judgment . . . on any co-ordinate branch of government." They argued that in other states whose constitutions include separation of powers provisions, those provisions "by necessary implication prohibits the rendition of advisory opinions, unless other clauses expressly authorize them." Further, the two dissenters took the opportunity to remark that "[i]t is impossible to read the opinions of the courts throughout the country without coming to the conclusion that the attitude of the judiciary generally has been unfavorable to the [advisory opinion] practice even in those states where it is expressly permitted by their constitutions."[142] The two justices would never again participate in advisory opinion proceedings, usually saying simply that they "decline to respond, for reasons set forth" in their 1923 dissent. Their observation that the attitude of justices to their advising duties "generally has been unfavorable" is accurate, as Chapter 3 will show. The majority view has held, however, and the Alabama justices have become the most prolific issuers of advisory opinions.[143]

MICHIGAN (1962)

The newest advisory opinion provision was introduced at the 1961 Michigan constitutional convention, where the judiciary committee proposed a provision closely modeled on that of Massachusetts. Two chief differences were that the governor and legislature may "request," not "require" advisory opinions, and that the "court," not the "justices,"

---

[139] *Id.* at 491–92.

[140] John F. Hagemann, *The Advisory Opinion in South Dakota*, 16 S.D. L. REV. 291, 295 (1971).

[141] C. Dallas Sands, *Government by Judiciary—Advisory Opinions in Alabama*, 4 ALA. L. REV. 1, 4 (1951).

[142] *In re Opinion of the Justices,* 96 So. at 497–98 (Sayre and Miller, J.J., dissenting).

[143] In the 1930s, for example, the Alabama justices rendered fifty-one advisory opinions, three times more than the next highest state, and in the 1940s they rendered fifty, double the next highest state. Overall, since 1923 the number of Alabama advisory opinions exceeds the total of each of the other advisory opinion states.

was to render the advice.[144] The debate over the advisory opinion proposal, the most extensive recorded in any advisory opinion state, began with a question about what "solemn occasion" means. Concerns about the phrase were surprisingly persistent. No other issue about advisory opinions was discussed more.[145] It survived, however, and is in the present constitution. Some changes were made in the course of debate, based on historical concerns about advising duties, with which delegates seemed thoroughly familiar. Debate evidenced concerns about deviating from case or controversy requirements, and about litigated cases raising the same questions as those addressed in advisory opinion proceedings. The replies were that the court would have authority to decide which questions to answer, that it would "undoubtedly" request briefs amicus curiae, and that advisory opinions would be nonbinding.[146]

Another concern was that advisory opinion authority would in effect make the court a de facto legislature, though this initially was left as a matter of opinion and so apparently not a major concern.

> MR. GADOLA: [I]sn't this pretty close to putting legislation in the hands of the supreme court?
>
> MISS MCGOWAN [speaking for the judiciary committee proposing the advisory opinion provision]: In my opinion it is not.
>
> MR. GADOLA: My opinion is, it is. (laughter)
>
> CHAIRMAN VAN DUSAN: That is what makes horse races. (laughter)[147]

The matter was left at that, but a motion was then introduced to strike the advisory opinion proposal altogether, based on concerns about separation of powers, doubts about whether it "facilitates an abdication by the legislature and the governor of their duty" to judge the constitutionality of pending statutes or actions, whether it gives the supreme court excessive power, and the dangers of the court addressing abstract and hypothetical questions, all questions that have dogged advisory opinions. The motion to strike, though, was soundly defeated, 66–39.[148]

The debate on the motion to strike, however, apparently created sufficient concern for the delegates to consider imposing limits on the proposed advisory opinion authority. The delegates immediately proceeded to create the most restrictive of all advisory opinion provisions. A motion to restrict the justices to constitutional questions was amended at the request of a delegate who wished to limit sharply the ability of the court to intrude on the legislature. "If we consider," he said, "that [an advisory opinion] would

---

[144] State of Michigan Constitutional Convention, 1961, Official Record, 1479 (Proposal 96, sec. k) (hereafter, Official Record). The chair of the convention's judiciary committee noted that "[s]imilar language appears in the Constitution of the State of Massachusetts." *Id.* at 1480.

[145] One delegate, perhaps reflecting the amount of attention given the phrase, joked that the vote to keep it (which passed 104–2) was a solemn occasion. *Id.* at 1550. "Solemn occasion" and its meanings played an important role in development of a jurisprudence of advisory opinions, discussed in Chapter 3.

[146] *Id.* at 1544.

[147] *Id.* at 1545.

[148] *Id.* at 1546–47.

be asked for before legislation was enacted, it would, of course, be an interference with the powers of the legislature, a violation of the separation of powers. If we consider that the opinion would be asked for after the enactment of the legislation, if the opinion is not restricted to the question of constitutionality, we would be in effect giving the supreme court a veto over matters of legislation." A compromise version of an advisory opinion provision, restricting advisory opinions to constitutional questions about legislation after enactment but before its effective date, passed by a vote of 82–23.[149]

A motion to limit authority to request advisory opinions to each branch of the legislature (omitting the governor), and a motion to authorize the "legislature" (rather than each branch separately) to submit requests were both defeated with little debate.[150] There was little debate over whether Michigan needed advisory opinions at all. Several times, though, one particular instance was invoked to show the need for them. This was a 1959 law, which, the chair of the judiciary committee said, imposed a "four cent sales tax which was passed and, in a short time thereafter, was declared unconstitutional."[151] When the tax was declared unconstitutional, as another delegate complained, "there was well over $20 million of moneys collected from taxpayers in small amounts that could not be refunded to them. It was collected from them unconstitutionally, but it could not be refunded to them."[152] The sales tax example must have impressed the delegates, and it is still preserved, if a bit cryptically, as part of a comment to the advisory opinion clause in the official state statutes.[153] After the defeat of the two motions to amend (omitting the governor and requiring the "legislature" to submit requests for advice), the proposal to include the advisory opinion provision in the constitution passed.[154]

NORTH CAROLINA

Finally, there is the curious instance of North Carolina, where there is no statutory or constitutional authority for advisory opinions, but where the supreme court has been rendering them since the mid-nineteenth century. There is no record of any establishment of the process. In an 1849 advisory opinion, apparently the first, the justices answered questions from the senate regarding a contested election, declaring the advising a "duty of courtesy and respect to the Senate." The justices' willingness to answer the questions seemed to come from their certainty that the answers were clear beyond reasonable dispute. If they had doubts, they said, "they would have been obliged to defer

---

[149] *Id.* at 1548.

[150] *Id.* at 1550–51.

[151] *Id.* at 1480.

[152] *Id.* at 1547.

[153] Michigan Compiled Laws Ann. (2002), Const. of 1963, Art. 3, sec. 8, "Convention Comment" ("An example of the possible exercise of this section would have been the matter of the 4-cent state use tax which was passed and later declared unconstitutional.").

[154] OFFICIAL RECORD, 1551. No vote recorded.

their answer until the parties or their counsel could submit their views."[155] They do not explain or defend their notion that the difference between an adjudicated decision and an advisory opinion is the judge's doubts. An 1870 advisory opinion, however, showed for the first time that the justices were divided on the propriety of their advising. The justices who were willing to advise referred again to their "duty of courtesy and respect," citing the 1849 advisory opinion as "precedent," and, oddly, suggested that "the question is more easy of solution now, when it can be treated as a dry matter of constitutional law, than it might be hereafter, when complicated with collateral considerations."[156] The collateral considerations, presumably, are those that would arise from a case or controversy. They noted, though, that they render their opinion "not as a *court*, but as *judges*."[157]

Three justices, however, refused to advise. One offered no explanation.[158] Another explained that he refused to advise "solely upon the ground that the Constitution forbids me to answer."[159] Invoking what would become the chief objection to advisory opinions everywhere—separation of powers—he cited the separation clause in the state's recent constitution, ratified in 1868, under which, he said, an advisory opinion is "substantially an interference with the legitimate business of the legislature, and . . . the Constitution forbids it."[160] This opposition, though in the minority, may have put a brake on the advisory opinion process in North Carolina. At any rate the justices issued only five advisory opinions over the next half-century, and thereafter rendered them regularly if infrequently, averaging one every five years, until 1985. In that year the justices refused to render an advisory opinion. It was the first time.[161] The question related to a statute providing for a "judicial trigger" requiring that statute not take effect until the supreme court holds that it is constitutional.[162] The justices, perhaps concerned by the potential for judicial triggers to become a regular part of the legislative process, refused to advise, noting that such an advisory opinion would have the force of law. After this refusal, the North Carolina justices have rarely rendered advisory opinions.

---

155 Waddell v. Berry, 31 N.C. (9 Ire.) App. (1849). Quoted in ELLINGWOOD, DEPARTMENTAL COOPERATION, 68. *See also* Preston W. Edsall, *The Advisory Opinion in North Carolina*, 27 N.C. L. REV. 297, 299–301 (1949).

156 *Opinions of the Justices of the Supreme Court in Regard to the Terms of Office of the General Assembly That Was Elected in April 1868*, 64 N.C. 785, 786 (1870). *See* Edsall, *The Advisory Opinion in North Carolina*, 304–8.

157 *Opinions of the Justices*, 64 N.C. at 786.

158 *Opinions of the Justices*, 64 N.C. at 796 (Settle, J., declining to advise).

159 *Id.* at 793 (Reade, J., declining to advice).

160 *Id.* at 792–93.

161 *See* Edsall, *The Advisory Opinion in North Carolina*, 1877–78.

162 *In re Advisory Opinion*, 335 S.E.2d 890, 890 (N.C. 1985) (quoting from the bill in question: "Section 5 and 6 shall become effective 30 days from the date the Supreme Court issues an advisory opinion on the constitutionality of those sections unless the opinion states that those sections are unconstitutional, in which event those sections shall not become effective.").

2 }

Danger of Grave Abuses

ATTACKS ON THE LEGITIMACY OF ADVISORY OPINIONS

At first, nothing much happened. The advisory opinion may have been originally constitutionalized owing to the heated controversy about plural office holding, but for decades advisory opinion provisions themselves garnered little if any attention either in constitutional conventions or "out of doors." From 1780 through the Federalist years and well into the nineteenth century, advisory opinions apparently were of little use and no interest. The Massachusetts justices rendered only eight reported advisory opinions during the first forty years. Several were not reported until many years later. The first Massachusetts advisory opinion, rendered in 1781, was reported in 1879; the next two, rendered in 1784 and 1787, were reported in 1817.[1] In New Hampshire, which had adopted a provision similar to that of Massachusetts in 1784, the justices issued one advisory opinion during the next four decades, and it was not reported until 1889.[2] There is no recorded debate, or even passing comment, anywhere on advisory opinion provisions for some forty years after first appearing in the Massachusetts constitution of 1780.

Then, in 1820, with striking suddenness, the advisory opinion became, as it remains, a problem and a target, so that by 1886 the Colorado justices can plausibly invoke the "danger of grave abuses" in the use of advisory opinions, and by 1889, at the constitutional convention of the new state of North Dakota, a delegate could, he said, "safely say that there is not a state in the Union where that [advisory opinion] provision prevails but not only the Supreme Court but every other person who has an intimate knowledge of the workings of that provision would wish it were not there."[3] There is no record of a judge

---

[1] *Opinion of the Justices to the Senate and the House of Representatives*, 126 Mass. 547 (1781); *Opinion of the Justices of the Supreme Judicial Court*, 14 Mass. 470 (1784); *Opinion of the Justices of the Supreme Judicial Court*, 14 Mass. 472 (1787).

[2] *Opinion of the Court*, 62 N. H. 704 (1816).

[3] Colorado: *In re House Bill No. 122*, 21 P. 478, 480 (Colo. 1886). This advisory opinion is actually a refusal to advise, in fact a diatribe against advisory opinions. It is discussed later in this book. North Dakota: *Proceedings and Debates of the First Constitutional Convention of North Dakota,* 231 (1889). The convention defeated the proposed advisory opinion provision. *See* Langer v. State, 284 N.W. 238, 251 (N.D. 1939) (citing the above quote with approval, reviewing the convention's arguments against advisory opinions, and noting that after debate "the proposal was finally defeated"). *Id.* at 251.

directly disagreeing. With remarkable consistency over nearly two centuries, the advisory opinion has been attacked not only for violating fundamental doctrines of American jurisprudence but for politicizing and thereby both threatening the independence of the judiciary and expanding judicial power, and only occasionally defended for its utility in the interests of efficient, cooperative, and open government. This began, not with concerns about advisory opinions' clash with separation of powers, due process, case or controversy, and other fundamental doctrines, but rather with fears of judicial politicization and consequent loss of independence. This attack surfaced at the 1820 Massachusetts constitutional convention, and with the chairman of its judiciary committee, U. S. Supreme Court Justice Joseph Story, whose hostility toward advisory opinions and whose role in the history of advisory opinion jurisprudence has not heretofore been explained, or even written about.[4]

The Most Costly Price: Politicization of the Judiciary

Joseph Story attacked advisory opinions not only as a threat to the Massachusetts judiciary but also as a direct assault on the integrity of the law. He was the first to lead a move not merely to remove outright an advisory opinion provision from a constitution but even to replace it with a positive prohibition. His exceptionally strong stand at the 1820 convention, after decades of no recorded opposition to advisory opinions anywhere, can be explained by major changes in perceptions and status of the law and especially by Story's profound guiding vision of a legal science and his commitment to its development as a protection against the politicization of the law as well as of the judiciary. To this vision and commitment advisory opinions were a menace.

Story's views no doubt carried great weight at the 1820 Massachusetts convention. Among its most prominent and respected members, he had been a U.S. Supreme Court Justice since 1812, which itself gave him considerable authority among the delegates.[5] At forty-two he was already known as the Court's "scholar in residence"[6] and for years had been the most prolific legal scholar in New England.[7] He had been a member of Harvard's board of overseers since 1818, beginning an association that would culminate in his becoming the law school's first head in 1829.[8]

---

[4] An exception is Mel A. Topf, *The Origins and Early History of Supreme Judicial Court Advisory Opinions in Massachusetts*, 7 Mass. Legal Hist. 21, 32–45 (2001), from which this discussion of Story is adapted. None of the studies of Story's life and work has addressed his view of advisory opinions or its place in his legal thought.

[5] R. Kent Newmyer, Supreme Court Justice Joseph Story: Statesman of the Old Republic 167 (1985). Newmyer discusses the 1820 convention at some length (164–170) but nowhere mentions either its deliberations on the advisory opinion clause or Story's concerns about it.

[6] *Id.* at 156.

[7] *Id.* at 7.

[8] *Id.* at 165.

At the convention he ran for its presidency and lost to Massachusetts Chief Justice Isaac Parker,[9] but he strongly wished to be accepted as the leader of the convention's conservatives. He was quickly accepted as such, successfully establishing his credentials as an opponent of republicanism.[10] Story brought his prestige and leadership, together with his considerable political and legal skills, to what was for him and his allies at the convention the overriding mission: to save the Massachusetts frame of government from the democratizing forces (or from radicalism, the term Story used) that were threatening the Republic itself.[11] It would be difficult to overemphasize the centrality of this mission to Story's theory of the judiciary. Story, along with Daniel Webster and others, led the conservative faction toward its goal of creating an alliance to protect the Massachusetts constitution from democratic extremes of the radicals, whose program was the convention's main agenda.[12]

For Story, among the most dangerous of the radicals' proposals was one to amend the state constitution to allow the legislature to reduce the salaries of the judges.[13] This subjection of the judiciary to the legislature aimed directly at the heart of judicial independence which for Story was the security that a state must give the judiciary against the state's own power, making the judiciary, he said, "as it were, something exterior to the state."[14] Story's alarm stemmed from his core concept of bench and bar as "the conservative counterweight to the tyranny of the majority."[15] The dichotomy was clear for Story: on one side the law, the constitution, and their protectors, the judiciary, all working together to develop America's commerce, improve its civilization, and support individual enterprise. On the other side, politics.[16] While the danger lay especially in the legislature, the problem for Story was not the legislature itself as a coordinate branch but rather the political control by parties over the legislature. Party was "the source of his anxiety and despair about the future of the Republic," and "lawyers, judges, the courts, and the common law were a corrective to, even an alternative to, the bumbling work of politicians and legislatures."[17] It was a longstanding fear. In the Revolutionary era "the desire for an independent expert judiciary was bred by the continuing and ever renewed fear of democratic politics."[18] Chief Justice Marshall began the move to

---

[9] Gerald T. Dunne, Justice Joseph Story and the Rise of the Supreme Court 205 (1970). The vote was 130 to 195.

[10] Newmyer, Supreme Court Justice Joseph Story, 162–164. (At the 1820 convention, "Story had to prove his dedication and his value to the conservative cause" (162).)

[11] Merrill D. Peterson, Democracy, Liberty, and Property: The State Constitutional Conventions of the 1820's at 6 (1966).

[12] Newmyer, Supreme Court Justice Joseph Story, 167–71.

[13] *Id.* at 167–68.

[14] Joseph Story, 3 Commentaries on the Constitution of the United States 436 (1833).

[15] Newmyer, Supreme Court Justice Joseph Story, 78.

[16] *Id.* at 154.

[17] *Id.* at 161, 163.

[18] Gordon Wood, The Radicalism of the American Revolution 323 (1991). On the movement at the time to separate politics from the law, see Morton J. Horwitz, The Transformation of American Law, 1780–1860 at 256–59 (1977). Although Horwitz views the "desire to separate law and politics" as a "central aspiration of the legal profession" since the early post-Revolutionary era, he attributes the conservatives' later

separate the legal and the political; indeed, William Nelson writes, his "creative act was to use the distinction between law and politics to circumscribe . . . the extent to which the political, majoritarian style could engulf all government, as it was threatening in 1800 to do."[19]

Story's enduring mission was to engage in the immunization of law against the disease of majoritarian politics by establishing and asserting the doctrine of the primacy of the judiciary in interpreting the constitution, perhaps the first to do so.[20] He was committed to legitimizing this primacy by making the law a science. Legal science "forms the core of Story's vision of constitutionalism. . . . Without science, there would be no reason to believe that the decisions of the [United States Supreme] Court could withstand the competing interests of other institutional actors."[21] It bordered on the Manichean: Story undertook the great project of basing law on scientific principles of uniformity, rationality, and objectivity, "a universal empire of judicial reason," so as to better oppose what he called the "[t]emporary delusions, prejudices, and excitements" that mark political discourse.[22] He worked to make legal thought and language a science and as such ontologically distinct from political discourse and concerns: law as a unique category of knowledge, requiring interpretation and application only by those trained in such interpretation and application. Story set forth what he called the "true rules of interpretation applicable to the constitution; so that we may have some fixed standard."[23] This served to institutionalize and professionalize the interpretation of the law, to give it a stability that would make it a building block of one nation indivisible. Legal interpretation was to become a technical mystery requiring an expertise possessed neither by common citizens nor by politicians. It was to be an objective and rational interpretation, the means of establishing a judicial authority that is not political—not partisan, unstable, biased, emotional, and personal. So it was that legal science became central to Story's vision of America as a constitutional republic. With it the judicial enterprise would be preserved. Without it Supreme Court decisions would not "withstand the competing interests of other institutional actors."[24]

It was a distinctly Enlightenment notion of science that Story held, with its values of harmony, lack of discord, and a scientific method that led to knowledge universally

---

program to depoliticize law partly to the rise of the codification movement after 1820 and that movement's view of the law as essentially political, as an instrument of power.

[19] William E. Nelson, *The Eighteenth-Century Background of John Marshall's Constitutional Jurisprudence*, 76 MICH. L. REV. 893, 935 (1978).

[20] *See* Michael Stokes Paulson, *The Most Dangerous Branch: Executive Power to Say What the Law Is*, 83 GEO. L.J. 217, 311–12 (1994) (arguing that judicial supremacy doctrine begins with Joseph Story). Judicial supremacy and its relation to advisory opinions are discussed in Chapter 6.

[21] PAUL W. KAHN, LEGITIMACY AND HISTORY: SELF-GOVERNMENT IN AMERICAN CONSTITUTIONAL THEORY 41 (1992).

[22] NEWMYER, SUPREME COURT JUSTICE JOSEPH STORY, 114; STORY, 1 COMMENTARIES ON THE CONSTITUTION OF THE UNITED STATES 410 (1833).

[23] Quoted in KAHN, LEGITIMACY AND HISTORY, 41.

[24] *Id.*

accepted, hence led to an end to history's sorry spectacle of searches for truth mired in controversy and rancor. For the Enlightenment,

> [t]he history of thought . . . was a history of discord, of endless fruitless wrangles. . . . [N]ow the sciences of nature promised a way to knowledge to which all reasonable men could assent. This is why the scientific method struck the eighteenth century as an invention unprecedented in its sheer magnificent effectiveness. . . . If scientific method was the sole reliable method for gaining knowledge in a wide variety of contexts, . . . it seemed plausible and in fact likely that it could be profitably exported to other areas of intense human concern.[25]

This understanding of scientific method is indispensable to understanding Story's vision of legal science as a bulwark against majoritarian threats against the judiciary, indeed against the Republic. Crucial was scientific method's promise of a "way to knowledge . . . to which all reasonable men could assent." Controversy here is a consequence of imperfect knowledge and not, as politicians would see it, opposing interests. Scientific method aims at and demands "judgments concerning which universal agreement can be reached."[26] To achieve this, science privileges methodology.[27] For Story legal science specified "a correct technique for judicial law-making. Scientific rules could assure the orderly unfolding of the genius of the law that was already present, if inchoate, in the material with which a judge had to work."[28] Scientific method would set law free from the assaults of politics, party, and policy, because the method is not merely observation but a means of detachment from ordinary experience, thereby the only way to objective, disinterested knowledge. This was scientific method's source of its enormous authority in the eighteenth and nineteenth centuries.[29] Morton Horowitz may be

---

[25] PETER GAY, 2 THE ENLIGHTENMENT: AN INTERPRETATION 163–64 (1969). Newmyer sees Story's concept of science as derived from the eighteenth-century notion of system, of any organized body of knowledge (the older, more general meaning of "science"). NEWMYER, SUPREME COURT JUSTICE JOSEPH STORY 285. But this concept was concurrent with the newer idea of science as a distinct and revolutionary method of deriving knowledge, and of knowing. I differ with Howard Schweber's view of Story's legal science as simply system in his *The "Science" of Legal Science: The Model of the Natural Sciences in Nineteenth-Century American Legal Education*, 17 LAW & HIST. REV. 421, 437 (1999). For a study of Enlightenment ideas of objectivity, rationality, abstraction, and replicability, and their relation to law, see Thomas D. Barton, *Troublesome Connections: The Law and Post-Enlightenment Culture*, 47 EMORY L. REV. 163 (1998).

[26] J. M. ZIMAN, PUBLIC KNOWLEDGE 30 (1968).

[27] *See generally* Robert Markely, *Objectivity as Ideology: Boyle, Newton, and the Languages of Science*, 16 GENRE 355–72; *see also* ZIMAN, PUBLIC KNOWLEDGE, 64–65.

[28] Richard S. Kay, *Book Review of Newmyer, Supreme Court Justice Joseph Story*, 18 CONN. L. REV. 207, 210 (1985).

[29] This view of science is based on Hannah Arendt's discussion of experimental method in THE HUMAN CONDITION 239–41 (1959). Arendt argues that experimental method differs from mere observation in requiring a separation (alienation, she calls it) from the world of observed phenomena in order to infer knowledge from the experimental findings only. It was this methodological detachment that was seen as the only true way to objective, disinterested knowledge, and as such it was the source of science's enormous authority. On the role of experiment (as distinct from mere observation) in the scientific revolution, see ALEXANDRE KOYRE, METAPHYSICS AND MEASUREMENT: ESSAYS IN THE SCIENTIFIC REVOLUTION 90 (1968); CHARLES GILLISPIE, THE EDGE OF OBJECTIVITY 79 (1960); STEVEN SHAPIN, THE SCIENTIFIC REVOLUTION 13 (1996).

correct in claiming that "there is no content or methodology to be found in [the] persistent claims to the scientific character of the law,"[30] but scientific method has always drawn its power and influence as much as a legitimizing ideology as an actual account of the search for knowledge.[31]

Story's legal science project culminated in his treatises, a leading part of the treatise tradition in the 1820s and 1830s admired as demonstrating the scientific nature of law.[32] His *Commentaries on Constitution of the United States*, with its influential, rigorous rules of interpretation and its distinct rejection of policy and "interest" in constitutional interpretation, required not only close textual analysis, but isolated, detached textual analysis. "It would be dangerous in the extreme," he wrote, to infer meaning "from extrinsic circumstances."[33] Just as two scientists separately performing the same experiment must arrive at the same result, so two judges, each analyzing the same law, must arrive at the same interpretation because they are bound by scientific rules of construction. The method affirms the objective legitimacy of the interpretation, and the rigorous rules of construction identify those who practice them as an autonomous group of experts alone qualified to interpret the law. As Newmyer observes, with "Story's *Commentaries* began the lawyers' monopoly on American constitutional law."[34]

Legal science legitimized judicial independence and contributed to countering the instabilities of a democratized Republic mired in faction and interest, securing the law against the widening vortex of politics. The stakes were high for Story. If the fundamental law is not judged "by the fair meaning of the words of the text" he wrote, then "there can be no security for the people."[35]

At the 1820 convention, Story was alarmed by the radicals' moves against the judiciary, which centered on the proposed amendment to empower the legislature to reduce judicial salaries by simple majority vote. The convention apparently understood, as Story of course did, that judicial independence itself was "the safeguard of the judiciary against the influence of popular clamor," as he put it years later, when he recalled the debate on judicial salaries as one that "I shall never forget. For eloquence, for vivid and powerful reasoning, for warm, vehement, and varied discussion, it was not exceeded by any debate at that Convention, on any subject, even if it was equaled. All the leading speakers addressed the Convention on that occasion. . . . In all my life I never heard any debate which excelled it."[36]

---

[30] Horwitz, Transformation of American Law, 257.

[31] *See, e.g.*, Richard H. Brown, Toward a Democratic Science 24–25 (1998) (on science and legitimation); Koyre, Metaphysics and Measurement, 144–50; Shapin, Scientific Revolution, 94–95. Shapin argues that scientific method served as much as a legitimizing ideology as it did a description of what actually happens in the search for knowledge. Even its actual practice by pioneering scientists in the seventeenth century is open to question. *See* Koyre, Metaphysics and Measurement, 144–50 (arguing that some of the famous experiments of Galileo, Pascal, and Torricelli produced doubtful results even if they were carried out at all).

[32] On this view of treatises, see Horwitz, Transformation of American Law, 257.

[33] Story, 1 Commentaries, 411.

[34] Newmyer, Chief Justice Joseph Story, 191–92.

[35] Story, 1 Commentaries, 391

[36] William H. Story, 1 Life and Letters of Joseph Story 387 (1851).

It was within this context that Joseph Story was the first to assert that an advisory opinion provision, with its potential for involving the judiciary in political controversy at the call of the executive and legislature, was a threat to judicial independence, even an instrument for the removal of justices, acting through the "popular clamor" that was the bane of the conservatives' vision of a constitutional republic and against which the legal science project was to be a bastion.

And so Story led the earliest attack on advisory opinions. Addressing the 1820 Massachusetts convention on the proposal to delete the advisory opinion provision, he put forth the arguments against them. It was, he said, "exceedingly important that the judiciary department . . . be independent of the other departments."[37] Speaking as chair of the convention's judiciary committee, he proposed not only that the advisory opinion provision be deleted but that it be replaced with a positive ban on advisory opinions.[38] This was because, he said, "[i]t is desirable as far as possible to remove the judges of the Supreme Court from any connection with the other Departments of Government either executive or legislative."[39] This argument is similar to that the Supreme Court Justices put to President George Washington in 1793, and for Story that separation principle was a given. His emphasis at the 1820 convention was not on the principle but rather on the concrete and dangerous opportunities the advisory opinion clause offered to the political branches, to have it in their power to "call in the Judges to aid them for any purpose."[40]

Story set out a dark vision of the political branches running rampant over the judiciary under writ of the advisory opinion clause, a vision of a judiciary whose independence is suppressed and of a system of legal science brought to ruin by the "extreme danger" of justices being "required to give opinions in cases which should be exclusively of a judicial character."[41] It was not only that the justices could be embroiled in political controversy. Worse, the advisory opinion clause could be taken up as a weapon willfully wielded by a demagogic legislature to cut down the justices' independence as surely as could the power to diminish their salaries. Not only so: for Story the power to require advice is the power to run judges out of court.

> The power of calling upon the judges for their opinion may be resorted to in times of political excitement with a view to make them odious, and to effect their removal from office. A better opportunity could not be afforded to an artful demagogue, for

---

[37] Journal of the Debates and Proceedings in the Convention of Delegates Chosen to Revise the Constitution of Massachusetts 1820–1821 at 220 (1853). Hereafter, Convention Journal.

[38] The deletion proposal is in Convention Journal, 220. ("[I]t is inexpedient to retain that article of the constitution which requires the Judges of the Supreme [Judicial] Court to answer questions proposed to them by the Governor and Council or either branch of the Legislature.") Prohibition proposal, which would become article nine of the convention's final draft, in Convention Journal, 278 ("The Governor and the two Branches of the Legislature respectively, shall not hereafter be authorized to propose questions to the justices of the Supreme Judicial Court, and require their opinions thereon.").

[39] Convention Journal, 72.

[40] *Id.* at 220.

[41] *Id.*

effecting the purpose of their removal, than by drawing from them opportunities, opposed to the strong popular sentiment, and subjecting them to popular odium.[42]

Here is Story's nightmare of democracy run amok, of a political maelstrom precipitated by demagogues inciting a turbulent public to despise the justices. The advisory opinion provision stood ready to be taken up to subvert an independent judiciary whose independence was grounded on the autonomous legal science that was Story's great project. The advisory opinion process could bring it all crashing down.

The resolution proposing the removal of the advisory opinion provision "was agreed to by a large majority" in the convention, and the clause expressly prohibiting advisory opinions easily passed as well.[43] At the polls the advisory opinion amendments were presented on the ballot together with three others as a four-point proposal for judicial reform. The proposal was defeated, 12,471 in favor and 14,518 against. This would happen at least twice again. Proposed amendments to remove the advisory opinion clause from the Massachusetts constitution and from the Rhode Island constitution, in 1853 and 1986 respectively, were tied in a package with other judicial reforms, the packages defeated at the ballot. In all cases it was other proposals that were controversial and not advisory opinions.[44] The 85-year-old John Adams was a member of the 1820 convention but apparently did not comment on the proposal to remove his advisory opinion clause, though he spoke on other topics. Perhaps this was owing to his poor opinion of what speaking he did. His appearance at the convention, he wrote to Jefferson, "was too ludicrous to be talked of. . . . I boggled and blundered more than a young fellow just rising to speak at the bar. . . . Feeling my weakness I attempted little and that seldom."[45]

The charge that advisory opinions politicize the judiciary, first raised by Story, would never go away. In Massachusetts, the next constitutional convention, in 1853, introduced proposals identical to those of 1820, to delete the advisory opinion clause and replace it with a positive ban. Again debate evidenced mistrust of the political branches, especially the legislature, reflected now in all states in a broadening trend to limit legislative power and expand judicial authority. One important move was toward elected state judges to remove selection from the legislatures, so that every state entering the Union from 1846 to 1900 provided for popular election of judges. By 1861 twenty-four of the thirty-four states elected their judges.[46]

---

[42] *Id.*

[43] *Id.*

[44] On the 1820 vote, see DUNNE, JUSTICE JOSEPH STORY, 207–08; PETERSON, DEMOCRACY, LIBERTY, AND PROPERTY, 124. The 1853 and 1986 proposals are discussed below.

[45] Letter, John Adams to Thomas Jefferson (Feb. 3, 1821), *in* ADAMS-JEFFERSON LETTERS 571–72 (Lester J. Capon ed., 1959).

[46] G. ALAN TARR, UNDERSTANDING STATE CONSTITUTIONS 122–23 (1998). *See also* James A. Henretta, *The Rise and Decline of "Democratic-Republicanism": Political Rights in New York and the Several States, 1800–1915*, *in* TOWARD A USABLE PAST: LIBERTY UNDER STATE CONSTITUTIONS 73, 79 (Paul Finkelman & Stephen E. Gottlieb eds., 1991); Caleb Nelson, *A Re-Evaluation of Scholarly Explanations for the Rise of the Elective Judiciary in Antebellum America*, 37 AM. J. LEGAL HIST. 190, 209 (1993).

At the 1853 convention one member argued that adding a positive prohibition against advisory opinions was necessary because, if the convention simply deleted the advisory opinion clause and left the constitution silent on this, "the legislature . . . may take it upon themselves to call upon the supreme court for an opinion, and there is nothing to forbid them. . . . [I]f the matter is thus left, without making any provision on the subject, it may give rise to a great deal of embarrassment between the legislature and the judiciary."[47] The convention's judiciary committee supported this argument based on the nature of state constitutions and especially the plenary powers they grant legislatures, in contrast to the enumerated powers of the federal Constitution. The need for a positive prohibition against advisory opinions, the committee said, arose because the Massachusetts constitution "does not confer specific powers and withhold others; but in our Constitution, the legislature have general powers and they do not have to look about and see a specific clause that authorizes them to do this or that. Therefore . . . lest the legislature should think proper to continue the old practice [of seeking advice], it was deemed but proper to insert a clause prohibiting the continuance of it."[48] Like Joseph Story, the 1853 opponents of advisory opinions expressed no concern more strongly than the capacity of the legislature to "drag the supreme court into politics."[49] One speaker evoked the image of the legislature "hounding [the justices] upon the circuit and pressing them, almost upon the instant, to give their opinions."[50] Speaker after speaker pointed to the danger of drawing the judiciary into the "vortex"[51] or the "maelstrom"[52] of politics. Repeated warnings were raised about the legislature's propounding questions to the high court on "some exciting topic which is creating a fever in the county,"[53] which might "agitate"[54] or "excite the community."[55] Aggravating this was the hot-potato problem that would frequently be raised over the next century: giving the political branches the opportunity through advisory opinions to "throw off responsibility"[56] and "put, in many important instances, the whole responsibility of their action upon the judicial department."[57]

In contrast to the 1820 convention, in 1853 several proponents rose to defend advisory opinions, but their numbers appear to be small: "I find I stand nearly alone," one defender said.[58] These appear to be the first recorded defenses of advisory opinions,

---

[47] 2 Official Report of the Debates and Proceedings in the State Convention Assembled May 4, 1853, to Revise and Amend the Constitution of the Commonwealth of Massachusetts, 690 (1853). Hereafter Official Report. The proposed amendment to ban explicitly advisory opinions is in *id.* at 684.

[48] *Id.* at 694.

[49] *Id.* at 695.

[50] *Id.*

[51] *Id.* at 694.

[52] *Id.* at 695.

[53] *Id.* at 689.

[54] *Id.* at 694.

[55] *Id.* at 685.

[56] *Id.* at 690.

[57] *Id.* at 687.

[58] *Id.* at 695.

focusing, as defenses always would, on the utility of advisory opinions.[59] Proponents at the convention did not directly counter opponents' arguments; none addressed the fears of dragging the judges into the vortex of politics. Rather they argued utility. One asserted that the "supreme court of the state can render no better service to the Commonwealth than in answering such questions as may be propounded by the legislature," without explaining why,[60] but others spoke of how advisory opinions allowed officials to "know how to perform their duties,"[61] and how they allowed the constitution to have "uniform application throughout the Commonwealth,"[62] and how they avoided "the necessity of parties having recourse to protracted and expensive litigation."[63] In contrast the advisory opinion process "is simple, easy, and perfectly practicable."[64] After all, said another proponent optimistically, "to what tribunal or what man or set of men can we go with so much confidence as to our supreme court."[65]

If proponents stressed, almost exclusively, utility, critics of advisory opinions would never leave off raising the red flag of a politicized judiciary.[66] In addition to advisory opinions' drawing the judiciary into politics which so concerned Story and the two Massachusetts conventions, later observers would also emphasize another problem: the damage to the political process and to public and discourse. "Perhaps the most costly price of advisory opinions," wrote Felix Frankfurter while a professor at Harvard Law School, "is the weakening of legislative and popular responsibility."[67] Other writers agree. For one thing, the legislature loses opportunities inherent in the "beneficent ordeal" of debate and negotiation, resulting in a diminished sense of responsibility.[68] The very availability of the advisory process invites the legislature to

---

[59] Defenses of advisory opinions are the subject of Chapter 4.

[60] OFFICIAL REPORT at 686.

[61] *Id.*

[62] *Id.* at 693.

[63] *Id.* at 687.

[64] *Id.* at 693.

[65] *Id.* at 695.

[66] *E.g.*, F. R. Aumann, *The Supreme Court and the Advisory Opinion*, 4 OHIO ST. L.J. 21, 48–50 (1937); Thomas R. Bender, *Rhode Island's Public Importance Exception for Advisory Opinions: The Unconstitutional Exercise of a Non-Judicial Power*, 10 ROGER WILLIAMS U. L. REV. 123, 158–62 (2004); Pascal F. Calogero, *Advisory Opinions: A Wise Change for Louisiana and Its Judiciary?*, 38 LOYOLA L. REV. 329, 367 (1992); Paul C. Clovis & Clarence M. Updegraff, *Advisory Opinions*, 13 IOWA L. REV. 188, 196 (1927); Preston W. Edsall, *The Advisory Opinion in North Carolina*, 27 N.C. L. REV. 297, 333 (1949); Felix Frankfurter, *A Note on Advisory Opinions*, 37 HARV. L. REV. 1002, 1004–07 (1924); John F. Hagemann, *The Advisory Opinion in South Dakota*, 16 S.D. L. REV. 291, 295 (1971); Robert H. Kennedy, *Advisory Opinions: Cautions About Non-Judicial Undertakings*, 23 U. RICHMOND L. REV. 173, 190–94 (1989); C. Dallas Sands, *Government by Judiciary—Advisory Opinions in Alabama*, 4 ALA. L. REV. 1, 37–38 (1951). For the minority view that this criticism lacks evidence to support it, see Note, *The Advisory Opinion and the United States Supreme Court*, 5 FORDHAM L. REV. 94, 110 (1936) ("That the advisory opinion will accentuate the pressure and impact of political issues upon the Court [if Supreme Court advisory opinions were permitted by New Deal–era proposed constitutional amendments] is an argument that cannot be buttressed by statistical proof."). The New Deal–era proposals to give the U.S. Supreme Court advisory opinion duties are discussed in Chapter 4.

[67] Frankfurter, *Note on Advisory Opinions*, 1007.

[68] Aumann, *Supreme Court and Advisory Opinions*, 48.

"dodge responsibility by passing the buck to the justices,"[69] and so to surrender their obligation to independently assess the constitutionality of a pending statute:[70] "It is not unknown for legislatures to abdicate their duty to act constitutionally in reliance upon eventual judicial review. Advisory opinions facilitate this process."[71] As well, it invites the executive to evade assessing the constitutionality of its acts.[72] One consequence is the capacity effectively to block governmental action "by ex parte interpretations of the constitution by a majority of that small group of government officials which is the least subject . . . to democratic political controls. This amounts . . . to too much government by judiciary."[73]

For another, the advisory process tends to diminish civil discourse essential to the political economy of a republic. This in turn contracts the political capacity of the people and deadens their public sense of moral responsibility.[74] Important questions sent to the justices are, after all, "virtually always political."[75] Even as the advisory process is in danger of politicizing the judiciary, it has a depoliticizing effect on civic discourse, withdrawing public questions from the political arena to the isolated realm of judicial deliberation, in which they are required to stay by virtue of the justices' disinterestedness. There the justices are at least formally unaffected by the variety of often conflicting and unpredictable assertions of public opinion that endlessly impinge on the legislative process. The advisory process relies on the wise man theory of government with its countermajoritarian temptation to evade the uncertainties and ambiguities of the democratic political process.[76] If advisory opinions were unavailable, "legislative and executive officials would be forced to face up to constitutional questions and take responsibility for the initial decisions on these questions, thereby giving at least some measure of evidence as to what the public understands the constitution to mean."[77]

THE ATTACKS AND THE RISING STATURE OF THE JUDICIARY

Why did advisory opinions, barely noticed and thoroughly uncontroversial during the first four decades since their initial appearance in 1780, become a focus of controversy during the next four decades? The answer lies not in any developments in the practice of advisory opinions but in the context in which the practice took place—the dramatic rise in the power and prestige of the judiciary in the early nineteenth century. The result of that rise was the anomaly of an independent, powerful, nonpolitical judiciary led, in

---

[69] Sands, *Government by Judiciary*, 38.

[70] Calogero, *Advisory Opinions*, 363. The question of coordinate review is discussed below.

[71] Kennedy, *Advisory Opinions*, 190.

[72] *Id.*

[73] Sands, *Government by Judiciary*, 38.

[74] James B. Thayer, Life of John Marshall, 103–10, cited in Frankfurter, *A Note on Advisory Opinions*, 1007.

[75] Bender, *Rhode Island's Public Importance Exception for Advisory Opinions*, 158.

[76] Sands, *Government by Judiciary*, 37.

[77] *Id.* at 38.

the advisory opinion states, by high court justices compelled to render advisory opinions at the demand of the political branches, especially legislatures, which were increasingly seen as a threat to judicial independence.

Important here is the significant alteration in the general understanding of the justices' greatly expanded authority as the judiciary came to be accepted as truly republican.[78] This broad acceptance of the authority of the judiciary is, one historian observes, "a remarkable story, . . . [o]ne of the great political and cultural transformations in American history, and it was accompanied by one of the great propaganda efforts in our history: to get people to believe that judges appointed for life were an integral and independent part of America's democratic government . . . was an extraordinary accomplishment."[79] In 1820, then, the advisory opinion jurisdiction created in 1780 was operating in a very different legal environment. Such developments as the broad acceptance of judicial review, perception of the judiciary as a truly coordinate and independent branch (no less, if no more, dangerous than the others), and the decline in the power of juries and concomitant rise in that of judges, together with the "growing perception that judges no longer merely discovered law; they also made it,"[80] intellectually legitimized by the view of law as a science, all effectively made the judiciary a branch with the authority, even the mandate, to check the partisan chaos of the political branches. Among the checks were law-making (not merely law-discovering) and policy-making. This went hand in hand with the popular election of judges. "This popular political base was essential for judges . . . because they were expected to make public policy." A delegate to the New York Convention in 1846 noted that in "re-organizing the legislative department we have made it less powerful for general legislation . . . [hence] a large share of judicial legislation will be inevitable."[81]

This expanded power maintained its legitimacy because, first, judges in the early nineteenth century "shed what had been a traditional political and magisterial role and adopted one that was much more exclusively legal."[82] Second, the judges' decisions came out of a judicial process hedged all about by restraints and limits. Hamilton's argument about the power of judicial review held for judicial powers in general: they would not be dangerous because the courts "should be bound down by strict rules and

---

[78] *See* Williams E. Nelson, Americanization of the Common Law 171 (1994).

[79] Gordon Wood, *The Origins of Judicial Review*, 22 Suffolk U. L. Rev. 1293, 1304 (1988).

[80] Horwitz, Transformation of American Law, 15. *See also* Leonard W. Levy, The Law of the Commonwealth and Chief Justice Shaw 290–95 (1957) (on the relation of judge and jury); John Philip Reid, Legislating the Courts: Judicial Dependence in Early National New Hampshire (2009) (studying the legislature's extraordinary dominance over the state's judiciary, including what a reviewer called "Reid's convincing account of an American version of republican [as opposed to Federalist] law that lifted legislatures and juries over courts and judges [that] generally prevailed in the early Republic." J. M. Opal, Book Review, 28 Law & Hist. Rev. 870, 871 (2010).

[81] Quoted in Tarr, Understanding State Constitutions, 124.

[82] Gordon Wood, *The Origins of Judicial Review Revisited, or How the Marshall Court Made Less Out of More*, 56 Wash. & Lee L. Rev. 787, 803 (1999). Wood notes that before 1800, judges were still seen as political magistrates, the early Congresses assigning "a surprisingly large number of nonjudicial duties to them."

precedents, which serve to define and point out their duty in every particular case that comes before them."[83] The problem regarding advisory opinions was of course that none of the restraints and limits applied. It would not matter so much with a weak judiciary but does matter greatly with a strong one.

The development of judicial review offers some insight here, owing to the resemblance of judicial review to rendering advisory opinions on the constitutionality of bills or acts. From the start justices rendering advisory opinions freely advised on constitutionality and set forth rules of statutory and constitutional interpretation.[84] Such opinions, whatever weight the requesting authority might have given them, would not yet evoke the concept of judicial review, a concept still inchoate and not yet widely accepted in the states. Judicial review "was a question for which the nation as a whole had no final answer in the 1780s [because the] conception of judicial review had not matured."[85] In the years 1776–1787 "few Americans believed that any State court had the right to declare an enactment invalid on the ground that it violated the Constitution."[86] It was still the era of virtually unquestioned coordinate review, by which, as Madison said, each branch "must in the exercise of its functions, be guided by the text of the constitution according to its own interpretation of it."[87] In this environment advice from the justices would appear to be, and could be taken as, simply advice, and whatever weight the requesting authority chose to give it the advice had no authority beyond the wisdom of the justices offering aid to the coordinate branches in their own efforts to determine the constitutionality of their acts.

---

[83] THE FEDERALIST No. 78 at 496 (Alexander Hamilton) (Benjamin Wright ed., 1961).

[84] On constitutionality: *e.g.*, *Opinion of the Justices to the Senate and House of Representatives*, 126 Mass. 547 (1781) (not unconstitutional for both houses to join in amending property valuations); *Opinion of the Justices*, 14 Mass. 470 (1784) (constitutional for legislature to fill council vacancies occurring from death or resignation of council members); *Opinion of the Justices*, 14 Mass. 472 (1787) (legislature commuting punishment fixed by law, after sentence given, violates constitution, Part 2, ch. 2, sec. 1, art. 8 [pardoning power] and Part. 1, art. XXX [separation of powers]. *Opinion of the Justices*, 7 Mass. 523 (1811) (on construing words in legislative acts). On rules of statutory and constitutional interpretation: *e.g.*, *Opinion of the Justices*, 7 Mass. 523 (1811) (While "words in any legislative act are to be construed according to the common usage," their import "may be enlarged or restrained, to express the real intention of the legislature, [which is] the law resulting from the act.").

[85] William E. Nelson, *Changing Conceptions of Judicial Review: The Evolution of Constitutional Theory in the States, 1790–1860*, 120 U. PA. L. REV. 1166, 1168 (1972). For a view challenging this "conventional history of judicial review" and arguing that judicial review "developed largely before 1776, see Philip Hamburger, *Law and Judicial Duty*, 72 GEO. WASH. L. REV. 1 (2003).

[86] ALLAN NEVINS, THE AMERICAN STATES DURING AND AFTER THE REVOLUTION 168–69 (1924). On the status of judicial review in this period, see also G. Alan Tarr, *Constitutional Theory and State Constitutional Interpretation*, 22 RUTGERS L.J. 841, 857–58 (1991) ("Judicial review of legislation and the idea of judges as prime protectors of rights are both anachronistic notions."); SYLVIA SNOWISS, JUDICIAL REVIEW AND THE LAW OF THE CONSTITUTION, chs. 1–3 (1990); Michael L. Buenger, *Friction by Design: The Necessary Contest of State Judicial Power and Legislative Policymaking*, 43 U. RICHMOND L. REV. 571, 573–85 (2009).

[87] JAMES MADISON, 4 LETTERS AND OTHER WRITINGS OF JAMES MADISON 349 (1865), quoted in SNOWISS, JUDICIAL REVIEW AND THE LAW OF THE CONSTITUTION, 98.

By 1820, however, "the doctrine of judicial review had attained general acceptance."[88] Similarly, the legislative supremacy of the 1780s, which the state constitutions so strongly embodied and which "had denied all judicial authority to regard or consider the Constitution" had, by 1825, been "completely rejected."[89] It was becoming widely accepted that the judiciary primarily (but not yet solely) held the formidable power of final review for constitutionality, including the power to invalidate unconstitutional acts by the other branches.[90] The parallel to advisory opinions on constitutionality must have become conspicuous enough to raise doubts. The perceived problem was that although the "strict rules and precedents" did not apply to advisory opinions, the difference between them and an adjudicated opinion regarding constitutionality was necessarily diminished enough to be a concern, especially as advisory opinions came to be regarded in and out of the legal community as authority carrying precedential force despite the justices' constant claims to the contrary.[91] The supreme courts' increasingly conspicuous power to invalidate laws they found unconstitutional, when combined with their power to advise on constitutionality, made advisory opinions too similar to judicial review and thus too formidable to ignore.

Before 1800, then, when the judiciary was generally seen as the weakest of the three branches, yet to emerge out of "its colonial insignificance,"[92] the duty to advise could not have seemed much of a problem. Even under the new national Constitution, "[t]he fact was that a national judiciary as a branch of government was still something of an abstraction, substantially less real than were the other two."[93] That a state legislature could demand advice from the justices would hardly have been an issue when few saw the judiciary, state or federal, as truly coordinate, whatever their independence. "It was one thing to render judges independent of the executive, another matter entirely to regard them as coequal in authority with the legislature."[94] A weak judiciary, relative to the legislature, was as it should be. Law and equity were to be enforced in the ordinary courts, but this did not, as James Wilson said, confer "upon the judicial department a power superior, in its general nature, to that of the legislature."[95] Leaders during the Revolutionary era "had no intention of curtailing legislative interference in the court structure and in judicial functions, and in fact they meant to increase it."[96]

---

[88] William E. Nelson, *Changing Conceptions of Judicial Review: The Evolution of Constitutional Theory in the States, 1790–1860*, 120 U. PA. L. REV. 1166, 1168–69, 1172 (1972) ("[J]udicial review was a question for which the nation as a whole had no final answer in the 1780s. . . . [B]y 1820 the doctrine of judicial review had attained general acceptance.").

[89] SNOWISS, JUDICIAL REVIEW AND THE LAW OF THE CONSTITUTION, 179.

[90] *See, e.g.*, CHRISTOPHER WOLFE, THE RISE OF MODERN JUDICIAL REVIEW 94–101 (1986).

[91] Chapter 5 is devoted to the issues surrounding claims that advisory opinions are nonbinding.

[92] WOOD, RADICALISM OF THE AMERICAN REVOLUTION, 323.

[93] STANLEY ELKINS & ERIC MCKITRICK, THE AGE OF FEDERALISM 64 (1993).

[94] JACK N. RAKOVE, ORIGINAL MEANINGS 305 (1996).

[95] Quoted in GORDON WOOD, CREATION OF THE AMERICAN REPUBLIC, 305 (1969).

[96] *Id.* at 161.

Twenty-first-century Americans, accustomed to judicial review as well as to judicial supremacy, would likely find it difficult to comprehend the low stature and weak power of the judiciary compared to the other two branches, especially the legislature, whose power over the judges in the states was, in the nation's early years, all but absolute. The new states did affirm judicial independence as against the executive, recalling as they did the history of the British Crown's conflicts with English judges. The states nevertheless accepted control of the judiciary by the legislature, seen as the people's branch and naturally a check on the other branches. New Hampshire was fairly representative.[97] The large fact about the stature of the judiciary there, and elsewhere, was that it was under the thumb of the legislature. This was a deep-seated value of republican ideology, which saw an elected legislature as the people's instrument of government, with a healthy suspicion of a branch of government dominated by elitist professional lawyers.[98] "[A]n independent judiciary was an obstacle to popular control."[99] In New Hampshire as in most states the legislature appointed the judges, who could be legislated out of office, as often happened to judges "belonging to a political party just defeated in the most recent election."[100] The legislature could impeach judges, but "addressing" them out of office, by which the legislature addressed to the governor a request to remove a judge, "was more direct, faster, cheaper, and far less complicated."[101] The addressing power, requiring neither cause nor trial, was an easily implemented provision of the constitutions of New Hampshire and several other of the early states.[102] In a remarkable exercise of another legislative power over the judiciary, the New Hampshire legislature in 1816 legislatively abolished the state's two highest courts, legislated all its members out of office, and then, by way of legislative overkill, also addressed from office all the judges of those courts.[103] This may have been extraordinary—"the most spectacular instance of legislative domination over courts of law, not just in New Hampshire but in all U.S. history"[104]—but it was entirely constitutional and well within the powers of the legislature. Further, the early national New Hampshire legislature was typical in engaging in adjudication, hearing cases and ruling on both law and fact,[105] and, in a state with only trial and no appellate courts,[106]

---

[97] Discussion of the judiciary in New Hampshire relies primarily on Reid, Legislating the Courts: Judicial Dependence in Early National New Hampshire. Reid notes that despite significant differences, "if written large, the judicial history of New Hampshire would mirror much of the judicial history of most other early-republic states." *Id.* at 7.

[98] *Id.* at 4–6.

[99] *Id.* at 11.

[100] *Id.*

[101] *Id.* at 118.

[102] *Id.* at 60, 118. Reid comments that this formidable power over the judges is not well known because it was rejected at the federal convention. *Id.* at 118.

[103] *Id.* at 160.

[104] *Id.*

[105] *Id.* at 65.

[106] *Id.* at 72.

the legislature freely passed "restoration of law" acts, by which the legislature could, for example, grant a new trial to a litigant.[107]

In short, in New Hampshire as in most of the new states, "[f]ar from being constitutionally independent, the judiciary was hardly recognized at all. To the extent that it was, it was at the will and pleasure of a majority of the legislature."[108] Advisory opinions from judges at this time could be of concern to few. It was only after 1800, when the judiciary began to be a "principle means by which popular legislatures were controlled and limited,"[109] that the legislature's power to compel advice from the justices became anomalous. Contributing indirectly but substantially to the rise of judicial status and power, and contributing in turn to the perception of political-branch-controlled advisory opinions as suspect, was the decline in the relative power of juries. During the colonial and Revolutionary periods juries had "vast power to find both the law and the facts" in nearly all cases.[110] The jury and not the judge decided applicable law, and "juries' power to find law was virtually unlimited."[111] Given the widespread functions of American courts at the time, "the jury may well have been regarded then as the true center of gravity in American political life: the institutional locus of a shared system of values."[112] By 1820, however, the relative power of jury and judge was virtually reversed, the courts now beginning to state the law to the juries and setting aside verdicts of juries failing to follow the courts' instructions.[113]

These developments were reinforced by the acceptance of a functionalist conception of the law in the early nineteenth century, raising the judiciary's stature and power as judges came openly to make law and policy and justify it in pragmatic terms. Developing quickly and steadily, the concept of law "as a means to the attainment of an end" by the 1820s "was first being confidently articulated."[114] This "fundamental shift in the conception of the law between 1780 and 1820"[115] saw judges expressly disregarding precedent in explicitly functional terms, and equally explicitly making, not merely discovering, law, and doing so on frankly functional grounds. By mid-nineteenth century the judiciary had undergone these enormous changes, the judges

---

[107] *Id.* at 64–65.

[108] *Id.* at 7.

[109] Wood, Radicalism of the American Revolution, 323.

[110] Nelson, Americanization of the Common Law, 21.

[111] *Id.* at 28.

[112] Robert L. Clinton, *Marbury v. Madison* and Judicial Review 55 (1989).

[113] Nelson, Americanization of the Common Law, 8. Compare the U.S. Supreme Court's decision in *Georgia v. Brailsford*, 3 U.S. 1, 4 (1794), recognizing in 1794 the jury's right to decide questions of law, with their rejection of that right in 1895 in *Sparf v. United States*, 156 U.S. 51 (1895). *See* Matthew P. Harrington, *The Law-Finding Function of the American Jury*, 1999 Wisc. L. Rev. 377 (recounting the history of the decline in the American jury's law-finding, and noting that the function endured into the early twentieth century in criminal cases but declined after 1820 in civil cases. Until then "many American lawyers and judges believed that juries had the power to declare both the law and the fact. The jury thus had the ability to take upon itself the right to determine the entire controversy.").

[114] William E. Nelson, *The Impact of the Antislavery Movement upon Styles of Judicial Reasoning in Nineteenth Century America*, 87 Harv. L. Rev. 513, 514, and 517 (1974).

[115] Horwitz, Transformation of American Law, 4.

accruing significant increases in status and power. The justices' duty to render advisory opinions remained as it was in 1780, but by 1820 was performed by judges with considerable power and prestige.

Doctrinal Attacks on Advisory Opinions: Separation of Powers and Due Process

American law has of course changed in important and fundamental ways since Joseph Story's move against advisory opinions at the 1820 Massachusetts convention. But the major points of attack against advisory opinions have remained remarkably constant over two centuries: advisory opinions infringe on separation of powers, and they violate due process. That is, on the one hand they offend the constitutional structure of government itself, with its otherwise carefully balanced system of separated and checked powers, and on the other they offend the ancient and fundamental right of individuals to notice and hearing before government may act against them. Separation and due process, as crucial restraints on arbitrary power, have been universally seen as the heart of a constitutional republic. Their relation to advisory opinions, since 1820, has never been an easy one.

SEPARATION OF POWERS

For these reasons, it is worth reviewing the grounds for the rejection of advisory opinions in the jurisprudence of judiciaries wherever they do not have an advisory opinion duty. On the federal level, the prohibition against advisory opinions is not merely an incidental consequence of Article III's case or controversy doctrine. It is itself a pillar of Supreme Court jurisprudence. "The [advisory opinion] ban is a rule that goes to the core of the legitimacy of the Supreme Court both as an institution and in its exercise of judicial review."[116] The federal ban is solidly based on separation of powers. It was always so. In 1787 the Constitutional Convention debated a proposed advisory body to review legislation and propose revisions. The motive was the fear, widely held at the Convention, of an overly powerful legislature, which Madison, for example, argued was "the real source of danger to the American Constitution." The experience of all the states, he said, evidenced "a powerful tendency in the Legislature to absorb all power into its vortex."[117] Madison earlier had supported (in the Virginia Plan) a council of revision comprising the executive and "a convenient number of the National Judiciary" with power to review and revise bills.[118] Despite Madison's belief that the council

---

[116] Richard W. Westling, *Advisory Opinions and the "Constitutionally Required" Adequate and Independent State Grounds Doctrine*, 63 Tulane L. Rev. 379, 391 (1988).

[117] 2 Records of the Federal Convention of 1787, at 74 (M. Farrand ed., 1987).

[118] 1 Records of the Federal Convention of 1787, at 21.

would provide "an additional check" against "unwise and unjust measures,"[119] other delegates, though agreeing with Madison about what Gouverneur Morris called "legislative usurpations," opposed the council proposal on separation grounds.[120] The proposal was put forth five times, but separation concerns prevailed and it never passed.

Charles Pinckney proposed an actual advisory opinion provision modeled on that of Massachusetts, giving the Supreme Court advisory powers. There was apparently no floor debate on it, and it was sent to the Committee on Detail, never to be heard from again.[121] The record reveals nothing about the "maneuvering and compromises which must have attended this abrupt termination of the issue."[122]

Absence of an advisory opinion provision notwithstanding, for several years after the new constitution took effect, the Supreme Court rendered advice, neither attracting comment nor commenting themselves on it. Washington in 1790 wrote the Justices inviting their opinions on the formation of the judicial system, especially on the Justices' own duty to ride circuit, imposed on them by Congress.[123] They thought the circuit duty constitutionally doubtful.[124] The general view seemed to have been that the president may seek advice, likely reflecting the centuries-old practice in England carried over to America.[125]

Judicial advising came officially to an abrupt and permanent end in 1793 when Secretary of State Thomas Jefferson wrote the Justices seeking advice on relations with France during its revolutionary wars. Certain legal questions, Jefferson wrote, have resulted in "much embarrassment and difficulty" for Washington's administration, requiring the Court's aid.[126] Chief Justice John Jay's response firmly rejected the invitation, refusing to advise, invoking separation of powers. The Court, Jay explained, considered as decisive "the lines of separation drawn by the Constitution between the three departments of government. These being in certain respects checks upon each other, and our being judges of a court of last resort, are consideration which afford strong arguments against the propriety of our extrajudicially deciding the question alluded to.[127]

---

[119] 2 RECORDS OF THE FEDERAL CONVENTION OF 1787, at 74.

[120] *Id.* at 76. Luther Martin, in an early reference to judicial review, argued that "as to the constitutionality of laws, that point will come before the Judges in their proper official character. In this character they have a negative on the laws," and to place them also on a council of revision would give them a "double negative." 2 RECORDS OF THE FEDERAL CONVENTION OF 1787, at 76.

[121] The advisory opinion proposal was introduced August 20. 2 RECORDS OF THE FEDERAL CONVENTION OF 1787, at 334. *See* STUART JAY, MOST HUMBLE SERVANTS: THE ADVISORY ROLE OF EARLY JUDGES 65–74 (1997).

[122] Note, *The Advisory Opinion and the United States Supreme Court*, 5 FORDHAM L. REV. 94, 102 (1936).

[123] Letter, Washington to the Justices, Apr. 3, 1790. Quoted in Robert P. Dahlquist, *Advisory Opinions as Extrajudicial Activity and Judicial Advocacy: A Historical Perspective*, 14 SOUTHWESTERN U. L. REV. 46, 50–51 (1983).

[124] Dahlquist, *Advisory Opinions as Extrajudicial Activity*, 51–52.

[125] Note, *Advisory Opinions and the United States Supreme Court*, 102.

[126] Letter, Thomas Jefferson to Supreme Court Justices, July 18, 1793. Quoted in Dahlquist, *Advisory Opinions as Extrajudicial Activity*, 59.

[127] Letter, Supreme Court Justices to President Washington, Aug. 8, 1793. The letter is quoted in its entirety in JAY, MOST HUMBLE SERVANTS, 179–80.

Perhaps, as some observers feel today, the Justices could well have advised and that there was no valid basis for refusing, certainly not separation of powers. But that is what the Justices did, setting forth what effectively remains the controlling federal precedent on advisory opinions. Though rendered in a letter, not an opinion, much less a reported and published opinion, Jay's refusal "established a tradition so firmly engrained in our constitutional law that the Court has never questioned and seldom bothered to discuss it in any detail."[128]

It was from the 1793 ban on advisory opinions that there would develop a jurisprudence of justiciability. The "oldest and most consistent thread in the federal law of justiciability," the Supreme Court has said, "is that the federal courts will not give advisory opinions."[129] Justiciability doctrine for the Court is the bulwark against advisory opinions. The doctrine exists "largely to ensure that the federal courts will not issue advisory opinions."[130] Repeatedly, as we will see, when the federal courts would interpret some action as moot, or unripe, or implicating a political question, or as independent and adequate state grounds, or as falling under several other justiciability doctrines, they would refuse to accept the case, citing the risk of rendering an advisory opinion. "Exploration of the categories of justiciability," as one prominent treatise puts it, "will reveal that opinions dealing with such problems as standing, ripeness, and mootness occasionally are expressed in terms of refusal to render advisory opinions."[131] The year before the outright ban in 1793, the Court in *Hayburn's Case* barred Congress from imposing duties of a nonjudicial nature on Article III judges, since "by the Constitution of the United States, the government is divided into three distinct and independent branches, and . . . it is the duty of each to abstain from, and to oppose, encroachments on either."[132] The Court, invoking *Hayburn*, tied separation of powers and nonjudicial

---

[128] P. C. McKeever & B. O. Perry, *The Case for an Advisory Function in the Federal Judiciary*, 50 Geo. L.J. 785, 803 (1962). Stewart Jay questions whether the Court's 1793 letter represents a flat rejection of advisory opinions on separation grounds, calling this "an unfounded assumption" because separation of powers was then "far less complex in its theoretical content and application than is the modern set of doctrines organized under the same rubric." Jay, Most Humble Servants, 173. Robert McCloskey suggests the rejection was asserted in order to preserve the distinction between the judiciary and the other two branches. Robert G. McCloskey, The American Supreme Court 33 (1960).

[129] Flast v. Cohen, 392 U.S. 83, 96 (1968), quoting C. A. Wright, Federal Courts 34 (1963).

[130] Erwin Chemerinsky, Constitutional Law: Principles and Policies 59 (2002). *See also* Note, *The Advisory Opinion and the United States Supreme Court*, 103–06 (reviewing Supreme Court case law rejecting advisory opinions on justiciability grounds).

[131] Charles A. Wright, et al., 1 Federal Practice and Procedure, sec. 3529.1 (2d ed. 1984).

[132] *Hayburn's Case*, 2 U.S. (2 Dall.) 409 (1792) (a violation of separation of powers for federal courts to make recommendations to the Secretary of War on veterans' benefits, if Secretary could refuse to follow recommendations). On *Hayburn's Case* and its role in defining the "distinctive judicial status" of the federal judiciary, *see* Gordon Wood, Empire of Liberty 453–54 (2009). Bickel comments that the "aspect of the 'case' concept emphasized in *Hayburn's Case*—namely, that the judgments the Court is asked to render must be final—merges with the prohibition against advisory opinions, insofar as judgments subject to revision elsewhere may be thought of as merely offering advice to the revising authority." Alexander Bickel, The Least Dangerous Branch 117 (2d ed. 1986).

duties to advisory opinions in *Muskrat*, its leading case on advisory opinions. Nonjudicial opinions, in short, are advisory opinions.[133]

However crucial it is in federal jurisprudence, the advisory opinion ban tends not to be enforced directly. "Instead it is usually implemented through other justiciability doctrines, such as standing, ripeness, and mootness."[134] But the federal (and state) courts rarely lose sight of the centrality of advisory opinion ban to it all. Courts, for example, see case or controversy requirements as diametrically opposed to advisory opinions. Indeed the very origins of case or controversy as a constitutional doctrine lies in its relation to advisory opinions: "[T]he case or controversy requirement ultimately found its way into the Constitution in order to prevent just such practices as the Privy Council's ex ante legislative review from taking root in federal courts. . . . The alternative to a case or controversy standard is to permit courts to issue advisory opinions."[135] The Supreme Court put the relation between case or controversy and advisory opinions directly in *Fruehauf*, noting that one basis for the federal rejection of advisory opinions is that they are on "issues which remain unfocused because they are not pressed upon the Court with that clear concreteness provided when a question emerges precisely framed and necessary for decision from a clash of adversary argument exploring every aspect of a multi-faceted situation embracing conflicting and demanding interests."[136] Judges, both state and federal, virtually idolize the value of what a Maine chief justice, in his 1908 article attacking his advisory duties, called "the shock of contention by adverse parties that lights the torch of truth. It is when every argument advanced, and every authority cited, is assailed by opposing counsel that the true reason and rule are most likely to be found."[137] It has been long and widely observed that the advisory opinion process, lacking all that the adversarial process provides, greatly increases the likelihood of error by the advising justices. "However great the talents of the judges," said Joseph Story, "however extensive their learning, they are never safe in deciding without an argument."[138]

An important consequence of the absence of adversarial process in advisory opinion proceedings is one that challenges the very nature of the judicial enterprise: the factual vacuum. Advising justices act in an abstract, hypothetical universe. Facts, wrote Frankfurter in his attack on advisory opinions, are decisive. Without them advisory opinions are responses to sterile legal questions "bound to result in sterile conclusions

---

[133] Muskrat v. United States, 219 U.S. 346, 362 (1911). Discussion of *Hayburn's Case* is at 352–53.

[134] Thomas Healey, *The Rise of Unnecessary Constitutional Rulings*, 83 N.C. L. Rev. 847, 896 (2005). Eugene M. Van Loan suggests that Article III's extension of judicial power to all cases "arising under this Constitution" (in addition to those arising under laws, treaties, and the enumerated cases or controversies) came out of the Framers' addressing the issue of justiciability. Their "intent in limiting the Court" to what Madison called "cases of a Judiciary nature" was "to prohibit advisory opinions." *See* Eugene M. Van Loan III, *Judicial Review and Its Limits: Part I (Legitimacy)*, N.H. Bar J. 52, 62 (Autumn 2006).

[135] Alison LaCroix, *The Authority for Federalism: Madison's Negative and the Origins of Federal Ideology*, 28 Law & Hist. Rev. 451, 467 (2010).

[136] United States v. Fruehauf, 365 U.S. 146, 157 (1961).

[137] Lucilius A. Emery, *Advisory Opinions from Justices*, 2 Me. L. Rev. 1, 3 (1908).

[138] Journal of the Debates and Proceedings of the 1820 Massachusetts Convention, 220.

unrelated to actualities."[139] The key here is *adversarial* fact, created within the frame of claim and counterclaim, "a proposition on one side denied on the other."[140] This is so partly because where judgment is required only when "an affirmative is met by a negative," the conflict represents the only legitimate means of disclosing facts.[141] But not only so. To speak of "disclosing" or "presenting" or "discovering" facts presumes that the facts are "out there," part of an objective, stable reality already awaiting the parties to a case to collect them and herd them into court. Judicial, adversarial facts, however, are judicial, adversarial constructions, existing insofar as they contribute to construction of judicial meaning. It is these facts that are crucially missing in advisory proceedings, so that the advisory justices' interpretations are what Story called the "retired speculations of ingenious minds."[142] A court properly relies on the core adjudicative acts of challenge and response, claim and denial, for its findings of facts. These are in contrast to the abstract, generalized facts offered by those requesting advisory opinions, "non-adjudicatory, hypothetical, and prospective."[143]

Justice Brandeis called attention to one insidious effect the factual vacuum has on advisory justices' consideration of the constitutionality of a proposed statute before it is enacted. It prevents constructive changes in laws based on the actual experience of a law in operation. Since the advisory justices consider the constitutionality of a proposed statute in a factual vacuum, there is, as Erwin Griswold said, describing Brandeis' view, "a tendency for the court (and counsel in their argument) to hunt out the worst factual assumptions, and to conclude that the statute, as drawn, would be invoked in such a case, leading to the result that the statute should be declared unconstitutional."[144]

---

[139] Frankfurter, *A Note on Advisory Opinions*, 1005.

[140] Hector L. MacQueen, *Pleadable Brieves, Pleading, and the Development of Scots Law*, 4 Law & Hist. Rev. 403, 413 (1986). On the historically central role of adversarial fact, see S. F. C. Milsom, Historical Foundations of the Common Law 42 (1981). The question of the place of advisory opinions in an adversarial legal system is discussed below in Chapter 6.

[141] Alessandro Guiliani, *The Influence of Rhetoric on the Law of Evidence and Pleading*, 7 Jurid. Rev. 216, 229 (1962).

[142] Journal of the Debates and Proceedings of the 1820 Massachusetts Convention, 392. On the idea of facts as constructions in legal contexts, see, e.g., A. Daniel Yarney, The Psychology of Eyewitness Testimony 57 (1979); Elizabeth F. Loftus, Eyewitness Testimony 21 (1979).

[143] Kennedy, *Advisory Opinions: Cautions About Non-Judicial Undertakings*, 192. For an opposing view, see McKeever & Perry, *The Case for an Advisory Function in the Federal Judiciary*, 812–13. McKeever and Perry are among the few observers who challenge the criticism of advisory opinions as operating in a vacuum. Advisory opinions do so, they say, "but this objection is not as important as it first appears. A study of the cases reveals that the objection has often been overemphasized. [Except for cases based on deprivations of human rights] the determination of the constitutional issue is infrequently dependent upon the factual pattern." This is based on the authors' analysis of U.S. Supreme Court opinions declaring acts of Congress unconstitutional. For the view that concrete cases tend to make bad law, see Charles A. Sullivan, *On Vacation*, 43 Houston L. Rev. 1143, 1201 (2006).

[144] Letter of Erwin J. Griswold, given in its entirety in D. L. Doernberg & M.B. Mushlin, *History Comes Calling: Dean Griswold Offers New Evidence About the Jurisdictional Debate Surrounding the Enactment of the Declaratory Judgment Act*, 37 U.C.L.A. L. Rev. 139, 141 (1989). Griswold's letter was a comment on the authors' *The Trojan Horse: How the Declaratory Judgment Act Created a Cause of Action and Expanded Federal Jurisdiction While the Supreme Court Wasn't Looking*, 36 U.C.L.A. L. Rev. 529 (1989). Brandeis argued that there is no understanding a law without knowing the facts relating to it, in his influential speech,

This absence of fact has the same source, in fact is essentially the same, as the absence of adversarial argument. Requests for advice need not be, and usually are not, briefed by parties in interest. Often the letter from the requesting authority is the sole source of information. The facts in such a request, if they are offered at all, might help explain the nature of the request, but they are not *adversarial* facts, put forth in contemplation of challenge from, or as a challenge to, opposing parties.

Advisory justices have been increasingly inviting briefs and oral argument,[145] but this raises its own problems. First, discretion to permit participation by interested parties remains with the justices. Second, even when participation is permitted, it is possible only after the question has been accepted by the justices. "No state provides any means for the public to address the jurisdictional question. Outside participation is possible only after a matter has been accepted for resolution."[146] Third, participation is hampered by the short time typical of the advisory opinion process. Fourth, there is no procedure for identifying interested parties, much less notifying them.[147] The best the justices can do is issue a general invitation, usually in their order accepting the request for advice. This may lead to due process concerns among the justices, which may impel them to restrict advisory opinions to the broadest and most general public issues (some advisory justices have made this a rule for accepting advisory opinion requests), making it all the more difficult to identify parties with a sufficient stake in the issue to effectively argue on it.[148] Fifth, briefs and oral argument in advisory opinion proceedings blur the "already imprecise distinction between decisions of the court and opinions of the justices."[149] Finally, briefs and arguments in advisory opinion proceedings may not be of the same quality and force as in adjudications. A former Massachusetts chief justice observed that briefing for an advisory opinion "sometimes is not so effective or so well-focused as that which follows thorough examination of the issues through the trial process."[150] At any rate, "inviting" holders of opposing views to participate in an advisory opinion proceeding is simply not the same as participating as an adversarial interested party in a litigated case.[151]

The Living Law, delivered to the Chicago Bar Association, Jan. 3, 1916. Reprinted in 10 Ill. L. Rev. 461 (1916). Declaratory judgments are discussed later in this chapter.

[145] Calogero, *Advisory Opinions: A Wise Change for Louisiana and Its Judiciary?*, 348. Only Florida's advisory opinion provision requires the justices to permit interested parties to be heard, but in no state are briefs or argument required in advisory opinion proceedings.

[146] Kennedy, *Advisory Opinions: Cautions About Non-Judicial Undertakings*, 184–85.

[147] *Id.* at 192; Calogero, *Advisory Opinions: A Wise Change for Louisiana and Its Judiciary?*, 348.

[148] *Id.* at 349.

[149] Charles M. Carberry, *The State Advisory Opinion in Perspective*, 14 Fordham L. Rev. 81, 101 (1975).

[150] Letter from Massachusetts Chief Justice Paul J. Liacos to Louisiana Chief Justice Pascal F. Calogero, May 17, 1991. Copy on file with the author.

[151] Joseph Jaconelli, *Hypothetical Disputes, Moot Points of Law, and Advisory Opinions*, 10 Law Q. Rev. 587, 610–11 (1985). *See also* Kennedy, *Advisory Opinions: Cautions About Non-Judicial Undertaking*, 192. McKeever and Perry disagree, suggesting that briefs in advisory opinion proceedings more accurately and more concisely frame a constitutional issue. McKeever & Perry, *The Case for an Advisory Function in the Federal Judiciary*, 814.

DUE PROCESS

The factual vacuum inherent in advisory opinions implicates not only justiciability, through which the advisory opinion ban runs like a red thread and which cannot be evaded or ignored without offending separation of powers. By tracking the separation issues that shadow advisory opinions we go through case or controversy and the whole spectrum of justiciablilty doctrines to this second great shadow—due process. "The concept that decisions are driven by facts lies at the heart of fairness and due process. Careful differential factual analysis is the common work of judges. . . . It cannot, however, be engaged in by an advisory court operating with abstract principles and hypothetical facts . . . [J]ustice requires that there be operative facts that ultimately control the results."[152] The relation of one of the core "fact" requirements of case or controversy, injury-in-fact, to advisory opinions was set out clearly by New York's high court. "The requirement of injury in fact is closely aligned with our policy not to render advisory opinions. . . . Injury in fact thus serves to define the proper role of the judiciary."[153] The key problem is of course that justices in rendering advisory opinions may approve a prospective statute or action without allowing affected parties to be heard. Often it is not the action of the advising justices that is the due process problem, but the action of the requesting authority that acts on the justices' advice.[154] Further, advisory opinions are prospective, and as such they "might foreclose issues on which interested parties in future litigation would not have had full opportunity to be heard."[155] Partly to mitigate this, all advisory justices have restricted requests for advice that affect private rights or pending litigation.[156] But the doubts as to its effect remain.

The due process dangers were first addressed at the 1820 Massachusetts convention. A "question proposed by the legislature or by the Governor and Council to the Judges may deeply affect private rights and interests," a delegate said. "It is contrary to the general theory of responsible government that the rights or property of any citizen should be taken away without an opportunity of being heard upon the questions of law which those rights and that property may involve." If a question manages to avoid private rights and is of a purely public character, then it involves "political power."[157] The concern has been a constant in the advisory opinion states ever since.

---

[152] Kennedy, *Advisory Opinions: Cautions About Non-Judicial Undertaking*, 193.

[153] Society of the Plastics Industry v. County of Suffolk, 573 N.E.2d 1034, 1040 (N.Y. 1991).

[154] *See* Note, *Extra-Judicial Opinions*, 10 Harv. L. Rev. 50 (1896); Note, *Constitutional Law—Powers of the Judiciary—Obligation of Courts to Give Advisory Opinions*, 655 (1912); Carberry, *The State Advisory Opinion in Perspective*, 101.

[155] Carberry, *The State Advisory Opinion in Perspective*, 101. Closely related to this is the problem of the inability of those affected to participate in resolving issues involved, an important element of what Eisenberg calls social ordering, "participation by persons who will be affected by decisions." Melvin Aron Eisenberg, *Participation, Responsiveness, and the Consultative Process: An Essay for Lon Fuller*, 92 Harv. L. Rev. 410, 411 (1978) (discussing Fuller's work, especially *The Forms and Limits of Adjudication*, 92 Harv. L. Rev. 353 (1978), in which Fuller develops his "participation thesis").

[156] Chapter 3 discusses the advising justices' restrictions.

[157] Journal of the Debates and Proceedings, 72, 220. Later observers commenting on increased likelihood of error in advisory proceedings include Frankfurter, *A Note on Advisory Opinions*, 1006; Smiljanich,

Aggravating the due process question is the frequent criticism that the justices may be prejudiced by their advisory opinions if the same issue comes before them in an adjudicated case. There is risk of the justices being "insensibly biased" by their earlier conclusions in advisory opinions, since the justices may be slow to overcome the pride of first conviction and admit the need to change their views.[158] Even if the advice were incorrect, the justices might be slower to see error in their own work than in that of others.[159] Advisory justices are aware of the problem. It was among the objections of the Rhode Island justices to their advisory duty that was reported to the 1986 state constitutional convention. "Once an advisory opinion is issued, it becomes very difficult [for the justices] to reconsider an issue and decide it differently, in light of an actual factual situation."[160] The Massachusetts justices have referred to their duty to "guard against" any influence of advisory opinions while considering an adjudicated case;[161] and two Alabama justices, declining to join their five brethren who affirmed the constitutionality of the state's advisory opinion statute, said that rendering advice "will constitute a moral obstacle . . . to stand in the way of a free and unbiased decision should the question now propounded hereafter recur in the course of litigation the court will be bound to decide."[162]

Not in This State: Rejections of Advisory Opinions on Separation of Powers and Due Process Grounds

In every state whose supreme court was not bound constitutionally or statutorily to advisory opinion duties, the court invoked separation of powers or due process or both to ground their refusal to render advisory opinions. These states include those where the justices had issued advisory opinions and then suddenly stopped, and those where the justices, faced with statutes imposing advisory opinion duties on them, declared the statutes unconstitutional.

Advisory Opinions in Florida, 337; Calogero, *Advisory Opinions: A Wise Change for Louisiana and Its Judiciary*? 366; Kennedy, *Advisory Opinions: Cautions About Non-Judicial Undertaking*, 186; Sands, *Government by Judiciary*, 31.

[158] Ellingwood, Departmental Cooperation, 254–55.

[159] Edsall, *The Advisory Opinion in North Carolina*, 332. *See also* Sands, *Government by Judiciary*, 26; Persky, *Ghosts That Slay*, 1211–12 (observing that the notion that justices will not be biased by their advisory opinions when subsequently addressing the same question litigated during appeals "surely reflects an optimistic view").

[160] Report of the Judicial Selection and Discipline Committee, Minutes of the Rhode Island Constitutional Convention, May 21, 1986.

[161] Massachusetts Hous. Fin. Agency v. New England Merchants National Bank, 249 N.E.2d 599 (Mass. 1969).

[162] *In re Opinions of the Justices in re Amendment to Section 93 of the Constitution*, 96 So. 487, 498 (Ala. 1923).

ADVISING, THEN STOPPING

Connecticut and Nebraska had issued advisory opinions, usually without comment on doing so, then, in response to a request for advice, announced they will henceforth refuse, without accounting for the sudden change. Connecticut rendered advisory opinions in 1862 and 1865 without remarking on the legitimacy of the process. For the 1862 opinion, the justices were "convened by the Governor, pursuant to the direction of the General Assembly, to advise him respecting the constitutionality of the act in question." The act permitted taking votes of soldiers serving out of state in elections for state officials. The justices held the act unconstitutional because the state constitution is sufficiently specific on the time, place, and manner of elections that the legislature may not alter them.[163] In 1865 the legislature asked the judges to advise on whether African-Americans are "citizens of the United States" under the Connecticut constitution, apparently in response both to the proposed Thirteenth Amendment to the U.S. Constitution, recently sent to the states for ratification, and to Congress's recently passed civil rights bill. The justices answered in the affirmative. Their reply is one sentence long, offering neither rationale for their opinion nor comment on their advising.[164]

Then, in 1867, the Connecticut justices flat out refused to respond to the legislature's request for advice on the validity of a tax bill. "There are in our minds," the justices wrote, such strong objections both to the legislature asking and to the justices giving opinions on proposed legislation, "that we feel it our duty . . . to decline to give the opinion requested." They rehearsed the problems. Advising would be "clearly extra-judicial," with no parties before the court and "nothing to adjudicate." The advice would be no more binding than "any other five judicious lawyers" but with the added defect that the judges might later be biased, "inclined to adhere to an opinion which we had expressed." These are "grave reasons" for regarding such advice as invalid. The justices defended their two earlier advisory opinions on grounds of exceptional public importance, without making clear if that would remain a standard for advising in the future.[165]

In Nebraska the justices, for a while, gave advisory opinions to nearly anyone asking, in the absence of either constitutional or statutory authority. In 1884, for example, the court reporter asked what expenses he could charge the state for publishing the court reporter volumes. Apparently taking seriously the traditional notion that advisory opinions are the separate opinions of each justice, four of the five justices each offered his own opinion (the fifth just concurring with another). One justice signed himself "attorney at law," perhaps to emphasize that while advising, the justices do not act in their judicial capacity.[166] A second opinion, issued the same year, advised the state board of education on proper investment of its funds. This request was submitted jointly by the

---

[163] *Opinion of the Judges of the Supreme Court*, 30 Conn. 591 (1862).

[164] *Opinion of the Judges of the Supreme Court*, 32 Conn. 565 (1865).

[165] *Reply of the Judges of the Supreme Court to the General Assembly*, 33 Conn. 586 (1867).

[166] *In re Brown*, 50 N.W. 273 (Neb. 1884).

governor, attorney general, secretary of state, and the Commissioner of Public Lands and Buildings. The justices, noting that the question was "not inconsistent with our duties," rendered the advice sought.[167] A third advisory opinion advised the state auditor on capital requirements for life insurance companies organized in the state.[168]

Then, a few years later the justices rendered another routine advisory opinion concerning the authority of two state boards. For the first time, however, one justice "dissents," not to the advice given but to giving advice at all. Citing the state constitution's separation of powers clause, Justice Norval argued that the constitution confers no advisory jurisdiction on the supreme court. After describing the due process challenges in some detail, he declared that "it is time for the court to call a halt" to advising. His brethren seemed unimpressed, issuing their advice with no response to the dissenter.[169] But they do not seem to have advised again, and a year later the court put forth a rule asserting that it will address questions only involved in litigation, and "no opinion will be filed in answer to any merely hypothetical question."[170]

DECLARING ADVISORY OPINION STATUTES UNCONSTITUTIONAL

The Minnesota supreme court in 1865 rejected the state's only statutory attempt to create advisory opinions, in what appears to be the first such action by a state supreme court. The state's advisory opinion law required the "court or judges" to advise either house of the legislature when so requested.[171] The justices had declined to advise twice before without referring to constitutional issues, perhaps hoping the legislature would take a hint. But on a third request for advice they stopped it altogether, declaring the statute unconstitutional, citing the state constitution's separation of powers clause. The clause, the court said, prohibits one department of government from imposing duties on another "not within the scope of its jurisdiction." Adopting the reasoning of every court rejecting advisory opinion duties, the court asserted that an advisory opinion is not a judicial act, "nor is it to be performed in a judicial manner," but rather transforms the supreme court into "the advisors of the legislatures, nothing more." The court's contempt for advisory opinions is transparent. Allowing advisory opinions would be "a dangerous precedent," and the "evils which might result to the people from such a source will suggest themselves on a moment's reflection." Observing that the only states which permit advisory opinions are those whose constitutions compel their justices to

---

[167] *In re School Fund*, 50 N.W. 272 (Neb. 1884).

[168] *In re Babcock*, 32 N.W. 641 (Neb. 1887).

[169] *In re Board of Public Lands and Buildings, and Board of Purchase and Supplies*, 37 Neb. 425 (1893), Norval, J., dissenting, 432–35.

[170] 37 Neb. XIII, Rule 23 (1894), quoted in Edsall, *The Advisory Opinion in North Carolina*, 336. Aumann, *The Supreme Court and the Advisory Opinion*, 32, writes that the supreme court's advisory opinions were "apparently discontinued in 1898 by 52 Neb. XVIII, Rule 32."

[171] *Minn. Comp. Stat.*, sec. 15, ch. 4 (1863).

render them, the court comments that they "confess that . . . such a constitutional provision does not address itself to our minds with any favor."[172]

Vermont is the only state that enacted an advisory opinion statute, repealed it, then passed one again, the latter to be declared unconstitutional. An 1864 law permitted the governor to require the opinions of the justices on questions of law related to the governor's duties.[173] It was repealed in 1915, but a new advisory opinion law was enacted in 1948. The governor signed it into law, and, expressing, on separation of powers grounds, "grave doubts about the constitutionality" of such a law, asked the court (the law referred to "Supreme Court," not to "justices") to render an advisory opinion. He did not comment on the paradox. The governor went on to request, should the law be found constitutional, an advisory opinion on an educational bill awaiting his signature. The advisory opinion statute was aggressive, requiring the court to consider requests for advice "forthwith," and if the court was not in session when the request arrived, it "shall be forthwith called in session" by the chief justice. The court's response was that rendering advisory opinions violates separation of powers, which restricts the judicial branch to judicial matters, hence to cases or controversies, "actual and bona fide litigation." By "no possible construction of the Constitution of this State can this power be enlarged to include the giving of an opinion on a question of law not involved" in litigation. The court was careful not to specify that the advisory opinion statute itself was unconstitutional, that is to answer the governor's questions (that would be giving the advice they ruled they cannot give), though it concluded obliquely by noting that the court had "incidentally but necessarily indicated" to the governor that his doubt about the constitutionality of the law "is well founded."[174]

In 1936 Kentucky enacted a law permitting the governor or either house of the legislature to obtain advisory opinions from the state supreme court. The sequence and rapidity of events suggest an intentional test. The law took effect January 22, 1936. The House of Representatives promptly submitted a request for advice regarding a tax bill on January 30, asking the justices to render the advice on February 4, giving them all of three workdays to consider their response. The court responded by the deadline, declaring advisory opinions unconstitutional. In what may be an American record, the time from the law taking effect to its being ruled unconstitutional was fourteen days. The court dispatched advisory opinions in a decision of little more than a page, advisory opinions never to be heard from again in Kentucky. The ruling declared advisory opinions to be a violation of separation of powers because they are not judicial acts, and the state constitution's separation provisions "forbid an assignment to the judiciary of any duties not properly judicial and to be performed in a judicial manner." The constitution

---

[172] *In the Matter of the Application of the Senate*, 10 Minn. Reports 78 (1865).

[173] *Vermont Revised Laws*, sec. 795 (1880). *See* Hugo A. Dubuque, *The Duty of Judges as Constitutional Advisors*, 24 AM. L. REV. 369, 377 (1890).

[174] *In re Opinion of the Justices*, 64 A.2d 169 (Vt. 1949).

limits the supreme court to appellate jurisdiction, the court said, and this is properly understood only as "a resort from an inferior tribunal justice to a superior."[175]

The new states of North Dakota and South Dakota, carved out of a large part of the Dakota Territory, held simultaneous constitutional conventions in the summer of 1889 and were admitted into the Union on the same day the following November. Both considered similar advisory opinions provisions. South Dakota (discussed earlier in this chapter) adopted it and retains it today. North Dakota rejected it, recording the debate in some detail.[176] One proponent of advisory opinions offered an expertise argument, one of increasing influence in the course of the nineteenth century, noting that a majority of those elected to the legislature "will be farmers, mechanics and laboring men," presumably those in need of expert legal advice. But the debate was in the main hostile to advisory opinions. It was the delegate responding to the one making the expertise argument who said that, while "a very few" states allowed advisory opinions, in all those states "not only the Supreme Court but every other person who has an intimate knowledge of the workings of that provision would wish it were not there."[177] Exactly a half-century later the North Dakota supreme court, in their rejection of advisory duties in *Langer v. State*, made clear the intent of the convention. "The debates of the Constitutional Convention leave no doubt that it was the deliberate judgment of the framers of the State Constitution that the Judges of the Supreme Court . . . should not be required, or authorized, to give advisory opinions."[178]

A JURISPRUDENCE OF REJECTION: FERRETING OUT COVERT ADVISORY OPINIONS

The vigilance against advisory opinions has been strong and steady among judiciaries in states where the justices have no explicit statutory or constitutional authority to advise.[179] In these nonadvisory jurisdictions courts have been especially wary of covert advisory opinions—requests for advice coming to them under cover of innocent procedural guises. With bloodhound alertness these courts have been vigilant in smelling out an advisory opinion request, tracking it down, declaring the proceeding to be such a request in camouflage, and chasing it out of court. They explain themselves mainly in separation of powers and due process terms, when they explain themselves at all.

---

[175] *In re Constitutionality of House Bill No. 222*, 90 S.W.2d 692 (Ky. 1936).

[176] Official Report of the Proceedings and Debates of the First Constitutional Convention of North Dakota, 230–35 (1889); Journal and Debates of the South Dakota Constitutional Convention, 77–81, 97–99, 157–73 (1889). The Illinois convention of 1869 introduced a proposed advisory opinion provision, but, like the similar proposal at the federal convention in 1787, it was sent to committee and not heard from again. Debates and Proceedings of the Constitutional Convention of the State of Illinois [of 1869], 174 (1870).

[177] Official Report, at 231.

[178] Langer v. State, 284 N.W. 238, 252 (N.D. 1939).

[179] North Carolina is something of an exception, as noted in Chapter 1.

In Louisiana in 1925 a new law required school districts to adjust their finances so that they operated on a fiscal year basis, beginning July 1, rather than a calendar year basis. The school board in one parish responded by ordering several schools simply to be shut down for a school year, claiming it was impossible to abide by the requirement in any other way. On an appeal in a mandamus action, the state supreme court ordered the school board to rescind its order to close the schools in its parish. The relators then requested a rehearing so that they could request that the court's order be changed to say that the fiscal year law was "not mandatory but only directory" regarding school districts changing to a fiscal year basis. The court denied the rehearing. In some states, it said, "the court of last resort renders advisory opinions at the request of the other departments of government, but not in this state." Why would a grant of a rehearing result in an advisory opinion? The court offered no explanation. It may have been that in holding that the statute was "directory" rather than "mandatory," or not, it would be advising. But they do not say so. At any rate the court took this opportunity to establish its position on advisory opinions, which holds today.[180]

The New York Court of Appeals, the state's high court, was more explicit about how the action before them constituted a de facto request for advice. In the court's leading case on advisory opinions, the question concerned the statutory authority of an agency to certify questions to an appellate court. In 1917 New York's industrial commission's enabling statute specifically provided for the commission to certify questions of law to the Appellate Division. A commission member introduced a proposal on the funding of the workers' compensation program. The commission, doubtful of its legal authority to act on the proposal, certified the question to the Appellate Division, the state's intermediate appellate court, which held the commission had the authority. The court also granted leave to appeal its holding to the Court of Appeals, and the commission certified the same question to that court.

Justice Cardozo, writing for a unanimous court, dismissed the action, leaving no doubt as to why. New York courts, he wrote, "do not give advisory opinions." The commission's enabling act allowed appeals, but subject to the same limits as on any civil action. Here, the opinion held, there was no case or controversy; opposing parties received no notice and did not appear; the commission made no decision; the appeals court's response "bound no one and settled nothing." The enabling act's provision on certifying questions in reality permitted the commission to seek advisory opinions. Cardozo, citing a half dozen U.S. Supreme Court cases, asserted that the function of the courts—all courts—is to "determine controversies between litigants. They do not give advisory opinions. The giving of such opinions is not the exercise of the judicial function." He took the trouble to distinguish New York from jurisdictions where advisory opinions may be legitimate, that is in England and the American advisory opinion states, arguing that in those places justices are not acting in a judicial capacity when they advise. But in New York the legislature may not "charge the courts with the

[180] State v. Rapides Parish School Board, 103 So. 757 (La. 1925).

performance of non-judicial duties." Certified questions under the commission's statute must, he said, "be incidental to a pending controversy with adverse parties litigant." Cardozo concluded by citing another unacceptable characteristic of advisory opinions—their too general and abstract, anticipatory nature. "We deal with the particular instance; and we wait till it arises."[181]

Justice Cardozo made the position of the Court of Appeals on advisory opinions clear enough, but the court would typically take great care to ferret out advisory opinion requests. Cardozo addressed the matter again in 1928. New York's governor directed a state judge to report to the governor on a citizen's complaint against the Queens borough president and demand for his removal. The governor was acting under a statute allowing the governor to appoint a judge to take evidence in proceedings for removal of a public officer. After this case began with Judge Scudder holding hearings and subpoenaing witnesses, legislation was enacted expanding the governor's power under the statute, allowing him to direct a judge to conduct a full investigation. On appeal, Justice Cardozo, again writing for a unanimous court, ordered the judge to cease the proceedings. Judges may not be made "adjuncts or advisors" to other agencies. Hence Judge Scudder is "disqualified, while retaining the office of judge, to act as a delegate of the Governor under one name or another." The argument that the judge was acting as an individual and not in a judicial capacity was unacceptable. "The prohibitions of the [New York] Constitution [on plural officeholding] are not to be evaded through the form of accepting as an individual what the judge must reject." The statute in question, Cardozo wrote, permits charging a judge with performing nonjudicial duties, making the judge a "delegate of the Governor in aid of an executive act [removal of a public officer]." The judge's findings "will be mere advice to the Governor." Cardozo distinguishes sharply between "what is of the essence of the judicial function"—deciding—and the "pallid opportunity to consult and recommend." The statute was therefore an encroachment on judicial power, in effect seeking to "annex the office of a judge. . . . As often as the Governor commands, the judge is to obey."[182] Cardozo's opinion typifies the manner in which a court will designate some statutorily defined action as a nonjudicial duty imposed on the judiciary, the fulfilling of which would be an advisory opinion.

In a 2008 Kansas case the camouflage was a statute's "judicial trigger" provision, which the Kansas supreme court rejected outright as effectively a demand by the legislature that the court issue an advisory opinion. That the court's rejection may have been, as a critic argued, inadequately grounded, only signals all the more the court's vigilance against advisory opinions.[183] Kansas, at least since 1980, has made clear its prohibition

---

[181] *Matter of State Industrial Commission*, 119 N.E. 1027 (N.Y. 1918). The Texas supreme court also expressed suspicion of the potential for certified questions to be covert requests for advisory opinions, in *Morrow v. Corbin*, 62 S.W.2d 641 (Tex. 1933). The court held that it is an advisory opinion if a judgment has not been rendered in the court below. The court traced this position back to when Texas was an independent republic.

[182] *In re Richardson*, 160 N.E. 655 (N.Y. 1928).

[183] *Kansas ex rel. Morrison v. Sebelius*, 179 P.3d 366 (Kans. 2008). The critique of *Morrison* is in Kenneth Burden, "State Constitutional Law – Separation of Powers – A 'Judicial Trigger Provision' Violates the

against advisory opinions.[184] In 2007, however, the state legislature enacted a statute to regulate protesters picketing at the funerals of soldiers who fell in Iraq or Afghanistan. The statute included a judicial trigger requiring that it not take effect until it was upheld by a court. The Kansas supreme court declared the trigger unconstitutional since it would not present a court with "an actual case or controversy" and in effect "would seek an advisory opinion," a violation of separation of powers,[185] which the court related, at considerable length, to case or controversy standards. It carefully distinguished a case or controversy from an advisory opinion, applying in detail the doctrines of standing including mootness and ripeness.

The court was careful to show that its rejection of advisory opinions in general, and specifically the judicial trigger at issue here, was based on state, not federal, constitutional doctrine. "Each state is free to define the judicial powers of its courts."[186] Citing differences between Kansas and federal standards, it concluded that while the "Kansas Constitution's provisions do not vary from those in the United States Constitution as drastically as other state constitutions," one distinction is that the Kansas constitution has no reference to "case" or "controversy."[187] But the Kansas courts have repeatedly held that the duty of the courts is to "decide actual controversies by a judgment which can be carried into effect, and not to give opinions upon moot questions or abstract propositions."[188] For its own case or controversy requirements, "Kansas courts have relied solely on the separation of powers doctrine embodied in the Kansas constitutional framework."[189] In the funeral picketing case, by holding the statute in question inoperative until a court rules on its constitutionality, separation of powers was infringed. "Power is shifted away from the legislature when the legislature does not reach its own independent conclusion, albeit preliminary, regarding the constitutionality of a statute."[190] The case or controversy requirements apply only to private parties. "When actions are brought on relation to the Attorney General or another government officer, there is no requirement of actual injury." The officer is, however, required to show that the question involves a specified duty imposed by law, regarding a question of great public importance, and (the key distinction from advisory opinions) the question must arise from an actual controversy.[191]

The ruling of the Kansas supreme court in *National Education Association—Topeka* against advisory opinions was also fairly typical in the way that the court found an

---

Kansas Constitution's Separation of Powers Doctrine by Requiring Courts to Issue an Advisory Opinion," 40 *Rutgers L.J.* 825 (2009) (arguing that the Kansas Supreme Court "merely adopts the federal case or controversy requirement, without any searching analysis of state constitutional pedigree on the issue. . . . [T]he basis for rejecting advisory opinions under [Kansas] state constitutional law is suspect.").

[184] *National Education Association—Topeka v. U.S.D. 501*, 608 P.2d 920 (Kans. 1980).

[185] *Kansas ex rel. Morrison v. Sebelius,* 179 P.3d at 390.

[186] *Id.* at 381.

[187] *Id.*

[188] *Id.* at 382.

[189] *Id.*

[190] *Id.* at 383, citing Frankfurter, "A Note on Advisory Opinions," 1003.

[191] *Kansas ex rel. Morrison v. Sebelius,* 179 P.3d at 389.

advisory opinion lurking in an appeal, in this case owing to what it found to be mootness. In a dispute regarding negotiations between a school board and a teachers union now at impasse, the trial court granted the union's motion and temporarily enjoined the school board from negotiating contracts with individual members of the bargaining unit, pending results of a fact-finding panel's efforts to resolve the impasse. The school board appealed the injunction. While the appeal was pending, the panel's report was rejected by the board (though accepted by the union), and the board proceeded unilaterally to offer the members of the bargaining unit contracts for the school year. Though the contracts were at variance with both the panel's report and the previous year's contracts, most teachers accepted them. The court said the contracts were properly issued, having been accepted and ratified by the teachers, and "nothing we can state in this opinion will alter the rights of the parties with respect to the contract." Therefore, the court concluded, the questions presented were moot and so without "actual case or controversy." Absent that, the court would be rendering an advisory opinion, which it may neither statutorily nor constitutionally do. "Such an opinion would . . . violate the doctrine of separation of powers."[192]

The Ohio supreme court's leading opinion rejecting advisory opinions showed extraordinary willingness to declare their repugnancy. In 1882 both houses of the legislature jointly sought the supreme court's opinions on four questions presented regarding a quo warranto proceeding. At the time the supreme court was constitutionally a court of original jurisdiction for certain actions including quo warranto. Two of the questions, though, were not actually related to the action but had to do with taxation to pay the salaries of the offices in question, rather than the authority of the offices themselves. The court apparently could have declined to answer just on those grounds. Instead, based on its smelling out a request for advisory opinions in the two irrelevant questions presented, it expanded its refusal to answer the two questions into a fully developed rejection of advisory opinions, choosing to understand the questions as a request for an opinion on matters not provided for in the constitution. At any rate they responded as if it were that, invoking the duty to decide only in judicial proceedings, since to do otherwise would offend separation of powers. Absent a judicial proceeding involving the taxation questions, the questions are hypothetical. "If the judiciary were to assume to decide hypothetical questions of law not involved in a judicial proceeding in a cause before it . . . it would . . . be an unwarranted interference with the functions of the legislative department that would be unauthorized and dangerous in its tendency." Further, it would raise the due process issue of settling questions of law "involving the rights of persons without parties before it." That the court had advisory opinions in mind is clear from the contrast it made to the Massachusetts justices, whose advisory duties are dictated by the constitution, but even there, the court said, the justices may not advise if the opinion would implicate private rights.[193]

---

[192] National Education Association—Topeka at 922–23.

[193] *State v. Baughman*, 38 Ohio 455 (1882).

Thereafter the Ohio supreme court joined the high courts of the other nonadvising states in refusing to render opinions in any matter that the court perceives as advisory, including hypothetical questions (as in *Baughman*), cases where there is no real prejudice to either party,[194] or where there is no real party in interest,[195] or where a relator put himself in the position of both relator and respondent so that there was no actual controversy.[196]

In Mississippi, among the states where the lieutenant governor presides over the senate, a parliamentary question arose. On the death of the governor in 1927, the lieutenant governor took his place, and a member of the senate became president pro tempore. Elections occurred that November and a new senate was elected, to take office January 3, 1928. The newly elected lieutenant governor would not be inaugurated, however, until some two weeks later. The question to the supreme court was: May the president pro tempore remain in office from January 3 until the new lieutenant governor is inaugurated? The court identified this as a request for advice and refused to answer, citing the state constitution's separation of powers provision, "impliedly prohibiting the giving of advisory opinions by one department to another." Further, advising on a question that may later be submitted for decision "is highly improper" unless the constitution requires it, and in Mississippi it does not.[197] The rule given here is vague. It is not accurate to say that no department may advise another—legislative and executive branches routinely do so. It is, presumably, that the *judiciary* may not do so, given the unique nature of judicial duties, but the court does not address this. Similarly, the court is not clear why any question on which advice is given may not be "submitted for decision" at some time in the future. But, the hazy reasoning notwithstanding, the court's position is clear enough: it simply will not answer requests for advisory opinions, whatever the form of the request put to them.

A dispute over a vetoed bill came to Maryland's high court. The governor's veto came after the legislative session ended, and under the constitution the bill therefore must be returned to the legislature when it reconvenes. The question was whether a bill, if it were returned and then passed over the governor's veto, would be null. If so, then the governor should not return the bill. On appeal, the supreme court ruled that this was a matter of legislative process with which "no court can interfere" before the process is completed. This, the court chose to emphasize, is an advisory opinion because it is being asked to address a question on pending legislation, and in Maryland "the courts will not, in the absence of constitutional mandate, render advisory opinions. Nor will the courts render advisory opinions unless there is an actual justiciable controversy between the parties."[198] The latter sentence seems gratuitous since it does not seem to follow from the pending legislation problem or from the question put to the court. At least the court

[194] *Tschantz v. Ferguson*, 566 N.E.2d 655 (Ohio 1991).

[195] *State ex rel. Court Index Press, Inc. v. Deters*, 565 N.E.2d 532 (Ohio 1990).

[196] *Cain v. Calhoun*, 401 N.E.2d 947 (Ohio 1979).

[197] *In re Opinion of the Justices*, 114 So. 887 (Miss. 1927).

[198] *Maryland–National Capitol Park and Planning Commission v. Randall*, 120 A.2d 195 (Md. 1956).

doesn't make the connection. But the court's animosity toward advisory opinions is the point, and it makes that point clear.[199]

The states' bars against justiciability infractions are rigorously grounded in advisory opinion prohibitions. The Arkansas supreme court, for example, noting that a city had rescinded and replaced a policy that had been challenged in court, upheld the trial court's dismissal of the challenge as moot. The "appellate courts of this state will not review issues that are moot. To do so would be to render advisory opinions, which this court will not do."[200] Ripeness is approached similarly with respect to advisory opinions. "The ripeness requirement prevents courts from issuing purely advisory opinions," ruled the California supreme court.[201] In Texas, a family planning service sought a declaratory judgment that a statutory provision prohibiting state funding of prescription drugs to minors without parental consent was unconstitutional. Since the provision had not yet been implemented, the supreme court held, the purported future injury to the planning service (who may have stood to lose funding, depending on how the provision was implemented) was too contingent or remote, hence not ripe. The court's rationale connects ripeness doctrine, which "serves to avoid premature adjudication," directly to advisory opinions, and through advisory opinions to separation of powers. "The constitutional roots of justiciability doctrines such as ripeness . . . lie in the prohibition on advisory opinions, which in turn stems from the separation of powers doctrine. The courts of this state are not empowered to give advisory opinions."[202]

A Pennsylvania court enjoined a county board of elections from placing proposed amendments to a town's home rule charter on the ballot, on grounds that the amendments, if adopted, would be unconstitutional. The state supreme court held that placing the amendments on the ballot was part of the local legislative process, in which "courts should not interfere." Until a law is enacted and "has been actually applied to a litigant,"

---

[199] Other states whose supreme courts have directly rejected advisory opinions include: Arkansas: *K.S. v. State*, 31 S.W.3d 849 (Ark. 2000); Illinois: *Oliviera v. Amoco Oil Co.*, 776 N.W.2d 151 (Ill. 2002); Iowa: *Hartford-Carlisle Sav. Bank v. Shivers*, 566 N.W.2d 877 (Iowa 1997); Mississippi: *Grant v. State*, 686 So.2d 1078 (Miss. 1996); Missouri: *State v. Self*, 155 S.W.3d 756 (Mo. 2005); Montana: *Northfield Ins. Co. v. Montana Ass'n of Counties*, 10 P.3d 813 (Mont. 2000); Nebraska: *Wilcox v. City of McCook*, 262 Neb. 696 (2001); New Jersey: *In re Requests to Judges in Chancery for Advisory Opinions*, 137 A. 151 (N.J. 1927); New Mexico: *City of Las Cruces v. El Paso Elec. Co.*, 954 P.2d 72 (N.M. 1998); Oklahoma: *Dank v. Benson*, 5 P.3d 1088 (Okla. 2000); Texas: *Brown v. Todd*, 53 S.W.3d 297 (Tex. 2001); Utah: *Richards v. Baum*, 914 P.2d 719 (Utah 1996); West Virginia: *State ex rel. West Virginia Deputy Sheriff's Ass'n, Inc. v. Sims*, 513 S.E.2d 669 (W.Va. 1998); Wisconsin: *State ex rel. La Follette v. Dammann*, 220 Wisc. 17 (1936); Wyoming: *Cathcart v. Meyer*, 88 P.3d 1050 (Wyo. 2004).

[200] *Cotton v. Fooks*, 55 S.W.3d 290, 292 (Ark. 2001) (citations omitted). Note the suggestion that the courts will not address moot issues *because* that would result in rendering advisory opinions. The Texas supreme court said as much when it dismissed an appeal as moot: "Because [petitioner] Valley Baptist's appeal of the discovery order became moot after the deposition occurred, the court of appeal's opinion is advisory. . . . Therefore [we] vacate the court of appeals' judgment and opinion." Valley Baptist Medical Center v. Gonzales, 33 S.W.3d 821, 822 (Tex. 2000). *See also, e.g., State v. Vicente*, 84 P.3d 1191, 1192 (Utah 2004) ("When an issue is moot, judicial policy dictates against our rendering an advisory opinion.").

[201] *Hunt v. Superior Court*, 987 P.2d 705, 715 (Calif. 1999).

[202] *Patterson v. Planned Parenthood of Houston and Southeast Texas, Inc.*, 971 S.W.2d 439, 442–43 (Tex. 1998) (citations omitted).

that is, "brought into operation so as to impinge upon the rights of some person or persons," a court should not "decide academically the unconstitutionality or other alleged invalidity of legislation." To do so is to "offer advisory opinions during the deliberative stages of the legislative process," however apparent the unconstitutionality of the proposed law may be.[203]

On the federal level, the Supreme Court's wariness about and hostility toward advisory opinions is at least as strong as in the supreme courts in the nonadvisory states, reflected in its responses to the variety of actions that the Court sees as camouflaged de facto requests for advisory opinions. In such instances the Court does not merely reject the action as inappropriate, because, say, it is nonjusticiable. It will assert, occasionally at some length, that to issue a ruling in the case would be to render advice. The Court, for example, holds to be advisory opinions the following: judgments subject to review by another branch; statements to another branch on contemplated actions by the branch; Court review when there is adequate and independent state grounds for a decision; and dicta, that is any part of an opinion not necessary to the disposition of the case at bar.[204] One commentator complains that the Supreme Court has been "extremely sloppy" in its use of the term "advisory opinion," arguing in part that of the many ways the Court uses the term, most are prudential and not constitutional requirements. Other observers affirm the constitutional ground, or at least a mix of constitutional and prudential grounds, for the limits the Supreme Court has imposed based on the advisory opinion rationale.[205] As with some state supreme courts, the doctrine and standards may not be entirely clear or consistent. But the rule certainly is: *Absolutely no advisory opinions*.

The adequate and independent state grounds doctrine, which the Supreme Court long ago called a "settled rule," requires that when a state court relies on both federal and nonfederal grounds, federal jurisdiction "fails if the nonfederal ground is independent of the federal ground and adequate to support the judgment."[206] The Court, much later in *Michigan v. Long*, clarified the doctrine so that when a state decision is interwoven with federal law, the adequacy and independence of a state law ground will not be reviewable if the state court decision "indicates clearly and expressly that it is alternatively based on bona fide separate, adequate, and independent grounds." In the absence of such a plain statement, the Court held, "we have jurisdiction."[207]

It is the advisory opinion ban that constitutes the rationale for the modern formulation of the state grounds doctrine. The Court established its new plain-statement rule "precisely" because it desires "to avoid advisory opinions" as well as because of its

---

[203] *Mt. Lebanon v. Country Board of Elections of Allegheny County*, 368 A.2d 648, 649–50 (Pa. 1977).

[204] *See* Evan Tsen Lee, *Deconstitutionalizing Justiciability: The Example of Mootness*, 105 Harv. L. Rev. 603, 644 (1992).

[205] *Id. See also* Bickel, The Least Dangerous Branch, 113–16.

[206] *Fox Film Corp. v. Muller*, 296 U.S. 207 (1935), quoted in Henry Hart & Herbert Wechsler, The Federal Courts and the Federal System 535 (3d ed. 1988). The Supreme Court notes that the state grounds rule goes back at least to *Klinger v. State of Missouri*, 13 Wall. 257, 263 (1871). The doctrine was more fully developed in *Murdock v. City of Memphis*, 20 Wall. 590 (1875).

[207] *Michigan v. Long,* 463 U.S. 1031 (1983). Quoted in Hart & Wechsler, Federal Courts, 540, 541.

respect for state courts. It calls these the two "cornerstones" of the state grounds doctrine.[208] An observer has explained this advisory opinion rationale as constitutionally required under Article III and not merely the Court's prudential policy.[209] He adopts Alexander Bickel's broad view that the sources of the federal advisory opinion ban are the constitutionally required checks on "the otherwise unbridled discretion of the judicial branch," especially regarding judicial review. The justiciability doctrines, themselves arising from Article III, prevent the Supreme Court from making pronouncements "in the large and in the abstract," or from giving opinions, "even in a concrete case, which are advisory because they are not finally decisive, the power of ultimate disposition of the case having been reserved elsewhere."[210] While case or controversy requirements have both prudential and constitutional sources, when the latter applies the Supreme Court's discretion is sharply limited. If, for example, in a case involving the constitutionality of a statute, both parties desire the same result, then the court may not constitutionally take the case, since that "could result in a constitutionally impermissible advisory opinion."[211]

Some commentators on the state grounds doctrine, however, are critical of the Court's use of the term "advisory opinion." One calls it useless as a rationale for the state grounds doctrine and suggests discarding it. The Supreme Court, he argues, explains adequate and independent state grounds doctrine "on the ground that decision of the federal question presented would be merely advisory. This use of advisory opinion terminology is essentially useless" since the state grounds doctrine "in fact rests on other foundations."[212] Another observer similarly argues that in the justiciability, state grounds, or dicta contexts, the Court's use of the term advisory opinion is "ill advised" because it should be limited to denoting federal cases "that fall beyond the grant of judicial power in Article III because of vulnerability to revision by another branch of government."[213] Another observer agrees that the Supreme Court has used the term in various ways, "leading to needless confusion of the term." The term does contain a core "with firm grounding in Article III, but also in penumbras with a far more tenuous connection to the constitution's text."[214]

---

[208] *Id.* at 545.

[209] Westling, *Advisory Opinions and the "Constitutionally Required" Adequate and Independent State Grounds Doctrine*, 391. *See also* Lisa A. Kloppenberg, *Avoiding Constitutional Questions*, 35 B.C. L. Rev. 1003, 1061 (1994) ("The doctrine [of adequate and independent state grounds] is generally grounded in efforts to avoid advisory opinions and unnecessary constitutional rulings.").

[210] Westling, *Advisory Opinions and the "Constitutionally Required" Adequate and Independent State Grounds Doctrine*, 392, *quoting* Bickel, The Least Dangerous Branch, 114–15.

[211] Westling, *Advisory Opinions and the "Constitutionally Required" Adequate and Independent State Grounds Doctrine*, 393.

[212] Wright, et al., Federal Practice and Procedure, 298 (sec. 3529.1) (1984).

[213] Lee, *Deconstitutionalizing Justiciability: The Example of Mootness*, 650. Lee argues that mootness should be deconstitutionalized and treated solely as a prudential doctrine, whether or not the Supreme Court characterizes decisions in moot cases as advisory opinions.

[214] Sam Kamin, "An Article III Defense of Merits—First Decisionmaking in Civil Rights Litigation: The Continued Vitality of *Saucier v. Katz*," working paper, 27 (2008), *available at* http://ssrn.com/abstract=1104042.

These attacks on the Supreme Court's use of advisory opinion terminology give inadequate recognition to the weight and centrality of the Court's animosity toward advisory opinions. The ban on advisory opinions is not some incidental consequence of doctrines on justiciability or on state grounds. It is a cause of and warrant for such doctrines, or at the least deeply integral to them and to the Court's jurisprudence on the doctrines. The core requirement is for "a real, live dispute between adverse parties, *in order to avoid an advisory opinion*," and that is "reflected in the standing doctrine's injury requirement and the justiciability doctrines of ripeness and mootness."[215] Court decisions must affect the outcome of the dispute "to avoid rendering an advisory opinion."[216] But it is sufficient for our purposes to note that even were we to agree that the Supreme Court has been wrong or "sloppy" or "ill advised" or confusing in its use of the term, that all the more declares how strong, central, and, over the decades, enduring the Court's hostility toward advisory opinions remains.

Another major field of federal, as well as state, jurisprudence under the shadow of the advisory opinion is the declaratory judgment. Judicial concerns about declaratory judgments from the start have frequently centered on the extent to which they may be de facto advisory opinions. During the early debate over declaratory judgments, proponents stressed the harm in restricting the jurisdiction of the courts to the common law limits on damages and injunctions as remedies for actual violations of rights. "Reformers argued that social equilibrium can be disturbed not only by direct violations of rights, but also by actions that leave persons in 'grave doubt and uncertainty' about their legal position." The reformers saw declaratory judgments as legitimately available to any party who did not have a common law claim for any one of three reasons. The opposing party held the claim but had not yet sued, or a party had no remedy because their controversy was not yet justiciable, or the parties were not seeking common law relief.[217] These proponents favored declaratory judgments as a means of broadening the jurisdiction of the courts so they could address disputes incapable of remedies at common law. Among proponents was the American Bar Association, which officially supported the federal Declaratory Judgment Act in 1919 when the first such bill was introduced, and the association repeatedly testified before Congress until the federal declaratory judgment law was enacted in 1934.[218]

Early proponents of declaratory judgments rarely seemed to have sensed the potential for advisory opinion problems, but federal and state judges, ever vigilant about

---

[215] Kloppenberg, *Avoiding Constitutional Questions*, 1010 (emphasis added).

[216] *Id.*

[217] D. L. Doernberg & M. B. Mushlin, *The Trojan Horse: How the Declaratory Judgment Act Created a Cause of Action and Expanded Federal Jurisdiction While the Supreme Court Wasn't Looking*, 36 U.C.L.A. L. Rev. 529, 551–52 (1989). The quote is from Edwin M. Borchard, *The Declaratory Judgment—A Needed Procedural Reform, Part I*, 28 Yale L.J. 3 (1918). Borchard was an early and influential proponent of declaratory judgments. *See* Edwin M. Borchard, *The Declaratory Judgment—A Needed Procedural Reform, Part II*, 28 Yale L.J. 105 (1918); and Edwin M. Borchard, Declaratory Judgments (1934). Doernberg & Mushlin discuss Borchard's role in *The Trojan Horse*, 550–56.

[218] Doernberg & Mushlin, *The Trojan Horse*, 550–51.

infringement on their judicial role, certainly did. The first case to test the constitutionality of a declaratory judgment act was in Michigan, which had recently passed such an act, where a street railway employee sought a declaration on the constitutionality of a state law limiting working hours. The Michigan supreme court noted that the defendant company admitted the allegations, that neither party was claiming violation of rights or threat of violation, and that no claim for damages was being made. The action, the court said, rested solely on the state's declaratory judgment act.[219] The court sharply attacked the act as unconstitutional, imposing on the judiciary a blatantly nonjudicial advisory duty in requiring it to consider what in fact was a moot case brought by friendly parties.

The court saw the act in effect permitting wholesale advisory opinions. The act "required that the time of the court shall be taken, not in the determination of actual controversies where rights have been invaded and wrongs have been done, but in the giving of advice to all who may seek it." The case before it, the court said, presented all the "objectionable characteristics" of a moot case, and indeed it amounted to a contempt of court. "Any attempt by a mere colorable dispute to obtain the opinion of a court upon a question of law, when there is no real controversy, is an abuse which courts have always reprehended and treated as a punishable contempt of court."[220] The court referred to cases from state after state making the connection to advisory opinions as forbidden by the principle that courts "may not tender advice upon matters not in litigation"—Minnesota, Maryland, New York, Louisiana, Illinois, Virginia, Montana, Tennessee, Ohio, California—and then provided citations to twenty-three additional cases, for those "who desire to pursue the subject."[221]

Though declaratory judgment acts would come to prevail, the courts have remained sensitive to any declaratory action that, in their judgment, in reality attempts to seek an advisory opinion from the judges. The jurisprudence of declaratory judgments in good part comprises attempts to distinguish them from advisory opinions.[222] The U.S. Supreme Court, in upholding the Declaratory Judgment Act of 1934, defended its ruling partly on the ground that the act did not permit advisory opinions, allowing declaratory judgments only in "a case of actual controversy."[223] But the requirement that declaratory judgments be granted only when there is an actual controversy has from the start been challenged as insufficient to distinguish it from advisory opinions. One writer has commented that the 1934 Declaratory Judgment Act is a "landmark in congressional

---

[219] *Anway v. Grand Rapids Ry. Co.*, 179 N.W. 350, 351 (Mich. 1920).

[220] *Id.* at 355, quoting 2 Bouvier's Law Dictionary 2245.

[221] *Id.* at 357–59.

[222] In Erwin Chemerinsky's Constitutional Law (2d ed. 2002), the only discussion of declaratory judgments in the 1250-page book is on efforts to distinguish them from advisory opinions (58–59 and 103). *See also* Edward A. Purcell, Jr., Brandeis and the Progressive Constitution 126 (2001) ("The appearance of declaratory judgments . . . raised [the question of] whether judgments that were merely 'declaratory' constituted unauthorized 'advisory opinions.'").

[223] *Aetna Life Ins. Co. v. Hawarth,* 300 U.S. 227, 241 (1937).

efforts to authorize federal courts to give advisory opinions."[224] The Supreme Court, however, reasoned that the act was constitutional because it provided a new procedure or remedy to be used in actual controversies. It acknowledged, though, that if the act were intended merely to require federal courts to render advisory opinions, then it was unconstitutional. Since the act itself referred to "cases of actual controversy" in defining the power to render declaratory judgments, the Court held the act did not establish advisory opinion jurisdiction and so was valid.[225]

Thereafter the Supreme Court would regularly be at pains to distinguish an "actual controversy" as contemplated by the Declaratory Judgment Act and an "abstract question," answering which would constitute an advisory opinion. The Court admitted, though, that "it would be difficult, if it would be possible, to fashion a precise test for determining in every case whether there is such a controversy."[226] Justice Brandeis had doubts about the Declaratory Judgment Act from the start, "largely based on his experience with the 'Advisory Opinion' practice in Massachusetts," because the act, despite its "actual controversy" requirement, had in common with the advisory opinion process a factual vacuum.[227]

In states with declaratory judgments acts, the courts have been vigilant in detecting advisory opinions in declaratory judgment clothing. A Pennsylvania case, entirely typical in this regard, was on the question of the defendant seller's liability to the real estate agents for the commission on an aborted sale of property to the plaintiffs. Under the sale agreement the sellers had the right to retain the plaintiffs' deposit (as liquidated damages for the plaintiffs' breach of the agreement), but the sellers offered to return the deposit to the plaintiffs provided the plaintiffs obtain a release from the real estate agents for any claim to a commission. Plaintiffs sought a declaratory judgment. The court held that the plaintiffs had no dog in this fight since the possible liability of the sellers to the real estate agents presented no actual controversy to justify a petition for declaratory judgment. The plaintiffs' only present interest was whether or not to accept the sellers' offer to return the money on a contingency. "In reality," the court said, "the plaintiffs seek an advisory opinion. . . . Organically, courts are not instituted to render advisory opinions, either by way of declaratory judgment or otherwise."[228]

In a 1936 Wisconsin dispute between the governor and the secretary of state over the governor's authority to make certain appointments, Governor LaFollette went to court

---

[224] Phillip M. Kannan, *Advisory Opinions by Federal Courts*, 32 U. Richmond L. Rev. 769, 774 (1998).

[225] *Aetna Life Ins.*, 300 U.S. at 240. The statute's reference to "actual controversy" is at 28 U.S.C. sec. 2201.

[226] *Golden v. Zwickler*, 394 U.S. 103, 108 (1969), quoting *United Public Workers of America v. Mitchell*, 330 U.S. 75, 89 (1947). *See* Kannan, *Advisory Opinions by Federal Courts*, 776–77, for a discussion of *Golden*.

[227] Letter of Erwin Griswold to D. L. Doernberg and M. B. Mushlin, commenting on their *The Trojan Horse*. The letter appears complete in Doernberg & Mushlin, *History Comes Calling: Dean Griswold Offers New Evidence About the Jurisdictional Debate Surrounding the Enactment of the Declaratory Judgment Act*, 140–42. Edward Purcell inquires extensively into Brandeis's hostility to declaratory judgments in Brandeis and the Progressive Constitution, 124–32.

[228] *Schoenbrun v. Nettrour*, 61 A.2d 868, 869 (Pa. 1948).

under the state's Uniform Declaratory Judgments Act. The state supreme court (observing that such acts are new) concluded that the governor had no interest that could be vindicated since the governor had not yet actually made appointments, so that there is no one who could "presently assert a legally protectable interest—a right to an office or emoluments thereof—which the court may vindicate by a declaratory judgment." Hence potential controversies involving actual claimants to the office in question would not be terminated. The court, then, is "impelled to the conclusion that any opinion which we might presently express would be merely advisory."[229]

Judicial sensitivity about being cornered into rendering advisory opinions is emphatic in a North Dakota declaratory judgment action, where the state supreme court held that the governor's petition under the state's declaratory judgment act was invalid, there being no justiciable controversy. The court asserted, as did the Wisconsin supreme court three years earlier, that declaratory judgments outside a justiciable controversy amount to an advisory opinion. But then the court went on to develop this assertion at such extraordinary length and with such striking animosity, it made the case the leading decision in North Dakota rejecting advisory opinions outright, in a declaratory judgment or in any other context. It several times made the point that the state's declaratory judgments act "does not authorize the rendition of advisory opinions. Indeed, if it did so authorize, it would be unconstitutional."[230] It is here that the court recalled in detail the extensive debate and explicit rejection of an advisory opinion provision at the state's founding constitutional convention, quoting favorably the statement by one member, a judge, that he could "safely say that there is not a state in the Union where that [advisory opinion] provision prevails but not only the Supreme Court but every other person who has an intimate knowledge of the workings of that provision would wish it were not there."[231]

---

[229] *State ex rel. LaFollette v. Dammann*, 264 N.W. 627 (Wisc. 1936). *See also Texas v. City of Frisco*, 2008 WL 828055 (E.D. Tex.) (ruling that the state's request for a declaratory judgment should be dismissed since it did not state a justiciable controversy, and the issue involved was not yet ripe, and that a declaratory judgment in this instance would therefore amount to an advisory opinion).

[230] *Langer v. State*, 284 N.W. 238, 250 (N.D. 1939).

[231] *Id.* at 251.

3 }

To Create a Power to Refuse

THE RISE OF A JURISPRUDENCE OF ADVISORY OPINIONS

The attacks on advisory opinions and their widespread rejections were reflected in the attitude of the advising justices. They came to express their reluctance, even their hostility, toward their advisory duties, to an extent that may be unique in American constitutional history. No other constitutional provision seems to have engendered such open animosity for so long by state supreme court justices. The attacks on advisory opinions, were, after all, grounded in indisputable, fundamental doctrines of American law—separation of powers, due process, and justiciability, among others. These doctrines hover over the advisory opinion jurisdictions, real and dark and huge, and the justices have tried to make their peace with them. The chief mode was to create, on their own initiative, the authority to refuse outright to answer requests for advisory opinions, even if the authorizing provisions made advising mandatory, accompanied by the remarkable development of an elaborate jurisprudence to ground their refusals. This chapter is about the animosity and the jurisprudence it engendered.

Contrary to the Plain Dictates of Justice: The Justices' Animosity

During the latter half of the nineteenth century, the advisory justices developed an extraordinarily open reluctance to advise, sometimes expressing outright hostility toward their advising duty that seems out of proportion for an activity that they insisted was merely nonbinding, personal advice-giving.[1] The reluctance, doubts, and hostility

[1] The justices' reluctance, doubts, and hostility regarding their advisory duties have always been widely noted. *See, e.g.*, James B. Thayer, *Advisory Opinions*, *in* LEGAL ESSAYS 42 (1908; 1st ed. 1885); Note, *Extrajudicial Opinions*, 10 HARV. L. REV. 50 (1896); Note, *Constitutional Law—Powers of the Judiciary—Obligation of the Courts to Give Advisory Opinions*, 26 HARV. L. REV. 655 (1912); Note, *Duty of the Court to Give Advisory Opinions*, 2 MASS. L. Q. 542, 543, 548–49 (1917); William H. Robinson, Jr., *Limitations upon Legislative Inquiries under Colorado Advisory Opinion Clause*, 4 ROCKY MTN. L. REV. 237 (1932); Preston W. Edsall, *The Advisory Opinion in North Carolina*, 27 N.C. L. REV. 297, 310–11 (1949); Note, *The Validity of Restrictions on the Modern Advisory Opinion*, 29 ME. L. REV. 305 (1978); Harry Lee Anstead, et al., *The Operation and Jurisdiction of the Supreme Court of Florida*, 29 NOVA L. REV. 431, 486 (2005).

have stood against the clearly mandatory nature of most advising provisions.[2] Further, in what one observer called the "most startling development," the justices took it upon themselves to decide when they would respond to requests for advice and when they would not, effectively nullifying the ability of the executive or legislature to make such decisions.[3] It was a kind of covert revolt. The justices simply assumed near-total authority over when to advise, often without offering defense or explanation, responding or not as they saw fit, based on standards they chose to set forth, and which they waived at will. The justices in all advisory states, "irrespective of firm statutory or constitutional dictate," created their own "power to refuse to answer otherwise proper requests under a variety of circumstances."[4] The connection to their animosity toward their advising duty and to their reluctance to advise has been clear enough all along.

It was not only a startling development but doubtfully grounded as well, and widely criticized. "It is difficult to find any logical basis for this assumption by the courts of the right to pass" on the qualifications for valid advisory opinion requests, wrote one observer.[5] Another, a half-century earlier in 1890, insisted that the Massachusetts justices' first refusal conflicted with a century's worth of rendering advisory opinions, and that the "obligation to answer" is simply absolute; it is the requesting authority that decides when a question is appropriate, not the justices.[6] In response to the Massachusetts justices' refusal to answer its questions, the house of representatives in 1890 ordered its judiciary committee to investigate and report. The committee recommended that the house affirm its constitutional authority to propound questions. It did so, passing a resolution "That the House of Representatives does not acquiesce in the conclusion of the justices . . . and affirms the authority of the House, under the constitution, to require their opinion upon said question."[7] The justices, not impressed, responded that "we cannot surrender our own judgment to that of the House . . . but must for ourselves finally decide whether the occasion contemplated by the Constitution in which our opinion may properly be required has arisen."[8] A 1932 law review article complained (in its first sentence) that the Colorado supreme court's long list of restrictions is "tantamount to

---

[2] All advisory opinion provisions created before 1923 were mandatory upon the justices. Alabama's 1923 statute and Michigan's 1963 constitutional amendment allow the requesting authority only to "request" advice rather than "require" it. In 1968 Florida amended its constitution's advisory opinion provision so that advice may only be "requested."

[3] R. K. Hoffman, *Why Not Advisory Opinions for Illinois?*, 31 CHI.-KENT L. REV. 141, 149 (1952).

[4] Charles M. Carberry, *The State Advisory Opinion in Perspective*, 14 FORDHAM L. REV. 81, 99–100 (1975).

[5] Hoffman, *Why Not Advisory Opinions for Illinois?*, 150.

[6] Hugo A. Dubuque, *The Duty of Judges as Constitutional Advisors*, 24 AM. L. REV. 369, 384, 386, 398 (1890).

[7] Cynthia R. Farina, *Supreme Judicial Court Advisory Opinions: Two Centuries of Interbranch Dialogue*, *in* THE HISTORY OF THE LAW IN MASSACHUSETTS: THE SUPREME JUDICIAL COURT 1692–1992 at 353, 375 (1992). Farina sees the justices' refusals as reflecting "a progressively stronger sense of judicial confidence and independence vis-à-vis the other branches, as well as an increased sophistication in manipulating constitutional doctrine." *Id.* at 374.

[8] *Opinion of the Justices in re Power of the Legislature to Require Opinion*, 150 Mass. 598, 601, 24 N.E. 1086 (1890).

saying that the court will refuse to entertain a question whenever the judges in their discretion decide not to answer it."[9] When the South Dakota justices refused to render an advisory opinion in 1920, a *Harvard Law Review* note declared that "the court flies in the face of the state constitution."[10] Maine's former chief justice insisted that the state's justices were simply wrong in refusing to advise, whatever the defects in the advisory opinion process.[11] The justices themselves, often on an irritable defensive, "have appeared perplexed, and often somewhat embarrassed, in explaining the scope of their advisory jurisdiction. Often, no explanation is provided," commented one writer as recently as 1989.[12]

But the justices' reluctance and hostility toward their advisory duties remained, and remains still, a constant. "We don't like to give advisory opinions," the Rhode Island chief justice said in open court in 2008.[13] Before 1840, justices rarely remarked on the advisory opinion process. After that, given the traditional circumspection of justices in commenting negatively on their duties, the frequency and intensity with which they expressed their doubts, and with which they acted on them, has been remarkable, likely because with constitutions requiring the justices to advise, the justices were, so to speak, up against a constitutional wall, which they did their best to undermine or at least redesign. The increasing expressions of the doubts and the hostility, together with the growing confidence with which the justices asserted their restrictions, were in good part owing to the rise in the stature and power of the judiciary (noted in Chapter 2). Observers were impressed with the justices' antipathy. One in 1896 noted the "extreme reluctance" with which the Massachusetts justices rendered advice.[14] Another, who favored advisory opinions, was critical of the advisory justices' tendency "in most jurisdictions . . . to discourage the practice."[15] Two Alabama justices, themselves dissenting to the majority's finding that the state's advisory opinion statute is constitutional, remarked that it "is impossible to read the opinions of the courts throughout the country without coming to the conclusion that the attitude of the judiciary generally has been unfavorable to the practice."[16] Another observer, writing on the Colorado court's advisory duties, noted in 1932 that the court, "in its reluctance to give advisory opinions has restricted the advisory opinion clause . . . to such an extent that any practical use of it is now impossible. . . . The court has at all times been exceedingly reluctant to give

---

[9] Robinson, *Limitations on Legislative Inquiries*, 237.

[10] Note, "Recent Cases," 34 HARV. L. REV. 670, 674 (1920).

[11] This is the main point of Chief Justice Emery's 1916 article, discussed further below.

[12] Robert H. Kennedy, *Advisory Opinions: Cautions About Non-Judicial Undertakings*, 23 U. RICHMOND L. REV. 173, 182 (1989).

[13] Rhode Island Chief Justice Frank Williams, in the supreme court, October 28, 2008, from notes of the author, who was present.

[14] Note, *Extra-Judicial Opinions*, 10 HARV. L. REV. 50 (1896).

[15] ALBERT R. ELLINGWOOD, DEPARTMENTAL COOPERATION IN STATE GOVERNMENT 256 (1918). Ellingwood also comments disapprovingly that in South Dakota (the most recent state to adopt advisory opinions when Ellingwood wrote) the supreme court's replies to requests for advisory opinions "have not been cordial." *Id.*

[16] *In re Opinions of the Justices*, 96 So. 487, 497 (Ala. 1923) (Sayre and Miller, JJ., dissenting).

advisory opinions, and in a number of cases it has frankly said so."[17] Another observer in 1937 said that "in all jurisdictions, jurists [who] face the perplexing task of formulating an opinion in advance of litigation have forcibly expressed the inadequacy of their positions."[18] Another wrote in 1959 that "one cannot read the cases set forth in the annotations to these [advisory opinion] provisions without sensing the opposition to the practice."[19]

A good number of justices joined in. The earliest justices to comment on advisory duties were those in Maine, who in 1840 complained that they were obliged to render advice in the absence of argument since their duty to advise was constitutionally mandated. The justices, the Maine constitution says with some redundancy, "shall be obliged" to advise "when required" by the governor, senate, or house. The only qualifications were that the opinions be given only "upon important questions of law" and only "upon solemn occasions."[20] The qualifications became, in the six states whose provisions included them, a window of opportunity.[21] Early on the justices seemed to assume the requesting authorities had the authority to determine solemnity and importance. At any rate no Maine justice made an issue of it in these terms until 1891 when the Maine justices boldly reversed this position. Simply asserting the authority to decide when to advise, they declared that they would refuse to answer the question put to them because the facts did "not indicate that any solemn occasion exists, within the meaning of the constitution of the state."[22] What was not solemn about the occasion? It was that the question may arise later in a litigated case, and so, establishing one general restriction on advisory opinions, they asserted that "we think it inexpedient to prejudice the question before any occasion has arisen calling for its legal determination."[23] The due process problem of advisory opinions affecting litigated cases had long been recognized by this time, but here the justices overcame the advisory opinion clause's mandatory language by applying the "solemn occasion" qualification. The phrase, though, was not defined generally either in this opinion or later. It simply was and remained a means to legitimize their refusals to advise, an umbrella under which they would gather their chosen restrictions to lend both the restrictions and the justices constitutional cover. Advising justices in other states would come to do the same. Those in Massachusetts, for example, said that there is no solemn occasion when: the requesting authority does not have "serious

---

[17] Robinson, *Limitations upon Legislative Inquiries*, 237.

[18] F. R. Aumann, *The Supreme Court and the Advisory Opinion*, 4 Ohio St. L. Rev. 21, 46 (1937).

[19] George Neff Stevens, *Advisory Opinions—Present Status and an Evaluation*, 34 Wash. L. Rev. 1, 11 (1959).

[20] Me. Const. art. VI, sec. 3 (1963).

[21] Besides Maine, the phrases also appear in the advisory opinions provisions of Colorado, Massachusetts, Michigan, New Hampshire, and South Dakota. In the other four states (Alabama, Delaware, Florida, and Michigan), the advisory opinion provisions limit the justices to constitutional questions. Only Michigan has both the phrases and the constitutional question restriction.

[22] *In re Removal and Appointment of Country Attorneys*, 27 A. 454, 454 (Me. 1891).

[23] *Id.*

doubts" about their authority to act;[24] when the governor has no present duty awaiting performance;[25] and when the question does not involve executive power or authority.[26]

The new attitude met with some justices' disapproval. In 1901 a majority of Maine justices refused to answer a question from the house of representatives because the question might subsequently come before the justices in a litigated case. They developed at length the theory stated briefly in 1891 and supported it by applying another long-standing difficulty with advisory opinions: separation of powers. They concluded that "it would not be proper for members of the court to give an official opinion, outside of judicial proceedings, which might have the effect of influencing the action of other departments of government, except upon such as are within the contemplation of the constitution." What the constitution contemplates are solemn occasions, and, the justices opined, while "it would not be wise to attempt to give a definition of this expression which would cover all cases," they knew what it means in this case: a solemn occasion "does not exist unless the body making the inquiry has occasion to consider and act upon the questions submitted in the exercise of the legislative or executive powers intrusted to it by the constitution and the laws of the state."[27] And in case the political branches did not see it, the justices affirmed their new position on who may decide when an occasion is solemn, rejecting any contention that "this preliminary question is a legislative, and not a judicial, one."[28]

Three justices disagreed. For them, taking a stand that was disappearing among advisory justices, a mandatory duty was a mandatory duty, notwithstanding whatever they disliked about the advisory opinion request before them or about advisory opinions in general. They had, they said, "regretfully come to the conclusion that [they] are obliged by the constitution to give the opinion required." (They were throwing the constitutional language in the majority's face. The advisory opinion clause specifies that the justices are "obliged" to advise whenever "required" by the requesting authority.) The minority proceeded to render a three-page advisory opinion, but only after they devoted six pages to defending their position, the first such extended defense of advisory opinions by advisory justices anywhere. The language providing for advisory opinions, they said, is "explicit and mandatory" and "leaves nothing to the discretion of the justices."[29] They did their duty "regretfully," however, only because the constitution so commanded, as they made clear in an attack on their advisory duty. The attack exemplifies advisory opinion provisions as perhaps uniquely the target of state supreme court justices' open animosity, unmatched in state constitutional history. The Maine advisory opinion provision, the three justices said,

[24] *In re Answer of Justices to Governor*, 302 N.E.2d 565, 569 (Mass. 1973).

[25] *In re Answer of Justices to Acting Governor*, 868 N.E.2d 444, 446 (Mass. 1997).

[26] *Id.*

[27] *In re Opinions of the Justices*, 51 A. 224, 225–27 (Me. 1901).

[28] *Id.*

[29] *Id.* at 227.

> is onerous upon the justices; that it may at times cause them great embarrassment to give opinions more or less hurriedly without the aid of opposing arguments, that it may injuriously affect personal or property rights without giving the person affected an opportunity to be heard, that it may be abused by those branches of the government entitled to use it, or, generally, that it has proved to be an unwise provision detrimental to the principle of the separation and independence of the three departments of government (if such criticisms be well founded) cannot, of course, justify any justice in refusing to render this constitutional provision complete obedience, or to effectuate its full purpose.[30]

As to deciding what occasions are solemn, this, the three justices said, is a political and not a judicial question, and at any rate it is "doubtful" that the justices might "override the judgment of the representatives of the people."[31] One of these three justices apparently felt strongly enough to publish two law review articles on the issue, the first while he sat as chief justice. That article, noting the reluctance and the "protests" with which the justices in Maine and Massachusetts exercise their advisory duties, frankly described Maine's advisory opinion provision as "undesirable" and called for "its most sparing use."[32] The chief justice reviewed all the difficulties, including infringement of separation of powers, absence of "argument or help of counsel," possibly determining "important rights, public and private" while interested parties have no opportunity to be heard, and the absence of adversarial process and its "shock of contention by adverse parties that lights the torch of truth." A further danger is of drawing the justices

> into the arena of politics. However diligent and sincere their efforts to give correct answers, they will give offence. If not openly accused they may be suspected of partisanship, of undue sympathy with a class or some powerful interest, or with some political or economic dogma. The submission of every such question is fraught with danger to the dignity of the Court and the reputation of the Justices for judicial integrity and impartiality.[33]

The (now former) chief justice's second article focused on his argument that, all the problems notwithstanding, the justices' advisory opinion duty is obligatory. The power to decide when a question is of sufficient solemnity and importance rests with the requesting authority, he argued, and not with the justices.[34]

In 1844, four years after the Maine justices first did so, the Massachusetts justices commented openly on their advisory duties after having rendered twenty-two reported advisory opinions since 1781 without comment. The justices said that they rendered advice on a question that was properly "to be decided in a regular course of judicial proceeding." Hence, they said in an early indication that they may refuse to advise

---

[30] *Id.*

[31] *Id.* at 228.

[32] Lucilius A. Emery, *Advisory Opinions from Justices*, 2 ME. L. REV. 1, 1 (1908).

[33] *Id.* at 2–3.

[34] Lucilius A. Emery, *Advisory Opinion of the Justices—No. II*, 11 ME. L. REV. 15, 16 (1917).

despite their advisory opinion clause's mandatory language, "we had doubts . . . whether it was a case coming within the intent of the constitution, pursuant to which questions of law are proposed." The doubts were about due process, lack of facts, and absence of argument. They declared that such an opinion, without notice to the parties, "would be contrary to the plain dictates of justice." The justices, likely feeling pressed by the mandatory nature of their duty, proceeded to render an opinion. They explained, adopting an approach to become widely used in all advisory states, that the opinion was at any rate nonbinding and so "cannot affect the rights of parties."[35]

The thin cover of the nonbinding rationale eventually gave way. In 1877 the Massachusetts justices declared their first refusal, after nearly a century of rendering advisory opinions. The question given them, they said, may arise later in litigation. They outright refused to answer on due process grounds, since, they said, quoting their 1844 opinion, to render the advice without notice to, or hearing from, parties affected by the opinion "would be contrary to the plain dictates of justice." Having created a power to refuse, they declined to define "the limits of the authority to require opinions of the judges," but the statement indicates that they were free to do so. They grounded their general imposition of limits on separation of powers and due process, and said that it could not have been the founders' intention to enable the political branches to compel the justices to advise in advance of a question that may arise later in litigation.[36] Not long after, in another advisory opinion, they continued their remarkably skeptical inquiry into the nature of their advisory duties by setting out an extraordinary, lengthy history of the advisory opinion from the Stuart kings through colonial Massachusetts to the state's 1780 convention. They took up this task because "some of us had doubts whether [the question propounded here] was one upon which we could properly express an opinion." They said that consideration of precedents, which they did not cite, dispelled their doubts, but they wished to show that in answering the question propounded, they did not exceed their constitutional authority.[37] In a pointed instance of judicial exclusivity if not supremacy, the justices said what the law is, and implied that they—not the political branches—are the ones to declare the law on advisory opinions. They here for the first time expressly instructed the political branches on what those branches' authority is regarding advisory opinions. Questions are limited to when the answers "are necessary" in the exercise of the requesting authority's powers. The ground for this is that the "opinions of the Justices can be required only 'upon important questions of law,' not upon questions of fact, 'and upon solemn occasions,' that is to say, when such questions of law are necessary to be determined by the body making the inquiry, in the exercise of the legislative or executive power entrusted to it by the Constitution and the

[35] *Opinion of the Justices*, 46 Mass. 596, 597 (5 Met.) (1844). The nonbinding doctrine is discussed later in this chapter and in Chapter 5.

[36] *Answer of the Justices*, 122 Mass. 600, 602–04 (1877). The question related to plural office holding, on whether a judge of a municipal, district, or police court could also hold the office of governor, lieutenant governor, or a seat in the legislature.

[37] *Opinion of the Justices*, 126 Mass. 557, 560–65 (1880).

laws of the Commonwealth."[38] Thereafter, the Massachusetts justices developed their jurisprudence of advisory opinions under color of these phrases.

The New Hampshire justices first commented on the advisory opinion process in 1852, based on the many defects they saw in a request from the senate.[39] The defects, however, were passed off as harmless because the advice would be nonbinding. The request, they said, for an opinion on the constitutionality of a bill was "considerably embarrassing," reflecting a pattern generally adopted by advisory justices over the next century: creating a restriction on advising after receiving a request for advice that seems inappropriate for reasons the justices will then first identify.[40] By discussing each of the "embarrassments" the New Hampshire justices for the first time put forth standards by which they would decide the propriety of requests for advice. First, the senate's inquiry was too general: the request was for an opinion on the constitutionality of a bill "of great length, embracing many new and untried provisions." Second, the request was vague. "[I]t is impossible to understand to what point in the principle or in the details of the bill it is the wish of the Senate that we should direct our attention." Third, "[w]e are also deprived of the aid which courts generally receive from the arguments of counsel."[41] They, something like the Maine justices, will advise anyway since the advisory opinion "must be regarded" as nonbinding in view of the defects noted.[42]

It is not clear whether that means advice would be binding were there no defects, but at any rate by 1875 the New Hampshire justices no longer seemed to think that declaring their advice nonbinding was acceptable protection against defects in advisory opinion requests. In that year the justices refused to respond to the house of representatives regarding the authority of the governor, because that "would obviously be an interference with the duties of the executive."[43] They relied on separation of powers, the importance of which they discuss at length. "There is no principle more fundamental, more thoroughly interwoven with the whole fabric of our republican institutions and form of government," and one branch cannot interfere with the duties and functions of the others "without striking a blow at the foundation upon which rests all security as well for private rights as the public welfare." The justices did not expressly suggest that the house might have been using the advisory opinion provision to make the justices the instrument of that interference, the sort of mischief that so concerned Joseph Story,[44] but the justices did assert that the "somewhat exceptional" advisory opinion clause may not be used to override separation of powers.[45] Over the next several years the New Hampshire

---

[38] *Id.* at 566.

[39] *Opinion of the Justices*, 25 N.H. 537 (1852). There was one prior refusal, an 1816 opinion (reported in 1883) in which they declined to advise because, they said, advisory opinions should not affect private rights of a party that may later litigate. *Opinion of the Court*, 62 N.H. 704, 705 (1883).

[40] *Opinion of the Justices*, 25 N.H. 537 (1852).

[41] *Id.* at 537–38.

[42] *Id.* at 538.

[43] *Opinion of the Justices*, 56 N.H. 574, 575 (1875).

[44] Story's criticism of advisory opinions is discussed in Chapter 2.

[45] *Id.* at 576–77.

justices would continue to develop their restrictions on advising, broadly applying due process principles as they earlier applied separation principles, to ground their new restrictions.

It was with extraordinary aggressiveness that the Missouri justices imposed limits on advisory opinions. Though that state's advisory opinion clause was the first to limit opinions to constitutional questions, this appears to have done nothing to mitigate the justices' "attitude of hostility" that, a writer notes, they maintained throughout the eleven-year life of the Missouri clause, and which was a likely cause of its repeal. He attributes the weakness of the Missouri advisory opinion process to the justices who rendered it "ineffective by narrow judicial construction."[46] Of the ten requests for advice during those eleven years (1865 to 1875), the justices refused four, more refusals than in all the other advisory states taken together to that time. But it was their "narrow construction" that stands out—narrow enough to constitute effective sabotage—such that the justices' jurisprudence of restrictions on their advisory power "fore-shadowed its doom by confinement."[47]

They rendered their first advisory opinion routinely, carefully answering all four of the governor's questions with no reference to or comment on their advisory duties and no expressions of difficulties with or doubts about the process, in fact no mention of the advisory opinion provision or process at all.[48] Within a few weeks the justices issued their second advisory opinion, like the first on an apparently unexceptional subject. (The first was on railroad financing, the second on the law of corporations.) Now the justices began by declaring that they "have met with difficulties" owing to the "general and indefinite nature" of the questions put to them.[49] The justices identified neither difficulties nor defects in the questions. They did not discuss the questions at all. Rather, simply refusing to answer, they launched into elaborate and detailed criteria and prohibitions on advisory opinion requests. It was the first time advisory justices approached their duty self-consciously and comprehensively, developing a full jurisprudence of advisory opinions, openly arising out of their discontent with the duty to advise.

The Missouri justices began by asserting the constitutional limits on rendering advice, declaring that requests for advice are limited to important questions of constitutional law, and to solemn occasions, "and then only when required by the Governor, the Senate, or the House of Representatives." They categorically reserved to themselves the authority to decide what question is important and when the occasion is solemn. These positions are not much different from those the justices in other advisory states

---

[46] Ellingwood, Departmental Cooperation, 46.

[47] Hoffman, *Why Not Advisory Opinions for Illinois?*, 144. For a summary of the ten Missouri advisory opinions, see Manley O. Hudson, *Advisory Opinions of National and International Courts*, 37 Harv. L. Rev. 970, 978–82 (1924).

[48] *In re Questions of Constitutional Law*, 37 Mo. 135 (1865).

[49] *Id.* at 136.

would take. But then the Missouri justices continued: The question propounded, they said,

> can scarcely be any other than some question of the proper construction and true meaning of some provision, clause, or words contained in the Constitution; and it must be, in its own nature, a judicial question, the final determination of which, by the organic frame of our Government, properly belongs to the Judiciary. In calling for such opinions, to be given in a manner somewhat novel and extra-judicial, and in matters not in litigation between contending parties, it must have been understood by the framers of that instrument, and would seem to be the clear intent of the section as it reads, that such questions should be important in reference to the public interest, and the necessary and immediate action of the Executive or Legislative branch of the Government, upon some matter of unusual and solemn concern for the public good, and on a pure question of law, which could only be finally determined by the Supreme Court as a judicial question.

Further, the justices assert they will simply refuse to advise whenever they believe the constitution did not permit advising. They will not permit themselves to become the legal advisors to the governor or legislature, they say. They will not perform the functions of the attorney general. They will refuse to answer questions about the general legislative or executive powers, or about private affairs. They will answer no question unless it concerns the "action" of the executive or legislature; answer no question "relating to the operation or effect of the Constitution or of any enactment proposed to be made by the General Assembly upon incorporated companies or private persons." The justices continue, emphatically if redundantly, that they would not answer "a general and indefinite question," but answer only a "distinct" question, and only on constitutional powers, and only if presented as a judicial question, and only if the question had "an immediate, direct and important bearing upon the action of the Governor, or either House of the General Assembly," and only if it depends "for its solution upon a judicial construction or interpretation of some [part] . . . of the Constitution." To answer questions failing to meet all these requirements, the justices conclude, "instead of being a light and a guide, might prove to be but a snare to the feet."[50]

Under this barrage of restrictions most if not all requests for advice might easily be judged defective and all answers snares to the feet. "But wait," they might well have said, "there's more." After this advisory opinion, the Missouri justices rendered three without commenting on the advisory process and then refused to answer three of the next five, substantially extending their restrictions, and their animosity. In the first of these three refusals the justices stated that to render advice in the face of one of their numerous restrictions would be advising "when not authorized by the Constitution," hence in "willful disregard" of their constitutional duties. This, they declare with some

---

[50] *Id.* at 136–38.

drama, "would subject themselves to impeachment and removal from office."[51] In their next refusal the justices go so far as to expressly criticize the language of the constitution's advisory opinion clause itself, calling the provision "somewhat anomalous in its character, and couched in terms vague, indistinct and hardly susceptible of definite interpretation."[52] A commentator, fascinated by Missouri justices' hostility, concluded that advisory opinions did not get a fair chance in Missouri, stultified by the justices.[53]

The Colorado supreme court (in that state the "court" is required to advise, not the "justices") was as openly displeased with its "anomalous and peculiar" advisory duties as were the Missouri justices, and like them it narrowly restricted the application of the constitution's advisory opinion clause. Even though the court ruled its advisory opinions to be binding since the court and not the justices give the advice, their complaints were similar to those made by justices in the nonbinding states, except with the added complaint that their advice was binding. The court observed with apparent envy the repeal in 1875 of Missouri's advisory opinion clause, attributing the repeal to that state's "profiting, we suppose, by experience."[54] They noted with some resentment that the great majority of states have no truck with advisory opinions. Only "five states of the entire Union besides Colorado imposed advisory duties on their high courts." Worse, in two respects Colorado had gone even further than those states in "this doubtful and perilous experiment." First, the advice carries "all the force and effect of judicial precedents." Second, the advisory opinion clause requires the court to answer all "important questions," in contrast to the other states' clauses, which limit questions to those relating to law or to the constitution or to both. This has the effect of requiring answers to questions of fact, and, taken together with advisory opinions having precedential force, "might lead to the ex parte adjudication of private rights by means of a legislative or executive question, without giving the party interested a day or voice in court." Further, the court said, the clause permits questions on policies relating to proposed legislation, answers to which inserts the court into the political arena, a challenge to separation of powers.[55]

The Colorado court, then, simply asserted its authority to restrict advice, the clause's mandatory language notwithstanding. Thereafter the court strongly and repeatedly declared itself the sole and final authority on what are important questions and what are solemn occasions, and they acted accordingly. That is, the court and the court alone will "determine for itself" what questions to answer.[56] Even so, the court warned, in advisory

---

[51] *In re North Mo. R.R.*, 51 Mo. 586, 588 (1873).

[52] *In re Resolution of the General Assembly*, 55 Mo. 497, 498–99 (1874).

[53] Hudson, *Advisory Opinions of National and International Courts*, 982.

[54] *In re Senate Resolution Relating to Senate Bill No. 65*, 21 P. 478, 479 (Colo. 1889).

[55] *Id.* at 479–80. Michigan created an advisory opinion clause in 1963 which designates the court and not the justices as the advice-givers. South Dakota amended its constitution in 1972 so that there too the court and not the justices render advice. The other seven advisory states designate the justices as advice-givers. Colorado remains the only advisory state whose advisory opinion provision does not limit advice to questions of law or constitution.

[56] *E.g.*, *In re Penitentiary Comm'rs*, 35 P. 915 (Colo. 1894); *In re Interrogatories of the House*, 162 P. 1144 (Colo. 1917); *In re Senate Resolution No. 2*, 29 P.2d 705 (Colo. 1934). As in Maine, not all

opinion practice "there is danger of grave abuses" that can be suppressed only if both those requesting advisory opinions and the court exercise "the utmost vigilance and caution . . . in acting under this novel constitutional authority . . . only as a *dernier* resort . . . should the court be requested to act." After all, the problems with rendering advice are many. Besides those relating to due process and separation of powers, the need for speed makes it impossible to give the questions sufficient research and deliberation. Hence, the court said, "our embarrassment is seriously enhanced" while the chances of "erroneous decisions" are increased. Even when the court did offer advice, a "false interpretation . . . may indirectly lead to the most grievous consequences."[57] The Colorado court proceeded to develop rules so restrictive that one observer declared that it "is difficult to comprehend how the advisory opinion clause can be warped to this extent."[58]

The Florida justices, though never as openly critical as their colleagues in Missouri or Colorado, began to join them in imposing restrictions on their advisory opinions in 1887, after having issued fifteen without refusals or restrictions. Earlier the justices declared that they had no discretion with regard to their duty to advise. Their second advisory opinion, for example, stressed that "there is no power in the court to decline to give an opinion upon the questions submitted by the Executive. . . . [I]t is plain that there is no discretion in the court."[59] But in 1887 they found some discretion, perhaps influenced by the justices in other advising states, and in that year the justices refused outright to answer a request for advice. The justices did not explain their turnabout, but they took advantage of an 1875 amendment to the advisory opinion clause which limited the governor to seeking advice only on constitutional questions relating to the office's executive duties and powers.[60] The 1877 advisory opinion exemplifies how narrowly the justices, when asked to advise, would construe a constitutional provision. The governor had sought advice on whether he should refuse to sign certain types of bills that appear to be unconstitutional. The justices, declining to advise, told the governor that signing bills into law is not an executive duty. It is a legislative duty, as part of the enactment process. "Any duty imposed by the constitution on the governor with reference to a bill, before it becomes law, is not an executive duty. The enactment of laws is a legislative duty, when your excellency is required by the constitution to do any act which is an essential prerequisite thereto, such act is legislative, and is performed by you as part of the law-making power, and not as the law-executing power."[61]

The South Dakota justices were quick both to impose limits on requests for advice and to express doubts about their advisory duties, the former clearly arising from the latter. They observed that few states have ventured to adopt advisory opinion provisions

---

justices agreed. *See, e.g.*, *In re Lieutenant Governorship*, 129 P. 811 (1913), in which a dissenting justice argued that the court has no discretion to decide whether to answer questions.

[57] *In re Senate Bill No. 65*, 21 P. 478, 480.

[58] Robinson, *Limitations on Legislative Inquiries Under Colorado Advisory Opinions Clause*, 244.

[59] *In re Executive Communication of the 9th of Nov. 1868*, 12 Fla. 653, 663 (1868).

[60] *In re Executive Communication*, 6 So. 925 (Fla. 1887).

[61] *Id.*

in their constitutions, and observed as well, using language identical to the Colorado justices', that Missouri repealed its advisory opinion clause, "profiting, we suppose, from experience."[62] An observer in 1918 noted that the justices' responses to advisory opinion requests "have not been cordial," the justices disposed to "restricted interpretations" of the advisory opinion clause.[63] In their first refusal to advise, they allowed that the governor and legislature may have some say as to what are appropriate questions, though they insisted that the justices must have "some voice" as well, and that their right to challenge the requesting authority "should not be denied." Promptly exercising that right, the justices adopted the constitutional phrases "important questions of law" and "solemn occasions" as umbrellas under which they developed an advisory opinion jurisprudence. The first refusal set forth due process and separation of powers concerns, asserting the impropriety of rendering advice when private rights are at issue and when it constitutes interference with the other branches of government. For these reasons "and [for] many others which might be with propriety urged," the justices refused to advise.[64]

The Rhode Island justices were something of an exception. They did not confront the issue of imposing restrictions until 1937, or express doubts about advisory opinions until well after that. For nearly a century after an advisory opinion clause was introduced in its 1843 constitution, the justices indicated no doubts or reluctance regarding their advisory duties or set down restrictions on rendering advice. They advised freely, answering nearly all questions put to them.[65] An 1881 advisory opinion, for example, concerned an existing statute prohibiting licenses for selling liquor "within four hundred feet of any public school." The governor asked the justices if this meant the entire space within a 400-foot radius, or just 400 feet measured along a street or highway, and if it meant the school building or the whole school lot. The entire space and the whole school lot, answered the justices in an advisory opinion two sentences long.[66] Writing in 1918, a commentator said that the Rhode Island justices "have never given any indication of a disposition to withhold advice," excepting only when the advice might impinge on pending litigation. He attributes this to the broad language of Rhode Island's advisory opinion clause (requiring advice on "any" question of law).[67] Then in 1937 the justices followed the other advisory states in imposing restrictions and refusing to advise when the restrictions were exceeded.[68] It is not clear why they did not follow the other states earlier, or why they began to do so in 1937. It may be because, compared to other states, the Rhode Island advisory opinion clause is unique, with no language limiting advice to

---

[62] *In re Construction of Constitution*, 54 N.W. 650, 651 (S.D. 1893).

[63] Ellingwood, Departmental Cooperation, 54.

[64] *In re Construction of Constitution*, 54 N.W. at 651–52.

[65] The Rhode Island justices refused to advise only twice from 1843 to 1936, in *In re Opinion of the Judges*, 4 R.I. 583 (1858); and *In re Legislative Adjournment*, 27 A. 324 (R.I. 1893).

[66] *Opinion of the Judges*, 13 R.I. 736 (1881).

[67] Ellingwood, Departmental Cooperation, 172.

[68] Beginning with *To Certain Members of House of Representatives in Gen. Assembly*, 191 A. 269 (R.I. 1937).

"solemn occasions" or "important questions of law," on which justices in other states can hang at least some of their restrictions.[69]

The Rhode Island justices therefore would eventually make considerable efforts to justify restricting their advice. They began to do so as did advising justices in other states, by expressing their uneasiness if not animosity toward advisory opinions. They may refuse to advise, they said with remarkable directness, because "this peculiar obligation" is "obviously" repugnant to the principle of separation of powers. Such a clause could not have been included, they believe, without reason. They suggest a reason, if without historical evidence to support it: "in order to enable the executive and legislative departments to more effectively discharge particular duties that are textually committed to them by the Constitution."[70] From this the justices infer an assistance rationale for determining when they may properly render advice. The effective performance of constitutional obligations by the executive and legislature "requires from time to time assistance from the judges, . . . assistance which the framers of the constitution contemplated as being best provided through the device of the advisory opinion." Their duty to advise, however, is joined, "in view of the separation of executive, legislative, and judicial departments of government," by an equal duty to refuse to advise when the request for advice does not "fall reasonably within the constitutional clause relating thereto." Hence the requirement that the justices advise on any question of law "was intended to be exclusory in effect," that is, excluding advice that does not assist the other branches in the discharge of specific constitutional duties.[71]

It is something of a stretch, and reflects the Rhode Island justices' reluctance to advise, which has been quite open. In addition to the Chief Justice Williams' outright declaration that "we don't like to give advisory opinions," several former and present Rhode Island justices were clear on this in 1986, when a proposal to repeal the advisory opinion clause was introduced at a constitutional convention. Delegates learned that the justices "reported that the obligation [to advise] . . . is not viewed favorably by the

[69] Another explanation may lie in one of the most dramatic events in the history of state supreme courts. In 1935 the Rhode Island legislature, for the first time in decades, was controlled by the Democrats. In that state the supreme court justices were appointed—and dismissed—at the will of the Grand Assembly (both legislative houses sitting in joint session). When the Democratic-controlled legislature convened in 1935, it promptly dismissed all of the five justices of the supreme court (whose justices had been consistently Republican appointees since the 1850s), and replaced them with five others. The new justices, perhaps sensitive to being seen as under the thumb of the legislature, may have decided to resist rendering advisory opinions simply at the request of either house. At any rate there appears to be no record explaining why the justices suddenly decided to refuse to advise in 1937. On the 1935 removal of the justices and the "Bloodless Revolution" of which it was a part, see WILLIAM G. MCLOUGHLIN, RHODE ISLAND: A HISTORY 201–04 (1978). Beginning in 1994, Rhode Island's judiciary achieved greater independence through two constitutional amendments. The first, passed in 1994, provides that justices hold office on good behavior, subject only to impeachment. The second, passed in 2004, establishes separation of powers. R.I. Const. art. X, section 5; and art. V.

[70] *Opinion to the Governor*, 191 A.2d 611, 614 (R.I. 1963).

[71] *Id.*

Justices," and that several justices "spoke out in opposition" to advisory opinions.[72] In practice the justices joined their colleagues in the other advisory states in imposing restrictions by asserting that the mandatory language of the advisory opinion clause is mandatory only when the questions sent to them conform to whatever restrictions the justices choose to impose from time to time. Following the general pattern of other advisory justices, they have typically imposed a new restriction in the same opinion where they first refuse to advise based on the restriction. Under their assistance rationale, the Rhode Island justices have converted a broadly mandatory constitutional clause into a broadly discretionary one, and have asserted their restrictions accordingly.

The Jurisprudence of Advisory Opinions

Each state's advisory justices came around to developing a jurisprudence of restrictions differently, if in all cases arising from, and reflecting, their doubts about their advisory opinion duty. They typically have done what one writer said of the South Dakota justices: "In imposing . . . limitations, the South Dakota judges also voice the standard objections to the advisory opinion process. They say that the process is contrary to the idea of separation of powers and that these advisory opinions should be given only in very unusual situations."[73] The development of advisory opinion jurisprudence has been a curious mix of the justices' self-regarding concerns about their roles as advisors on the one hand, and a set of doctrines that is essentially a negative space. Advisory opinions are *not* opinions of the court, *not* decisions in litigated cases, *not* binding on those seeking the advice (or on anyone), *not* to be rendered on questions affecting private rights or on issues involved in litigation or in a broad range of other circumstances. By 1937 the justices in all the advisory states developed a jurisprudence centered on groups of restrictions on when they will advise. Most of the restrictions are correctives to, and compensations for, the criticisms and attacks on advisory opinions, their own and others', so that whether or not to accept a request for advice became the threshold issue, "the most important decision," one "quite different in its implications from any substantive advice the justices may ultimately provide."[74] The rest of this chapter reviews that jurisprudence.

---

[72] The first quote is in the REPORT OF THE JUDICIAL SELECTION AND DISCIPLINE COMMITTEE, MINUTES (May 21, 1986). The second quote is in the CONVENTION PROCEEDINGS (June 4, 1986). Neither record identifies the justices. The convention would approve the repeal measure, but it would be voted down at the polls owing to it being tied to another, more controversial, measure regarding judicial selection. This was similar to the defeats of the advisory opinion repeal measures in Massachusetts in 1820 and in 1853.

[73] John F. Hagemann, *The Advisory Opinion in South Dakota*, 16 S.D. L. REV. 291, 298 (1971).

[74] Kennedy, *Advisory Opinions: Cautions About Non-Judicial Undertakings*, 184.

THE NONBINDING DOCTRINE

This may be the most controversial of advisory opinion doctrines and standards, as we will see.[75] Most advisory opinion provisions are not explicit about whether advisory opinions are binding on those who have requested the advice or on others, that is, whether they carry the force and effect of precedent. Most advisory justices, however, have made the nonbinding nature of advisory opinions a centerpiece of their advising jurisprudence, beginning with New Hampshire in 1852.[76] Its importance to advisory opinion jurisprudence has been evident ever since. The nonbinding doctrine was the strongly stated central argument of the earliest law review article on advisory opinions, going so far as to note this about the advice from the British judges to the Law Lords: "No one supposes" that when they seek the judges' advice, that "the Law Lords are bound by the opinions given."[77]

This has essentially been the—often heavily, even defensively, emphasized—position of advisory judges of eight of the ten advisory states (all but Colorado and South Dakota), and mostly asserted early on.[78] Advisory opinions, the doctrine says, are merely advisory and consultative, binding on no one, including the courts.[79] "An advisory opinion is not precedentially binding on the court," as the Michigan justices put it. "It represents only the opinions of the parties signatory framed in a factual void."[80] The two exceptions, the supreme courts of Colorado and South Dakota, hold their advisory

---

[75] Chapter 5 is devoted to issues regarding nonbinding doctrine.

[76] *Opinion of the Justices*, 25 N.H. 537 (1852) (Justices' advisory opinions "must be regarded as impressions by which we should not feel ourselves bound."). It is not clear whether this position was taken owing to the vagueness of the particular question presented here. (The justices complain about the "considerably embarrassing" nature of the inquiry sent to them, since it is "impossible to understand" what the senate was requesting of them.) At any rate the New Hampshire justices have held to the nonbinding doctrine ever since.

[77] Thayer, *Advisory Opinions*, 47.

[78] The justices in Alabama asserted the nonbinding doctrine in their first advisory opinion in 1923; in Delaware in one of the earliest reported advisory opinions in 1930; in Florida in 1869 in the third advisory opinion; in Maine in 1870; in New Hampshire in 1852, in the fifth advisory opinion; in Rhode Island the justices adopted nonbinding doctrine in 1918, their first general statement about advisory opinions. *Opinion of the Justices*, 96 So. 487 (Ala. 1923); *State ex rel. Satterthwaite v. Highfield*, 152 A. 45 (Del. 1930); *In re Matter of the Executive Committee of the 28th January, 1869*, 12 Fla. 686 (1869); *State v. Cleveland*, 58 Me. 564 (1870); *Opinion of the Justices*, 25 N.H. 537 (1852); *In re Election of United States Senators*, 103 A. 513 (R.I. 1918).

[79] *Alabama Educ. Ass'n. v. James*, 373 So.2d 1076 (Ala. 1979); *Opinion of the Justices*, 417 So.2d 936 (Ala. 1981); *Opinion of the Justices*, 424 A.2d 663 (Del. 1980); *Petition of Kilgore*, 63 So.2d 30 (Fla. 1953); *Opinion of the Justices*, 396 A.2d 219 (Me. 1979); *Commonwealth v. Welosky*, 177 N.E. 656 (Mass. 1932); *In re Requests of the Governor and the Senate on the Constitutionality of Act No. 294 of the Public Acts of 1972*, 208 N.W.2d 469 (Mich. 1973); *Opinion of the Justices*, 25 N.H. 537 (1852); *Romeo v. Cranston Redevelopment Agency*, 254 A.2d 426 (R.I. 1969); *Opinion to the Governor*, 174 A.2d 553 (R.I. 1961).

[80] *Request for Advisory Opinion on the Constitutionality of 1979 PA 57*, 281 N.W.2d 322, 325 (Mich. 1979). The fact that Michigan's advisory opinion provision refers to the "court" and not the "justices" has not impelled the justices to hold their advisory opinions to be binding, in contrast to Colorado and South Dakota.

opinions to be binding.[81] The sole textual basis for the justices' positions is the references in the authorizing provisions, not to the advisory opinions, but to the justices themselves. All advisory opinion provisions refer to the advice-givers either as the justices or the judges on the one hand, or as the supreme court on the other. In all the states whose advisory opinion provisions refer to the "justices," the term has been held to mean that the advice is the personal, individual opinion of each justice, hence not a decision of the court, and so not binding. They are, as the Delaware justices put it, "nonadjudicative expressions of personal points of view."[82] The justices of all seven of the advisory states whose provisions refer to the "justices" or "judges" (all but Colorado, Michigan, and South Dakota) adopt the position that advisory opinions are nonbinding because they are the justices' opinions, not the court's.[83] The advisory opinion provisions in the other three states refer to the advice-giver as the supreme court, but Michigan holds notwithstanding that its advisory opinions are nonbinding.[84] Hence Colorado and South Dakota are the two states where advisory opinions are binding.[85]

In addition to references to justices rather than courts, the nonbinding advisory opinion states rely on two other grounds to justify the doctrine. One is the nonjudicial nature of advisory opinions. The Alabama justices' statement in their first advisory opinion is fairly representative. "The performance by the Justices of the function the [advisory opinion] act contemplates is non-judicial, this for the obvious reason that advisory opinions given do not conclude or vindicate any right or remedy, result in no judgment or decree, bind no one whatsoever."[86] The other nonbinding states generally agree.[87] The other ground, in some nonbinding states, is the assistance rationale for giving advice. The justices are offering, they say, noncourt, nonjudicial, and therefore nonbinding,

---

[81] In re Senate Resolution Relating to Senate Bill No. 65, 21 P. 478 (Colo. 1889); *In re Request for the Opinion of the Supreme Court Relative to the Constitutionality of SDCL 21-32-17*, and *Construction of SDCL 21-32-16*, 379 N.W.2d 822 (S.D. 1985).

[82] *Opinion of the Justices*, 413 A.2d 1245, 1248 (Del. 1980).

[83] In re Opinion of the Justices, 96 So. 487 (Ala. 1923); Opinion of the Justices, 417 So.2d 936 (Ala. 1981); Opinion of the Justices, 413 A.2d 1245 (Del 1980); In re Advisory Opinion to the Governor, 509 So.2d 292, 315 (Fla. 1987). Opinion of the Justices, 281 A.2d 321 (Me. 1971); *Bowe v. Secretary of Commonwealth*, 69 N.E.2d 115 (Mass. 1904); *Piper v. Town of Meredith*, 251 A.2d 328 (N.H. 1969); *Opinion to the Governor*, 191 A.2d 611 (R.I. 1963).

[84] In re Requests of the Governor and the Senate on the Constitutionality of Act No. 294 of the Public Acts of 1972, 208 N.W.2d 469 (Mich. 1973).

[85] In re Senate Resolution Relating to Senate Bill No. 65, 21 P. 478 (Colo. 1889); In re Request for Opinion of the Supreme Court Relative to the Constitutionality of SDCL 21-32-17 and Construction of SDCL 21-32-16, 379 N.W.2d 822, 828 (S.D. 1985) (Henderson, J., dissenting). As I argue in Chapter 5, the distinction has little practical effect.

[86] In re Opinion of the Justices, 96 So. 487 (Ala. 1923); *see also State ex rel. Bozeman v. Hester*, 72 So.2d 61 (Ala. 1954).

[87] *Opinion of the Justices*, 424 A.2d 663 (Del. 1980); *Laughlin v. City of Portland*, 90 A. 318 (Me. 1914); *Bourne v. Secretary of Commonwealth*, 69 N.E.2d 115 (Mass. 1946); *In re Requests of the Governor and the Senate on the Constitutionality of Act No. 294 of the Public Acts of 1972*, 208 N.W.2d 469 (Mich. 1973); *Opinion of the Justices*, 25 N.H. 537 (1852); *Opinion to the Governor*, 191 A.2d 611 (R.I. 1963).

advice to the requesting authorities to guide them in the proper exercise of their duties.[88]

RESTRICTIONS AND STANDARDS

In light of the nonbinding doctrine, the restrictions at first glance seem "puzzling," as a commentator calls one of them,[89] since advisory opinions do not bind and have no legal effect on individuals or on the government. But no one, it seems, has thought the nonbinding doctrine sufficient. However often or emphatically the doctrine was invoked, the justices have generally appeared to have little faith that it effectively addresses their doubts about rendering advisory opinions.[90] They all came to rely on a fully developed set of concrete restrictions and standards determining when they will advise and when they will refuse.

1. The Advisory Justices, Not the Requesting Authorities, Are the Sole Judges as to When the Justices Will Advise and When They Will Refuse

This straightforward projection of primary authority to decide when to advise is now the position in all the advisory states. It appears to fly in the face of the mandatory nature of the justices' duties in most advisory states, and, as we have seen, in fact the rule appeared only late in the nineteenth century (before which the requesting authority was generally presumed to determine when to request advice), a likely result of the justices' growing doubts about their advising duties along with the judiciary's expanding power and status. Former Maine Chief Justice Emery's 1917 article on the subject argued that the justices are not the ones to choose when to answer questions. The political branches have "the duty and hence [the] right" to decide whether a question is important and the occasion solemn. Emery complained that the Maine justices' first refusal was rendered "in a rather curt manner without stating any ground for assumption of such power."[91] The problem is that the constitutional requirement that the question be important is a fact question, for the legislature or executive to decide, not the judges.

---

[88] *Opinion of the Justices*, 394 So.2d 957 (Ala. 1981); *Answer of the Justices*, 122 Mass. 600 (1877); *Request for Advisory Opinion on the Constitutionality of 1979 PA 57*, 281 N.W.2d 322 (Mich. 1979); *Opinion of the Justices*, 68 A.2d 859 (N.H. 1949); *To Certain Members of the Senate in the General Assembly*, 191 A. 518 (R.I. 1937).

[89] Farina, *Supreme Judicial Court Advisory Opinions*, 378–79 (referring to the Massachusetts justices' refusal to advise if there is possible pending litigation involving the question presented).

[90] Chapter 5 shows that the lack of faith in nonbinding doctrine is fully justified.

[91] Emery, *Advisory Opinions of the Justices*, 18. Emery was referring to the Maine justices' first refusal in *In re Removal and Appointment of Country Attorneys*, 27 A. 454 (Me. 1892). This is discussed in Jonathan D. Persky, *Ghosts That Slay: A Contemporary Look at State Advisory Opinions*, 37 CONN. L. REV. 1155, 1190–91 (2005); and Note, *The Validity of the Restrictions on the Modern Advisory Opinion*, 313.

The justices themselves do not have the capacity to decide if a question is important merely by reading a request for advice.[92]

Emery's position did not prevail. Eventually in all advisory states with mandatory advisory opinion provisions, despite those provisions the justices would assert their sole authority and discretion over answering requests for advice, so that, as the Alabama justices put it, whether "the question falls within the purview of advisory opinion jurisdiction is determinable alone by the justices."[93]

2. *Advisory Opinion Provisions Must Be Strictly Construed*

Recognizing the extraordinary if not doubtful nature of their duty to advise, the justices in several states have adopted an explicit interpretive standard of narrowness and strictness, typically stated in strong terms. "The most extraordinary caution and conservatism should be exercised in propounding and answering" requests for advice, the Colorado court said.[94] The Delaware justices similarly held that they "have clearly emphasized that advisory opinions are outside the mainstream of our responsibilities as judicial officers and, for that reason, the [advisory opinion] Statute has traditionally been given a very narrow construction."[95]

3. *Questions Propounded Must Relate to Important Questions of Law and to Solemn Occasions*

Aiding advising justices in some of the states in asserting strict construction are two phrases. In six states the advisory opinion provisions state that advice must be on important questions of law, or on solemn occasions, or both. The justices there have long

---

[92] Emery, *Advisory Opinions of the Justices*, 18. *See, e.g.*, C. Dallas Sands, *Government by Judiciary—Advisory Opinions in Alabama*, 4 ALA. L. REV. 1, 19 (1951).

[93] *Opinion of the Justices*, 198 So.2d 269 (Ala. 1967); *In re Interrogatories of the Governor Concerning Chapter 89, Session laws 1935*, 51 P.2d 695 (Colo. 1935); *Opinion of the Justices*, 437 A.2d 597 (Me. 1981); *Opinion of the Justices*, 24 N.E. 1086 (Mass. 1890); *Opinion of the Justices*, 72 A. 754 (N.H. 1909); In Delaware the justices "may" but are not required to render advice, and they have presumed their sole discretion. *See Opinion of the Justices*, 330 A.2d 769 (Del. 1974). In Michigan the court has similarly assumed (though the constitutional provision is not specific on this) that its advisory power is "discretionary." *In re Request for Advisory Opinion, Enrolled House Bill No. 5250*, 235 N.W. 321 (Mich. 1975). The Rhode Island justices do not appear to have expressly stated their sole authority over whether to advise, but they have freely adopted restrictions and standards, silent on the issue of sole authority. This may be owing to their not adopting restrictions until relatively late (1937), when the question was no longer at issue in other advisory states. In South Dakota, where the opinions are from the court (not the justices) and are held to be binding, the court appears to have presumed they have the same sole discretion to rule on the appropriateness of requests as they would on any justiciability issue in litigated cases. *See, e.g.*, *In re House Resolution No. 30*, 72 N.W. 892 (S.D. 1897).

[94] *In re Senate Resolution Relating to Senate Bill No. 65*, 21 P. 478 (Colo. 1889). *Also: Answer of the Justices*, 276 N.E.2d 694, 695 (Mass. 1971) (The Massachusetts advisory opinion provision must be "strictly construed."); *Advisory Opinion to Governor*, 8 So.2d 26 (Fla. 1942); *Opinion to Governor*, 191 A.2d 611 (R.I. 1963); *In re Chapter 6, Session Laws of 1890*, 66 N.W. 310 (S.D. 1898).

[95] *Opinion of the Justices*, 413 A.2d 1245, 1247 (Del. 1980).

relied on these as grounds for imposing their restrictions.[96] What one observer noted about Maine's justices accurately applies to the others. "The Justices have restricted the scope of the advisory opinion through construction of the phrase 'solemn occasion,' . . . [and] by a narrow construction of the phrase 'important questions of law and upon solemn occasions' the Maine Justices have limited the availability of the advisory opinion."[97] The justices, that is, use the phrases to legitimize a restriction they are asserting. "Jurisdiction over advisory questions is governed less by explicit litmus tests and more by gestalt evaluations of what constitutes 'important questions of law' and 'solemn occasions.'"[98] Another commentator was critical about this, noting in 1918 that "the only tangible harvest from the refusals founded on this discretion is a collection of paraphrases and the rule which follows. . . . [T]he failure to establish definite rules leaves the other departments completely at a loss to know when they can obtain extra-judicial counsel and when not."[99] A justice-made restriction on advising is typically attached to one or the other phrase. The Massachusetts justices, for example, have held that there is no solemn occasion when the legislature seeks advice on legislation no longer pending, or when there was no time for interested parties to file briefs before the legislative session ended. For a broad set of restrictions, in short, "solemn occasion" has been the legitimizing pretext.[100]

The question of just what "solemn occasion" means, and what the distinction is between that phrase and "important questions of law," arose in the debate over the Michigan provision at the constitutional convention in 1962. The proposed provision, expressly modeled on that of Massachusetts, included the two phrases.[101] One delegate inquired about what "solemn occasion" means. The judiciary committee member leading discussion replied that the definition of the phrase is "some serious and unusual urgent need. It has been held to be such urgent need when either branch of the legislature having some action in view has serious doubts as to their power and authority to take

[96] Both "important questions of law" and "solemn occasions" are in the advisory opinion provisions of Colorado, Maine, Massachusetts, Michigan, and New Hampshire. South Dakota's refers just to "important questions of law." Of the other four states, Alabama's provision refers to "important constitutional questions," Delaware's specifies that the question must relate to a constitutional clause or to the constitutionality of legislation or proposed constitutional amendments. Florida's refers to "any question" relating to the governor's duties, and Rhode Island's refers simply to "any question of law."

[97] Note, *The Validity of the Restrictions on the Modern Advisory Opinion*, 316.

[98] Persky, *Ghosts That Slay*, 1190.

[99] Ellingwood, Departmental Cooperation, 208.

[100] *Opinion of the Justices*, 150 N.E.2d 693 (Mass. 1958); *Opinion of the Justices*, 502 N.E.2d 936 (Mass. 1987). *See also Opinion of the Justices*, 302 N.E.2d 565 (Mass. 1973), where the justices refuse to answer, holding that the question was important but the occasion not solemn; *In re Opinion of the Justices*, 29 P.2d 705 (Colo. 1934); *Opinion of the Justices*, 339 A.2d 439 (Me. 1975); *In re Request for Advisory Opinion, Enrolled House Bill No. 5250*, 235 N.W.2d 321 (Mich. 1975); *In re Construction of the Constitution*, 54 N.W. 650 (S.D. 1893). The South Dakota court relies heavily on "solemn occasions"; one opinion sets out eight standards for determining solemn occasion. *In re Request of Governor William J. Janklow for an Advisory Opinion Concerning the Constitutionality of House Bill 1163*, 530 N.W.2d 367 (S.D. 1995).

[101] *State of Michigan, Constitutional Convention of 1961, Official Record*, 1480 (1962). Hereafter, *Official Record.*

such action under the constitution or existing statutes."[102] The delegate replied that he was "a little bit puzzled over 'solemn.' It injects an atmosphere in the section which I am not quite certain of." He also noted that the distinction between "solemn occasions" and "important questions of law" is not clear. "Isn't there some tendency to be redundant here? . . . Wouldn't 'question of law' take into account ['solemn occasion']?" The judiciary committee member's response was that the definition of "solemn occasion" came from "a case, and the case is found at 290 Massachusetts 601."[103] The delegate suggested a possible religious influence, perhaps impressed by the great age of the Massachusetts constitution and its advisory opinion clause. (In effect since 1780, the constitution was, and remains, the world's oldest surviving written constitution.) He commented that "there is a very strong flavor of religious sentiment expressed in the old [Massachusetts] constitution, and I don't know that the word 'solemn' has the same connotation today as it might have had when it was first introduced in the Massachusetts constitution."[104] Later in the debate on the advisory opinion proposal, another delegate defended inclusion of "solemn occasion," insightfully commenting that it would give the justices a foundation for exercising restraint in rendering advisory opinions. "What these words will do is give the court sound legal doctrine for hanging their hat on in refusing to give an opinion."[105] This is in fact a fair description of what advising justices have done, in the states where the advisory opinion clauses include the phrase, when they refuse to answer requests for advice.

4. The Justices Will Not Exercise Fact-Finding Power When Advising

Most advisory justices have established that they will render advisory opinions only on questions of law or constitution, never on questions requiring findings of facts. One writer attributes this restriction to the justices' lack of resources,[106] but more likely is the straightforward fact that all advisory opinion provisions specify that opinions are to be on questions of law or on interpretations of constitutions. Also, the advisory justices take care to distinguish the nonjudicial function of advising from the judicial function of fact finding. The Rhode Island justices, for example, said that their duty to advise "does not apply to inquiries that can be answered only through an exercise of the factfinding power, inasmuch as the justices of this court, in so doing, are acting as individuals and not exercising the judicial power of the state. . . . [T]he factfinding power inheres in the court as the judicial branch of state government and . . . may not be

---

[102] *Id.* at 1543.

[103] *Id.* The response, which drew laughter, perhaps because it could mean little to most delegates, referred to a 1935 Massachusetts advisory opinion in which the justices refused to advise because the legislature had been prorogued, so that the solemn occasion that gave rise to the request "ceased to exist." Early in the opinion the justices discuss what constitutes a solemn occasion. *In re Opinion of the Justices*, 195 N.E. 357, 290 Mass. 601 (1935).

[104] *Official Record*, 1543–44.

[105] *Id.* at 1548.

[106] Ellingwood, Departmental Cooperation, 218.

exercised by justices when acting as individuals pursuant to [the advisory opinion provision]."[107]

5. The Justices Will Not Answer Questions Affecting Private Rights

This fundamental element of due process—the right to be notified and heard if one's rights may be at issue—has always been held to be infringed by the advisory opinion process. The earliest recorded refusal to advise, by the New Hampshire justices in 1816, identified the possible interference of their advice, with private rights as their reason.[108] This restriction was not without some controversy. A strong proponent of advisory opinions was critical of it, especially if it merely bars advisory opinions on the mere possibility that the question may arise in litigation at some later date.[109] Another critic, writing on advisory opinions in Colorado, complains that the court, "in its reluctance to give advisory opinions," included among its many restrictions one regarding private rights, which he called an "unfortunate limitation."[110] On the other hand an opponent of advisory opinions is among those who believe that "nearly every question raised in a request for an advisory opinion would affect very real private interests in some fashion."[111] Another critic offers a middle ground, recommending that the justices should refuse to advise only when the effect on individual rights is "direct, immediate, and possibly detrimental."[112] No justices have adopted such positions. The aura of illegitimacy surrounding the advisory opinion process impels advising justices to give due process a wide berth. While the justices have not addressed specifically the problem that many if not most advisory opinions are likely to affect private rights at some point, they nonetheless hold that they will not advise when, in their view, private rights are, or may be, affected.[113] They do, however, occasionally answer questions directly affecting

---

[107] *In re Advisory Opinion to the Governor*, 324 A.2d 641, 647 (R.I. 1974). If the question mixes fact and law, the Rhode Island justices have said, they will refuse to advise. *Opinion to the Governor*, 191 A.2d 611 (R.I. 1963). *See also People ex rel. Engley v. Martin*, 36 P. 543 (Colo. 1894); *Opinion of the Justices*, 382 A.2d 1364 (Del. 1978); *Opinion of the Justices*, 369 A.2d 233 (Me. 1977); *Dinan v. Swig*, 112 N.E. 91 (Mass. 1916); *Opinion of the Justices*, 45 N.H. 607 (1864); *Opinion of the Justices*, 463 A.2d 891 (N.H. 1983); *In re Limitation of Taxation*, 54 N.W. 650, 652 (S.D. 1893).

[108] *Opinion of the Court*, 62 N.H. 704 (1816).

[109] ELLINGWOOD, DEPARTMENTAL COOPERATION, 180–205. Sands discusses this in *Government by Judiciary*, 20.

[110] Robinson, *Limitations upon Legislative Inquiries under Colorado Advisory Opinion Clause*, 237 and 244.

[111] Sands, *Government by Judiciary*, 22. Ellingwood, in 1918, calculated that, of the 410 advisory opinions rendered in the advisory opinion states, 207 "involved dealing with obvious questions of private rights, including both personal rights and property rights." ELLINGWOOD, DEPARTMENTAL COOPERATION, 181.

[112] T. A. Smiljanich, *Advisory Opinions in Florida: An Experiment in Intergovernmental Cooperation*, 24 U. FLA. L. REV. 328, 331 (1972).

[113] *Opinion of the Justices*, 198 So.2d 269 (Ala. 1967); *In re Senate Resolution No. 4*, 130 P. 333 (Colo. 1913); *Opinion of the Justices*, 413 A.2d 1245 (Del. 1980); *Advisory Opinion to the Governor*, 196 So.2d 737, 739 (Fla. 1967); *Opinion of the Justices*, 121 A. 912 (Me. 1923); *Answer of the Justices to the Council*, 366 N.E.2d 730 (Mass. 1977); *Request for Advisory Opinion on the Constitutionality of 1979 PA 57*, 281 N.W.2d 322 (Mich. 1979); *Opinion of the Justices*, 66 A.2d 76 (N.H. 1949); *Opinion to the House of Representatives*, 433 A.2d 944 (R.I. 1981); *In re Opinion of the Justices*, 182 N.W.2d 849 (S.D. 1971).

criminal rights.[114] Some of the justices also distinguish the opposite side of the coin, positively requiring that requests for advice be only on matters of what the Alabama justices call "a general public nature."[115]

6. The Justices Will Refuse to Answer Questions on Issues Directly or Indirectly Involved in Pending Litigation

Closely related to due process concerns about private rights is the parallel concern about the "grave difficulties" arising from advising when the question is also pending in litigation. The former is usually identified as the rationale for the latter. It is one of the oldest of restrictions (in the seventeenth century Lord Coke as Chief Justice complained of having to advise the king or House of Lords on matters pending before the courts), and advising justices strictly adhere to it.[116] The Rhode Island justices set out the rationale:

> [G]rave difficulties would follow if we were to give a purely advisory opinion on the proposed question, only to be confronted later with the necessity of deciding the same question after a hearing, upon review or otherwise, in the litigated case. In such event, the defendant conceivably might have some ground to complain that his legal and constitutional rights had been unnecessarily prejudiced by our having reached a considered opinion, even though only advisory, upon a material question of law which we know to have been involved in his conviction, without yet affording him a full hearing.[117]

---

[114] *E.g., Opinion of the Justices*, 355 A.2d 341 (Me. 1976) (detaining suspected drunk drivers); *Opinion of the Justices to the House of Representatives*, 142 N.E.2d 770 (Mass. 1957) (wiretapping); *Opinion of the Justices*, 431 A.2d 144 (N.H. 1981) (right to counsel for indigent minor defendants); *In re Advisory Opinion to the Governor (Appointed Counsel)*, 666 A.2d 813 (R.I. 1995) (right to counsel for indigent defendants, misdemeanor charges). *See also Opinion of the Justices*, 294 So.2d 578 (Ala. 1975) (refusing to answer question regarding death penalty, as too serious a question for abstract response).

[115] *Opinion of the Justices*, 384 So.2d 1056 (Ala. 1980). Besides Alabama, Colorado and Maine specify the requirement. *In re Advisory Opinion*, 21 P. 478 (Colo. 1888); *In re Opinion of the Justices*, 128 A. 691 (Me. 1925).

[116] *Opinion of the Justices*, 431 So.2d 496 (Ala. 1982); *In re Interrogatories by the Governor*, 245 P.2d 1173 (Colo. 1952); *State v. Cleveland*, 58 Me. 564 (1870); *Opinion of the Justices to the Senate*, 486 N.E.2d 1109 (Mass. 1985); *Opinion of the Justices*, 91 A.2d 458 (N.H. 1952); *In re Advisory Opinion to the Governor*, 492 A.2d 134 (R.I. 1985); *In re Opinion of the Judges*, 275 N.W. 633 (S.D. 1937). Delaware, Florida, and Michigan appear to place pending litigation restrictions under private rights restrictions. On the resistance of the English judges to advising when the question may arise in adjudication, see STUART JAY, MOST HUMBLE SERVANTS: THE ADVISORY ROLE OF EARLY JUDGES 13–16 (1997) (discussing the judges' refusal to advise the House of Lords on this ground, and noting a 1718 instance where the Lords themselves decided not to put a question to the judges because it may come before the judges judicially). This view of advisory opinions is in Lord Coke's INSTITUTES: "Judges ought not to deliver their opinions before-hand of any criminal case, that they may come before them judicially." COKE, THIRD INSTITUTES (1644). Quoted in JAY, MOST HUMBLE SERVANTS, 16.

[117] *Opinion to the House of Representatives (Resolution H-1225)*, 149 A.2d 343, 346 (R.I. 1959).

7. The Question Must Seek Advice That Relates Directly to the Requesting Authority's Duties Presently Awaiting Performance

Many advising justices are emphatic in requiring a clear connection between the question propounded and the duty that is awaiting performance, sometimes called the "live gravity" requirement.[118] The executive must have a *present* duty to perform for which the advice is needed, and the legislature's need for advice must be on legislation *currently* being considered. The action of the requesting authority must depend on the advice. This suggests that a requesting authority cannot seek advice for a third party, which would amount to the justices intruding into the affairs of that party, which the Rhode Island justices called "grossly gratuitous" and "inexcusable."[119] Some justices accordingly specify that advice to the legislature must be on pending—not passed—legislation.[120] The Rhode Island justices explain this on the ground that, according to "the universally accepted rule," enacted legislation is presumed constitutional unless it is shown otherwise.[121] The justices accordingly will not advise if the legislature has adjourned *sine die*, since at that point no legislation can be pending.[122] Correspondingly, advice to the governor involving legislation must be about passed—not pending—legislation.[123] This, however, may provide "an executive with unlimited standing to obtain constitutional assessment of new [enacted] legislation," by which the executive "may employ the judiciary to supervise the legislative process."[124]

---

[118] *Opinion of the Justices*, 319 So.2d 709 (Ala. 1975); *In re Interrogatories by Governor*, 206 P. 383 (Colo. 1922); *Opinion of the Justices*, 355 A.2d 341 (Me. 1976); *Opinion of the Justices*, 168 N.E. 536 (Mass. 1929); *Opinion of the Justices*, 83 A.2d 738 (N.H. 1950); *In re Request for Advisory Opinion Regarding House Bill 83-H-5640*, 472 A.2d 301 (R.I. 1984); *In re Opinion of the Justices*, 210 N.W. 186 (S.D. 1926).

[119] *In re Opinion to the Governor*, 284 A.2d 295 (R.I. 1971) (The governor "improperly" sought advice on behalf of city council members, in which instance "the giving of opinions would be grossly gratuitous and an inexcusable participation by the judges in the affairs of a municipality.").

[120] *Opinion of the Justices*, 665 So.2d 1387 (Ala. 1995); *In re Senate Resolution No. 4*, 130 P.333 (Colo. 1913); *Opinion of the Justices*, 150 N.E.2d 693 (Mass. 1958); *Opinion to the Justices*, 463 A.2d 891 (N.H. 1983); *Opinion to the House of Representatives*, 208 A.2d 126 (R.I. 1965). Michigan is an exception since its constitutional clause on advisory opinions provides for advice after enactment, though "before its effective date."

[121] *Opinion to the House of Representatives*, 208 A.2d 126 (R.I. 1965).

[122] *In re Senate Bill No. 416*, 101 P. 410 (Colo. 1909); *Opinion of the Justices*, 281 A.2d 321 (Me. 1971); *Answer of Justices to Senate*, 371 N.E.2d 772 (Mass. 1978); *Opinion of the Justices*, 193 A.2d 880 (N.H. 1963); *In re Advisory Opinion to the House of Representatives*, 272 A.2d 925 (R.I. 1971). New Hampshire makes an exception if the legislature requests advice on possible legislation to be considered at a future session if the legislature specifically requests it, and it might be of benefit. *Opinion of the Justices*, 37 A.2d 478 (N.H. 1944).

[123] *Opinion of the Justices*, 238 So.2d 326 (Ala. 1970); *In re House Resolution No. 12*, 298 P. 960 (Colo. 1931); *Opinion of the Justices*, 305 A.2d 608 (Del. 1973); *Opinion of the Justices*, 396 A.2d 219 (Me. 1979); *Opinion of the Justices*, 463 A.2d 891 (N.H. 1983); *Advisory Opinion to the House of Representatives*, 264 A.2d 920 (R.I. 1970); *In re Construction of the Constitution*, 54 N.W. 650 (S.D. 1893). The Florida justices ruled that under the 1968 constitution the justices may advise the governor on constitutionality of legislation not yet enacted. *Opinion to the Governor*, 239 So.2d 1 (Fla. 1970). Previously, the justices had held that the governor could not seek advice on whether to sign a bill, since that was a legislative and not an executive function. *Advisory Opinion to Governor*, 8 So.2d (Fla. 1942).

[124] Kennedy, *Advisory Opinions: Cautions About Non-Judicial Undertakings*, 195.

8. The Question Propounded Must Refer Directly to Pertinent Constitutional Provisions or to a Specific Constitutional Duty

The justices dislike unduly broad questions, especially blanket questions on whether a statute, taken as a whole, is constitutional, and most will not answer blanket questions generally inquiring if anything in a statute is unconstitutional for any reason.[125] They generally require that the requesting authority cite specifically the constitutional clauses which might be violated by particular provisions of the legislation being considered or by the action the executive is contemplating.[126] As the Alabama justices put it, to "leave to the justices to search for all possible avenues of constitutional tests, imposes a task with . . . doubt and uncertainty."[127] The New Hampshire justices are among those who have long been strict on this point, complaining in 1852 about receiving from the senate a copy of a bill to regulate "drinking houses and tippling shops," the senate simply asking if the bill was constitutional. "It is impossible to understand," they said, "to what point in the principle or in the details of the bill it is the wish of the Senate that we should direct our attention."[128] Though they answered the question, later they would join other advisory justices in applying this restriction. They refused two requests on this ground within a few weeks in 2001, in which the senate included among its questions whether the bills at issue would "violate any other provision of the New Hampshire Constitution." The justices replied, simply, that in "accordance with our long-standing practice, we respectfully decline to answer this question because of its generality."[129] Delaware is an exception, allowing for an entire statute to be submitted for general review against all possible constitutional limitations.[130]

9. Questions Should Not Be Hypothetical, Unclear, or Speculative

In another application of the "live gravity" requirement, justices will not answer questions too abstracted from actual, concrete concerns. "The anticipated need for the advice must not be tentative, hypothetical, and abstract," the Maine justices said.[131]

---

[125] *Opinion of the Justices*, 251 So.2d 759 (Ala. 1971); *In re Senate Resolution No. 2 Concerning Constitutionality of House Bill No. 6*, 31 P.2d 325 (Colo. 1934); *Opinion of the Justices*, 176 N.E. 649 (Mass.1931); *In re Opinion of the Judges*, 210 N.W. 186 (S.D. 1926).

[126] *Opinion of the Justices*, 373 A.2d 1050 (Ala. 1979); *In re Interrogatories of Governor Concerning Chapter 89, Session Laws*, 51 P.2d 695 (Colo. 1935); *Opinion of the Justices*, 330 A.2d 769 (Del. 1974); *Opinion of the Justices to the Senate*, 484 N.E.2d 95 (Mass. 1985); *In re Request for Advisory Opinion, Enrolled House Bill No. 5250*, 235 N.W.2d 321 (Mich. 1975); *Opinion of the Justices*, 254 A.2d 273 (N.H. 1969); *Advisory Opinion to the Governor*, 437 A.2d 542 (R.I. 1981).

[127] *Opinion of the Justices*, 238 So.2d 326, 327 (Ala. 1970).

[128] *Opinion of the Justices*, 25 N.H. 537, 537 (1852). The justices answered anyway. The Michigan justices in 1975 were similarly simply sent a copy of a bill. They expressed the same complaints as did the New Hampshire justices, but they refused to render advice. *In re Request for Advisory Opinion Regarding Constitutionality of 1975 PA 227*, 235 N.W.2d 321, 322 (Mich. 1975).

[129] *Opinion of the Justices*, 765 A.2d 673, 676 (N.H. 2001); *Opinion of the Justices*, 765 A.2d 706, 709 (N.H. 2001).

[130] *Opinion of the Justices*, 330 A.2d 769 (Del. 1974).

[131] *Opinion of the Justices*, 330 A.2d 912, 915 (Me. 1975).

They refused to answer questions on the applicability of a statute to a candidate for state attorney general. Whether the application of the statute "will ever come in issue remains in the realm of speculation. . . . [T]he questions here posed are at a stage yet too tentative, hypothetical, and abstract to have achieved the 'live gravity' necessary for the existence of a 'solemn occasion.'"[132] The justices in most other advisory opinion states agree, though none has been precise on what constitutes a hypothetical question.[133]

10. Questions Should Not Be on the Wisdom or Expediency of Proposed Legislation

In a parallel to the U.S. Supreme Court's political question doctrine, advising justices will on occasion resist questions that deviate from narrowly statutory or constitutional matters, that is, when questions are too strongly or exclusively political. As the justices put it, questions must relate closely to the constitutional powers and authority of the requesting authority, and must not relate to such matters as the wisdom, expediency, or desirability of legislation.[134] "With the wisdom of the policy which the Legislature seeks to establish we are not concerned," said the Maine justices. "Our task is to give our opinion upon the constitutionality [of the statute in question] and no more."[135]

Some Other Restrictions

The Colorado supreme court has refused to advise when the request included questions excessive in number or complexity. To a request to answer four questions on four sections of the constitution, the court said that "a satisfactory response, would require [of the court] vast research and extraordinary caution. . . . In view of the fact that we must act as both court and counsel, and in view of the other duties we must necessarily perform, the period of time provided for a legislative session would hardly be sufficient to return safe and satisfactory answers to more than one such inquiry."[136] The court readily referred to this position when they were sent forty-one questions regarding the constitutionality of an act.[137]

---

[132] *Opinion of the Justices*, 96 A.2d 219, 229 (Me. 1979) (internal quotes and cites omitted).

[133] *Opinion of the Justices*, 468 So.2d 883 (Ala. 1985); *In re Opinion of the Justices*, 88 A.2d 128 (Del. 1952); *Answer of the Justices to the Governor*, 829 N.E.2d 1111 (Mass. 2005); *Advisory Opinion to His Excellency, Frank Licht, Governor of the State of Rhode Island*, 289 A.2d 430 (R.I. 1972). "Manifestly," the South Dakota justices said, they will not answer questions on future legislation, "the exact terms of which rest entirely in speculation and conjecture." *In re Opinion of the Justices*, 210 N.W. 186 (S.D. 1926).

[134] *In re Senate Resolution Relating to Senate Bill No. 65*, 21 P. 478 (Colo. 1889); *Opinion of the Justices*, 132 A.2d 47 (Me. 1957); *Answer of Justices*, 66 N.E.2d 358 (Mass. 1946); *Rossner v. Federal Collateral Society*, 300 N.W. 45 (Mich. 1941).

[135] *Opinion of the Justices*, 132 A.2d 47, 49 (Me. 1957). Thanks to Prof. Robert H. Whorf for pointing out the similarity between this rule and the political question doctrine.

[136] *In the Matter of the Senate Resolution on the Subject of Irrigation*, 21 P. 470 (Colo. 1886).

[137] *In re House Bill No. 99*, 56 P. 181 (Colo. 1899). *See* Robinson's discussion of this in *Limitations upon Legislative Inquiries under Colorado Advisory Opinion Clause*, 242. In this opinion the justices complained also of the frequency with which they were sent requests for advisory opinions. They had answered about eighty since their first advisory opinion in December 1886. After this 1899 opinion, they declined to answer frequently, refusing to answer six of the next eight requests. The complaint and the refusals apparently had

The Delaware justice will not answer a purely federal question. Subject matter of advisory opinions must be within the jurisdiction of the Delaware courts.[138]

The Michigan supreme court may not advise if the enactment in question has an effective date prior to the date it was sent to the court for advice.[139] Michigan's constitution limits advisory opinions to advice on legislation only after it has been enacted but before its effective date.[140]

The Massachusetts justices refused to advise on whether proposed legislation violated the state constitution, when the Supreme Judicial Court already ruled that the legislation violated the federal constitution. Hence the question was "academic."[141]

The New Hampshire justices will not advise if the requesting authority has determined not to consider the advice,[142] or if the request is for advice in interlocutory matters.[143]

The Rhode Island justices refused to advise when the question was propounded by the presiding officer of a legislative house, without a formal assembled meeting in which the house voted for the request.[144]

* * *

The elaborate pattern of restrictions on advisory opinions may seem puzzling in light of the nonbinding doctrine. Advisory opinions may be the nonjudicial statements binding on no one that the justices say they are. But in addition to doubts about even that, discussed later in this book, the justices understandably wish to maintain some authority, some boundaries, and some discretion over their advice-giving in the face of the mandatory nature of the duty in most advisory states.

EXCEPTION: PUBLIC IMPORTANCE

Having established a jurisprudence of restrictions defining when the justices will advise, the justices in several of the advisory opinion states have introduced a public importance exception. The exception permits them to waive their restrictions. What constitutes public importance sufficient to warrant waiving a restriction appears to be entirely at the call of the justices, and in fact application of the exception tends to be ad hoc if not

---

some effect. Over the following twelve-year period (1890 to 1901) they received only six requests for advice.

[138] *Opinion of the Justices*, 413 A.2d 1245 (Del. 1960).

[139] *In re Enrolled Senate Bill 933*, 236 N.W.2d 62 (Mich. 1975).

[140] Mich. Const., art. II, sec. 8.

[141] *Opinion of the Justices*, 257 N.E.2d 94 (Mass. 1970). The legislation related to limiting welfare payments to people arriving from other states.

[142] *In re School Manual*, 4 A. 878 (N.H. 1885).

[143] *Opinion of the Justices*, 373 A.2d 642 (N.H. 1977) (advice sought in the midst of proceedings for removal of a state official by the governor).

[144] *In re Certain Members of the House of Representatives*, 191 A. 269 (R.I. 1937).

simply arbitrary.[145] None of the advisory justices have formulated a rule, standard, or policy on the exception, usually just vaguely referring to public interest or importance, only occasionally offering factual grounds. The typical rationale, though by no means a consistently applied standard, is that the advice is warranted to avoid the undesirable effects of waiting until the issue involved can be resolved in regular adjudication. Hence the cases noted below are simply a few instances where the justices have invoked the exception.

The Colorado court issued an advisory opinion even though they would not normally do so regarding an already passed statute, owing to the "disastrous effects" if the statute were later found to be unconstitutional after being implemented.[146] The Alabama justices advised despite pending litigation on the same question because the question "is one of great public interest."[147] The Delaware justices similarly did so because the question presented, though failing to raise a constitutional issue as the justices require, "presents a current issue of general public interest," and the advisory opinion is needed to preclude unnecessary litigation and to prevent "inequitable disenfranchisement of otherwise eligible voters."[148]

In several cases the Florida justices have waived their restrictions owing to "the great public interest" in the state's financial stability; to the "irreparable harm to the public" if the statute in question was implemented and it turned out to be in error; and to the need to avoid "the potentially chaotic impact" on the governor's duties if the statute in question waited for litigation to test its constitutionality.[149] The Maine justices advised even though a bill was still in committee and therefore not pending before the senate, since it involved "a question of great public concern,"[150] and the Massachusetts justices did so regarding an already enacted statute, in order to avoid needlessly spending the time, effort, and public funds should the statute be later found unconstitutional.[151]

---

[145] Problems and challenges with the public importance exception, including, in some states, its ill-defined and excessive use, are discussed in Chapter 6. *See also generally* Thomas R. Bender, *Rhode Island's Public Importance Exception for Advisory Opinions: The Unconstitutional Exercise of a Non-Judicial Power*, 10 Roger Williams Univ. L. Rev. 123 (2004); Mel A. Topf, *The Advisory Opinion on Separation of Powers: The Uncertain Contours of Advisory Opinion Jurisprudence in Rhode Island*, 5 Roger Williams Univ. L. Rev. 385, 397–408. As shown in Chapter 6, Rhode Island's advisory opinion process is subject to extraordinarily frequent use of the public importance exception.

[146] *In re House Bill No. 168*, 39 P. 1096 (Colo. 1895).

[147] *Opinion of the Justices*, 624 So.2d 107, 109 (Ala. 1993). In another instance involving pending litigation the justices said they would render advice anyway because the governor's request "involves questions vitally important to the people of the State of Alabama." *Opinion of the Justices*, 558 So.2d 390, 391 (Ala. 1989). *See also Opinion of the Justices*, 599 So.2d 1166, 1167, (Ala. 1992) (advising despite legislature being not in session and no legislation pending, because "matters of great public concern are involved requiring immediate resolution").

[148] *Opinion of the Justices of the Supreme Court in Response to a Question Propounded by the Governor of Delaware*, 202 A.2d 276 (Del. 1964).

[149] *In re Advisory Opinion to the Governor*, 239 So.2d 1, 8–9 (Fla. 1970); *In re Advisory Opinion to the Governor*, 374 So.2d 959 (Fla. 1979); *In re Advisory Opinion to the Governor*, 509 So.2d 292 (Fla. 1987).

[150] *Opinion of the Justices*, 370 A.2d 654 (Me. 1977).

[151] *Opinion of the Justices to the Senate*, 493 N.E.2d 859, 863 (Mass. 1986).

The Rhode Island justices rendered an advisory opinion to the governor despite it being about pending and not enacted legislation, and despite it having no relation to a present constitutional duty of the governor, because it involved "a significant constitutional issue of great public interest sufficient to transcend these infirmities."[152]

[152] *In re Advisory Opinion to the Governor*, 732 A.2d 55, 59, and 71–72 (R.I. 1999). The two advisory opinions that the Connecticut justices rendered before stopping the practice were explained (in their later first refusal to advise) as dealing with "acts of great importance . . . where an immediate opinion was needed." *Reply of the Judges of the Supreme Court to the General Assembly*, 3 Conn. 586, 587 (1867). The two advisory opinions are discussed in Chapter 2.

4 }

Useful Instrument of Government

DEFENDING ADVISORY OPINIONS

Explanations about the value of advisory opinions came only after the attacks, requiring justification only after being questioned.[1] And they came after the development of the justices' restrictions as well. The attacks and restrictions responded to the challenges to the legitimacy of advisory opinions. The defenses, however, arose elsewhere, largely from changing notions of the role of the judiciary in modern government. It has always been a curious trait of the defenses that they rarely address the attacks directly. Proponents of advisory opinions have largely declined to deal with separation of powers, due process, case or controversy, or other challenges raised by opponents of advisory opinions. The proponents, usually observers—rarely the advising justices whose animosity toward their advising duties remain a constant—have generally limited themselves to "practical arguments, as opposed to the theoretical arguments made against them."[2] Almost without exception the proponents have avoided the doctrinal questions and focused solely on "the practical and empirical."[3]

The Defenses of Advisory Opinions

ALL THE AGONY: THE PROBLEM OF JUDICIAL REVIEW'S DELAY AND INEFFICIENCY, AND ADVISORY OPINIONS AS A SOLUTION

The defenses largely boil down to the claim that advisory opinions are a cure for the delay and consequent uncertainty inherent in the process of judicial review.

[1] James L. Huffman & Mardi Lyn Saathoff, *Advisory Opinions and Canadian Constitutional Development: The Supreme Court's Reference Jurisdiction*, 74 MINN. L. REV. 1251, 1273 (1990). Huffman and Saathoff are writing about Canadian advisory opinions (called "references" there, denoting a question that is referred to a court for advice), but the point about the rise of defenses applies to the United States as well. Appendix B, a note on foreign advisory opinion practices, includes a brief account of advisory opinions in Canada.

[2] T. A. Smiljanich, *Advisory Opinions in Florida: An Experiment in Intergovernmental Cooperation*, 24 U. FLA. L. REV. 328, 338 (1972).

[3] "Proponents of advisory opinions focus on the practical and empirical, rather than the theoretical, underpinnings of the doctrine." Jonathan D. Persky, *Ghosts That Slay: A Contemporary Look at State Advisory Opinions*, 37 CONN. L. REV. 1155, 1172 (2005). Advising justices themselves "rarely attempt to explain why the exercise of advising jurisdiction is likely to result in a more useful governmental product than what might be expected from adjudication." Robert H. Kennedy, *Advisory Opinions: Cautions About Non-Judicial Undertakings*, 23 U. RICHMOND L. REV. 173, 186 (1989).

This argument for advisory opinions surfaced in the 1880s. "To wait two or three years to find out that the law is unconstitutional," said a proponent at the 1889 North Dakota constitutional convention, "is not wise."[4] This criticism of the delay in settling the meaning and validity of legislation—more exactly, settling them only after the legislation is enacted and put into effect, violated, and then challenged—goes back at least to Bentham's utilitarian criticism of the judicial process. A judicial decision, he wrote, is something like the way you make laws for your dog. "When your dog does anything you want to break him of, you wait till he does it, and then beat him for it. This is the way you make laws for your dog: and this is the way the judges make law for you and me. They won't tell a man beforehand what it is *he should not do*—they won't so much as allow of his being told."[5]

Putting this in terms more germane if less memorable than Bentham's, proponents of advisory opinions seem to see law in this realist perspective, as setting forth rules or norms for regulating conduct.[6] Important to the success of law in this respect is the ability of those subject to the law to obtain answers to the inevitable questions on the meaning of a given law. From this viewpoint the problem in the American judicial system is that it has retained from English common law the retrospective process of determining authoritatively the law's meaning, and has added to it the cumbersome process of judicial review to determine the law's own validity as well as its meaning. Before the meaning may become clear or its validity confirmed, a law may be passed, promulgated, and then, before the judiciary may say "what the law is," it must be allegedly violated, tested at trial, appealed, and perhaps appealed again. All future application of the law will depend on the ruling. This remedial notion of law requires the judiciary to "stand mute in the face of an unconstitutional statute, ignoring its possible harm until a justiciable issue is presented."[7] Proponents put forth advisory opinions as a corrective. They see the advisory opinion process as preventative jurisprudence, permitting those who make and those who execute the law to learn of constitutional difficulties, and be guided accordingly, before harm is done.[8] The harm for which advisory opinions are put forth as the best remedy is serious.

> Laws are brought into existence at much travail and expense only to be declared nullities as soon as brought before the court of last resort. . . . [O]ne out of every three

---

[4] Official Report of the Proceedings and Debates of the First Constitutional Convention of North Dakota 233 (1889).

[5] Jeremy Bentham, *Truth versus Ashhurst; or Law as It Is, Contrasted with What It Is Said to Be*, *in* 5 The Works of Jeremy Bentham 232 (1823). Quoted in Pascal F. Calogero, *Advisory Opinions: A Wise Change for Louisiana and Its Judiciary?*, 38 Loyola L. Rev. 358 (1992).

[6] For two prominent treatments of law in this respect, see generally H. L. A. Hart, The Concept of Law (1976); Hans Kelsen, General Theory of Law and State (1949) (especially *General Norms Created by Judicial Acts*, at 149–53).

[7] P. C. McKeever & B. O. Perry, *The Case for an Advisory Function in the Federal Judiciary*, 50 Geo. L.J. 785 (1962).

[8] *See, e.g.*, Albert R. Ellingwood, Departmental Cooperation in State Government 254 1918); R. K. Hoffman, *Why Not Advisory Opinions for Illinois?*, 31 Chi.-Kent L. Rev. 141 (1952); McKeever & Perry, *The Case for an Advisory Function in the Federal Judiciary*, 785 and 794; Persky, *Ghosts That Slay*, 1161.

> hundred statutes passed by our lawmaking bodies is declared never to have been law at all. What is still worse, often these unconstitutional "laws" go unimpeached for years, while private rights are based upon their validity, only to meet disaster in the crucial test. Meanwhile, in our jurisprudence, there is a conclusive presumption that every citizen, including the officials of the executive and legislative departments, knows the law, although in fact it is impossible for anyone to know it.[9]

The delay of judicial review has always been the target for defenders of advisory opinions because "resolution of doubts as to the constitutionality of a statute must await the time-honored and time-consuming machinery of judicial review."[10] Delegates at the Michigan constitutional convention which proposed the state's advisory opinion provision defended it in good part by arguing that it gave the governor and legislature "an opportunity to get a decision rather than to plunge ahead regardless of what the legal outcome may be." Questions may be settled "in advance without the necessity for going through all the agony of setting up divisions and departments [provided for by a law later found unconstitutional] and then having to dismantle them."[11] Proponents see advisory opinions as "preventative jurisprudence" and call for advisory opinion duties for the federal courts, much needed there owing to the "fundamentally remedial" nature of the legal system, which "must lie dormant until activated by the commission of a legal wrong. . . . This remedial concept of law . . . has severely limited judicial exploration of the uncharted areas of what may be called preventative law."[12] The uncertainty as to judicial perception of a law's constitutionality itself seems to call for the remedy of advisory opinions. If the legislature, say, has doubts about the constitutionality of a bill, it may wish it could seek an advisory opinion. The wish, though, often as not is likely to arise from the need for insurance. "Those who support advisory opinions . . . assume that unconstitutional laws are passed because of legislative ignorance regarding

[9] ELLINGWOOD, DEPARTMENTAL COOPERATION, 251. Ellingwood quoted from the British writer James Bryce's study of American government, I THE AMERICAN COMMONWEALTH, 352–53 (1888): "Since the doubtful point may be the construction of the fundamental law of the Union, the President and Congress may be left in uncertainty as to how they shall shape their course. With the best wish in the world to act conformably to the Constitution, these authorities have no means of ascertaining before they act what, in the view of its authorized interpreters, the true meaning of the Constitution is." Bryce suggested that advisory opinions might be more useful for the states rather than the federal government, owing to the "minuteness of the state constitutions," giving more opportunities for issues of constitutionality to arise, and also owing to what he called the "inconsiderate haste" with which state legislation is passed. I AMERICAN COMMONWEALTH, 263–65. Quoted in J. E. Rhodes, *Advisory Opinions*, 6 ME. L. REV. 28, 35 (1912). Bryce was regius professor of civil law at Oxford University when he wrote AMERICAN COMMONWEALTH. He became Britain's ambassador to the United States in 1907.

[10] McKeever & Perry, *The Case for an Advisory Function in the Federal Judiciary*, 793.

[11] STATE OF MICHIGAN, CONSTITUTIONAL CONVENTION OF 1961, OFFICIAL RECORD, 1544 (1962). The speaker may have had in mind the fate of New Deal legislation, discussed below.

[12] McKeever & Perry, 785. These authors see advisory opinions and judicial review as similar in nature, one accepted and the other rejected for political rather than doctrinal reasons (at 809). Chapter 6 below offers comparisons between the two.

their constitutional status."[13] The requesting authority, however, can just as plausibly be sure that a bill is constitutional but still seek insurance—a prior commitment from the state's highest court that it will not invalidate the bill. A legislature may be sure about the constitutionality of a bill, but it can rarely be sure of the judiciary's view of the constitutionality of the bill.

Opponents of advisory opinions do not deny the problem, but they do not accept advisory opinions as the cure. A commentator, writing in 1912 in opposition to advisory opinions, admitted nonetheless that to "settle at once and forever a disputed point of constitutional law would often be a gain both to private citizens and to the organs of government. Under the present system there is no certainty when, if ever, such a point will be settled. . . . [T]he President and Congress may be left in uncertainty as to how they shall shape the course."[14] For proponents, however, curing the law's delay and its consequent mischief is sufficient warrant for advisory opinions. "By providing an early determination of the constitutionality of legislation, an advisory opinion can avoid the harm which is frequently caused by unconstitutional statutes [which] . . . may be in effect for years before they are struck down," wrote one proponent in 1956.[15] Another proponent agrees, stressing the lack of alternatives: "There is no other way of testing the constitutionality of a statute in its incipient stages. . . . With advisory opinions the judiciary need not stand mute in the face of injustice created by an unconstitutional statute."[16]

Part of the harm avoided is the litigation process itself and its propensity especially to provide "piecemeal answers" to constitutional questions. In a rare favorable comment by an advising justice on advisory opinions as a cure for judicial delay, the justice, disagreeing with the majority's refusal to advise the Michigan House of Representatives, favored rendering advice because, if the legislation in question is unconstitutional, "the propriety of countless decisions throughout Michigan may be called into question. At the least, countless motions and appeals will be filed and immeasurable litigative energy will be exercised in discovering piecemeal answers to the constitutional inquiries [here] set forth by the House of Representatives."[17] Advising justices tend to be pragmatic about their advising duty, much like the nonjudicial proponents stressing the practical consequences of delaying rather than addressing doctrinal difficulties. The Massachusetts justices defended their rendering an advisory opinion despite the request being about legislation already passed, and so against their standards. The statute was on the disposal of radioactive waste and would require legislative and voter approval of certain executive decisions regarding disposal. "If [these requirements] are unconstitutional,"

---

[13] Michael A. Bamburger, Reckless Legislation: How Lawmakers Ignore the Constitution 170 (2000). Bamberger discusses advisory opinions at 169–83.

[14] Rhodes, *Advisory Opinions*, 35.

[15] Note, *Advisory Opinions and the Constitutionality of Statutes*, 69 Harv. L. Rev. 1302, 1304–05 (1956).

[16] Smiljanich, *Advisory Opinions in Florida*, 339.

[17] *In re Request for Advisory Opinion Regarding Constitutionality of 2002 PA 678*, 658 N.W.2d 124, 126 (Mich. 2003).

the justices said, "considerable time, effort, and public funds necessary to obtaining legal certification and voter approval would be expended needlessly."[18]

Virtually all proponents of advisory opinions are enamored of the relative speed of advisory opinions as a means of "heading off" constitutionally doubtful legislation.[19] Calogero, for example, notes that defenders of advisory opinions favor "its speedier method of passing upon the constitutionality of proposed legislation or executive action" compared to the "traditional trial and appeal process."[20] And all proponents worry about the practical consequences, the "waste," of delay.

ADVISORY OPINIONS AND THE NEW DEAL ERA

The problem made a surprisingly prominent appearance on the national stage during the Progressive and New Deal eras, and, for the first time since the Constitutional Convention of 1787, proposals were made to confer constitutional advisory opinion jurisdiction on the U.S. Supreme Court. Several such proposals found their way into Congress in the 1930s. The immediate issue was the "elaborate machinery" set up by New Deal legislation. Before the Court's famous "switch" in 1937, it declared eleven New Deal acts unconstitutional, from the Economy Act of 1933 to the Bituminous Coal Act of 1935.[21] Among them was the National Industrial Recovery Act of 1933 (NIRA), which would testify to the consequences of the delay of judicial review. Before the Supreme Court ruled the NIRA unconstitutional in 1935, over one thousand national and local authorities were created under the statute, and for some two years they administered regulations with significant impact on the economy.[22] One observer later complained that "the whole fiasco could have been avoided had the federal supreme court been empowered, or

---

[18] *Opinion of the Justices to the Senate*, 493 N.E.2d 859 (Mass. 1986). Cynthia R. Farina offers this case as exemplifying how the Massachusetts Supreme Judicial Court "tends to take a pragmatic view of institutional needs, interests and capacities." Cynthia R. Farina, *Supreme Judicial Court Advisory Opinions: Two Centuries of Interbranch Dialogue, in* THE HISTORY OF THE LAW IN MASSACHUSETTS: THE SUPREME JUDICIAL COURT 1692–1992, 353, 378 (Russell K. Osgood ed., 1992).

[19] The quote is from Bentley W. Warren, "Memorial to Arthur Prentice Rugg," 302 Mass. 635 (Supplement), 635, 638 (1940).

[20] Calogero, *Advisory Opinions: A Wise Change for Louisiana and Its Judiciary?*, 329, 355 (1992).

[21] *See generally* LEONARD BAKER, BACK TO BACK: THE DUEL BETWEEN FDR AND THE SUPREME COURT (1967); BARRY CUSHMAN, RETHINKING THE NEW DEAL COURT: THE STRUCTURE OF A CONSTITUTIONAL REVOLUTION (1998). The Court famously reversed its antagonism toward New Deal legislation in *West Coast Hotel v. Parrish*, 300 U.S. 379 (1937), possibly—though by no means certainly—in response to FDR's "court packing" plan, proposed to Congress in "A Recommendation to Reorganize the Judicial Branch of the Federal Government," H.R. Doc. No. 142, 75 Cong., 1st Sess. (1937). The media called the *West Coast Hotel* reversal the "switch in time that saved nine." *See* William E. Leuchtenberg, *The Origins of Franklin D. Roosevelt's "Court-Packing" Plan*, 1966 SUP. CT. REV. 347; Richard D. Friedman, *Switching Time and Other Thought Experiments: The Hughes Court and Constitutional Transformation*, U. PA. L. REV. 1891 (1994); KEN I. KERSCH, CONSTRUCTING CIVIL LIBERTIES 134 (2004) (arguing that seeing New Deal constitutional developments as a linear process going from "outmoded economic liberties" to solicitude for "personal individual liberties" is Whiggish history).

[22] The NIRA was ruled unconstitutional in *A.L.A. Schechter Poultry Corp. v. United States*, 295 U.S. 495 (1935).

required, to first express an opinion on the constitutionality [of the NIRA] before it was imposed on a helpless public." He further lambasted "the economic waste, not to mention the upheaval, the country suffered."[23]

The complaints spread well beyond legal actors. Heywood Broun, then a widely read syndicated columnist, lamented in 1935 that

> [f]or better or worse, our economic system is a very complicated one. Any measures which vitally affect money rock the whole structure. Sometimes months or even years elapse before the gears and flywheels have been readjusted to the new rhythm. And at this exact point up steps some litigant with an appeal to the Supreme Court and again there is fear of earthquakes. . . . If the Court is going to speak forever with the authority which it now possesses, it should at the very least, be obligated, to make its voice known at the time of the controversy, or forever after hold its peace.[24]

Among legal writers, one writing in 1937 spoke with Depression-era urgency about the burden of judicial review's delay.

> With dozens of laws before the Court and the interests of millions of people involved the time element becomes a matter of the greatest importance. . . . When hopes have been raised for great masses of people only to be dashed to the ground by a judicial veto, dissatisfaction is bound to arise; or if the people are compelled to live in fear and uncertainty over a large period until the Court speaks, the result will be the same.[25]

Congress passing a bill without the Supreme Court's advice is "a leap in the dark." The "time factor possessed large potentialities for evil."[26] While the remedy may be "the prompt settlement of doubts," the writer had doubts about the efficacy of advisory opinions in this regard, questioning the apparent assumption of proponents "that the Supreme Court's opinions in advance of legislation will grind our controlling legal principles, which will resolve all doubts for good and all." But the way that the American constitutional system works "does not seem to bear this out" because "attempts to deal with constitutional questions abstractly are bound to meet difficulties and result in conclusions that are quite unrelated to reality."[27]

Nonetheless, after the controversy triggered by *Schechter*, Congress, for the only time in its history, engaged in "a major effort to overturn the rule against advisory opinions."[28] Since the Supreme Court long before (in 1793) established the

---

[23] Hoffman, *Why Not Advisory Opinions for Illinois?*, 141. Hoffman's 1952 article proposed introducing advisory opinions in Illinois.

[24] Heywood Broun, *It Seems to Me* [newspaper column], THE COLUMBUS CITIZEN, Jan. 23, 1935. Quoted in F. R. Aumann, *The Supreme Court and the Advisory Opinion*, 4 OHIO ST. L. REV. 21, 24 (1937).

[25] Aumann, *The Supreme Court and the Advisory Opinion*, 25.

[26] *Id.* at 28.

[27] *Id.* at 42–43.

[28] Robert P. Dahlquist, *Advisory Opinions as Extrajudicial Activity and Judicial Advocacy: A Historical Perspective*, 14 SW. U. L. REV. 46, 68 (1983).

federal ban on advisory opinions on constitutional grounds, a ban strictly adhered to ever since, overturning the ban would require a constitutional amendment. Several proposals to do so were introduced in the summer of 1935, soon after the unanimous *Schechter* opinion came down in May of that year.[29]

The first proposal provided that the "President or either House of Congress, at any time may require from the Supreme Court an opinion upon the constitutionality of any Act passed by Congress, and the Supreme Court shall render such opinion in writing."[30] "At any time" was strong. Not only was the advising duty mandatory but the Court would be required to convene to consider the legislation in question whether or not it was in session, an indication of how intense feelings were about judicial review's delay. A second proposal introduced in July went so far as to require the president to submit *every* act of Congress to the court for its opinion on the act's constitutionality, the Court to respond within sixty days.[31] No act may become law absent the Court's opinion. A third proposal was similar to the first, requiring the Court to render advisory opinions on acts. Here, however, both houses must jointly request the opinion, though only one-third of each house was needed to approve the request.[32] The Senate in 1935 also considered several bills to address the issue, but, perhaps owing to concerns about the elaborate amendment process, most of the Senate bills did not propose advisory opinions, seeking other ways to press the Court to rule quickly on constitutionality of legislation. Senator George W. Norris introduced a bill to require a two-thirds vote by the Justices to permit judicial review of federal laws, and would require also that such review take place only within six months of the bill's enactment.[33] Senator LaFollette introduced a bill to

---

[29] Discussion of the Supreme Court's 1793 decision is in Chapter 1. Discussion here of the proposed amendments is drawn from several sources addressing advisory opinions in the New Deal era. *See* Aumann, *The Supreme Court and the Advisory Opinion*; Dahlquist, *Advisory Opinions as Extrajudicial Activity*; J. F. Davison, *The Constitutionality and Utility of Advisory Opinions*, 2 U. Toronto L.J. 254 (1937); Note, *The Advisory Opinion and the United States Supreme Court*, 5 Fordham L. Rev. 94 (1936); Hoffman, *Why Not Advisory Opinions for Illinois?*; McKeever & Perry, *The Case for an Advisory Function in the Federal Judiciary*; Edward A. Purcell, Brandeis and the Progressive Constitution: *Erie*, the Judicial Power, and the Politics of the Federal Courts in Twentieth Century America 127–29 (2001). The advisory opinion amendment bills were a few of many bills intended to check the Supreme Court's review power. "Proposals to counteract the Court were widely discussed, and congressmen introduced more than 100 bills aimed at expanding congressional authority and limiting judicial review." Purcell, Brandeis and the Progressive Constitution, 34. As we will see later in this chapter, these proposals, like much that was on the New Deal agenda, came out of the Progressive Movement.

[30] H.J. Res. 317, 74th Cong., 1st Sess. (1935).

[31] H.J. Res. 344, 74th Cong., 1st Sess. (1935).

[32] H.J. Res. 374, 74th Cong., 1st Sess. (1935). Opponents as well as proponents of the New Deal favored Supreme Court advisory opinions, the opponents hoping the opinions would give New Deal legislation short shrift. As early as 1933 Senator Vandenberg, Republican from Michigan and a leading adversary of the New Deal, favored an advisory opinion amendment owing to the "grave danger *today* from the lack of a 'short cut' to conclusive constitutional determination." Letter, Arthur H. Vandenberg to William D. Mitchell, Jan. 30, 1934. Mitchell Papers, Box 1. Emphasis in original. Quoted in Purcell, Brandeis and the Progressive Constitution, 128.

[33] S.J. Res. 149, 74th Cong., 1st Sess. (1935). Senator Norris, chairman of the Judiciary Committee, was among the most influential of the Senate's New Dealers. Purcell calls him "possibly the most successful legislator in the Senate's history." Purcell, Brandeis and the Progressive Constitution, 77. The proposals

fast-track any federal statute to the Supreme Court for a ruling on its constitutionality, if the attorney general certifies it is in the national interest.[34] The Senate later considered a proposal authorizing the Senate to receive advisory opinions on legislation pending before either house. The bill simply asked the Supreme Court to amend its own rules to permit this.[35] None of these proposals made it out of Congress.

There were also calls for, and opposition to, advisory opinion amendments "out of doors." In 1935 Harold G. Hoffman, governor of New Jersey, made the advisory opinion as public a controversy as it ever would be on either state or federal levels, when he published a letter he had sent to the National Republican Committee (NRC), asking the NRC to add to its party platform a constitutional amendment requiring all bills passed in Congress to be certified as constitutional before they could take effect. Governor Hoffman, a New Deal opponent, apparently hoped to make the Supreme Court a fast-acting barrier to New Deal legislation.[36] The day after Hoffman's letter was reported in the news on October 7, the *New York Times* carried an editorial opposing Hoffman's proposal. The editorial depicted Hoffman's rationale for the amendment, tongue-in-cheek, as the one thing needed to save the Republic. "In Mr. Hoffman's opinion the adoption of his amendment would remove uncertainty, prevent governmental encroachment on private rights, stop illegal expenditure and taxation, 'make forever impossible any attempt by a President to change the form of the Government of the United States by a series of revolutions *ad interim*, each conducted by the enforcement of an unconstitutional law for the usual two years intervening between its enactment by Congress and its rejection by the Supreme Court.'"

The editorial rejected Hoffman's proposed amendment out of hand, claiming plausibly enough that neither the public nor the Congress would support it. "It is not worth while [*sic*] to consider seriously a proposal that has no public sentiment behind it and that no Congress is ever likely to submit to the people."[37] The *Times* that month carried three letters on the issue, two opposed to advisory opinion amendment and one favoring it. The letters neither denied the problem of judicial review's delay nor addressed such doctrinal issues as separation of powers. One letter, making the argument that Felix Frankfurter had made a decade before, said that the amendment would force the Supreme Court to decide on a "law's validity entirely along hypothetical lines." The law in question could not receive "the proper defense which it would otherwise receive if it were being argued by our ablest constitutional lawyers."[38] The emphasis, though, was

---

addressing judicial review were reflective of the New Deal supporters' general hostility toward the federal judiciary. Norris, for example, proposed that all federal district and circuit courts be abolished. *Id.* The relation of advisory opinions to the Progressives' and New Dealers' antagonism toward the federal judiciary is discussed later in this chapter.

[34] S. Res. 3211, 74th Cong., 1st Sess. (1935).

[35] S. Res. 103, 75th Cong., 1st Sess. (1937).

[36] New York Herald Tribune, Oct. 7, 1935, at 16. The Herald Tribune that day also carried an editorial disagreeing with Governor Hoffman.

[37] Editorial, New York Times, Oct. 8, 1935, at 22.

[38] Letter from Lester Jashnoff, New York Times, Oct. 12, 1935, at 16. The other two letters appeared Oct. 27, 1935, sec. 4, at 9 (unfavorable toward advisory opinions) and Nov. 3, 1935, sec. 4, at 9 (favorable).

on judicial review's delay. Another letter, in response to the Gold Clause Cases then being argued before the Supreme Court, argued that if "advisory opinions are not allowed on a critical matter like the gold clause, Congress must take steps of momentous import, to which business must make far-reaching adjustments, with the possibility that everything that has been done may be later overturned."[39] Another letter opposed federal advisory opinions but admitted to the "seriousness of our constitutional procedure—that a law becomes a nullity as of the date of its enactment, years after the economic and social activities of our community have built upon and around it. Because if its importance, I have pondered for years about it. The solution, to me, seems further off than ever."[40]

To those for whom the advisory opinion is the solution, overcoming the delay inherent in adjudicated judicial review and its consequences is one side of that solution. Another is the virtues of speed and efficiency themselves, and many proponents of advisory opinions argue their virtues in their own right regardless of whether the delay has harmful consequences. One proponent wrote simply that there "can be no question that the advisory opinion has a great advantage over regular judicial procedure so far as time is concerned."[41] The writer, calling the time between "enactment of a statute and the judicial determination of its validity" among "the most glaring defects" of judicial review, compares advisory opinions with judicial review in that respect. His research found that between request and advisory opinion, the average period ranged from 7.4 days in South Dakota to 45.4 days in New Hampshire, with the average for all advising states coming out to just under 30 days. For adjudicated judicial review, his analysis of ten selected states showed an average of seventeen and a half years. On the federal level, statutes were "on the books, on an average, ten years before they were declared invalid."[42]

---

[39] Letter from Charles E. Ozanne to New York Times, Jan. 16, 1935, at 16. The Gold Clause Cases were argued jointly before the Supreme Court in January 1935, coming out of the Roosevelt administration's restrictions on the ownership of gold. These included the surrender of gold coin, bullion, and certificates to the government, and the cancellation of gold clauses in contracts. The cases were: *Norman v. Baltimore and Ohio RR Co.* and *United States v. Bankers Trust Co.*, 294 U.S. 240 (1935); *Nortz v. United States*, 294 U.S. 317 (1935); and *Perry v. United States*, 294 U.S. 330 (1935). The 5–4 decision was in favor of the government's position. For a summary discussion, see The Oxford Companion to the Supreme Court of the United States, *Gold Clause Cases*, 107 (Kermit L. Hall ed., 1992). *See also* Richard D. Friedman, *Switching Time and Other Thought Experiments: The Hughes Court and Constitutional Transformation*, 142 U. Pa. L. Rev. 1891, 1923–27 (1994) (calling the Gold Clause Cases a "daring change" in constitutional protections of private contracts, an example for Friedman of the Supreme Court undertaking major constitutional changes supporting the New Deal before the 1937 "switch").

[40] Letter from Emanuel Redfield to New York Times, June 11, 1935. *See also* Letter from James L. Nesbitt to New York Times, Sept. 18, 1935 (favoring advisory opinions so that "the issue over governmental powers and prerogative might be less frequently joined"). This influential defense of advisory opinions, as a means of reducing conflict and increasing governmental cooperation and harmony, is discussed later in this chapter. *See also* Nesbitt's article, *Due Process of Law and Opinion*, 26 Colum. L. Rev. 23 (1926).

[41] Oliver P. Field, *The Advisory Opinion—An Analysis*, 24 Indiana L.J. 203, 207 (1949).

[42] Field, *Advisory Opinions*, 206–07. Field was writing in 1949, based on his WPA study of pre-1937 advisory opinions in five states. *See* Farina, *Supreme Judicial Court Advisory Opinions*, 371. McKeever and Perry, writing in 1962, calculated the time between federal enactment of a statute and Supreme Court

Advisory opinion proponents have largely accepted speed as an advantage in itself, usually without acknowledging at least the possible wisdom of occasional delay. A critic of advisory opinions invoked the value of the time required by judicial review by calling attention to the "political value of some delay between passage [of a statute] and judgment [on its constitutionality]," which, he said, "is obvious. That is, before being tested by litigation, an otherwise new statute will not only have been seasoned by use which will provide a real factual context, but will provide a useful space between enactment and judgment."[43] Proponents, though, correlate speed with efficiency, and view advisory opinions as "a method of promoting governmental efficiency."[44] One of them has argued that advisory opinions "lend to the operations of the government at least some semblance of efficiency, a quality most conspicuously absent in our present system."[45] Another, noting the "efficiency and expediency" of the advisory opinion process, says that in this respect advisory opinions are especially useful for legislative responses to rulings on constitutionality. "When the legislature enacts laws designed to remedy defects previously identified by the court, in either an adjudicative or advisory setting, the advisory opinion is a useful and efficient mechanism by which the legislature or executive can test the conformity of the new legislation with the prior doctrine."[46]

EXPERTISE OF THE JUSTICES

Occasionally joining arguments for the speed and efficiency of advisory opinions is one for expertise. Some proponents defend the value of advisory opinions on the basis of the justices' purported expertise, usually put forth as a taken-for-granted assumption rather than a verifiable proposition. One, writing in 1890 effused over how, with advisory opinions, the political branches are "aided and enlightened by the wisdom and learning of able and impartial jurists."[47] A delegate at the 1889 North Dakota constitutional convention supported an advisory opinion provision for the new state's constitution, lamenting the legal ignorance of the legislature. "The people," he said, "don't as a rule elect constitutional lawyers to the legislature." But if any legislator could ask the legislature to request advice from the knowledgeable justices, then "he would be perfectly independent, and equal to the best lawyer in the body."[48] An opponent replied by noting the opinion of a judge is "not worth more than that of any other lawyer of like

---

nullifying decision to be 8.7 years. McKeever & Perry, *The Case for an Advisory Function in the Federal Judiciary*, 800.

[43] Kennedy, *Advisory Opinions: Cautions About Non-Judicial Undertakings*, 199. Kennedy, focusing on a 1987 Florida advisory opinion, argues that advisory opinions "have a potential to hazard substantive error," in part because the justices' render advice on constitutionality without waiting for appropriate litigation. *Id.* at 176.

[44] McKeever & Perry, *The Case for an Advisory Function in the Federal Judiciary*, 792.

[45] Hoffman, *Why Not Advisory Opinions for Illinois?*, 150.

[46] Persky, *Ghosts That Slay*, 1176.

[47] Hugo A. Dubuque, *The Duty of Judges as Constitutional Advisors*, 24 Am. L. Rev. 369, 375 (1890).

[48] Proceedings and Debates, 230.

standing and ability."[49] The notion, however, that justices have expertise by virtue of their positions has endured, so that two proponents decades later could defend advisory opinions as a means by which "the number of unconstitutional laws is minimized by expert advice to the legislature by the justices."[50]

INTERBRANCH COOPERATION AND HARMONY

Prominent among arguments in support of advisory opinions is that they foster cooperation and harmony among the branches of government. Albert Ellingwood, in his "undiluted enthusiasm for advisory opinions,"[51] made it the central argument of his 1918 book on advisory opinions, the only full-scale study of the subject in the twentieth century, which he straightforwardly entitled *Departmental Cooperation in State Government*. The cooperation defense seems to be a reply to the chief attack on advisory opinions—separation of powers—but the call for cooperation among branches through advisory opinions seems to pass off the risks to separation rather too easily. The argument presumes that separation of powers is successful only when the departments, as Ellingwood put it, are "working in harmony towards a common end."[52] This presupposes a kind of corporate-bureaucratic view of government, where cooperation is prerequisite to rational efficiency, and efficiency is a means of maximizing productivity of services to the public. Separation of powers, however, was conceived presuming the contrary. Madison, for example, defended separation as a protection against the "dangerous tendency" toward the accumulation and concentration of power. This tendency necessitates a defense that "must be commensurate with the danger of the attack."[53] This is not the

---

[49] *Id.* at 232. The North Dakota convention would defeat the advisory opinion proposal.

[50] Paul C. Clovis & Clarence M. Updegraff, *Advisory Opinions*, 13 IOWA L. REV. 188, 198 (1927). These authors wrote in the 1920s, clearly influenced by the Progressive era's fascination with government by experts. This fascination is discussed later in this chapter. For a recent skeptical view of this rationale for judges advising the political branches, see Abner J. Mikva, *Why Judges Should Not Be Advicegivers: A Response to Professor Neal Katyal*, 50 STANFORD L. REV. 1825 (1998). Mikva is critical of the opinion that "there is something in judges' status or stature that qualifies them to give . . . advice to elected officials." (at 1826). Mikva's article responded to Neal Kumar Katyal, *Judges as Advicegivers*, 50 STANFORD L. REV. 1709 (1998). For a contemporary (Depression-era) skeptical British view of the purported value of advisory opinions as contributing to either efficiency and expertise, see Carleton K. Allen, *Administrative Consultation of the Judiciary*, 47 LAW Q. REV. 43, 43 (1931) ("It is exactly from the executive officer's efficiency and zeal that we must save ourselves. . . . [H]e is the expert, with special means of knowledge at his command: and when principles of law are put in his way, he is apt to be impatient of them as mere pedantic obstructions."). Allen was writing against use of advisory opinions in Britain, in reply to E. C. S. Wade, *Consultation of the Judiciary by the Executive*, 46 LAW Q. REV. 169 (1930).

[51] C. Dallas Sands, *Government by Judiciary—Advisory Opinions in Alabama*, 4 ALA. L. REV. 1, 30 (1951).

[52] ELLINGWOOD, DEPARTMENTAL COOPERATION, 252.

[53] THE FEDERALIST No. 47, 301, and No. 51, 321–22 (James Madison) (Clinton Rossiter ed., 1961). Hans Linde offers advisory opinions as a means of resolving "disputes over institutional structures." This, however, suggests that questions of "institutional structures" are purely intragovernmental and would not implicate due process issues, and assumes that resolving such disputes through intervention of the judiciary is wise. Hans A. Linde, *Symposium: Structures and Terms of Consent: Delegation, Discretion, Separation of Powers, Representation, Participation, Accountability?*, 20 CARDOZO L. REV. 823, 835 (1999).

language of harmony or efficiency but rather suggests that these virtues, to the extent that they are political virtues at all, must if anything be curtailed by a tripartite check on the accumulation and concentration of power.

Nonetheless the cooperation defense has remained a strong support of advisory opinions, in good part owing to prioritizing efficiency, often in contrast to the purported inefficiency inherent in separation of powers. "We witness a deplorable lack of cooperation between the different organs of state," Ellingwood wrote, "a deficiency of which the expense to the people is enormous."[54] The problem for Ellingwood is the hindrances of separation of powers, which he curiously likens to "the economic principle of a division of labor," which is "only a success when all the groups are complementary, working in harmony towards a common end. . . . Our present political problem is to build up a cordial sympathy and mutual cooperation between the three departments."[55] The answer is advisory opinions. "It is a fundamental of the efficient government of the future, in a representative democracy, that there shall be harmony and cooperation between its component parts. . . . The experience and skill of the judiciary should be at the service of the other departments in time of need. . . . [The advisory opinion] will go far towards furnishing a solution of this difficult problem."[56] A contemporary reviewer of Ellingwood's book commented that he "appears to attach too great an importance to the influence of the advisory opinion in efficient cooperative action of the three departments of the state government."[57] But Ellingwood was not exceptional, and among proponents, the faith in the capacity of advisory opinions to contribute to interbranch cooperation, and thereby to efficiency, has been a constant.

Equally constant among proponents has been the presumption that government is defective unless running without conflict, that conflict is merely disruptive and advisory opinions merely an instrument for a dispute-resolution approach to government, government perceived as a matter of addressing difficulties. The "manifest purpose of the advisory opinion," writes one defender, ". . . is to obviate those difficulties which can arise among the several departments."[58] Another defender considers advisory opinions valuable since the "political process is not very good at resolving disputes about the legal meaning of constitutional rights and obligations. An advisory opinion can serve to take these sorts of questions off the table. This frees the political process to go forward."[59]

These proponents reveal an almost sentimental attachment to cooperation alone as a virtue regardless of its contribution to governmental efficiency, a desirable alternative in itself to the unfortunate train of conflicts and disputes that for them characterizes the political process. Some speak of advisory opinions in a rhetoric of harmony. For one

---

[54] Ellingwood, Departmental Cooperation, 251.

[55] *Id.* at 252.

[56] *Id.* at vi.

[57] J. M. Matthews, review of Albert R. Ellingwood, Departmental Cooperation in State Government, 12 Am. Pol. Sci. Rev. 155 (1919).

[58] Hoffman, *Why Not Advisory Opinions for Illinois?*, 150.

[59] Farina, *Supreme Judicial Court Advisory Opinions*, 387.

writer "acting in harmony" through advisory opinions allows a "uniformity of construction" to prevail among government departments. Not only future conflicts but "various forms of injustice may be avoided."[60] Another speaks of the "cooperation of the individual justices with the people's elected representatives" in offering their advice.[61] Another praises the advisory opinion for its capacity to bypass the case or controversy requirement and thereby "to obviate to some degree the necessity for social conflict inherent in the requirement that legal injuries shall precede appeal to the courts."[62] Some see advisory opinions as improving communication, thereby presumably facilitating interbranch cooperation. "In many respects the advisory opinion process is an ongoing conversation between two branches of government."[63]

Sanctimonious Reverence: Attacks on the Constitutional Arguments Against Advisory Opinions

To the limited extent that defenders of advisory opinions have left off their arguments about harmony and efficiency in order to confront directly the opponents' doctrinal arguments, a strange aspect of their defenses is how they demean the doctrines, including separation of powers, case or controversy, and judicial review. Attacks on advisory opinions always have been grounded on the constitutional demands of these doctrines, which for the critics may not be set aside for the conveniences offered by the advisory opinion process. The defenses of advisory opinions—which appeared only after the attacks—have tended to evoke the relatively bland, pragmatic, and decidedly nonconstitutional virtues of cooperation, harmony, expertise, and efficiency. Proponents have rarely had much to say about how their defenses stand up to the doctrinal attacks. Rather, and surprisingly, they seem to have entered a demurrer, not denying the attacks but suggesting that the attacks are just not relevant in our time. They argue that separation of powers and such doctrines are old stuff, not suitable to modern government, surviving only by an "attitude of sanctimonious reverence and exclusive devotion to the past," which, said one proponent of advisory opinions in 1936, is "apt to impoverish our outlook on the present."[64]

The argument that advisory opinions violate separation of powers has received especially hostile attention. The unknown 1936 writer, critical of the Supreme Court's recent decisions on New Deal programs and the widespread uncertainty the decisions caused, accused the Court of deliberately suspending "the note of finality which accounts for the atmosphere of confusion attending the administration of the law and which is becoming progressively more and more inept to solve the increasing social need of security."

[60] Dubuque, *The Duty of Judges as Constitutional Advisors*, 375.
[61] McKeever & Perry, *The Case for an Advisory Function in the Federal Judiciary*, 786.
[62] Note, *The Advisory Opinion and the United States Supreme Court*, 96.
[63] Persky, *Ghosts That Slay*, 1175.
[64] Note, *The Advisory Opinion and the United States Supreme Court*, 113.

Opponents, the writer claims, have attacked the best solution to the problem—a federal advisory opinion process—on separation of powers grounds only because "there has clustered around it [separation of powers] a eulogistic flavor and an honorific association which has tended to envelope it in a nimbus of ivory tower inviolability."[65] Another contemporary commentator, also writing in response to the Supreme Court's invalidating of New Deal legislation, put the separation of powers problem more succinctly, complaining that the barrier to accepting federal advisory opinions is "due to the Montesquieu doctrine," by which "Congress could only pass the law, take a leap in the dark and wait developments."[66]

In contradiction to Brandeis and others, some defenders of advisory opinions asserted with doubtful historical accuracy that separation of powers "is meant to serve governmental efficiency and not vice versa."[67] ("The doctrine of separation of powers," Brandeis wrote in his dissent to *Myers v. United States*, "was adopted by the convention in 1787, not to promote efficiency but to preclude the exercise of arbitrary power."[68]) Albert Ellingwood, in his 1918 book on advisory opinions, echoed the call to sacrifice separation of powers on the altar of efficiency with his argument that separation has gone "too far." Separation "should be an instrument of both democracy and efficiency. There are daily evidences that the separation has gone too far in the United States, that it is responsible for a great waste of governmental energy."[69] In addition, he argued a bit inconsistently, separation of powers may be safely discounted since it is "not affected in the slightest by the advisory opinion," because advisory opinions are extrajudicial, are nonbinding, and anyway any interference with the legislature or executive branches is "insignificant," apparently because they may accept the advice or not, as they wish. Also, he wrote (in contrast to the urgent concerns of Joseph Story a century before), the effect on the independence of the judiciary, "must be remote."[70] A New Deal–era supporter of federal advisory opinions argued that separation of powers is a bit of a fiction anyway, since the branches of government are really interwoven despite the "theory" of separation.[71]

Judicial review and due process also tend to get short shrift by defenders of advisory opinions, in the face of charges that the advisory opinion process is a questionable substitute. One defender calls judicial review "seriously inadequate" and another declares that "the Anglo-Saxon judicial system has certain serious defects. This is especially true

---

[65] *Id.* at 112–13.

[66] Aumann, *The Supreme Court and the Advisory Opinion*, 28, quoting James M. Beck, "The Future of the Supreme Court," address to the Pennsylvania Society of New York, Dec. 20, 1924. The "Montesquieu doctrine" is of course separation of powers.

[67] Clovis & Updegraff, *Advisory Opinions*, 196.

[68] Myers v. United States, 272 U.S. 52, 292–93 (1926) (Brandeis, J., dissenting).

[69] Ellingwood, Departmental Cooperation, 251.

[70] *Id.* at 169–70. Story's views of advisory opinions and its dangers to judicial independence are discussed in Chapter 2. The issue of the purportedly nonbinding nature of advisory opinions is the subject of Chapter 5.

[71] E. F. Albertsworth, *Advisory Functions in Federal Supreme Court*, 23 Geo. L.J. 643, 667–68 (1935).

in the United States where the courts may declare [a statute unconstitutional]. . . . The very particularism of the case-system may bring about grave inconvenience."[72]

Advisory opinion defenders similarly held the cooperative virtues of advisory opinions in higher esteem than due process or case or controversy. Responding to the advising justices' due process ban on advisory opinions if they would affect private rights, a defender asked, "Should not consideration for the general welfare prevail over too scrupulous a regard for private rights?"[73] Another passed off the case or controversy argument against advisory opinions. He raised the significant point that when a court declares a statute unconstitutional, its unconstitutionality applies not only with respect to the case before the court "but also with respect to other cases to which the questioned provisions apply." The question arises about the necessity of "actual litigation" in judicial review, and about whether courts "could not pass upon the constitutionality of legislation even before a clash has arisen among interests affected by the statute; and if this step should be taken, whether competence could be conferred on American courts to pass upon the constitutionality of proposed legislation before its enactment, so as to prevent a process of legislative stultification."[74] The anonymous 1936 proponent of federal advisory opinions agreed, complaining that the case or controversy requirement hinders achieving social goals owing to its adversarial nature. "Under the advisory opinion procedure, the [Supreme] Court would be less hampered by the tensity of litigation and the contentiousness of parties and freer to build its decisions in conformity with the social and economic fabric of the times."[75]

The Maintenance of a Harmony: Advisory Opinions and the Progressive Attack on the Constitution

The pragmatic defenses of advisory opinions, with their concern for such practicalities as delay and inefficiency on the one hand, and their devotion to governmental harmony and cooperation on the other, seem weak, even irresponsible, in light of the defenders' indifference if not hostility toward such fundamental doctrines as separation of powers, case or controversy, due process, and judicial review. That those doctrines have long been, and remain, the challenges to the legitimacy of advisory opinions seems to have had little influence on advisory opinion proponents. Or even, apparently, on the advising justices themselves. The rise in numbers of advisory opinions in the late nineteenth century, notwithstanding the development of restrictions on their use during the same period, is striking. In the sixty years of rendering advisory opinions before 1840, a total

---

[72] Field, *The Advisory Opinion—An Analysis*, 221; Ellingwood, Departmental Cooperation, vii.

[73] *Id.* at 189.

[74] Manley O. Hudson, *Advisory Opinions of National and International Courts*, 37 Harv. L. Rev. 970, 974–75 (1924).

[75] Note, *The Advisory Opinion and the United States Supreme Court*, 109.

of thirty-two were reported in the three advisory opinion states.[76] In the following twenty years, 1840–1859, the (now five) advisory states issued thirty advisory opinions.[77] In the next twenty-year period, 1860–1879, the advising justices issued seventy-four, more than in the previous eighty years taken together.[78] From 1880 to 1899 the number of advisory opinions, 176, more than doubled the previous twenty years.[79] The rise generally continued in the twentieth century.[80] After falling somewhat during 1900–1919 (143), the dramatic rise resumed during 1920–1939 (241), 1940–1959 (358), and 1960–1979 (509). The century's final twenty-year period saw a falling off, to 246 advisory opinions. This overall growth over a century and a half, both in the number of advisory opinions and in the number of advisory states, occurred despite doctrinal challenges, weak pragmatic defenses, and the justices' expanding restrictions on rendering advisory opinions and their often open reluctance and occasional outright hostility toward their advisory duty.

The sharp rise in the number of advisory opinions in the late nineteenth century and into the twentieth was accompanied by the pragmatic defenses, which, we have seen, often included dismissive views of separation of powers and other fundamental doctrines that challenged the legitimacy of advisory opinions. What could make credible such dismissive views? What could account for the force of what seem like pretty lightweight defenses of advisory opinions? Mere efficiency and cooperation, whatever their pragmatic value, would not seem to project intellectual or moral force sufficient to stand against such principles as separation of powers. But they did project that force. This is because the proponents of advisory opinions joined with, in fact usually were, adherents of a major intellectual and political force that adopted the same views and values, the same hostility to those constitutional principles: the Progressive movement.

The Progressives pressed for and legitimized their calls for government reforms with the same arguments and principles that proponents employed in support of advisory opinions. The advisory opinion proponents adopted and extolled Progressives' influential rhetoric of efficiency and cooperation, core principles of the movement.[81] The Progressives, with their "fascination with efficiency," made it into an overriding moral and political, as well as pragmatic, virtue. "They equated efficiency with virtue

---

[76] Massachusetts adopted an advisory opinion provision in 1780, New Hampshire in 1784, and Maine in 1820. The history of adoptions is addressed in Chapter 1.

[77] Rhode Island adopted an advisory opinion provision in 1842, and Delaware in 1852.

[78] Missouri adopted an advisory opinion provision in 1865 (abolished in 1875), and Florida in 1868.

[79] Colorado in 1886 and South Dakota in 1889 introduced advisory opinion provisions. The dramatic rise in numbers of advisory opinions between 1880 and 1899 is in good part accounted for by Colorado, where the court issued eighty-three advisory opinions in this period, thirty-one of them just in the state's first three years. South Dakota's justices issued ten in the decade after joining the Union.

[80] Alabama adopted advisory opinions in 1923, Michigan in 1963.

[81] On the values of the Progressive movement, especially regarding efficiency, see, e.g., M. S. LARSON, THE RISE OF PROFESSIONALISM 141 (1977) (noting that in the Progressive era the "impact of the ideology of efficiency was profound"); SAMUEL HABER, EFFICIENCY AND UPLIFT 104–07, 116 (1964); ELDON J. EISENACH, THE LOST PROMISE OF PROGRESSIVISM (1994) (studying the movement's intellectual foundations); DAVID B. DANBOM, THE WORLD OF HOPE (1987); MICHAEL J. SANDEL, DEMOCRACY'S DISCONTENTS 201–27 (1996).

and inefficiency with vice."[82] The application of efficiency as a remedy for the ancient complaint of what Hamlet calls the law's delay was central to the Progressives' reforms.[83] Woodrow Wilson expressed the Progressive notion of efficiency in 1887 when he called for the law to be administered "with equity, with speed, and without friction."[84] For Progressives efficiency was closely tied to cooperation, efficiency valued for its purported capacity to diminish conflict, political or legal. Harmony and conflict-avoidance was central to the Progressives' reform program, and indeed the "fascination with efficiency" bordered on the utopian. "The efficient society . . . would be composed of happy, productive people which would cooperate with one another harmoniously. . . . Efficiency was a . . . means to a united, cooperative society."[85] Good government itself "would necessarily flow from efficient machinery."[86]

A key barrier to the Progressive program was judicial review, seen by Progressives and their New Deal descendants as the very model of inefficiency. This was owing to the Progressive's model of reform through legislation, the legislation created out of the research and knowledge of experts on the one hand, and administered by experts on the other. The characteristic nonpartisanship of the Progressives was "an expression of belief in the underlying harmony of society," but "it was a harmony put into force by legislation."[87] The faith in efficiency famously called for replacing conflict-ridden politics and adversity-ridden adjudication with "administration" of public affairs by the experts. The ideology of, and nearly absolute faith in, expertise was grounded in the equation of efficiency with virtue.[88]

Hence the Progressive antipathy to the judiciary. The expertise so central to the Progressives' reform agenda both in the creation and in the administration of reform

---

[82] The phrases are from DANBOM, THE WORLD OF HOPE, 119.

[83] Hamlet's complaint is in William Shakespeare, *Hamlet*, act. III, scene I.

[84] Woodrow Wilson, *The Study of Administration*, 2 POL. SCI. Q. 197 (1887). Quoted in Eric R. Claeys, *Progressive Political Theory and Separation of Powers on the Burger and Rehnquist Courts*, 21 CONST. COMMENTARY 405, 412 (2004).

[85] DANBON, THE WORLD OF HOPE, 192. On the relation between the calls for "a united, cooperative society" and the broad process in early twentieth-century America "of relocating sovereignty from the communities and voluntary associations in which the people had governed themselves to the agencies and experts who would rule on their behalf," see generally Christopher Capozzola, *Uncle Sam Wants You: World War I and the Making of the Modern American Citizen* (2008). The quote is from James T. Sparrow's review of the book in 28 LAW AND HIST. REV. 1092, 1093 (2010).

[86] Danborn, The World of Hope, 133.

[87] HABER, EFFICIENCY AND UPLIFT, 102.

[88] DANBOM, THE WORLD OF HOPE, 125. On the Progressives' view of experts, see, e.g., STEVEN BRINT, IN AN AGE OF EXPERTS: THE CHANGING ROLE OF PROFESSIONALS IN POLITICS AND PUBLIC LIFE 7–15 (1994). Brint argues that "for the Progressives, expertise had both a technical and a moral aspect" (at 7) in contrast to the post–World War I era, where the latter gradually disappeared. *See also* M. S. LARSON, THE RISE OF PROFESSIONALISM 143–44 (1977) (on the idea of a "transpolitical state" run by experts); MICHAEL J. SANDEL, DEMOCRACY'S DISCONTENTS 209 (1996) ("Professionals armed with scientific method would [for the Progressives] . . . make it possible to dispense with the conflict and uncertainty that had always characterized the political realm."); H. H. HYMAN & WILLIAM WIECEK, EQUAL JUSTICE UNDER LAW: CONSTITUTIONAL DEVELOPMENTS 1835–1875 at 335 (1982) (noting that the call for "government run largely by means of apolitical commissions, staffed by appointed experts," as a remedy for the "excesses of elective democracy," occurred as early as 1860).

legislation stood in hostile relationship to the courts. "One of the central aims of thirty years of Progressive and Legal Realist thought was to bring independent technological and scientific knowledge to bear on social problems. . . . [S]ome form of faith in science characterized the critique . . . of the abstraction and formalism of traditional legal thought."[89] For Progressives the reform agenda was properly the purview of the legislature, "popularly elected and hence closer to the people," able to "investigate social problems methodically and ameliorate them broadly."[90] Progressives idealized the legislative process as amenable to the influence of expertise, both as to the experts' claims to science and to their reliance on efficiency and cooperation, but they were correspondingly hostile to the judiciary. Progressives "pictured legislatures and their expert administrative agencies relatively abstractly and as they wished them to be, as authentically popular, problem-solving and even 'scientific' branches of government. They scrutinized the courts, in contrast, with a searing realism that revealed judicial work as ill-informed and socially biased."[91] By the late nineteenth century they saw state and federal courts as anti-reform and pro-business—*Lochner* purportedly constitutionalized that bias under claims of liberty of contract—so that one inescapable requirement for ensuring reform was controls on the courts. Therefore the call for expanded legislative power, and correspondingly diminished judicial power, by Progressive leaders including Woodrow Wilson (in his *Congressional Government*), Theodore Roosevelt, Robert Lafollette, Felix Frankfurter, and Louis Brandeis.[92]

Brandeis's and Frankfurter's constant calls for judicial limits were grounded in this Progressive vision. For Frankfurter "courts have to stop imposing their own view of economic theory on legislation that has been designed to deal with the real, rather than an abstract world."[93] Frankfurter's devotion to judicial restraint, already central to his thought as a young Harvard law professor and never diminished or qualified, demanded that the courts limit themselves strictly to a deferential rational-basis standard for review of legislation. As a justice he insisted in his *Barnette* dissent the Supreme Court's "only and very narrow function [is] to determine whether within the broad grant of authority vested in the legislature they have exercised a judgment for which reasonable justification can be offered."[94] Brandeis similarly never deviated from his

---

[89] Deborah C. Malamud, *Engineering the Middle Classes: Class Line-Drawing in New Deal Hours Legislation*, 96 Mich. L. Rev. 2212, 2246 (1998).

[90] Purcell, Brandeis and the Progressive Constitution, 13.

[91] *Id.* at 16. Purcell attributes the view that courts were "formalist" between 1877 and 1937 to this Progressive critique of the court. *Id.* at 312, note 29.

[92] *See* M. J. C. Vile, Constitutionalism and the Separation of Powers 265, 268 (1967).

[93] Melvin I. Urofsky, Felix Frankfurter: Judicial Restraint and Individual Liberties 7 (1991).

[94] *West Virginia Board of Education v. Barnette*, 319 U.S. 624, 649 (1943). *Barnette* effectively reversed the Supreme Court's flag salute decision three years earlier in *Minersville School District v. Gobitis*, 310 U.S. 586 (1940), which had upheld the authority of a school district to require schoolchildren who are Jehovah's Witnesses to salute the flag in a daily classroom ceremony, even if doing so violated the children's religious beliefs. *Barnette*, perhaps in response to criticism of *Gobitis* and to reports of hundreds of assaults on Jehovah's Witnesses, upheld the right to refuse to salute, or to repeat the Pledge of Allegiance, on free speech grounds. Frankfurter, in the majority in *Gobitis*, held to his judicial restraint philosophy even as the Court

Progressive belief that judicial restraint was fully justified if only, he said in his 1916 "Living Law," speech, because courts were "largely deaf and blind" to social conditions and changes, and "continued to ignore newly arisen social needs."[95]

The Progressives' faith in legislatures as agents of reform was not of course inconsistent with their suspicion of politics and its tendencies toward corruption, cronyism, machines, and waste. While reform programs were to be developed and reform legislation passed by the legislators, the programs were to be executed and administered by emphatically apolitical agencies and commissions whose legitimacy and authority came directly from their expertise and commitment to efficiency and intergovernmental cooperation. That is where the problem with the judiciary arises. The Progressives' sharp distinction between administration and politics meant that "government operates best when the Constitution is construed to stop elected politicians from interfering with expert bureaucrats."[96] Roscoe Pound put forth the Progressive relation between legislatures and administration when he predicted in 1908 that "there is coming to be a science of modern legislation, and modern statutes were the result of detailed legislative investigation and long patient study by experts."[97]

The Progressive vision of legislative reform achieved through apolitical administration had little place for the judiciary, the vision creating a two-function system of government. The vision "provided the basis for a new functional division . . . consistent with the dominant trends of political thought at the end of the [nineteenth] century. . . . The distinction between the State will and its realization in action lay behind the whole structure of thought in this period of the development of 'public administration.'"[98] The role of the judiciary was diminished by default, a branch of government seen as no longer capable of playing a contributive role in government in a Progressive, reformist era. In such times, the courts playing their traditional role could only be a hindrance and a snare, inefficiently miring reforms in delay, and—worst of all—institutionally

---

turned its attention away from economic issues to individual rights. Urofsky notes that Frankfurter's strong position in his *Barnette* dissent, "if taken literally, nearly denies the Court any role in enforcing the Bill of Rights." UROFSKY, FELIX FRANKFURTER, 56. Urofsky says—it is a theme of his book—that Frankfurter's "view of judicial restraint . . . became a rigid and insurmountable obstacle to dealing with changing social concerns." *Id.* at 32. Thomas M. Keck similarly views Frankfurter's judicial restraint doctrine and judicial deference to Congress as "a relic of the past" by the time of the Warren Court. Keck argues that modern conservative demands for judicial restraint are belied by the conservative justices own activism. THOMAS M. KECK, THE MOST ACTIVIST SUPREME COURT IN HISTORY: THE ROAD TO MODERN JUDICIAL CONSERVATISM 65 (2004). The title refers to the Rehnquist Court.

[95] Louis Brandeis, "The Living Law," address to the Chicago Bar Association, Jan. 3, 1916, from the website of the Cardozo Law Review, http://www.cardozolawreview.com/index (retrieved Apr. 4, 2010). Published in 10 ILL. L. REV. 461 (1916). The quote is at 464. While many Progressives favored advisory opinions, as we will see, because of their ability to circumvent judicial review, Brandeis and Frankfurter opposed them, seeing advisory opinions as giving the justices too much discretion.

[96] Claeys, *Progressive Political Theory*, 407 (arguing that the Burger and Rehnquist courts "continued to use the Progressive theory of apolitical administration to decide hard separation of powers cases").

[97] Roscoe Pound, *Common Law and Legislation*, 21 HARV. L. REV. 383, 384 (1908). Quoted in PURCELL, BRANDEIS AND THE PROGRESSIVE CONSTITUTION, 13.

[98] VILE, CONSTITUTIONALISM AND THE SEPARATION OF POWERS, 278. This concept was developed by a leading Progressive writer, Frank Goodnow, in his POLITICS AND ADMINISTRATION (1900).

incapable of adapting to or even being aware of new conditions and new demands on government.

Inherent in Progressivism, then, was what Learned Hand called its "suspicion of courts."[99] Judges were seen as "incapable of investigating the facts, freeing themselves from old and hardened conceptions, and designing intelligent and systemic reforms."[100] Professor Frankfurter complained that "[i]t is beyond belief what the courts don't know . . . I do not mean their views but their ignorance of facts and events."[101] Brandeis too stressed the judges' systemic ignorance. He argued that social and economic changes created a demand for social justice in America rather than legal justice. He invoked Goethe's condemnation of past customs and laws that injure present society. His "Living Law" address was "the Progressive era's clearest and most cited critique of the failure of the courts to take into account the facts of the real world."[102] Judicial review served merely to void legislation that state assemblies passed to address the people's needs, causing popular hostility toward the courts.[103]

Leading Progressive writers and theorists were in full accord. Frank Goodnow, in his *Politics and Administration*, saw the judiciary as simply part of the administrative process, best functioning when it refrains from intervening in state programs.[104] Herbert Croly passed off the judiciary as simply incapable of contributing to or engaging in social reform. The common law judge, he wrote, "cannot become a satisfactory or sufficient servant of a genuinely social policy." This is in good part because courts "cannot be sure of being confronted by the real facts or all the facts."[105] The theme of Croly's influential *Progressive Democracy* is the call to recover legislative over judicial primacy. He lamented what happened in the nineteenth century, when "The Law" was "stupendously magnified," and when "such phrases as due process of law and equal protection of the laws were tortured in order to serve as legal pretexts for judicial control over legislation." In a Progressive era, for Croly, the courts remained inflexible, "loath" to modify their precedents "because they do not like to abandon the secure footing of an accepted and tested rule." Courts have difficulty obtaining sufficient facts about real conditions, in contrast to legislative and administrative bodies, because "they are obliged to accept any group of facts certified to them in the record, and they cannot be sure of being confronted by the real facts or all the facts."[106] At least one judge agreed. Charles Amidon, a Progressive federal judge in North Dakota writing to Oliver Wendell

---

[99] Learned Hand, The Spirit of Liberty: Papers and Addresses of Learned Hand 15 (Irving Dillard ed., 1959). Quoted in Purcell, Brandeis and the Progressive Constitution, 13.

[100] *Id.*

[101] Felix Frankfurter, letter to Benjamin Flexner, Feb. 16, 1921. Frankfurter Papers, Box 55, folder 1038. Quoted in Purcell, Brandeis and the Progressive Constitution, 13.

[102] Melvin I. Urofsky, Louis D. Brandeis: A Life 431 (2009).

[103] *Id.* at 432.

[104] Frank Goodnow, Politics and Administration, 7, 16, 23 (1900). *See* Vile, Constitutionalism and the Separation of Powers, 279.

[105] Herbert Croly, Progressive Democracy 366, 368 (1914).

[106] *Id.* at 139, 366.

Holmes, complained that judicial opposition to reform legislation made "the courts odious."[107]

Animosity toward the judiciary was not at all limited to the writing of Progressive intellectuals. Though largely forgotten, it was in fact a major, perhaps decisive, campaign issue among Progressive candidates for the presidency of the United States. In early 1912, as Theodore Roosevelt was planning his campaign to become Republican Party candidate for president, he gave an important speech in Ohio in which he took care to moderate his Progressive positions (often attacked as leftist if not downright socialist) in order to win over conservative Republicans. With one exception: support for the recall of state judicial decisions by popular ballot.[108] This relatively extreme position (modified a bit by not applying to the federal courts) would be crucial to his failure to capture the Republican nomination, a position that one biographer called "an egregious mistake" which "impaired considerably Roosevelt's chances of securing the nomination."[109]

A month prior to the Ohio speech, Roosevelt was still coy about whether he would run for president, contributing to what later would be called news media buzz.[110] During that month he wrote an opinion piece attacking the judiciary.[111] Referring to court rulings that overturned Progressive legislation, he attacked the state courts' power of judicial review, "a power which may give [the judges] the right to nullify the wishes of enormous majorities of their ninety million fellow citizens.[112] He called for revisions to state constitutions to permit the recall of decisions by ballot, in order to "enable the people to decide for themselves, . . . finally and without appeal, what the law of the land shall be."[113] Roosevelt, as a biographer observed, "felt that no comprehensive program

---

[107] Charles Amidon, Letter to O. W. Holmes, Jr., Jan. 19, 1911, Holmes Papers, Box 37, folder 20. Quoted in PURCELL, BRANDEIS AND THE PROGRESSIVE CONSTITUTION, 14.

[108] Theodore Roosevelt, speech, Columbus, Ohio, February 21, 1912, discussed in George E. Mowry, *Theodore Roosevelt and the Progressive Movement* 213 (1946).

[109] *Id.* at 213, 217. Regarding Roosevelt's attempt to moderate his anti-judicial position by limiting it to state courts, see Carol Chomsky, "Progressive Judges in a Progressive Age: Regulating Legislation in the Minnesota Supreme Court, 1880–1925," 11 LAW AND HIST. REV. 383, 384 (1993) (noting that many state courts "had their own *Lochners*, striking down statutes that limited working hours, regulated manufacturing, or proscribed certain unfair employer practices"). While some modern observers challenge the view that state courts were hostile to Progressive legislation (see Chomsky, 383–84), the perception of contemporary Progressives was that state courts were generally anti-Progressive. These included, besides Roosevelt, Roscoe Pound and Louis Brandeis. (Chomsky, 440). Roosevelt would become the presidential candidate of the new Progressive ("Bull Moose") Party in the 1912 election, where he lost to Democrat Woodrow Wilson.

[110] *See, e.g.*, "Roosevelt Refuses to Declare Himself," *New York Times,* January 6, 1912. Retrieved from the *New York Times* Website March 30, 2011.

[111] Theodore Roosevelt, "Judges and Progress," *Outlook* (magazine), Jan. 6, 1912, 40. Roosevelt had become an editorial writer for *Outlook*, a Social Gospel journal. Much in demand as a writer after he left the presidency in 1909, he received a very substantial $12,000 salary. See Kathleen Dalton, *Theodore Roosevelt: A Strenuous Life,* 339–40, 348 (2002). The *New York Times* quoted extensively from the piece on the day of its publication. "Roosevelt on the Courts," *New York Times,* Jan. 6, 1912. Retrieved from the *New York Times* website March 30, 2011.

[112] Roosevelt, "Judges and Progress," 41.

[113] *Id.* at 45.

of reform could be achieved unless the nation's courts were first curbed," a likely response to his experience while president (1901-1909), when "the nation's courts were shaping the federal and state constitutions into an almost impenetrable barrier against social legislation," and when the Progressive movement became increasingly "hostile to the whole judicial hierarchy."[114]

The Progressive view of the courts continued prominently in the 1924 presidential campaigns. Progressive Party candidate Robert M. La Follette called for a constitutional amendment to sharply limit the U.S. Supreme Court's authority to invalidate federal legislation, including allowing Congress to overturn an invalidation of legislation. When he announced his candidacy for president as an Independent Progressive, La Follette's platform included the following plank: "A constitutional amendment giving Congress power to reenact a statute over a judicial decision."[115] His Progressive rationale was clear. In 1921, echoing Roosevelt, he said that the "old fight" against monopoly and special privilege "had been brought to ignominious defeat" by recent Supreme Court decisions.[116] After the Supreme Court ruled unconstitutional a federal child labor law whose passage was a major Progressive achievement, he asked, on the floor of the Senate, "Which is supreme, the will of the people or the will of the few men who have been appointed to life positions on the Federal bench?"[117] As with Roosevelt in 1912, La Follette's plank on the judiciary would injure, perhaps fatally, his candidacy. The plank was "perhaps the most controversial of the entire platform." It was "so contrary to the fundamental notions of American government and its system of checks and balances . . . that it destroyed any glimmer of hope for a successful La Follette candidacy."[118]

La Follette's challenge to the courts was important enough in the 1924 election that U.S. Solicitor General James M. Beck commented weeks after the election (as *Time Magazine* reported it) that "the Supreme Court has survived a real crisis in its existence." As he put it, 28 million voters supported the Supreme Court, while four million "turned against it." He was apparently referring to those who voted for the Republican or Democratic candidates on the one hand, as opposed to those who voted for La Follette.[119] Beck's speech went on to propose (without explaining the connection) that Congress have authority to pass a joint resolution, ratified by the president, to seek an

---

[114] Mowry, *Theodore Roosevelt and the Progressive Movement*, 214.

[115] *See* Nancy C. Unger, *Fighting Bob La Follette: The Righteous Reformer,* 288–90 (2000).

[116] *Id.* at 289.

[117] *Id.* at 289–90. The child labor decision was *Bailey v. Drexel Furniture Co.*, 259 U.S. 20 (1922).

[118] *Id.* at 290.

[119] James M. Beck, speech to the Pennsylvania Society of New York, New York City, December 1924, reported in *Time* magazine, Dec. 29, 1924, with no exact date. Retrieved from the website of *Time* magazine Dec. 10, 2010. The actual figures were somewhat lower than the 28 million that Beck offered for the Republican and Democratic candidates, and higher than the 4 million he gave for La Follette. Republican Calvin Coolidge, the winner, received 15,725,016 votes; Democrat John W. Davis 8,386, 503; and La Follette 4,822,856. See Thomas A. Bailey, *The American Pageant: A History of the Republic,* 979 (1956). Slightly different figures are in other sources. Beck (or the *Time* reporter) may have mistakenly given the total votes for the three candidates (28 million) when just the total for Coolidge and Davis (24 million) was intended.

advisory opinion from the Supreme Court on any bill that the Court may overturn. The Court would have the right to decline the request for advice.[120]

Why Beck made the advisory opinion proposal is not clear. It may have been a response to the likely disturbing fact that the Progressive attack on the courts reached the point of a major campaign issue asserted by a credible (if third party) candidate for the presidency. He may have seen advisory opinions as a compromise position, preferable to the more extreme proposal to empower Congress to override a Supreme Court decision. Beck might have received a scare by La Follette's anti-judicial plank, in light of the substantial vote the candidate received. At any rate his position favoring Supreme Court advisory opinions contradicted a position he had earlier in that year. Beck, a lifelong conservative and leading antagonist of the Progressives and, later, the New Deal, wrote the best-selling *The Constitution of the United States,* which went through seven printings within ten months of its publication in June 1924. (A special edition of 10,000 copies, with a foreword from president-elect Coolidge, went to schools and libraries around the country.) Ostensibly the story of the creation of the constitution, it reflected his strong conservatism, looking longingly to a past when there were giants in the earth. His remarks on the sort of candidates who run for president nowadays (1924) would doubtless have brought La Follette, among others, to the minds of his readers. "Today," he wrote, "men are mentioned for the Presidency who even a generation ago would not have been regarded as worthy of more than a subordinate place in a State. Men are seriously considered for the first place in the gift of the American people who, judging by their past records, are little more than political adventurers."[121] Referring to Progressive, or at least popular, laws that the Supreme court overturns, then, Beck wrote, "threats are made, as are now being made, to destroy this power [of judicial review], or at least to impair it."[122]

Beck's book mentions the possible virtues of U.S. Supreme Court advisory opinions but opposes them nonetheless. If the Court had advisory authority, it "would mean that whenever the passage of a law is under consideration and great and powerful racial and class interests are arranged on either side the Court would be plunged into a heated political controversy by being obliged to give an anticipatory opinion whether the law was or was not invalid. Under these circumstances its prestige would be quickly shattered."[123] Beck's reversal between completion of his book in June 1924 and his speech at the end of the year may have been sparked by what happened in between: La Follette's campaign for President and the prominence of its anti-judicial plank, which may have alarmed Beck enough to call the election results a referendum on the Supreme Court, and to propose advisory opinions as a more moderate means of curbing the Supreme Court's power of judicial review.

---

[120] Beck, speech to the Pennsylvania Society of New York.

[121] James M. Beck, *The Constitution of the United States,* 275 (1924).

[122] *Id.* at 225.

[123] *Id.* at 227.

Later, the New Deal Congress accorded with Progressive hostility toward the judges. The hostility was pervasive even before the Supreme Court decisions overturning major New Deal legislation. Proposals to amend the Constitution were introduced in Congress with the intent of radically undermining three enduring constitutional pillars of judicial independence. Of the four amendments proposed in the 73rd Congress that applied to the judiciary, two would permit Congress, at will, to reduce federal judges' salaries during their term of office.[124] Another would remove life tenure, giving judges six-year terms.[125] The fourth would authorize Congress to decide how to choose federal judges, rather than merely rendering advice and consent to the president's choices.[126]

The judges' own skepticism toward Progressive and New Deal reform legislation, often quite open, contributed to antipathy toward the judiciary. The general suspicion of legislative power that characterized much of the judicial response to Populism and Progressivism mirrored the Progressives' and New Deal proponents' view of their programs being beleaguered by a judicial-review wielding federal judiciary and its suspicion of Congress's intrusion into the states' police powers.[127] That suspicion impelled the Progressive and New Deal eras' Supreme Court to discontinue its deference to legislative judgment about police power legislation. Rather, the federal courts began demanding fact-based proof that federal or state legislation that restricted the Ninth Amendment's "retained liberties of the people were actually pursuing a legitimate purpose rather than merely purporting to do so. . . . [T]hey began requiring of legislation a showing of actual means-end fit, rather than merely deferring to legislative judgment that measures were necessary to achieve a proper purpose. . . . [T]hese decisions came to be reviled . . . by political progressives and populists."[128] Hence the "Brandeis brief"; not so much an *ex nihilo* creation of a brilliant lawyer as a necessary, and not necessarily happy, response to the judges' demand for factual information. It was a demand that signaled less a desire to be better informed about social and economic problems needing reform and more a pronounced distrust of a Congress intruding wholesale on state police powers. "Brandeis himself believed that while such material might be of assistance to a judge in understanding a statute, in fact the court should not even have to consider the material, since it ought to defer to the wisdom of the legislature exercising its authority. . . . [E]xcept in occasional cases, there should be no need for a Brandeis brief, because courts, exercising judicial restraint, ought not to be second-guessing the legislatures."[129]

---

[124] H.J.R. No. 144 and No. 164, 73rd Cong., 2nd sess. (1934).

[125] H.J.R. No. 215, 73rd Cong., 2nd sess. (1934).

[126] S.J.R. No. 38, 73rd Cong., 2nd sess. (1934). On the anti-judiciary proposals, see generally Paul M. Giddens, *Constitutional Amendments Proposed in the 73rd Congress*, 9 U. Cin. L. Rev. 213 (1935).

[127] Stephen Gardbaum, *New Deal Constitutionalism and the Unshackling of the States*, 64 U. Chi. L. Rev. 483, 488 (1997). *See also* Randy E. Barnett, Restoring the Lost Constitution 216 (2004) (on the "Progressive Era's [Supreme] Court's skepticism about legislation").

[128] Barnett, Restoring the Lost Constitution, 222.

[129] Urofsky, Louis D. Brandeis, 221. *See also* Barnett, Restoring the Lost Constitution, 218 ("In response to the Progressive Era [Supreme] Court's demand for some proof that the legislation in question was a reasonable means of pursuing an appropriate end, lawyers began presenting courts with empirical support

The Progressives' and their New Deal descendants' hostility toward the judiciary included surprisingly open attacks on such fundamental constitutional doctrines as separation of powers. The attacks were not from outlier reformists asserting their reform ideology at any cost. To the contrary, what one scholar calls the assault on the Constitution was a carefully considered foundation of the Progressive enterprise from the late nineteenth until well into the twentieth century. The crucial element was interbranch efficiency and cooperation. One of the "major objectives of the Progressive attack on the Constitution [was] . . . the need to achieve an effective, harmonious relationship between the branches of government."[130] The problem was typically seen as one of government structure, a barrier to reform as such. Social and economic crises may have been the basis for demands for reform, but "the proximate problems were thought to lie in the political realm and, in particular, within the design and operation of political institutions, which were viewed as incapable of responding appropriately to changing conditions."[131] The problems were the "existing arrangements" that were stumbling blocks to an "entirely new set of economic and political conditions" besetting government institutions.[132]

This may be traced back to the post–Civil War years when already there were doubts about such doctrines as separation of powers and checks and balances on the branches of government. "Both represented points of view fast becoming inadequate in the face of the tasks of government in the modern world. . . . The Civil War . . . ushered in a long, intense period of criticism and attack upon the established constitutional theory, of an unprecedented ferocity, conducted alike by practical politicians, journalists, and academics."[133] By the late nineteenth century the call for government to address social and economic crises simply overrode constitutional niceties. The call itself "was an attack on a constitutional system that allowed these problems to be shelved, or indeed required them to be shelved. . . . [I]t was directed . . . against [separation of powers] . . . as one of the factors making for an ineffectual and weak system of government." The call was for "a system in which the unity of the powers of government would be as important a consideration as their separation."[134] Similarly, in the Progressive era the state constitutional conventions "began, for the first time, to question the traditional belief that . . . executive and judicial checks worked to foster deliberation in the public interest. . . . [I]n the early twentieth century the view began to take hold that governors and judges were acting to thwart the enactment of a number of well-intended statutes."[135]

---

for particular legislation. The most famous of these litigators was future justice Louis Brandeis.") On the relation of Brandeis's emphasis on empirical support for legislation to his views of states as "laboratories" of democracy and to his Progressive interest in scientific management, see G. Alan Tarr, *Laboratories of Democracy? Brandeis, Federalism, and Scientific Management*, 31 PUBLIUS 37 (2001).

[130] VILE, CONSTITUTIONALISM AND SEPARATION OF POWERS, 272.

[131] John Dinan, *Framing a "People's Government": State Constitution-Making in the Progressive Era*, 30 RUTGERS L.J. 933, 942 (1999).

[132] *Id.*

[133] VILE, CONSTITUTIONALISM AND THE SEPARATION OF POWERS, 263.

[134] *Id.* at 264.

[135] Dinan, *Framing a "People's Government,"* 946.

The Progressive era's constitutional conventions echoed the attacks on such old notions as separation of powers as a guarantee against arbitrary governmental power. "Progressive-era constitution makers concluded that the public interest was less likely to be secured through reliance on separation of powers, bicameralism, indirect representation, and constitutionalism than by a direct representation of the popular will."[136] One delegate at the 1917–1919 Massachusetts convention put it directly: "The times demand efficiency, and you cannot have efficiency with a government composed entirely of checks and balances."[137]

The primary target was separation of powers, which made the "concerted action" required to address modern social problems "impossible."[138] The Progressive intellectual leaders' rejection of separation of powers is striking in its severity. For Frank Goodnow, the three-branch separation "has been proven to be incapable of application to any concrete political organization."[139] Woodrow Wilson complained that the framers had "no clear analysis of the matter in thoughts when they implemented Montesquieu's separation of powers in the Constitution."[140] James Landis's 1938 study of New Deal administration, *The Administrative Process*, "fairly drips with contempt for the idea of a limited national government subject to a formal, tripartite separation of powers."[141] It is, these writers believed, modern administration that enables government to deal efficiently with the problems of an industrial economy. For Landis, the commission form of public administration that he favored "was an industrial pattern of organization adopted to meet the needs of an industrial society when the outmoded political divisions of Montesquieu had failed."[142] Herbert Croly was fairly typical in claiming that he did not call for outright rejection of separation of powers, but only what he believed was the extreme separation doctrine, that is a doctrine that interfered with his "demand for unity and harmony in the system of government."[143] For Croly, under separation of powers "government was prevented from doing harm, but in order that it might not do harm it was deliberately and effectively weakened. The people were protected from government; but quite as much was the government protected from the people. In dividing the government against itself by such high and rigid barriers, an equally substantial barrier was raised against the exercise by the people of any easy and sufficient control over

---

[136] *Id.* at 945.

[137] III Debates in the Massachusetts Constitutional Convention of 1917–1919, at 65 (1919). Quoted in Dinan, *Framing a "People's Government,"* 949.

[138] Vile, Constitutionalism and the Separation of Powers, 266.

[139] Frank J. Goodnow, Politics and Administration, 13. Quoted in Claeys, *Progressive Political Theory*, 420.

[140] Woodrow Wilson, Constitutional Government in the United States 167–68 (1911). Quoted in Claeys, *Progressive Political Theory*, 420.

[141] Gary Lawson, *The Rise and Rise of the Administrative State*, 1231.

[142] Vile, Constitutionalism and the Separation of Powers, 284.

[143] *See* Herbert Croly, Progressive Democracy 38–41 (1915). *See also* Vile, Constitutionalism and the Separation of Powers, 272–73. Vile notes that while the cohesiveness of the Progressive movement declined after World War I, "the criticism of separation of powers continued unabated." *Id.* at 282.

their government."[144] The Progressives would not permit separation of powers to get in the way of the movement's agenda.[145] The "destruction," by the late 1930s, of the principle of separation of powers that Madison had set forth "is perhaps the crowning jewel of the modern administrative revolution."[146]

Practically speaking, the greatest constitutional snare to the Progressives' reform ambitions was judicial review. As the courts increasingly exercised their review power, "conflicts between the legislative and judicial branches of government dominated debate."[147] Progressive-era state constitutional conventions increasingly saw judicial review as an anti-Progressive weapon, concerned that as they saw it, "beginning in the final decades of the nineteenth century, the federal and state courts had begun to exercise judicial review to strike down a number of laws that were seen as beneficial to the public."[148] Among the many calling for limiting or abolishing judicial review, or at least for recall of judicial decisions, was William Jennings Bryan, in a speech significantly entitled "The People's Law," in 1912.[149] The year before, L. B. Boudin, a Progressive attorney, in an article disparagingly entitled "Government by Judiciary," declared that the "most momentous question before the people of this country today is undoubtedly the question of the limits of the power of the judiciary to annul legislation for alleged unconstitutionality."[150] And in Congress during the Progressive and New Deal eras, over one hundred bills were introduced to limit judicial review or otherwise diminish

---

[144] Croly, *Progressive Democracy,* 40.

[145] Brandeis was the prominent exception, asserting in his dissent in *Myers* that separation of powers was "not to promote efficiency, but to preclude the exercise of arbitrary power. The purpose was, not to avoid friction, but, by means of the inevitable friction incident to the distribution of the governmental power among three departments, to save the people from autocracy." *Myers v. United States*, 272 U.S. 52, 293 (1926) (Brandeis, J., dissenting). It was not long after that the British writer Carleton K. Allen responded to a proposal to allow English judges to advise the government in order to increase efficiency. It is, he wrote, "exactly from the executive officer's efficiency and zeal that we must save ourselves." Carleton K. Allen, *Administrative Consultation of the Judiciary*, 47 L. Q. Rev. 43, 43 (1931) (replying to E. C. S. Wade, *Consultation of the Judiciary by the Executive*, 46 L. Q. Rev. 169 (1930)).

[146] Gary Lawson, *The Rise and Rise of the Administrative State*, 1248.

[147] Purcell, Brandeis and the Progressive Constitution, 12.

[148] Dinan, *Framing a "People's Government,"* 949. Dinan notes the connection between separation of powers and judicial review in the minds of Progressive constitutional convention delegates. Among the "heavily contested" principles on the state levels, he writes, was separation of powers, which "was subject to a series of assaults during the course of the Progressive-era state constitutional conventions particularly in regard to the power of judicial review." *Id.* at 944. Dinan also observes that the era's constitutional conventions "considered all sorts of proposals to limit judicial power—including efforts to abolish judicial review altogether," along with recall of judges, recall of decisions, and requiring supermajority or unanimous votes by the justices. On Progressive-era constitutional convention proposals to abolish judicial review, see *id.* at 951–54. For examples of Progressive-era states imposing limits on judicial review, see John J. Dinan, The American State Constitutional Tradition 127–30 (2006). For a treatment of major judicial decisions in this context, see William G. Ross, A Muted Fury: Populists, Progressives, and Labor Unions Confront the Courts, 1890–1937 at 1–48 (1994).

[149] William Jennings Bryan, "The People's Law," address at Columbus, Ohio, Mar. 12, 1912, Bryan Papers, Box 49. Cited in Purcell, Brandeis and the Progressive Constitution, 20. *See also* Barry Cushman, Rethinking the New Deal Court 12–24 (1998) (discussing measures to curtail judicial review).

[150] L. B. Boudin, *Government by Judiciary*, 26 Pol. Sci. Q. 238 (1911). Quoted in Purcell, Brandeis and the Progressive Constitution, 20.

judicial power.[151] These included the bills to give advisory opinion jurisdiction to the Supreme Court.

* * *

We see that the advisory opinion proponents' attacks on separation of powers, judicial review and other constitutional doctrines were not eccentric or marginal. The defenses of advisory opinions as instruments of efficiency, interbranch cooperation, and governmental harmony were far from some naïve cry for government by sweetness and light, oblivious to any constitutional principle standing in the way. Rather, the defenses of advisory opinions were invocations of mainstream Progressive thought, simply joining in the attacks on the Constitution that, with the rise of the administrative state, turned out to be widely perceived as legitimate, even innovative.

For those who favored advisory opinions, as for many other Progressives and New Dealers, the dominant bar to reform was "the persistence of outdated constitutional clauses and doctrines" imposed and enforced by an obstructionist judiciary exercising judicial review of laws greatly needed to address social and economic crises.[152] For some Progressives, as we have seen, the advisory opinion was a practical cure for the mischief of judicial review, inducing the advising justices' opinions on constitutionality before legislation has passed, or soon after, and so avoiding the long and cumbersome road to judicial review, so injurious to the Progressive and New Deal legislative agendas.

Felix Frankfurter was one Progressive who doubted that advisory opinions were worth the cost, mainly because he saw advisory opinions increasing, not decreasing, judicial power against his life-long devotion to the principle of judicial restraint.[153] He shared the Progressives' suspicion of judicial interference in reform legislation and held strictly to James B. Thayer's notion of judicial review as a last resort, to be exercised only instances of indisputable clear error. "Professor Frankfurter [at Harvard Law School] believed this in 1922; Mr. Justice Frankfurter still believed it four decades later when he retired from the bench."[154] Frankfurter saw any form of accelerated judicial review as a violation of judicial restraint. Hence his steady opposition to declaratory judgments. Such acceleration, he believed, "served primarily to strengthen the power of the judiciary over the legislature and to restrict the possibilities of intelligent social legislation; accelerated adjudication of constitutional issues meant that legislative

[151] *See* Purcell, Brandeis and the Progressive Constitution, 34. For the argument that much of the earlier New Deal legislation was overturned because it was much too poorly drafted to survive judicial scrutiny, see Cushman, Rethinking the New Deal Court, 36–39.

[152] Dinan, *Framing a "People's Government,"* 977. Dinan is writing about the Progressive-era constitutional conventions, but his statement holds for the period in general.

[153] *See generally* Urofsky, Felix Frankfurter (on the principle of judicial restraint as the dominant force in Frankfurter's legal thought even as the post-Depression Supreme Court addressed civil rights and due process, explains his striking lack of influence on the Court's jurisprudence).

[154] *Id.* at x. On Frankfurter's adoption of Thayer's standard, *see id.* at 30–31. Thayer's clear error standard of judicial review and its relation to advisory opinions are discussed in Chapter 5.

questions would be determined 'abstractly,'" and it "deprived legislatures of their 'creative function,' prevented growth of social knowledge through legislative experiments, and weakened legislative and popular responsibility. . . . '[G]rave dangers' loomed if the courts did not rigorously restrict its [judicial review's] use."[155] Frankfurter, though, stood in contrast with most other defenders of advisory opinions, who, we have seen, believed that they were worth the candle.

There was one significant difference, however, between advisory opinions and declaratory judgments, in fact between advisory opinions and almost any other type of judicial ruling, which seems to eliminate the problems of defending or opposing advisory opinions. Advisory opinions are, purportedly, nonbinding. They carry no precedential force or weight. They are the judges' personal views. They are extrajudicial and not enforceable. At least that is what the justices say.

[155] PURCELL, BRANDEIS AND THE PROGRESSIVE CONSTITUTION, 127. In summarizing Frankfurter's views on accelerated review, Purcell quotes from Frankfurter's article on advisory opinions where Frankfurter does not discuss declaratory judgments. Purcell does not make this clear in his own text, where he is ostensibly discussing declaratory judgments. Both advisory opinions and declaratory judgments, though, are forms of accelerated review, and Frankfurter was hostile to both for similar reasons.

5 }

An Offer That Can't Be Refused

JUDICIAL REVIEW AND THE FAILED ATTEMPTS TO DISTINGUISH ADVICE AND DECISIONS

This chapter looks critically at the nonbinding doctrine, which governs the advisory opinion process in most of the advisory states.[1] It is the chief contrast between advisory opinions and adjudicated decisions, frequently cited by the advising justices. Since modern advisory opinions are usually on questions of constitutionality, we need first to consider further their uneasy relationship to judicial review.

Advisory Opinions and Judicial Review

Advisory opinions and judicial review have had a close if awkward relationship. They have at least one obvious parallel. Both involve an inquiry into whether a statute, rule, or action violates the constitution on the one hand, and construction of constitutional provisions on the other, often leading to a pronouncement about the constitutionality of a challenged act.[2] Advisory opinions have routinely made such pronouncements, and from the start advisory justices often discussed and applied principles and standards of constitutional construction that would become regular features of judicial review. In the earliest reported advisory opinion, in 1781, the Massachusetts House of Representatives disagreed with the Senate on the construction of the state constitution's provision that "all money bills shall originate in the House of Representatives." The two houses together sought the advice of the justices since "the Legislature should, on the present occasion, unite in their construction of the Constitution without delay." The justices opined simply that there was no "unconstitutional impropriety" in both houses joining in the valuation process.[3] The justices, however, in their second reported advisory opinion commented in 1784 on how they were to construe the constitution, including incorporating original intent. This opinion addressed the question of whether the Massachusetts constitution permitted the legislature to fill vacancies in the Council. The justices

[1] A brief overview of nonbinding doctrine is in Chapter 3.

[2] *See, e.g.*, Michael J. Perry, The Constitution in the Courts: Law or Politics 15 (1994).

[3] *Opinion of the Justices*, 126 Mass. 547, 553 (1781; reported 1878).

advised that since the constitution was silent on the specific question, they judged the original intent to be that the offices in question should always be filled, so that the legislature had the authority to fill the vacancies.[4]

From this beginning the Massachusetts justices' advisory opinions grew increasingly explicit on both original intent and standards of constitutional construction. An 1807 advisory opinion asserted that the justices' answer to the governor's question must "solely depend on the construction of the constitution," and they replied in the negative to the governor's question on whether inhabitants of unincorporated plantations had the right to vote for governor and lieutenant governor. Extending the voting privilege to these inhabitants, they advised, is "without [i.e., outside of] the letter of the constitution, and is required neither by the principles, nor spirit of it."[5] An 1811 advisory opinion expounded on original intent, which is "to be ascertained by a reasonable construction, resulting from the application of correct maxims, generally acknowledged and received," including, for example, the rule that words are to be construed according to common usage though their import may be "enlarged or restrained" to express real intention, which, when ascertained, "must have the force of law."[6]

These pronouncements are obviously similar to pronouncements that underlie judicial review. The distinctions between advisory opinions and judicial review are neither in the construing nor in the pronouncing regarding constitutionality. In those respects, an advisory opinion differs little from adjudicated judicial review. The differences lie in two other elements of judicial review. First, judicial review incorporates the power to void the act in question and to declare it unenforceable. James Bradley Thayer's influential defense of the clear error standard of judicial review emphasized a crucial conceptual distinction between judges, on the one hand, "merely and nakedly" ascertaining the meaning of a constitutional provision and of an impeached legislative act in order to determine if the two were in conflict, which he called an "academic question," and on the other hand deciding "the really momentous question" of whether the court "can disregard the Act."[7] For Thayer, the clear error standard was an important check on this formidable judicial review power. To void legislation, he argued, judges should not nullify an act "merely because it is concluded that upon a just and true construction the law is unconstitutional. . . . It can only disregard the Act when those who have the right to make laws have not merely made a mistake, but have made a very clear one."[8] With the decline of the clear error standard[9] Thayer's distinction has lost its concreteness. A court's construction resulting in a finding of unconstitutionality, clear

---

[4] *Opinion of the Justices*, 14 Mass. (13 Tyng) 470 (1818; dated 1784).

[5] *Opinion of the Justices*, 3 Mass. (2 Tyng) 568, 571 (1807).

[6] *In re Opinion of the Justices*, 7 Mass. (6 Tyng) 523, 524–25 (1811).

[7] James B. Thayer, *The Origins and Scope of the American Doctrine of Constitutional Law*, 7 Harv. L. Rev. 129, 143–44 (1893).

[8] *Id.* On the history of the clear error standard, see generally Sylvia Snowiss, Judicial Review and the Law of the Constitution (1990); *Symposium: One Hundred Years of Judicial Review: The Thayer Centennial Symposium*, 88 Nw. U. L. Rev. (1993) (articles and commentaries on Thayer and judicial review).

[9] *See* Snowiss, Judicial Review and the Law of the Constitution, 62–65.

error or not, has virtually become equated with nullifying and voiding the impeached act, rendering the act without force and effect, and setting aside actions arising from the impeached act.

The second element of judicial review that distinguishes it from advisory opinions is its broad binding force. A high court's construction regarding constitutionality is binding on parties to the case at hand, and also "binds parties beyond those to the instant case."[10] Hence when an opinion states, for example, that "[o]ur conclusions are that sections 18 and 19 of the act referred to are clearly unconstitutional and void, and must be entirely disregarded," the statement may comfortably sit either in an advisory opinion or in an opinion in a case under judicial review.[11] But when an advisory opinion makes this kind of statement, the justices have not actually engaged in judicial review and in the "momentous" decision to nullify the challenged statute. The constitutional status of the statute has not changed at all because the "advice" has no force or effect. Advisory opinions may adopt such apparently strong judicial-review terminology as "unconstitutional" and "void" and "disregarded," but the jurisprudence of advisory opinions disengages and sets aside the nullifying so that the interpreting and opining on constitutionality stand alone.

"It's just advice," these advisory justices seem to say. "Take it or leave it." The justices are applying an apparently self-evident principle: advisory opinions are not binding. These opinions nullify nothing, the advisory justices repeatedly tell us. They have no force or effect whatever. This is key to the legitimacy of advisory opinions. It is also the most troublesome challenge to that legitimacy, and it reflects the inevitable tension between advice as helpful guidance and as inescapable exercise of power, notwithstanding claims to the contrary.

The Nonbinding Doctrine

It has been the most frequent and forceful statement advisory justices make about advisory opinions. That might be, to use Henry James's phrase, the eagerness of insecurity, but the doctrine is clear. Advisory opinions are simply advice. They bind no one and carry no weight of precedent. They are not even a decision of the court.[12]

Why *don't* advisory opinions bind? No advisory opinion provision requires them to be nonbinding. At first glance, though, the answer seems self-evident, requiring no doctrine. If the opinions are indeed advisory, then the very term indicates their discretionary nature. "To recommend; suggest" are typical definitions in dictionaries both legal and

---

[10] Barry Friedman, *The History of the Countermajoritarian Difficulty, Part One: The Road to Judicial Supremacy*, 73 N.Y.U. L. Rev. 333, 352 (1998).

[11] The quote is from the South Dakota supreme court's first advisory opinion, *In re Construction of Revenue Law, sec. 18 and 19*, 48 N.W. 813, 817 (S.D. 1891).

[12] Colorado and South Dakota are exceptions; as discussed in Chapter 3, each of these courts, not their justices, gives advisory opinions. James's phrase is from his novel The Bostonians (1886).

general, and *Black's Law Dictionary* takes care to note that "'[a]dvise' imports that it is discretionary or optional with the person addressed whether he will act on such advice or not."[13] "[C]ounseillyng is no comandement," says Chaucer's Wife of Bath.[14] Advisory opinions themselves often suggest that being advisory and being nonbinding, like a horse and carriage, just go together. The Massachusetts Supreme Judicial Court, for example, has held that the "familiar rule" is that "such opinions are wholly advisory . . . and are not decisions of the court,"[15] apparently assuming it is obvious that one follows from the other. It is, however, not *that* obvious. That the justices' answers are advice is in the first place, strictly speaking, an assumption. No advisory opinion provision has ever employed such terms as "advisory," "advice," or "advise."[16] No such terms were used in advisory opinions themselves for nearly a century after their first appearance in 1781. The justices seem to have begun using these terms only in the course of explaining the nature and extent of their advisory duties, that is, when they begin to be defensive about their advisory powers.[17]

Neither did early advisory opinions refer to advisory opinions as nonbinding. The first reference to this appears to be in an 1828 litigated case, about a half-century after the creation of the first advisory opinion provision (that of Massachusetts in 1780), where the Massachusetts justices held that they were not bound by an earlier advisory opinion in the litigated case before them.[18] The reason for the early lack of interest in whether advisory opinions were binding or not is that it was only in the 1820s, with its "outburst of judicial review,"[19] that advisory opinions' similarities to judicial review would have raised concerns sufficient for the justices to feel impelled to articulate distinctions between the two. In the era presuming coordinate review just ending, whereby each branch, as Madison put it, must be guided by "its own interpretation" of the Constitution,[20] advisory opinions would be necessarily seen as aids to the coordinate branches in *their* determination of the constitutionality of their acts. Originally the advisory opinion process may in fact have presupposed coordinate review. The advisory justices began asserting the nonbinding doctrine only after it became generally accepted that the judiciary held final authority to review for constitutionality and to nullify acts of

---

[13] Black's Law Dictionary 54 (6th ed. 1990) (at "advise"). The first quoted definition is in American Heritage Dictionary 26 (3d ed. 1992) (at "advise").

[14] Geoffrey Chaucer, Canterbury Tales, "Wife of Bath's Prologue," line 67.

[15] City of Boston v. Treasurer and Receiver Gen., 130 N.E. 390, 391 (Mass. 1921).

[16] The sole, partial, exception is the Delaware advisory opinion statute, to which was added in 1953 some procedural requirements that include the term "advisory opinion." *See* Del. Code Ann. tit. 10, sec. 141(c), (d) (2000).

[17] *See, e.g.*, Opinion of the Justices to the Senate and House of Representatives, 126 Mass. 557, 566 (1878) ("In giving such opinions, the Justices do not act as a court, but as the constitutional advisors of the other departments of the government.").

[18] *Adams v. Bucklin*, 24 Mass. (7 Pick.) 121, 122 (1828). The advisory opinion referred to is *Opinion of the Justices*, 24 Mass. (7 Pick.) 125, 126 (1825).

[19] Lawrence M. Friedman, A History of American Law 316 (1973).

[20] James Madison, The Federalist No. 78, at 98 (1788; Benjamin Wright ed., 1961).

other branches.[21] As judicial review evolved away from coordinate review and from the clear error standard toward the notion that constitutions have a determinate meaning that only supreme courts can divine, the courts would come to be viewed as "a board for answering legislative conundrums."[22]

The chief, and doubtful, textual foundation for the justices' nonbinding rule has been the references to the justices themselves. Most advisory opinion provisions confer the duty on the "justices" or "judges" of the supreme court rather than on the court itself. Hence supreme courts do not render advisory opinions, says the nonbinding doctrine, the justices do. This has been generally put forth as sufficient warrant to declare advisory opinions nonbinding. The justices have consistently held that in responding to advisory opinion requests, each justice gives his or her personal response, and therefore are responses that are extrajudicial and do not represent the opinion of the court, and so they cannot bind. They are "non-adjudicative expressions of personal points of view," as the Delaware justices put it.[23]

The two exceptions—Colorado and South Dakota—confirm this. The high court in Colorado, where the advisory opinion clause provides that "the supreme court" is the advice giver,"[24] declared in 1889 that advisory opinions "have all the force and effect of judicial precedents." This derives, the court observed, from one of the "peculiar features" of the Colorado advisory opinion provision, that "[i]n this state . . . it is the court, not the justices, that must answer."[25] Because, the court noted, advisory opinions are not pronounced by the court in the other advisory states, "they are not technically judicial decisions, nor do they necessarily constitute judicial precedents."[26] This view, however, was not evident to everyone. The reference to "justices" rather than "court" was quickly attacked as a weak foundation for the nonbinding rule. A few months after the Colorado court issued its interpretation, Thayer wrote in a letter to the editor of *The Nation* that "one may well doubt whether the Court is not over-emphasizing the effect of using the word 'court' instead of 'justices of the court.'"[27] A member of the Colorado legislature, replying, agreed. The state's advisory opinion provision, he wrote to *The Nation*, "was injected into the bill by a hasty amendment in a committee of the whole," and anyway, "[i]n legislative parlance" it was customary to use the term supreme court in conferring any power "upon the Court as a whole, or upon any of its members."[28] He suggested that the legislature favored the advisory opinion clause solely for "the purpose of avoiding

---

[21] Chapter 2 discusses the relation of advisory opinions to growing judicial power. *See also* Christopher Wolfe, The Rise of Modern Judicial Review 94–101 (1986); Snowiss, Judicial Review and the Law of the Constitution 179 (discussing judicial review in this period).

[22] Thayer, Origin and Scope, 146. *See also* Robert A. Schapiro, *Judicial Deference and Interpretive Coordinacy in State and Federal Constitutional Law*, 85 Cornell L. Rev. 656, 673 (2000).

[23] *Opinion of the Justices*, 413 A.2d 1245, 1248 (Del. 1980).

[24] Colo. Const. art. VI, sec. 3 ("The supreme court shall give its opinion. . . .").

[25] *In re Senate Resolution*, 21 P. 478, 479 (Colo. 1889).

[26] *Id.*

[27] James Bradley Thayer, Letter to the Editor, 49 The Nation 476 (1889). Thayer's interest in advisory opinions and especially in its nonbinding doctrine was sparked by specific events, reviewed in Chapter 6.

[28] O. F. A. Green, Letter to the Editor, 50 The Nation 51 (1890).

breakers as to its own acts" with the aid of nonbinding advice. Given the "hostility of the Legislature to the court at the time," he wrote, the legislature would not have intended to enlarge the court's power by making advisory opinions binding.[29]

Thayer's and Green's comments confirm that there is nothing in the terms themselves semantically determining that "court" signifies binding opinions and "justices" nonbinding. When a majority of the Alabama justices upheld the constitutionality of the state's new advisory opinion statute in 1923, the two apparently irritated justices in the minority (they would thereafter refuse to participate in any advisory opinion proceeding) attacked the distinction between "court" and "justices" as empty. "[W]e beg leave to say that in our opinion the suggested discrimination is illusory and unsubstantial. . . . We think the suggested difference between opinions by the court and by the Judges rests upon a distinction without a difference. It rests upon a difference in mere form of words."[30]

South Dakota is the more curious exception. The state altered its constitution's advisory opinion provision in 1972 so that the court and not the justices renders the advice.[31] The records of the South Dakota Constitutional Revision Commission, which proposed the amendment, are not clear as to why the commission favored the change. Former South Dakota Chief Justice Jon Fosheim, who was the commission's vice chair, responded to my query: "As I recall, it was felt that if the Supreme Court as a body issues an official opinion to the Governor on an important question of law, it could be taken by the Governor as binding interpretation in the exercise of his power."[32]

Notwithstanding the ambiguous nature of this textual basis for the nonbinding doctrine, the advisory justices have marshaled the doctrine against challenges to the legitimacy of advisory opinions. One challenge, for example, is the haste with which the justices are often expected to render advisory opinions. Early advisory opinions simply commented on this; later ones would defend advising with insufficient time by citing the nonbinding doctrine. In the 1781 Massachusetts advisory opinion three of the four justices responding commented on the short time they had, one reflecting that he did "as well as [he] could in the short space allowed."[33] The Maine justices in 1840 expressed

---

[29] *Id.* Greene used "breakers" figuratively referring to heavy ocean waves breaking violently near a rocky coast. A ship sailing toward breakers was on a dangerous course. For a contemporary dictionary's definition, see Oxford English Dictionary at "breakers," definition 5. The volume of the OED with this definition was published in 1888.

[30] *In re Opinion of the Justices*, 96 So. 487, 498–99 (Ala. 1923) (Sayre and Miller, JJ, dissenting). On the tendency of justices and requesting authorities to use the terms interchangeably, *see, e.g.*, Margaret M. Bledsoe, *The Advisory Opinion in North Carolina: 1947 to 1991*, 70 N.C. L. Rev. 1853, 1884 (1992); C. Dallas Sands, *Government by Judiciary—Advisory Opinions in Alabama*, 4 Ala. L. Rev. 1, 13 (1951); Mel A. Topf, *The Jurisprudence of the Advisory Opinion Process in Rhode Island*, 2 Roger Williams U. L. Rev. 201, 247–48 (1997).

[31] S.D. Const. of 1889, art. V, sec. 13 ("The governor shall have the authority to require the opinions of the judges of the Supreme Court . . ."; amended 1972 by deleting "the judges of.").

[32] Letter from Jon Fosheim to the author (Apr. 2, 1999) (on file with author). My thanks to Justice Fosheim for his response, and my thanks to Ann Eichinger of the South Dakota State Library for her assistance.

[33] *Opinions of the Justices*, 126 Mass. 547, 548 (1879) (opinion rendered 1781).

concern that the haste in which advisory opinions were prepared might damage the "respect" due the opinions. Further, a request for advice, they said, "cannot be allowed the time for that extensive research and patient examination and reflection, which the importance of the questions . . . may demand."[34] Later, as doubts about advisory opinions grew, advisory justices would invoke the nonbinding doctrine to mitigate this complaint. The New Hampshire justices asserted that "[i]t is manifestly impossible to give the subject adequate consideration in the time that can be taken before an answer to your inquiries must be returned. But it has seemed to us to be in conformity with the duty laid upon us by the Constitution to express to you such tentative views on the subject as we now have, with a repetition of the caution that the opinion given is not a judicial decision of the questions propounded."[35]

Later and more substantial challenges to advisory opinions were the absence of argument and the concurrent factual vacuum in which the advice is rendered.[36] Here too the justices applied the nonbinding doctrine in response, but now occasionally seeming to argue that the doctrine is grounded not in the text of the advisory opinion provision, but is in fact a response to the challenges themselves. An advisory opinion is "formed without the aid of counsel or the benefit of argument," the Maine justices said. "It often has been decided that an opinion formed and expressed under such circumstances is liable to incorrectness and must be regarded, not as conclusive and binding."[37] The Rhode Island justices similarly made the connection in defending their "overturning" an 1883 advisory opinion in 1935. An advisory opinion, "given, as it must be, without the aid which the court derives, in adversary cases, from able and experienced counsel, . . . can have no weight as precedent."[38]

The nonbinding doctrine has also been invoked in response to the due process challenges, liable as the advisory process is to the risk of affecting private rights of those without opportunity to be heard.[39] A Maine justice in 1881 expressed doubts about giving the requested advice in part for due process reasons, but gave the advice anyway, noting that the advice given "can have no effect if the matter should be judicially brought before the court."[40] The New Hampshire justices, responding in 1852 to a request for advice about the constitutionality of a bill, cautioned that "[we] feel it due to ourselves in justice to say that whatever opinions we might express on this bill, must be regarded as impressions by which we should not feel ourselves bound, if the bill should become law, and if the rights of a citizen should depend on its construction."[41] In similar manner the nonbinding doctrine has been held to cure separation of powers problems inherent

[34] *In re Justices' Opinion*, 16 Me. 479, 479–80 (1840).

[35] *In re Opinion of the Justices*, 138 A. 284, 291 (N.H. 1927).

[36] These issues are discussed in Chapter 2.

[37] *Opinion of the Justices of the Supreme Court*, 460 A.2d 1341, 1345 (Me. 1982).

[38] *Opinion of the Court to the Governor in the Matter of the Constitutional Convention*, 178 A. 433, 440 (R.I. 1935) (in reference to *In re The Constitutional Convention*, 14 R.I. 649 (1883)).

[39] Due process issues are discussed in Chapter 2.

[40] *Opinion of the Justices*, 72 Me. 543, 562 (1881).

[41] *Opinion of the Justices*, 25 N.H. 537, 538 (1852).

in the advisory opinions process. The Alabama justices ruled the state's advisory opinion statute is constitutional notwithstanding the state constitution's separation provisions, in great part on grounds of nonbinding doctrine.[42]

Quacking Like a Duck: The Failure of the Nonbinding Doctrine

The problem with the nonbinding doctrine is this: No one believes it. The angular fact about the doctrine is that it is pretty much ignored in judicial practice. The study of state constitutionalism may offer no comparable instance of the clear if not blatant disparity between judicial doctrine and judicial practice. Entirely typical is an example from the South Dakota justices, who have long asserted the nonbinding doctrine. In 1895 they advised that a statute providing for the issue of warrants to defray current state expenses, based on revenues not yet collected, was not a debt within the meaning of the constitution.[43] This advisory opinion has been regularly cited as binding authority in litigated cases ever since. A student of South Dakota advisory opinions cited a line of these cases extending from 1895, the same year the advisory opinion was issued, through 1969, two years before his article appeared.[44] This is entirely reasonable. Something like the conclusion about what looks like a duck, walks like a duck, and quacks like one, advisory opinions have been perceived and responded to as if they were adjudicated decisions, and so in turn they have inexorably come to look and behave like adjudicated decisions. For one thing, the advisory opinion process has steadily acquired the traits of appellate adjudication, including briefs and oral argument from opposing parties, which has blurred "the already imprecise distinction between decisions of the court and opinions of the justices."[45] The Florida justices may well have been speaking for the legal community as well as the public, indeed merely pointing out the obvious, when they commented that use of briefs and arguments in the advisory process has "enabled us to treat such requests [for advice] in somewhat the nature of an adversary proceeding."[46]

For another thing, and perhaps more important, advisory opinions are written in the style and form of adjudicated decisions. The principle forms of reasoning, analysis, and reliance on case law are nearly, if not fully, identical. An observer noted more than a half-century ago that for both lawyers and the public it is "difficult and awkward" to

---

[42] *In re Opinion of the Justices in re Amendment to Section 93 of the Constitution*, 96 So. 487, 489 (1923). *See* Sands, *Government by Judiciary—Advisory Opinions in Alabama*, 4–6; Jonathan D. Persky, *Ghosts That Slay: A Contemporary Look at State Advisory Opinions*, 37 Conn. L. Rev. 1155, 1210–12 (2005) (noting that the nonbinding doctrine "was dispositive" in the Alabama justices' ruling that the advisory opinion statute was constitutional, so that "their advice giving power . . . did not affect the constitutional relationship between the judiciary and the other branches of government, and thereby did not violate the constitutional provision that 'the judicial [department] shall never exercise the legislative and executive powers'").

[43] *In re State Warrants*, 62 N.W. 191 (1895).

[44] John F. Hagemann, *The Advisory Opinion in South Dakota*, 16 S.D. L. Rev. 291, 302–03 (1971).

[45] Charles M. Carberry, *The State Advisory Opinion in Perspective*, 14 Fordham L. Rev. 81, 105 (1975).

[46] *In re Advisory Opinion to Governor*, 243 So.2d 573, 576 (Fla. 1971).

keep in mind the difference between what the justices are doing when they're a "court" and when they're "justices" of the court, "especially when there is so little in external appearances to flag the difference. Advisory opinions are published in the official court reports, interspersed with no distinction among the written opinions which announce decisions in litigated cases. The techniques of legal rationalization used in writing advisory opinions are indistinguishable from those used in other opinions. They are all just "cases."[47]

The similarities have been attributed to "force of habit" and to "judicial propensity for exactness and dependence on precedent."[48] But it is more than that. It is a matter of credibility, a question of responding to the ever-present shadow of the illegitimacy of advisory opinions. "The legitimacy of judicial decrees depends . . . in considerable part on public confidence that the judges are predominantly engaged not in making personal political judgments but in applying a body of law."[49] Not surprisingly, then, the advisory justices have adopted in their opinions the style and devices honed through centuries of adversarial proceedings, adopted as a balance to the inescapable reality that the advisory process lies outside normative judicial activity. The advising is not made sufficiently "safe" by the justices' policy of strict interpretation of advisory opinion provisions and by the concomitant set of restrictions, or by insistence on advisory opinions as nonbinding.

Writing advisory opinions so that they are like judicial decisions rhetorically co-opts the legitimacy of the adjudicative process for the advisory process. It is because advisory opinions lie outside traditional judicial limits and disturb longstanding notions of judicial legitimacy that the justices take up a communications ethos that sustains the authority of the court when the justices issue advisory opinions. There is nothing unusual about this. Those in positions of authority naturally communicate in ways that recall the grounds of their authority, and they do so more or less depending on the perceived need to assert their legitimacy. The carryover of the justices' careful, limiting, highly circumscribed manner of writing their adjudicated decisions to advisory opinions provides them with a legitimizing rhetoric. What Justice Frankfurter said of the U.S. Constitution in his dissent in *Baker v. Carr* holds true for the states: "The Constitution's authority ultimately rests on sustained public confidence in its moral sanction. . . . [T]here is nothing judicially more unseemly nor more self-defeating than for this Court to make *in terrorem* pronouncements."[50] Advisory opinions come disturbingly close to being just such pronouncements, operating under thin cover of claims of nonbinding, nonadjudicative, personal advice-giving. Carrying the rhetoric of adjudicated decisions over to advisory opinions helps the justices speak as if they were a court acting within the proper judicial bounds. Advisory opinions, in short, are written to have "a normative impact" not distinguishable from a decision.[51]

---

[47] Sands, *Government by Judiciary—Advisory Opinions in Alabama*, 26.

[48] Ellingwood, Departmental Cooperation, 146–47.

[49] Archibald Cox, The Court and the Constitution, 362 (1987).

[50] Baker v. Carr, 369 U.S. 186, 270 (1962) (Frankfurter, J., dissenting).

[51] Sands, *Government by Judiciary—Advisory Opinions in Alabama*, 31.

Adjudicated decisions are hedged all around by limits. That was one reason Alexander Hamilton argued that the judiciary would not be as dangerous as the other branches. The courts "should be bound down by strict rules and precedents, which serve to define and point out their duty in every particular case that comes before them."[52] Benjamin Cardozo, 133 years later, affirmed that in fact that is what has happened. We accept judicial lawmaking in our legal system, he said, because the judge is restrained by "the bulk and pressure of the rules that hedge him on every side."[53] These constraints on legal decision-making "curb judicial excesses and ensure that constitutional doctrine remains, by and large, governed by the rule of law rather than by the whim of the judges."[54] The advisory justices are impelled to communicate that they are not engaged merely in personal or arbitrary pronouncements. In a government of balanced and limited powers, they must constantly express that they are keeping within limits. That is the general condition of legitimacy, and on that "the legitimacy of judicial decrees depends."[55]

Advising justices, freed from the constraints of the adjudicative process, rhetorically and to some extent procedurally reintroduce the constraints and make clear they are doing so. The advising justices' recourse to the forms and language of precedent invokes a fundamental tenet of Anglo-American judicial reasoning, which requires the court to limit itself to "finding" the basis for its decision in previous cases. Supreme court opinions, to the extent that they assert new legal doctrine, must do so in ways that respect "one of the half-truths of the common law," that judges may not make law, they must find it.[56] This is a key protection because the "legitimacy of judicial decrees depends" not merely on the judges not being engaged in "making personal political judgments," but on "public confidence" that they are not doing so. Put in other terms, judicial opinions' function "is to defend specific structures, processes and practices by suggesting they are good, natural, traditional, in the general interest or a matter of common sense."[57]

---

[52] THE FEDERALIST No. 78, 496 (1788) (Benjamin F. Wright ed.,). "Define" is used in the senses of "to limit" or "to restrict," and "to state precisely." *See* OXFORD ENGLISH DICTIONARY, "Define" (definitions 3 and 5).

[53] BENJAMIN CARDOZO, THE NATURE OF THE JUDICIAL PROCESS 137 (1921). On the relation of judicial restraints to judicial activism, and the relation of both to advisory opinions in one state, see June F. Entman, *Flawed Activism: The Tennessee Supreme Court's Advisory Opinions on Joint Tort Liability and Summary Judgment*, 24 MEM. ST. U. L. REV. 193, 194–200 (1994).

[54] Suzanna Sherry, *Putting the Law Back in Constitutional Law*, 25 CONSTITUTIONAL COMMENTARY 461 (2009).

[55] Cox, 362. *See also* Mel A. Topf, *Communicating Legitimacy in U.S. Supreme Court Opinions*, 12 LANGUAGE AND COMMUNICATION 17 (1992); G. Edward White, *The Evolution of Reasoned Elaboration: Jurisprudential Criticism and Social Change*, 59 VA. L. REV. 279, 298–300 (1973) (A judge's legitimacy arises from one "traditional means of protecting the public from judicial fiat: the requirement . . . that the judges give reasons for their results, and consequent disqualification of certain types of reasons as nothing more than illegitimate statements of personal preference. . . . [L]egitimacy is tied to the reasoning process in opinions.").

[56] P. A. Hamburger, *The Development of the Nineteenth-Century Consensus Theory of Contract*, 7 LAW AND HIST. REV. 241, 243 (1989).

[57] HOWARD GILLMAN, THE CONSTITUTION BESIEGED: THE RISE AND DEMISE OF LOCHNER ERA POLICE POWERS JURISPRUDENCE 16 (1993).

Another way of accomplishing this is for advising justices to rely on the agonistic grammar operating within the judicial context. Permitting briefs and arguments in the advisory opinion process not only allows interested parties to have their say (recruiting to the advisory process the legitimating force of due process). They also allow the justices to compose advisory opinions integrating the often opposing arguments of the participants into their reasoning, thereby grafting onto advisory opinions not merely a customary mode of writing judicial decisions but grafting also a core characteristic of the Anglo-American judicial process—its adversarial nature. A court has few formal means of discovering facts or truth other than through disputing parties.[58] By carrying over to advisory opinions such devices from the adjudicative process, the advisory justices are informing the advisory process with adjudicatory constraints, the "strict rules and precedents," which the advisory opinion process in and of itself so clearly lacks and which are the hallmarks of limits on judicial power.[59] Justice Cardozo, on the bench of New York's high court, confirmed the state's rejection of advisory opinions in part because of the ease of confusion of judicial roles, with the propensity of judges to remain, or fall back into, being a judge rather than an advisor.[60] In short, advisory justices are engaged in grafting on to the advisory process the adjudicatory constraints that the advisory opinion process lacks.

Another important factor in the blurring of distinctions between advisory opinions and adjudicated decisions is the stature of the judiciary. It is simply difficult to accept that a pronouncement by the justices of a state's supreme court on the constitutionality of an act carries no legal weight. Justices rendering advisory opinions sit in the same court, on the same bench, in the same robes of office, publish their advice in the same reports, and use the same rhetoric and reasoning, as they do when they sit as a court. Yet in asserting the nonbinding doctrine the justices are insisting that the world accept advisory opinions as entirely nonjudicial expressions of individual opinions, completely outside the supreme court's "real" work, the justices rendering advice, as it were, in their off hours, when they may "go fishing, play golf, or advise the governor and legislature on matters of constitutional law."[61]

---

[58] The role of adversarial conflict in legitimizing advisory opinions is discussed in Chapter 6. On the historically central role of adversarial fact, see S. F. C. MILSOM, HISTORICAL FOUNDATION OF THE COMMON LAW 42 (1981). *See also* A. S. Miller & J. A. Barron, *The Supreme Court, the Adversary System, and the Flow of Information to the Justices: A Preliminary Inquiry*, 61 VA. L. REV. 1187, 1189 (1975); Two authors who discuss the continental, inquisitorial, system's omission of indication of argument in opinions are Bernard Rudden, *Courts and Codes in England, France, and Soviet Russia*, 48 TULANE L. REV. 1010, 1015 (1974); and J. GILLIS WETTER, THE STYLES OF APPELLATE JUDICIAL OPINIONS 50–51 (1960).

[59] The Florida supreme court adopted, by rules amending the advisory opinion procedure, several indicia of litigated proceedings. The rules now require that advisory opinions be in writing, signed by the justices agreeing to the opinion. Also, "concurrence of four Justices shall be required in all advisory opinions." The latter rule seems to be at odds with the view that advisory opinions are the opinions of individual justices. Fla. Stat. Ann., Rule 2.1(h).

[60] *Connolly v. Scudder*, 160 N.E. 655, 662 (1928).

[61] Sands, *Government by Judiciary—Advisory Opinions in Alabama*, 4.

The insistence has long gone unheeded. In the earliest of law review articles on advisory opinions, Thayer referred in 1885 to "a popular impression that [advisory opinions] are on the same footing as decisions in litigated cases."[62] Few if any have ever disagreed. A half-century later a writer observed that "the [advisory] opinions are talked of by the recipients and the press as official action."[63] Another quarter century later, another wrote that "[p]ublic attitude on advisory opinions indicates that they are considered as official court pronouncements binding on future governmental action."[64] And two decades after that (in 1992), another writer confirmed that "the citizenry does not distinguish between advisory opinions and real cases."[65] Even the scholars who study supreme courts freely refer to advisory opinions as "decisions" and "rulings," as do the media who quote the scholars.

The Massachusetts senate sought an advisory opinion on a bill to establish civil unions for same-sex couples. The bill distinguished civil unions from marriages but provided that the former would have all "benefits, protections, rights and responsibilities" of latter. The senate's question was whether this accords with equal protection and due process requirements of the state constitution. The justices advised that the bill violated those requirements and was unconstitutional.[66] The *New York Times* had three articles on the opinion, and, its reputation for accuracy notwithstanding, all three consistently referred to the advisory opinion as a "decision" or a "ruling" and nowhere made clear that it was an advisory opinion, much less that it was not binding on anyone. The online article appearing the same day as the advisory opinion referred to the "decision" a half dozen times.[67] The following day the *Times* reported the advisory opinion as its page one lead article, referring to it consistently as a "ruling," again with no indication that the opinion was advisory only.[68] The day after that, the *Times* published a feature article on what it called the decision, with focus on the animosity between the majority and minority justices. (Four of the seven justices joined in the majority opinion; two justices wrote "separate" opinions advising that the senate bill was constitutional, with the seventh justices joining one of them.) The article quoted several scholars, one of whom "follows the [Supreme Judicial] court closely," and another of whom edited a history of the three-hundred-year-old Massachusetts high court. Both described the

---

[62] James Bradley Thayer, *Advisory Opinions*, *in* LEGAL ESSAYS 58 (1908; 1st ed. 1885). A Note in *Harvard Law Review* a few years later agreed, observing that "the daily press is apt to forget" that advisory opinions are "of a merely advisory character." Note, 3 HARV. L. REV. 228 (1889).

[63] Preston W. Edsall, *The Advisory Opinion in North Carolina*, 27 N.C. L. REV. 297, 332 (1949).

[64] T. A. Smijanich, *Advisory Opinions in Florida: An Experiment in Intergovernmental Cooperation*, 24 U. FLA. L. REV. 328, 333 (1972).

[65] Cynthia R. Farina, *Supreme Judicial Court Advisory Opinions: Two Centuries of Interbranch Dialogue*, *in* THE HISTORY OF THE LAW IN MASSACHUSETTS: THE SUPREME JUDICIAL COURT 1692–1992 at 353, 389 (Russell K. Osgood ed., 1992).

[66] *In re Opinion of the Justices to the Senate*, WL 202184 (2004).

[67] Terence Neilan, *Gays Have Full Marriage Rights, Massachusetts Court Says*, NYTIMES.COM, Feb. 4, 2004. Retrieved from NEW YORK TIMES website Feb. 5, 2004.

[68] Pam Belluck, *Massachusetts Gives New Push to Gay Marriage*, NEW YORK TIMES, Feb. 5, 2004, at A1.

opinion as a decision, and the article nowhere indicates that it was an advisory opinion.[69] The *New York Times* and the scholars it quoted were wrong only in the technical and theoretical senses. The world quite simply treats advisory opinions as decisions, that is, as binding, precedent-setting supreme court rulings. Writers on legal issues may often disagree with each other, but not here. One writer after another concurs. Entirely typical is one, among many, who comments that advisory opinions are only "superficially voluntary and advisory," but in fact are "binding upon the branch seeking the opinion";[70] and another notes simply that in Florida "The Governor . . . considers advisory opinions binding."[71]

Thayer was concerned about this even in 1885. He believed it to be "of grave importance that the notion of their binding quality should be dispelled."[72] But it never would be. It would be relevant here to consider the observers who have counterargued that the nonbinding doctrine is in fact more than empty declarations of the advising justices, but this author could find none. The nonbinding doctrine is a failure. The Maine chief justice complained in 1908 that advisory opinions, though "theoretically only advisory, . . . are often cited as judicial authority and the people are prone to regard them as adjudications to be adhered to despite all argument to the contrary."[73] As the chief justice intimates, it is not only a matter of an ignorant public and superficial media. The requesting authorities and the legal community have always cited advisory opinions as binding. A researcher's study of five advisory states found that advisory opinions were cited as authority an average of six times each, and he concluded that they "are used as precedents by the bar, by the courts, and by the public. They are cited in briefs, in decisions of the courts, and despite the fact that they are sometimes carefully distinguished from judicial decisions, they are relied on as fully as decisions are, so far as precedent is concerned."[74] A Michigan justice complained in his concurring advisory opinion that although "an advisory opinion is not an adjudicative decision of the Court and is not binding . . . our advisory opinions are read by the public, the profession, the Governor and the Senate as a definitive expression of our views."[75] The Massachusetts justices assert their refusal to allow advisory opinions to influence them when they have the same questions before them in litigated cases;

---

[69] Pam Belluck, *Court Majority v. Dissenters in Bitter Massachusetts Case*, NEW YORK TIMES, Feb. 6, 2004, at A17 (quoting R. Michael Cassidy of Boston College Law School on "how much they [the justices] struggled over this decision," and Russell K. Osgood, President of Grinnell College, on the justices' "bold decision"). The news account in the *Providence* [Rhode Island] *Journal* refers to "the court's advisory opinion," correctly noting the opinion was advisory, though incorrectly indicating it was the court's, rather than the individual justices,' opinion, and nowhere noting that it was nonbinding. Raphael Lewis, *Court Reaffirms Same-Sex Marriage*, PROVIDENCE JOURNAL, Feb. 5, 2004, at A1.

[70] Bledsoe, *The Advisory Opinion in North Carolina: 1947 to 1991*, 1896.

[71] Smiljanich, *Advisory Opinions in Florida*, 333.

[72] Thayer, *Advisory Opinions*, 59.

[73] Lucilius A. Emery, *Advisory Opinions from Justices*, 2 ME. L. REV. 1, 2 (1908).

[74] Oliver P. Field, *The Advisory Opinion—An Analysis*, 24 INDIANA L.J. 203, 216 (1949).

[75] *Advisory Opinions re Constitutionality of 1972 PA 294*, 208 N.W.2d 469 483 (Mich. 1973) (Levin, J., concurring).

as they themselves say, they "carefully . . . guard against any influence flowing from" the advisory opinion.[76] But, one writer observes, "in Massachusetts advisory opinions are freely cited."[77] Another notes that the extent to which the Alabama justices disregard their clearly stated nonbinding doctrine is an "eye-opener."[78] The advisory justices, in short, "do, in fact, treat their advisory opinions as very forceful precedent."[79] This can hardly be unexpected. Even "if the advice were incorrect, rumor has it that judges of high courts are slower to see error in their own work than in that of others."[80] At any rate, observers without exception have confirmed this not only in advisory states but in nonadvisory states as well.[81]

This may place lower courts in the advisory opinion states in an awkward position when a case pending before one of them addresses the same question that the supreme court justices are asked to answer in response to an advisory opinion request. One writer offers several examples where lower courts in Florida simply announce, apparently as a matter of policy, that they would abide by whatever advice the Florida supreme court gives on a pending issue.[82] A case in Rhode Island provides a remarkable instance of a trial court, in mid-proceeding, waltzing around an expected advisory opinion, also in mid-proceeding. In 1999 a trial court judge granted the governor a preliminary injunction blocking the state lottery commission's approval to increase the number of video slot machines at a dog-racing track and at a jai alai fronton, both private commercial enterprises. The governor had argued that the lottery commission violated the state constitution's separation of powers provision because it was an executive body with legislators not only sitting on it, but comprising a majority of its nine members. At that point in time the justices were preparing an advisory opinion on separation of powers,

---

[76] *City of Boston v. Treasurer & Receiver Gen.*, 130 N.E. 390, 391 (Mass. 1921).

[77] Edsall, *The Advisory Opinion in North Carolina*, 380.

[78] Sands, *Government by Judiciary—Advisory Opinions in Alabama*, 14.

[79] Hagemann, 297. Smiljanich notes cases in which the Florida justices stated that advisory opinions are persuasive as judicial precedents and usually adhered to. Smiljanich, *Advisory Opinions in Florida*, 312.

[80] Edsall, *The Advisory Opinion in North Carolina*, 332.

[81] *E.g.*, Pascal F. Calogero, *Advisory Opinions: A Wise Change for Louisiana and Its Judiciary?*, 38 Loyola L. Rev. 329, 331 (1992) (citing litigated decisions relying on advisory opinions in Colorado, Louisiana, Maine, Massachusetts, Texas, Washington, and Wyoming); Hagemann, *The Advisory Opinion in South Dakota*, 302–03 (South Dakota justices, despite assertions that their advisory opinions are nonbinding, have cited their own advisory opinions as precedent.); Mel A. Topf, *The Advisory Opinion on Separation of Powers: The Uncertain Contours of Advisory Opinion Jurisprudence in Rhode Island*, 5 Roger Williams U. L. Rev. 385, 410 (2000) (The Rhode Island justices rely extensively on advisory opinions as precedent.); George Neff Stevens, *Advisory Opinions—Present Status and an Evaluation*, 34 Wash. L. Rev. 1, 6–7 (1959) (As "a practical matter . . . the courts . . . recognize that advisory opinions carry real weight . . . and are cited quite frequently in later cases both at home and in other jurisdictions."). Farina's study of advisory opinions in Massachusetts concludes that the justices do not have a history of reversing their advisory opinions in litigated decisions. Farina, *Supreme Judicial Court Advisory Opinions*, 369. For a qualifying view, see Persky, *Ghosts That Slay*, 1232–33, arguing that references to advisory opinions in litigated cases are merely persuasive rather than dispositive. Persky's analysis shows that, of advisory opinions rendered since 1990, 30 percent are never cited, 68 percent are cited fewer than three times, and the typical advisory opinion is cited only once. *Id.* at 1207–08.

[82] Robert H. Kennedy, *Advisory Opinions: Cautions About Non-Judicial Undertaking*, 23 U. Richmond L. Rev. 173, 194, notes. 61, 66 (1989).

involving just the issue raised in the litigated case involving rights of private parties. In an instance of the tail wagging the dog, the trial judge announced he would suspend proceedings until the advisory opinion was rendered. He issued the preliminary injunction because he wanted to "hold matters approximately in the status quo" in light of the "pendency of the request by the Governor for an advisory opinion."[83] The judge was "looking to the Supreme Court for ultimate guidance," so he ordered a status conference scheduled for the day after whatever day the advisory opinion would be issued, "for the purpose, basically in seeing what the advisory opinion . . . has said and what steps, if any, should be taken as a result thereof."[84] The lottery commission, however, appealed the judge's preliminary injunction to the supreme court, which scheduled oral argument on the appeal.[85]

The supreme court justices issued their advisory opinion on separation of powers on June 29, and the hearing on the lottery commission's appeal was held on June 30. At the hearing, the awkwardness was apparent. The attorney representing the lottery commission, which supported allowing legislators to serve on the commission, noted that the trial judge had repeatedly referred to the expected advisory opinion and argued that the advisory opinion rendered the previous day supported the lottery commission's position.[86] When the trial judge later ruled that the injunction be lifted, he said that he had "read and reread" the purportedly nonbinding advisory opinion, and he "inescapably" concluded that "it would be intellectually and legally wrong" to keep the injunction in force since the justices "inferentially" answered the question at issue in the trial court. (In the advisory opinion the justices expressly declined to answer the question.) The judge issued a final decision in the case several months later, ruling that the statute in question was unconstitutional in that it improperly required that members of the legislature be appointed to the lottery commission.[87] The extent to which the trial judge's decision danced around the elephant in the room is impressive. Over half the decision's section on the history of the case is devoted to the advisory opinion, and the decision makes considerable efforts to juggle reliance on relevant statements in the advisory opinion on the one hand with those statements being officially nonbinding on the other. "The court is aware that Advisory Opinions issued by our Supreme Court . . . are of 'limited precedential effect.'"[88] (The phrase the judge adopted was one of the supreme court's recent, weaker assertions of nonbinding doctrine. Previous statements, including the court's first, were categorical: advisory opinions, the justices said in 1856, "can have

---

[83] Transcript of hearing before Hon. Michael A. Silverstein, June 9, 1999, at 18–19. Background on the lottery commission case is taken from the transcript and from Tom Mooney, *Court Blocks Expansion of Video Slots*, Providence Journal Bulletin, June 10, 1999, at A1; and Tom Mooney, *Ruling on Slots Heads to Top Court*, Providence Journal Bulletin, June 11, 1999, at A1. The advisory opinion on separation of powers itself is discussed in Chapter 6.

[84] Transcript of Hearing, 19.

[85] *See Almond v. Rhode Island Lottery Comm'n*, No. PC 99-2323, at 3–4 (July 27, 1999).

[86] From notes of the author, who attended the supreme court hearing on June 30, 1999.

[87] *Almond* at 14–15 (Oct. 27, 1999).

[88] *Id.* at 2–5; 9 (quoting from *In re Advisory to the Governor*, 732 A.2d 55, 73 (R.I. 1999).

no weight as a precedent."[89]) "Be that as it may," the judge's decision continues, "the Majority Advisory Opinion . . . represents the view of four of the five justices presently sitting on our Supreme Court and is highly persuasive, if not binding, upon this Court."[90] Since the justices said they declined to answer the question at issue, while the trial judge said they did answer it "inferentially," the judge's decision goes on awkwardly to note that the majority justices "declined to respond to certain questions propounded to them." But while they did not "directly" answer the questions, the justices "did make particular reference" to legislators serving on boards and commissions, and appointing others to do so, and the justices did say that proper procedure for changing this practice is a constitutional amendment. The decision then notes that none of this is dispositive for the case at hand. Then the judge goes on to decide the case on other grounds.[91]

Thus the ambiguity and strain arising from advisory opinions that are nonbinding in theory but impossible to disregard in practice. All this notwithstanding, the justices in most advisory opinion states persist in declaring their nonbinding doctrine. It may be unique in state constitutional jurisprudence. Justices insist on the truth and effect of a doctrine that is universally disbelieved, rejected, or merely ignored, even by the justices themselves, who seem to invoke the nonbinding doctrine with "an all-too-cavalier attitude toward the unique circumstances by which advisory opinions are issued."[92] It is, if nothing else, unreasonable to expect anyone to accept the doctrine when even the justices do not do so in practice, whatever their assertions about their theory. Advisory opinions are, after all, as the Delaware justices said, "what one would expect the Justices to say if the issue had been presented to them in litigation."[93] It would indeed be "absurdly naïve" to believe that an advisory opinion of a majority of the justices does not indicate "how that court would hold if the same questions were to come up later in actual litigation."[94] It is an easy prediction, then, that the requesting authorities comply with the advice rendered, and that indeed is the fact. They rarely take action not consistent with the justices' advice.[95] "Legislative and executive action is almost certain to be based on it."[96] And, in his comprehensive study of all advisory opinion states, Albert Ellingwood concluded in 1918 that advisory opinions "have been received, for the most part, with all the deference accorded to the solemn decision of a court of last resort. Both the legislative department and the executive department have usually treated the pronouncement of these opinions as final, and shaped their course of action accordingly."[97] A 1927 Maine decision in a litigated case followed closely the advice rendered in an

---

[89] *Taylor & Co. v. Place*, 4 R.I. 324, 362 (1856) (emphasis added).

[90] *Almond* at 9.

[91] *Id.* at 10–11.

[92] Persky, *Ghosts That Slay*, 1215.

[93] *Opinion of the Justices*, 413 A.2d 1245, 1248 (Del. 1980).

[94] Sands, *Government by Judiciary—Advisory Opinions in Alabama*, 25.

[95] Note, *Advisory Opinions on the Constitutionality of Statutes*, 69 Harv. L. Rev. 1302, 1311 (1956).

[96] P. C. McKeever & B. O. Perry, *The Case for an Advisory Function in the Federal Judiciary*, 50 Geo. L.J. 785, 791 (1962).

[97] Ellingwood, Departmental Cooperation, 154.

earlier advisory opinion on a similar question. The decision was direct on why this should be so.

> [Advisory opinions,] given to guide the Governor in the performance of a public and constitutional function of government, and having been followed, public policy, at least, requires that strong and compelling reasons be presented before the court sitting en banc will hold an act by the Chief Executive of this nature invalid when taken in pursuance of a construction of the organic law given upon request under the Constitution by a majority of the court.[98]

This is a reasonable functional definition of precedent.

A New Hampshire supreme court decision in a litigated case contradicted the advice the justices had given in an earlier advisory opinion on the same question. The court, significantly, felt the need to account for this, and of course it invoked nonbinding doctrine. "We reiterate that opinions of the justices are advisory opinions on the constitutionality of proposed legislation, and may not be entitled to weight equal to that given to judicial decisions following full adversary process."[99] The point here is that advisory justices can go either way, by way of having their judicial cake and eating it too. If the justices "decide to adopt a certain view in subsequent litigation, they can justify that adoption by appealing to the persuasiveness of the earlier [advisory] opinion. If they decide to abandon that view, they can dismiss the earlier opinion as nonbinding dicta."[100]

The only argument proffered to justify advisory opinions being binding in fact if not in theory is their "pure merit." If "because of the excellence of the opinions, great weight is accorded them, this is not a defect of the system."[101] But there is no evidence whatever that justices have ever sorted out advisory opinions according to their "merit." On the contrary, the inescapable fact is that "there is strong compulsion in these opinions" whatever their merit. Engaging in an act after the justices have advised that it is unconstitutional would be "rash indeed in a land where the judicial veto is universal."[102]

---

[98] *Fellows ex rel. Cummings v. Eastman*, 136 A. 810, 812 (Me. 1927).

[99] *Schoff v. City of Somersworth*, 630 A.2d 783, 785 (N.H. 1993); referring to *Opinion of the Justices*, 592 A.2d 180, 186 (N.H. 1991).

[100] Persky, *Ghosts That Slay*, 1175.

[101] Paul C. Clovis & Clarence M. Updegraff, *Advisory Opinions*, 13 Iowa L. Rev. 188, 195 (1927). Ellingwood takes as evidence that advisory opinions are "remarkably sound" that, despite being nonbinding, "as a rule, . . . they are commonly cited in regular cases, and have rarely been overruled in later cases." Ellingwood, Departmental Cooperation, 202. But, as Sands puts it, one "may question the fact that the courts themselves have tended to follow their own advisory opinions presents any evidence of the soundness of those opinions." Sands, *Government by Judiciary—Advisory Opinions in Alabama*, 21.

[102] Edsall, *The Advisory Opinion in North Carolina*, 331 (remarking that his study of North Carolina advisory opinions showed that those requesting the advice have followed it irrespective of merit, and in every case save one there has been no subsequent action contrary to the advice). Farina writes that with very few exceptions when the Massachusetts justices advised that a bill would be unconstitutional, the legislature either revised the bill according to the advice or put it aside. Farina, *Supreme Judicial Court Advisory Opinions*, 386, 388.

An offer of advice from the justices of the state's highest court is an offer that can't be refused.[103]

In light of all this, advisory opinions turn out to be illegitimate judicial review. The nonbinding doctrine is little more than a jurisprudential fig leaf, and it fails. The advisory opinion process, to the extent that it pronounces the constitutionality of an act, is de facto judicial review. As such it is difficult to defend the legitimacy of the process. Advisory opinions approach the judicial *in terrorem* pronouncements which Justice Frankfurter warned against as self-defeating,[104] and they do so under flimsy cover of claims of nonbinding, nonjudicial, individual advice-giving. The justices' purported personal opinions are asserted in the face of a fundamental principle of judicial self-restraint: the "rejection of personal preference."[105] True, the opinions are limited by the restrictions discussed earlier in this book, but these are nearly all justice-made and may be justice-waived, either one with or without explanation. Disturbingly, justices declare acts unconstitutional in advisory proceedings more freely than they do in adjudicated decisions.[106] This de facto judicial review is undertaken without such case or controversy limits as standing, ripeness, and mootness, often cited as important checks on judicial review.[107] The advisory justices' freedom from such constraints is aggravated by the abstract and hypothetical nature of advisory opinions, "the effect of which can neither be predicted nor controlled."[108] All this is rationalized by doubtful claims that the advice is nonbinding. At any rate, to the extent that advisory opinions are subject to criticism as inappropriate, courts cannot excuse this by declaring that those whom they advise are free to disregard it.[109]

---

[103] It is in some part a problem of ambivalence. Advice and rulings tend to employ the same imperative forms of language. Hobbes devotes most of a chapter of his *Leviathan* to "the confusion of Counsels and Commands, arising from the Imperative manner of speaking them both. . . . For the words *Doe this*, are the words of not onely him that Commandeth; but also of him that giveth Counsell." THOMAS HOBBES, LEVIATHAN, ch. XXV, 134 (1651; Everyman's Library ed. 1914).

[104] *Baker v. Carr*, 369 U.S. 186, 270 (Frankfurter, J., dissenting).

[105] HENERY J. ABRAHAM, THE JUDICIAL PROCESS 345 n. 52 (5th ed. 1986) (quoting PHILIP B. KURLAND, MR. JUSTICE FRANKFURTER AND THE SUPREME COURT 5 (1971)).

[106] Field, *The Advisory Opinions—An Analysis*, 212–13.

[107] *See, e.g., Ashwander v. Tenn. Valley Authority*, 297 U.S. 288, 345–46 (1936).

[108] Kennedy, *Advisory Opinions: Cautions About Non-Judicial Undertakings*, 198.

[109] *Id.* at 197–98.

6 }

Advisory Opinions and Judicial Supremacy

CONSTITUTIONALISM, A POLITICIZED JUDICIARY, AND THE ECLIPSE OF CIVIC DEBATE

Those who have given up on ordinary politics and the legislative process will not be unduly distressed if the most important controversies are entrusted to the courts for decision.[1]

The failure of the nonbinding doctrine leaves the justices' restrictions on rendering advice as the mainstay of the legitimacy of advisory opinions, which for all practical purposes, and notwithstanding all claims to the contrary carry, the force and weight of binding precedent. But what restrictions the justices may give, the justices may take away, raising major questions of the legitimacy of the advising jurisdiction and of the role of advisory opinions in an era of judicial supremacy.

Without Explanation: The Public Importance Exception and the Descent into Jurisprudential Fog

We have seen in chapters 2 and 3 that the advising justices developed restrictions on rendering advisory opinions, and did so to a great extent in response to the attacks and to their own reluctance to engage in advising, both grounded in concerns about due process, separation of powers, and politicization of the judiciary. We saw also that the justices developed a public importance exception, allowing for advisory opinions when a request violated one or more of their restrictions, in light, as the Florida justices put it, "of the irreparable harm to the public" that might result from permitting an unconstitutional law or action to go forward.[2] The public importance exception may have been intended to be exercised only rarely, but it may easily turn into a license to render advisory opinions beyond all limits regardless of purported standards and restrictions. That is in fact what has happened in some advisory states, and there is no reason doctrinally that it cannot happen in all of them. The Florida justices, for example, have since 1987

[1] MARY ANN GLENDON, RIGHTS TALK: THE IMPOVERISHMENT OF POLITICAL DISCOURSE 182 (1991).

[2] *In re Advisory Opinion to the Governor*, 374 So.2d 959, 962 (Fla. 1979).

begun advising in response to inappropriate questions "without explanation."[3] "The need for articulation of the purpose and standards is especially important," writes a critic, "where . . . the propriety of an advisory opinion request can no longer be determined by parsing the enabling language, by tracking constitutional history, or by analysis of the case law."[4] Going against their 1942 ruling that "emergencies do not create [judicial] power or authority,"[5] the Florida justices in 1987 asserted jurisdiction to advise the governor owing to "the chaotic impact on your constitutional duties" caused by the delay in waiting for a litigated case to result in a finding of unconstitutionality of the statute in question.[6] This assertion of the public importance exception, especially if it is without express standards or even without explanation, represents a significant expansion of judicial power.[7]

EXTREME EXAMPLE: RHODE ISLAND

Rhode Island represents an extreme example of this standardless and arbitrary application of the public importance exception. But it represents as well what may easily happen in any advisory opinion state. The public importance exception can readily turn into what one critic called an unconstitutional exercise of a nonjudicial power.[8] Let us look in Rhode Island at the development of a line of advisory opinions applying the public importance exception to see how an exception may slide from something extraordinary and requiring explanation, even defense, to something that is so routine as not even worth a passing comment. The development of the exception spotlights the tension in the dynamics of the political and the judicial inherent in the advisory opinion process but exacerbated by the questionable application of the public importance exception.

During their 1998–1999 term, the Rhode Island justices had before them one of the most politically contentious issues in the state's modern history: the common and longstanding practice of legislators serving, and appointing others to serve, on public and quasi-public executive branch boards and commissions. The governor requested an

---

[3] Kennedy, *Advisory Opinions: Cautions About Non-Judicial Undertakings*, 23 U. RICHMOND L. REV. 173, 182–84 (1989).

[4] *Id.* at 182.

[5] *In re Advisory Opinion to the Governor*, 9 So.2d 172, 176 (Fla. 1942), cited in this context in Kennedy, 183.

[6] *In re Advisory Opinion to the Governor*, 509 So.2d 292, 301 (Fla. 1987).

[7] On the similar use of the public importance exception to overcome mootness doctrine in state courts, see GEOFFREY C. HAZARD, JR., ET AL., PLEADING AND PROCEDURE: STATE AND FEDERAL 1366 (8th ed. 1999) (citing cases, e.g., *People ex rel Guggenheim v. Mucci*, 298 N.E.2d 109 (N.Y. 1973), holding that "an appeal should not be dismissed as moot if a question of general interest and substantial public importance is likely to recur"). "Likely to recur" is a qualification not adopted by the advising justices. On the federal level, Article III holds the courts to a stricter standard on mootness, and there is no public importance exception. HAZARD, PLEADING AND PROCEDURE, 1366.

[8] Thomas R. Bender, *Rhode Island's Public Importance Exception for Advisory Opinions: The Unconstitutional Exercise of a Non-Judicial Power*, 10 ROGER WILLIAMS U. L. REV. 123, 126 (2004) ("[O]n every occasion that the [Rhode Island] justices issue an advisory opinion pursuant to that exception they act outside their constitutional authority; that is, they themselves engage in an unconstitutional exercise.").

advisory opinion on the extent, if any, to which the practice violated the state constitution's separation of powers provision.[9] The justices' advisory opinion was "much anticipated." The state's major newspaper even had a lead article when the justices were "close to" issuing their opinion (or as the article put it, when the "Court" was close to "ruling").[10] The opinion came on June 29, 1999. The events leading to it began in October 1995, when the nine-member Rhode Island Ethics Commission voted unanimously to issue a revised draft of the code of ethics for public comment. Among its provisions was a new prohibition against legislators serving on or appointing others to serve on state boards and commissions.[11]

Ethics Commission members apparently had concerns early on, both about their authority to subject the legislature to the ban, and about the constitutionality of the ban itself. At a public hearing the following month on the proposal, they asked the governor, who was present, to seek an advisory opinion from the justices of the state supreme court. He promised to do so.[12] The following January the commission agreed to move ahead with developing the required procedures to implement the ban.[13] This triggered a quite public disagreement between the commission and its executive director, who strongly expressed doubts about the constitutionality of the commission's rule. It made page one: "According to [commission executive director] Healey, it would be a grave mistake for the commission to adopt broad rules that would ban legislators from serving on so-called quasi-public agencies. . . . Not only would the ban be unconstitutional, said Healey, but it would also severely damage the commission's credibility."[14] In a strange incident, the commission's legal counsel refused to offer his advice, without explanation and in the face of the executive director's insisting that it was his duty to do so. The legal counsel simply suggested that the commission hire a legal expert, and recommended Professor Geoffrey Hazard.[15] The commission retained Hazard, who agreed

---

[9] R.I. Const. art V (stating that "the powers of the government shall be distributed into three departments: the legislative, executive and judicial").

[10] Tom Mooney, *Court Close to Ruling on "Power" Case*, PROVIDENCE JOURNAL BULLETIN, June 18, 1999, at B1.

[11] Rhode Island Ethics Commission, *Code of Ethics (proposed)* 24 (Oct. 10, 1995). The record of the vote is in Rhode Island Ethics Commission, Minutes, Oct. 10, 1995. The proposed rule was: "No members of the general assembly shall serve as a member or participate in the appointment of any other person to serve as a member of the governing board of a quasi-public board, authority, or corporation while serving in the general assembly, said prohibition as to a member of the general assembly shall continue for a period of one (1) year after he or she leaves legislative office."

[12] Rhode Island Ethics Commission, *Proceedings at Hearing in re Code of Ethics (Proposed)* [transcript], Nov. 16, 1995, at 7.

[13] Rhode Island Ethics Commission, Minutes, Jan. 31, 1996.

[14] Randall Richard, *Ethics Panel Votes to Hire Legal Expert*, PROVIDENCE JOURNAL BULLETIN, July 27, 1996, at A1.

[15] Rhode Island Ethics Commission, Public Hearing [transcript], July 26, 1996, at 60. *See also* Randall Richard, at A1 ("Gary Yesser [Commission legal counsel]. . . demurred when [executive director] Healey suggested it was Yesser's job to advise the commission on the constitutionality of the proposed ban."); Rhode Island Ethics Commission, Minutes, July 26, 1996. No explanation was ever given for the legal counsel's refusal.

that the proposed ban exceeded the commission's constitutional authority.[16] Hazard's opinion notwithstanding, the commission adopted the ban on May 5, 1997 to take effect July 1, 1998.[17]

The governor asked the justices for an advisory opinion in November 1997. His letter inquired about the commission's authority to create the rule (Question 1) and about the constitutionality of legislators serving on boards and commissions (Questions 2 and 3). The governor did not inquire about the constitutionality of the regulation itself (Regulation 5014).[18] Soon after receiving the letter, the court issued an order inviting briefs.[19] In addition to those from the governor and ethics commission, twelve briefs amici curiae were filed, reflecting the degree of public interest. They included briefs from the senate, the house of representatives, the current and past attorneys general, the Rhode Island State Council of Churches, and the Rhode Island affiliate of the American Civil Liberties Union. Oral arguments before the justices took place in November 1998, lasting some five hours, with five proponents of the ban and seven opponents arguing. Nearly eight months later, on June 29, the justices rendered their advisory opinion. This was nearly four years after the ethics commission first put forth the ban, in this instance anyway belying the wisdom that advisory opinions are produced more speedily than litigated decisions.

During these four years there was almost no interest expressed in the fact that what the justices were asked to issue was an advisory opinion. No one seemed concerned that the justices' opinion would simply be advice, purportedly nonbinding and without force of precedent, or that the governor's request overstepped at least two prohibitions the justices imposed on such requests (discussed later). None of this played any part in the considerable public debate and media coverage over the nearly four years. Two of the briefs submitted did argue that the governor's questions were not proper. The governor's reply brief, somewhat defensively if not disingenuously, and perhaps owing to the failure to address the matter in his main brief, claimed to be surprised that the matter came up at all since the "Court did not appear to seek briefing on the propriety of the questions."[20] Yet the advisory opinion was an important step in the decade—long deviation by the justices from the carefully established restrictions on issuing advisory opinions, under the doubtful cover of the public importance exception.

The procedural deficiencies in the governor's request were substantial, and the justices' advisory opinion carefully noted them all. In the governor's Question 1, on

---

[16] Letter from Geoffrey C. Hazard to Rhode Island Ethics Commission, Aug. 9, 1996, quoted in *In re Advisory Opinion to the Governor*, 732 A.2d 55, 67 (R.I. 1999).

[17] Rhode Island Ethics Commission, Minutes, May 5, 1997. The regulation, codified as Regulation 36-14-5014, is hereafter referred to as Regulation 5014. The lengthy period between adoption and taking effect was apparently to permit time for the passage of the legislation required to change memberships of boards and commissions that included legislators or legislative appointees.

[18] Letter from the Governor to the Justices of the Supreme Court, Nov. 20. 1997.

[19] Rhode Island Supreme Court, *Order*, Nov. 26, 1997.

[20] *Reply Brief of the Governor to the Justices*, Nov. 20, 1997, 4–5. The two briefs that raised the issues were those from the Senate's majority leader and from the ACLU.

whether the ethics commission had authority to adopt Regulation 5014, the justices found two defects. First, the justices said, they will not advise the governor on pending legislation, but will advise the governor only when the governor's questions "concern the constitutionality of *existing* statutes which require implementation by the Chief Executive."[21] This restriction, wherein the justices will advise the governor only on laws already enacted and the legislature only on pending legislation, is one the justices have applied at least since 1965.[22] Second, the justices will not advise the governor unless the question propounded has "a bearing upon a present constitutional duty awaiting performance by the Chief Executive." Here, they said, at "the time of your request [November 20, 1997], and indeed at the present time, Regulation 5014 has not become effective and this does not concern any constitutional duty presently awaiting performance by Your Excellency."[23]

The governor seemed not to be concerned. His attempts at identifying his purported constitutional duties awaiting performance were perfunctory and vague. His letter to the justices said only that the presence of legislators or their appointees on public boards and commissions exercising executive power "affects the constitutional responsibility of the Executive branch to execute faithfully the law passed by the General Assembly," and that "whether the regulation [5014] is constitutional is a question that directly affects the performance of my duties." The only duty the governor referred to was the duty to make "numerous appointments to boards and commissions exercising executive powers."[24] But the justices had already made clear in 1993, and in fact decades before, that this is not a constitutionally vested duty.[25] The senate's brief forcefully and accurately pointed to this deficiency, arguing that "*none* of the questions propounded has *any* relationship to the official duties of the Governor."[26] In his reply brief, the governor was indignant but evasive and vague. "It is difficult to take this [the senate's] position seriously. Never has a question been more relevant to the official constitutional duty of the Governor of the State of Rhode Island than the separation of powers question presently before this Court."[27] During oral argument the governor's legal counsel was entirely silent on this point until the chief justice asked, "Should the court answer the questions? . . . Does the governor have an imminent duty?" The counsel replied, yes, and without identifying any such duty promptly left the subject and moved on.[28] A third defect in the governor's request for advice was one the justices did not mention, that the governor was seeking the advice for a third party, the ethics commission, as the governor's letter to the justices made clear (the "Commission requested that I seek the advice

---

[21] *In re Advisory Opinion to the Governor*, 732 A.2d at 59.

[22] *Opinion to the House of Reps.*, 208 A.2d 126, 128 (R.I. 1965).

[23] *In re Advisory Opinion to the Governor*, 732 A.2d at 59.

[24] Letter from the Governor, at 1.

[25] *In re Advisory from* [*sic*] *the Governor*, 633 A.2d 664, 666 (R.I. 1993), quoting *In re Decision of Justices*, 69 A. 555, 559 (R.I. 1908).

[26] *Brief of the Majority Leader*, at 11. The brief of the ACLU makes the same point, at 6–7.

[27] Governor's reply brief, at 4–5.

[28] Oral argument, Nov. 10, 1998. From notes of the author, who attended.

of the Justices . . ."), and the ACLU brief emphasized it pointedly. (The "mere fact that the request is on the Governor's stationery does not change the underlying reality that the request has, in essence, emanated from the Ethics Commission.")[29]

The governor was right in not being concerned about all these clear defects to his Question 1. Usually, the justices said in their advisory opinion, in light of a defective question, "consistent with long established precedent of this Court, we would ordinarily refrain from responding to Your Excellency's request." But the justices proceeded to give an answer, asserting the public importance of the question, which, they said, "is a significant constitutional issue of great public interest sufficient to transcend these infirmities. Therefore, in deference to Your Excellency's concern, we proceed to respond to your inquiry notwithstanding the significant procedural deficiencies."[30]

The justices found a defect in the governor's Questions 2 and 3 as well. The questions, on whether legislators sitting on public boards and commissions offend separation of powers, were defective because answering them would require the justices to engage in fact-finding. The justices (or "this Court," they say) "will not issue advisory opinions which require a direct or indirect exercise of our fact-finding power." The basis for this is that the justices render advisory opinions "as individuals and not as the judicial department of state government," and fact-finding inheres in the court as the judicial branch. The justices in their individual capacities "therefore lack the power to issue advisory opinions which implicate fact-finding," they say, citing their 1963 opinion setting this standard.[31]

The fact-finding that would be required to answer Questions 2 and 3, the justices stated, is to determine which of the public boards and commissions were executive in nature. The "classification of the boards as executive or otherwise requires fact-intensive investigation of the nature, purpose, membership, and operation of each board and commission." Further, "even determining the number of boards to which our advisory opinion would apply would require the exercise of fact-finding powers." Therefore the justices refuse to answer Questions 2 and 3.[32]

The justices' explanation clarifies little or nothing. Why is it necessary to identify all the state's executive boards, in order to advise on the general question of whether it is constitutional for legislators to sit on *any* executive branch board? The justices did not say. Even less relevant is the number of executive boards. Why is it necessary to determine the number to which they advisory opinion may apply? The governor's questions

---

[29] ACLU brief at 7–8. On the justices' bar against third-party requests, see *Opinion to the Governor*, 284 A.2d 295 (R.I. 1971), where the justices refused to advise since the governor sought advice for a city council on a matter that had no relation to the governor's duties.

[30] *In re Advisory Opinion to the Governor*, 732 A.2d at 59. The justices' answer to Question 1 was that the ethics commission lacked the power to enact Regulation 5014, since it "fundamentally alters the constitutional structure of the state. . . . The ethics commission is not a constitutional convention." *Id.* at 71–72.

[31] *In re Advisory Opinion to the Governor*, 732 A.2d at 72, quoting *Opinion to the Governor*, 191 A.2d 611, 614 (R.I. 1963).

[32] *In re Advisory Opinion to the Governor*, 732 A.2d at 72 and 73.

would seem to apply whether there are two boards or two hundred. Why was the question of whether the governor has a present constitutional duty requiring performance not an issue for Questions 2 and 3 if they were an issue for Question 1? The justices did not say. Having established purported defects in Questions 2 and 3, the justices refused to answer those questions, in obvious contrast to Question 1. Why did they not waive the defects on the same public importance grounds that they waived the defects of Question 1? The public importance they identified is of course the same. The justices did not say. They simply waived the defects in one question, and not in the other two, without explanation.

Further, the justices in fact did not refrain from answering Questions 2 and 3. They offered at some length their opinion about the constitutionality of legislators sitting, and appointing others to sit, on state boards and commissions. Then, they later declared their refusal to answer the questions. In their answer they looked into the history of the state's fundamental law and found no bars to the legislature's power of appointment, by separation of powers principles or otherwise.[33] They went back to the state's original royal charter of 1663, which, they said, gave the legislature unlimited powers, including the power "to appoint persons, including from its own membership, to all governmental bodies."[34] Why a colonial charter, with no semblance of anything relating to separation of powers, would be at all relevant the justices did not say. The justices further noted that the legislature, under the state's first constitution, of 1842, like legislatures in most states, have plenary and reserved, rather than enumerated, powers. This, they said, did not change with the new constitution of 1986, which retained the legislature's reserved powers.[35] In short, the justices concluded that the legislature appointing its members or others to executive boards and commissions is constitutionally sound, and that the only way to bar the legislature from doing so is by constitutional amendment.[36] Why did the justices in fact answer the questions, then later in their opinion say they refuse to do so? They did not say.

The justices also answered a question the governor did not ask, about the constitutionality of the ethics commission's Regulation 5014 itself. They volunteered that the regulation is unconstitutional, not owing to issues regarding separation of powers or the limits of the ethics commission's authority, but rather because it has a "self-executing presumption of universal conflict of interest and conclusive guilt based on status as a legislator," in violation of the "ancient and venerable principle" that a person is presumed innocent until proven otherwise.[37]

---

[33] *Id.* at 63–65.

[34] *Id.* at 63.

[35] *Id.* at 63–64. *See* R.I. Const. art. VI, sec. 10. Rhode Island was one of the two states (with Connecticut) that retained its colonial charter after Independence in 1776, ratifying its first constitution in 1842. The 1842 constitution established a three-branch government, but it included no clear statement of separation of powers. A separation provision would be added by amendment to the 1986 constitution in 2004.

[36] 732 A.2d at 62–63.

[37] *Id.* at 66.

Among the many problems with this advisory opinion, the public importance exception stands out. The apparently inconsistent if not arbitrary way the exception was employed requires a closer look at just what the Rhode Island justices were doing. What they were doing was significantly, if somewhat crudely, expanding judicial supremacy. In the separation of powers advisory opinion the justices invoked the exception to answer one defective question and ignored it when they refused to answer the other two questions. The justices did not account for why they invoked the exception in one instance, or why they did not in the others. This lack of clarity, explanation, definition, or predictability would be fairly typical of the justices' invocations of the public importance exception. There is nothing inherent in the advisory opinion jurisdiction, in Rhode Island or in the other advisory states, that governs, defines, or in any way limits this sort of invocation of the public importance exception.

Since developing their set of restrictions on rendering advisory opinions beginning in 1937, the Rhode Island justices adhered to them until 1986 with few exceptions. In the half-century from 1937 through 1985 the justices received ninety-nine requests for advisory opinions. They refused, in all or in part, thirty of the requests, about 30 percent, nearly all for failing to comply with one or more of their restrictions. During these years the justices waived their restrictions only twice, in neither instance basing it on a public importance exception.[38] This changed dramatically in 1986. In the twenty-five years from 1986 through 2010, the justices waived their restrictions in seven advisory opinions, out of total of twenty-eight requests for advice sent to them. They refused to answer five requests (about 18 percent), all or in part (including the partial refusal in the opinion on separation of powers).[39]

The ground for all seven waivers of the justices' restrictions since 1986 has been the same, and it is unprecedented and unique among the advisory opinion states in its scope—public importance. Since the inception of the advisory opinion clause in the state's first constitution of 1842, the justices applied that exception only once before 1986, in 1893, owing to what they called the "gravity of the situation" in that case.[40] The evolution of the justices' increasingly standardless use of the exception since 1986

---

[38] *Opinion to the Governor*, 170 A.2d 908 (R.I. 1961) (waiving the restriction against advising when the request does not specify the particular provision of the constitution implicated); *In re Opinion to the House of Reps.*, 5 A.2d 455 (R.I. 1939) (waiving restriction against rendering advice involving case pending in court). In a third instance the justices said they would have rendered advice to the senate despite restriction against doing so when a house has adjourned *sine die*, except that the answer would have been moot by the time the justices could have given it. *Opinion to the Senate*, 271 A.2d 810 (R.I. 1970).

[39] Persky similarly analyzes Rhode Island advisory opinions from 1990 to 2004, and finds that of the sixteen requests for advice during that time, thirteen were answered. Five of them had defects which were waived on public importance grounds. "Only twice did the [Rhode Island] justices find no public importance that could cure the procedural defects in the request." Jonathan D. Persky, *Ghosts That Slay: A Contemporary Look at State Advisory Opinions*, 37 Conn. L. Rev. 1155, 1192–93 (2005).

[40] *In re Legislative Adjournment*, 27 A. 324, 325–26 (R.I. 1893) (holding that the justices need not "take notice" of a question from the house of representatives since the house was not in session because the governor prorogued the legislature, but that they will answer owing to the "gravity of the situation" and "the importance of the principles and rights involved," which "are a sufficient warrant").

is significant. In the first of the seven advisory opinions with waivers on public importance grounds, the justices took considerable care in accounting for the waiver. The question presented to them was whether the state's conflict of interest statute required a state-appointed official, who was a member of a state agency, to resign from the agency when a business in which the official had an interest came before the commission, or whether he need only recuse himself. The same issue was being litigated before the state ethics commission, so that advising would violate the justices' restriction against advisory opinions when the question asked is involved in pending litigation either judicially or administratively.[41] But the issue, they explained, pointed to a threat to the governor's ability to persuade qualified people to assume public office. Hence, the "public interest," the justices said, "requires us to respond."[42]

In this and in the second and third advisory opinions that applied the public importance exception, the justices suggested that the exception is to be invoked only with deliberateness and in exceptional circumstances. In the first opinion applying the exception the justices referred to the "extreme conditions" that would warrant such an exception.[43] They cited a 1959 refusal to advise, in which the justices indicated that answering a question while the question was involved in pending litigation would require "*more extreme conditions than now appear*."[44] The italicized standard, emphasized in 1959 and applied without qualification a quarter century later, would suggest the justices were setting a reasonably clear, and high, bar for invoking the public importance exception. The second advisory opinion applying the exception seems to confirm this. The justices were responding to a question concerning the removal of the chief justice, jointly submitted by the governor and both houses of the legislature. The justices said that the request violated their restriction against joint requests, and also against requests where the governor lacks a constitutional duty awaiting performance, and against requests made absent a formal vote in either house requesting the advice. Here, though, the justices rendered advice, citing "the profoundly important substantive issues." Perhaps because this was the second time within one year that they applied the public importance waiver, they stressed that they were not binding themselves to the waiver. The justices "shall not consider this action as a precedent indicating that in the future we shall render an advisory opinion when the requesting petition is improperly before this court."[45]

In the third advisory opinion applying the public importance exception, the justices waived the pending litigation restriction citing the "public importance" of the question. They referred to the first opinion applying the exception, where, they said, "this court noted that, despite our established practice of refraining from rendering advisory opinions when the questions propounded are involved in litigation, there are extreme

---

[41] *E.g.*, *Opinion to the House of Representatives*, 443 A.2d 944 (R.I. 1981) (refusing advice owing to pending litigation in superior court); *In re Advisory Opinion to the Governor*, 492 A.2d 134 (R.I. 1985) (refusing advice owing to pending litigation in administrative proceeding).

[42] *In re Advisory Opinion to the Governor*, 504 A.2d 456, 459 (R.I. 1986).

[43] *Id.* at 458–59.

[44] *Opinion to the House of Reps.*, 149 A.2d 343, 345 (R.I. 1959).

[45] *In re Advisory Opinion*, 507 A.2d 1316, 1318–19 (R.I. 1986).

circumstances involving the public interest in which we shall respond."[46] These three advisory opinions each clearly asserted two conditions for invoking the public importance exception. First, it requires "extreme" circumstances. Second, any such invocation establishes no precedent. The justices did, however, leave the exception open-ended, never addressing standards for determining "extreme circumstances," or for when the exception may be invoked and when not, so that requesting authorities could have some guidance. They did not explain an earlier refusal to advise the governor despite a claim from the governor of public importance, telling him in 1959 that if he thought his questions were "of such pressing public interest and importance" despite pending litigation involving the questions, then he could take them to the attorney general, who could certify the questions to the justices.[47] The vagueness of the public importance exception was reflected in one justice's "dissent" in the third of the advisory opinions applying the exception. The question from the house of representatives, he said, had nothing to do with pending legislation but was actually about the duty of the governor under the enacted legislation, and the governor not only had sought no advice but had objected to the house's request.[48] The justices did not account for any of this.

The intellectual and doctrinal laxity with which the justices applied the public importance exception grew steadily, becoming less restrained and more expansive, to the point that the exception has become an arbitrary catchphrase for whenever the justices wish to ignore their restrictions. The fourth opinion invoking the exception did not bother with any warning about not establishing a precedent. The justices rendered advice to the governor despite finding that he had no present constitutional duty awaiting performance for which the advice was needed.[49] The justices applied the public importance exception using language nearly identical to that in the second exempted opinion: "In spite of the procedural deficiency ingrained in this request, we shall exercise our discretion and waive the defect . . . because this is an instance in which the public and constitutional importance is paramount."[50] This time, however, the justices were silent about not establishing precedent. They would never again express such caution.

The justices also became vaguer, in fact downright obscure, in the fourth advisory opinion about the grounds for applying the public importance exception. In this advisory opinion the governor's request for advice in effect challenged the state ethics commission's authority to create revolving-door regulations (which bar public officials from accepting employment from private organizations over which they had authority while in office). The challenge was unsuccessful, the justices upholding the authority of the commission.[51] The governor justified his request for advice by his purported need for advice pursuant to his constitutional duty to appoint qualified people to certain

[46] *In re Advisory Opinion to the House of Representatives*, 576 A.2d 1371, 1372 (R.I. 1990).

[47] *Opinion to the Governor*, 149 A.2d 341 (R.I. 1959).

[48] *In re Advisory Opinion to the House of Representatives*, 576 A.2d at 1376 (Weisburger, J., dissenting).

[49] *In re Advisory from* [*sic*] *the Governor*, 633 A.2d at 667. The opinion concerned the powers of the state ethics commission, of which the author was a member during this time.

[50] *Id.*

[51] *Id.* at 678.

government positions, but the justices found no such constitutional duty. "[N]o power of appointment [is] vested in the governor, save to fill vacancies temporarily existing." The state constitution, the justices said, does not make appointments to office an executive function. Hence, they held, the governor had no present constitutional duty awaiting performance.[52] Further, the brief from the ethics commission noted two other defects in the governor's request. One was that advising in this case would require the justices to engage in fact-finding, specifically the need to make "an ad hoc evaluation of each and every appointment." The other was that the question was "vague in form," against the justices' restriction on answering questions insufficiently specific or clear.[53]

The justices nonetheless chose to give the governor an advisory opinion on grounds of public importance. They applied their public importance exception in this fog-bound way. First, they simply ignored completely the ethics commission's points about fact-finding and vagueness. As to the governor's purported constitutional duty, they made clear there was none: "[T]he Governor has no present constitutional duty awaiting performance." Then the justices immediately proceeded to waive this defect on public importance grounds. This time they offered no elucidation at all, merely a footnote cryptically citing the second exempted opinion, without comment or explanation.[54] Citing that opinion, though, appeared to signal that the second exempted opinion was a precedent, thereby perhaps asserting the precedent the justices had said they would not establish. Or perhaps not. There is, again, no effort at explanation.

The fifth exempting advisory opinion continued in this arbitrary direction. The governor asked the justices if the state was constitutionally required to provide free counsel to indigent defendants even when the trial judge determined that no incarceration would be imposed. The governor made the dubious claim that he needed the answer in order to provide sufficient funding in the state budget, the preparation of which was a constitutional duty awaiting performance.[55] The governor's question, though, was not really about his budgetary duties, and one justice in her own "dissenting" opinion made the point: "The Governor's argument [on his need for advice] . . . is unconvincing. The question propounded was simply whether the state has an obligation to provide legal representation to indigent misdemeanor defendants. The question, therefore, did not bear upon the Governor's duty to present a balanced budget to the General Assembly." Hence "this case is a definitive textbook instance in which the Governor's question is not properly the subject of an advisory opinion."[56]

Against this clear identification of a defect in the governor's request, the majority's advisory opinion is a model of obscurity. The opinion put forth accurately the justices'

---

[52] *Id.* at 667.

[53] *Brief and Appendix of Amicus Curiae R.I. Ethics Commission*, at 12. The justices' rule about vague questions is in *Advisory Opinion to the Governor*, 289 A.2d 430 (R.I. 1972).

[54] *In re Advisory Opinion from the Governor*, 633 A.2d at 667 (R.I. 1993).

[55] *In re Advisory Opinion to the Governor*, 666 A.2d 813, 815 (R.I. 1995). The Rhode Island constitution (Art. IX, sec. 15) requires the governor annually to "prepare and present" a budget to the legislature.

[56] 666 A.2d at 818–19.

standard: they "will generally refrain from advising the Governor" on issues not bearing on a present constitutional duty awaiting performance.[57] Did the governor have such a duty here? The opinion observed merely that "Your Excellency has presented legitimate concerns that impede your ability to prepare a budget absent clarification of the requirements imposed by article I, section 10 [the right of the accused to counsel]." Since that article specifies no duty of the governor, the justices seemed to have opened the door of the advisory opinion process to virtually every item in the state budget, for both the governor and the legislature. The justices, though, quickly tried to close this door. "Although we are responding to your request for advice in this instance, we would not consider that every issue affecting the state budgetary duties of the Governor or of the General Assembly would be a proper subject for an opinion."[58] By what standard are the governor and legislature to determine which sorts of budgetary issues are proper and which are not? The justices did not say. It might be public importance, it might not. At any rate the justices then, without explanation, invoked their public importance exception, but, curiously, only in a footnote: "This Court has exercised its discretion to issue advisory opinions even on questions arguably improperly before the court, but of great public importance."[59] The statement sits isolated in the footnote, unsupported and unexplained. Is it the standard by which the justices will decide when budget-related questions, otherwise out of bounds for advisory opinions, will be answered? The justices did not say. What is the relevance of the public importance exception to the governor's request for advice on funding for indigent defendants? Is there some exceptional public importance to this question? The justices did not say. The justices, though, having simply recited the exception like some incantation that magically overcomes all advisory opinion restrictions, proceeded to answer the governor's question.

With this fifth instance of the justices answering an improper question based on their public importance exception, the exception has developed in two fog-ridden ways, both confirmed by the sixth excepting advisory opinion, on separation of powers, discussed above. The exception, whatever its nature, now trumps all the justices' restrictions on advisory opinions. And it has become freewheeling and expansive beyond all limits and with little definition or clarity as to what constitutes public importance, or what warrants applying the exception to one defective request for advice and not another. There is a diminished likelihood that a requesting authority, or the public, can reasonably determine what a proper request for advice is, or understand why some questions failing to adhere to the justices' restrictions are rejected for that reason and why some are not. In short, this jurisprudential fog makes it impossible to determine the scope of the Rhode Island justices' advisory opinion jurisdiction. The justices in effect are engaging in de facto judicial review, without constraints or limits.

In the seventh advisory opinion applying the public importance exception, the force and effect of the justices' restrictions on advising are so weak, the public importance

---

[57] *Id.* at 814–15.

[58] *Id.* at 815.

[59] *Id.* (note 1). The note cites the first, second, and fourth exempted advisory opinions, but not the third.

exception so expansive, that the justices for the first time simply ignore the whole matter. They barely bother to note the defects in the questions presented, and they invoke the public importance exception without explanation or support despite briefs strongly raising the issues. Two briefs were wholly devoted to the defects, and one of them devoted wholly to arguing against applying the public importance exception. This 2007 request for advice came from the Rhode Island House of Representatives, which had a bill pending that would permit members of the legislature to sit on the state's Coastal Resources Management Council (CRMC), and permit the Speaker of the House to appoint members of the public to the CRMC. The CRMC is a relatively powerful regulatory body with considerable authority over the small state's thousand miles of coastline. It creates and enforces policies and regulations affecting nearly all coastal activity. It rules on billions of dollars worth of coastal investments including marinas, condominiums, and wind farms.

The proposed bill was immediately attacked on separation of powers grounds, since the CRMC is purportedly an executive branch agency, and in response the house sought the advisory opinion. The justices, however, prohibit the legislature from seeking advice on already enacted legislation, and the bill in question was in fact no more than an exact copy of a statute already on the books. The house apparently introduced the bill so that it would have "pending" legislation as a pretext to permit seeking an advisory opinion. The house not surprisingly foresaw that this would be an issue, and its brief included a section devoted to noting that the justices have asserted their discretion to waive their restrictions on public importance grounds in the past, and that they should do so here since the questions from the house "raise issues of such profound importance" to the government and citizens "that they are appropriate for consideration by the Justices at this time." The briefs from the governor and the attorney general both point out the defect, though the governor agreed that it should be waived on public importance grounds.[60] One public interest organization submitted both a brief and a reply brief devoted to attacking the house's questions as defective requests for advice. It was an unusual instance of briefs in an advisory opinion proceeding arguing wholly in terms of the threshold of the appropriateness of the questions presented. The briefs argued, first, that the questions lacked clarity sufficient to warrant a response; second, that the questions failed to identify a specific constitutional provision of concern to the house; third, that two of the questions failed to be related to any pending legislation; and fourth, one of those questions involved fact-finding. Further, answering the questions would involve the justices so closely in public policy disputes as to offend separation of powers.[61] Since the brief of the house raised the public importance exception, and in light of the justices' growing use of the exception to waive defective requests, the public interest organization filed a twenty-two-page reply brief, probably unprecedented in the history of advisory opinion jurisprudence in any state, wholly devoted to arguing that the

---

[60] *Brief of the Speaker of the House of Representatives*, Mar. 14, 2008, 3–5; *Brief of Governor Donald L. Carcieri*, Jan. 31, 2008, 2; *Brief of the Attorney General* (n.d.), 2–3.

[61] *Brief of the Rhode Island Statewide Coalition as Amicus Curiae*, Jan. 31, 2008.

justices should not invoke the public importance exception to waive the defects of the house's questions.[62]

All this notwithstanding, the justices' advisory opinion barely bothers with the defects in the questions from the house, or with the public interest exception to waive the defects. They note that the bill at issue is simply a copy of an existing statute (a "reenactment," they call it, of a statute already in force), and, they say, the legislature may not seek advice on existing statutes. "In view of that principle," they conclude with some understatement, the house's authority to seek the advice "is somewhat less than self-evident." "However," they go on to say, "the existence of significant questions of law in an area of important public concern has convinced us, not without some hesitation, that we should respond." That is the sole reference to the public importance exception or to their unexplained hesitation about invoking it. The justices have reached the point where they can note one of the violations of their restrictions (ignoring all the others without explanation), then simply make an enigmatic reference to public importance and they are done. They compound and confuse the matter by warning vaguely that in the future they "may be less inclined" to respond to advisory opinion requests from the legislature "under circumstances similar to those here present."[63] This is an impressively vague account of how "circumstances" relate to the public importance exception, but it does serve to assert their position that in future they may be more inclined, or perhaps less inclined, to advise, as they please.

The uncertainty of the public importance exception in Rhode Island comes in the face of its remarkably frequent use. Compare its use in the other advisory states. During the period of 1986–1999, when the Rhode Island justices undertook their aggressive expansion of the public importance exception, the justices in each of the other nine advisory opinion states applied a public importance exception to defective requests for advice either rarely or not at all. Justices in seven of these states applied no such exception during this time. Of the other two states, the Alabama justices applied the exception three times, while refusing to advise twelve times out of a total of thirty-nine requests for advice during this period.[64] The Massachusetts justices applied the exemption once in this time, while refusing to advise eight times out of a total of twenty-nine requests

[62] *Reply Brief of the Rhode Island Statewide Coalition as Amicus Curiae*, Apr. 24, 2008. The author was co-counsel in the preparation and submission of this brief.

[63] *In re Request for Advisory Opinion from the House of Representatives (Coastal Resources Management Council)*, 961 A.2d 930, 932 (R.I. 2008). Contrast the Alabama justices, who have refused to advise on proposed bills that had provisions identical to those in existing statutes, since it would effectively be advising on existing law. *Opinion of the Justices*, 115 So.2d 524 (Ala. 1959); *Opinions of the Justices*, 132 So.2d 381 (Ala. 1961).

[64] The three opinions applying the exception are: *Opinion of the Justices*, 624 So.2d 107, 109 (Ala. 1993) (Despite pending litigation, question "is one of great public interest."); *Opinion of the Justices*, 599 So.2d 1166, 1167 (Ala. 1992) (Legislature not in session and there is no pending legislation, but "matters of great public concern are involved requiring immediate resolution."); *Opinion of the Justices*, 558 So.2d 390, 391 (Ala. 1989) (Governor's questions involve pending legislation, but the questions are "vitally important to the people of the State of Alabama.").

for advice.[65] In sum, from 1986 through 1999 the justices of the nine advisory states other than Rhode Island responded to a total of 134 advisory opinion requests, and applied the public importance exception a total of four times. In Rhode Island the justices, responding to nineteen requests in this time, applied the exception six times, to nearly a third of the total requests. In short the Rhode Island justices applied the exception in this period more than the other nine advisory states taken together.

There is nothing in the advisory opinion jurisprudence of the other advisory states that would bar such an expansive and fog-bound application of the public importance exception. They all have similar sets of restrictions, and while most claim that nonbinding doctrine obviates the difficulties attending advisory opinions, we have seen, in Chapter 5, that the claim fails. The advisory opinion jurisdiction in this context, then, necessarily implicates two important issues regarding judicial power—judicial supremacy and the politicization of the judiciary. In Rhode Island the justices' expanding use of the public importance exception, and the consequent weakening of their restrictions on advisory opinions, contributes to judicial supremacy in their exercise of de facto judicial review, and it intensifies advisory opinions' effects on the political process, by providing each of the two political branches with an open-ended opportunity to supervise the other branch. Reporting on the CRMC advisory opinion in Rhode Island, a journalist accurately if dramatically described it "a tug-of-war for power between the executive and legislative branches."[66] The justices, advising that legislators may constitutionally serve on state boards and commissions, effectively rendered the deciding blow in the dispute between the two political branches over essentially political appointments. The justices placed themselves in a position of significant political influence if not control through their rendering of a preemptive, nonadjudicatory advisory opinion. Advisory opinions, we see here (just as was stated at the 1853 Massachusetts convention), "have this further objection—that it is very little different from permitting the judiciary to control the legislative and executive powers."[67]

The public importance exception, with its propensity toward waiving whatever restrictions that might have served to limit the politicization of the justices, enables the use of the advisory opinion as an instrument of judicial supremacy. The political process—its debates, negotiations, compromises, lobbying, editorializing, and other risky and frustrating activities—is substantially marginalized if not altogether bypassed when questions of public importance are withdrawn from the political realm to the open arms of the advising justices. In 1997 panelists on a local television program discussed the "power struggle" between the governor and the legislature in Rhode Island over appointment power to fill a vacancy in the position of lieutenant governor. One panelist,

---

[65] Exemption applied in *Opinion of the Justices to the Senate*, 493 N.E.2d 859, 863 (Mass. 1986). (Question is defective as on an existing statute, but advice needed to avoid needless expenditure of time, effort, and public funds should statutes be found unconstitutional later.).

[66] Tom Mooney, *Justices Refuse to Ban Legislators from State Boards*, PROVIDENCE JOURNAL BULLETIN, June 30, 1999, at A1.

[67] 2 *Official Report of the Debates and Proceedings in the* [Massachusetts] *State Convention* 687 (July 11, 1853).

the chair of the senate's judiciary committee, perfectly depicted the relation between the disdain for political controversy and the desire to shift political issues to the justices for resolution through the advisory opinion process. She said that her "inclination would be for us [the senate] to seek an advisory [opinion]. . . . We need to be sensitive to public opinion. . . . People feel . . . all we're doing is fighting. . . . My personal inclination would be to receive some direction from the supreme court, [in] *a non-controversial manner*, as to whether or not the legislation I've introduced [on the appointment of the lieutenant governor] is in fact—would be valid."[68] Those who disdain the political, who want things done in a noncontroversial manner, will also want the justices to intervene in politics and "will not be unduly distressed if most important controversies are entrusted to the courts for decision."[69] From the time the Rhode Island Ethics Commission first promulgated a draft of what would become Regulation 5014 in October 1995 until their justices issued their advisory opinion in June 1999, there was considerable public discussion on the issues involved. But of course it all did not matter, formally speaking, because the questions went before the justices, who in principle must not be influenced by the public discussion. The only effective discussion was in the briefs and arguments of some fourteen attorneys, all addressed to the five attorneys who comprise the court, who in turn deliberated among themselves. Nineteen attorneys were the participants in the process leading to the advisory opinion that resolved a major political controversy.

The public importance exception, then, especially when it is employed as loosely as do the Rhode Island justices, strengthens the capacity of the advisory opinion process to contract or impoverish civic discourse even as it skews advisory opinion jurisprudence and reinforces judicial supremacy. The public importance exception, however extreme its use in Rhode Island, is, given the nature of advisory opinion authority, available to all advisory justices. The Rhode Island chief justice in 1991, corresponding with the Louisiana chief justice, said that the justices "only answer requests for advice if they meet the criteria set forth in our cases,"[70] and the justices in Rhode Island claimed in 1993 that they avoid rendering advisory opinions in circumstances not constitutionally mandated.[71] But this was not true then and is not true now.

This trackless and dubious exercise of the public importance exception, devouring the whole of advisory opinion jurisprudence in a single swallow, is permissible in all the advisory states even if overused so far only in Rhode Island. But it also imposes additional burdens on the legitimacy of advisory opinions.

---

[68] Video recording, *Lively Experiment* (television program broadcast, Jan. 30, 1997) (emphasis added).

[69] GLENDON, RIGHTS TALK, 182.

[70] Letter from Rhode Island Chief Justice Thomas F. Fay, to Louisiana Chief Justice Pascal Calogero, May 29, 1991 (copy on file with author).

[71] *In re Advisory from Governor*, 633 A.2d at 666.

Advisory Opinions and the Problem of Legitimacy

We saw earlier in this book that the history of the jurisprudence of advisory opinions is in great part of a history of responses to challenges to the legitimacy of advisory opinions. The responses include a broad range of restrictions curtailing the use of advisory opinions, the nonbinding doctrine, and the advising justices' borrowing from the rhetoric of adjudicated opinions and from devices of adjudication such as briefs and argument. But the failure of nonbinding doctrine, together with the capacity of the public importance exception arbitrarily to swallow up the carefully wrought restrictions on advisory opinions, leaves the advisory opinion process naked to the attacks on its fundamental legitimacy. Further, given the inevitable tension between the advice-giving as guidance on the one hand and as assertion of power on the other, advisory opinion jurisdiction leaves the advising justices open to charges of exercising raw judicial power. It has to do with the character of legitimacy in the assertion of political power.

Students of political science have not treated legitimacy in the exercise of power with much success, neither defined with precision nor much studied empirically.[72] It has long been a concern regarding judicial power, given the suspicion of "judicial decisions as undemocratic and hence illicit."[73] Since what I want to focus on here is the legitimacy of a written judicial document—the advisory opinion—I will first look at the role of communication in establishing legitimacy.

Usually taken for granted but nonetheless crucial is that the primary institutional space within which supreme court decisions operate is the common law adversarial system.[74] "Truth in the judicial process comes from the clash of opposites, in the arena of the courtroom."[75] In the common law system, much less reliant on or committed to "formal rationality" compared to the inquisitorial system,[76] judgment is required "only when an affirmative is met by a negative," when there is both claim and denial to be contested.[77] Only in such a system can a conflict of views represent a "means of discovering truth."[78] That is why, as Richard Posner observes, rhetoric is important in

---

[72] C. McEwen & R. Maiman, *In Search of Legitimacy: Toward an Empirical Analysis*, 8 Law and Policy 257 (1986); A. Hyde, *The Concept of Legitimation in the Sociology of Law*, 1983 Wisc. L. Rev. 379.

[73] G. J. Jacobsohn, The Supreme Court and the Decline of Constitutional Aspiration 75 (1986).

[74] For overviews of the adversarial system, especially in contrast with the civil law legal system, see generally Henry J. Abraham, The Judicial Process, ch. 3 (5th ed. 1986); Leonard Levy, The Origins of the Fifth Amendment, ch. 1 (1968); Stephan Landsman, The Adversary System (1984).

[75] A. S. Miller & J. A. Barron, *The Supreme Court, the Adversary System, and the Flow of Information to the Justices*, 61 Va. L. Rev. 1187, 1189 (1975).

[76] P. Birks, *Fictions Ancient and Modern, in* The Legal Mind 83, 85 (D. N. MacCormick ed., 1986).

[77] A. Guiliani, *The Influence of Rhetoric on the Law of Evidence and Pleading*, 7 Juridical Rev. 216, 229 (1969). Quoted in Hector L. MacQueen, *Pleadable Brieves, Pleading, and the Development of Scots Law*, 4 Law and Hist. Rev. 403, 411 (1986). *See also* S. F. C. Milsom, Historical Foundations of the Common Law 42 (1981) (on the "standard sequence of claim and denial, oath and test").

[78] Guiliani, *The Influence of Rhetoric*, 229. American courts have often commented on what the Supreme Court called the need for issues to be pressed "with that clear concreteness provided when a question emerges precisely framed and ready for decision from a clash of adversary argument." *United States v. Fruehauf*, 365 U.S. 146, 157 (1961). The requirement is often attributed specifically to the case or controversy requirement

Anglo-American law, since "legal questions cannot be resolved by logical or empirical demonstration."[79]

This central ethos of conflict is carried over into supreme court opinions, which communicate through a grammar of conflict. By the time a case reaches a supreme court, its adversarial character has been reified on several levels, typically beginning with the transformation of everyday circumstances into legal facts.[80] This is familiar enough to legal actors, but it is worth pointing out several aspects relevant here. An appellate opinion is not only constructed out of the facts and arguments presented by petitioner and by respondent, but it's rhetoric is shaped in part as a series of responses to their opposing arguments. Take this excerpt from a concurring opinion in *Bakke*, in which the Supreme Court ruled on the extent to which a university may consider racial criteria as part of its admissions procedures.

> Respondent [Allan Bakke] argues that racial classifications are always suspect and, consequently, that this Court should weigh the importance of objectives served by [the University of California at] Davis' special admissions program to see if they are compelling. In addition he asserts that this court must inquire whether, in its judgment, there are alternatives to racial classifications which would suit Davis' purposes. Petitioner [Davis' medical school], on the other hand, states that our proper role is simply to accept petitioner's determination that the racial classifications used by its programs are reasonably related to what it tells us are its benign purposes. We reject petitioner's view."[81]

This binary grammar ("Respondent argues . . ."; "Petitioner, on the other hand, states . . ."; "We reject petitioner's view . . .") develops as the opinion moves through arguments and counterarguments brought before the Court, arguments that are the supra-text for which the two or more levels of prior legal argument, in the courts below, are subtext. An opinion is written to show that its rulings are derived through accepting or rejecting contending arguments and by applying precedents from prior cases, these precedents deriving in turn from contending arguments or other precedents. In short, an appellate opinion asserts knowledge in agonistic structures.

American appellate court opinions, in striking contrast to Continental civil law opinions, are written so that their decisions are reached paratactically, a progression of points connected in added-on style, by overt and explicit deliberations on this argument and

---

and to various justiciability standards such as mootness and ripeness, but beyond them conflict is deeply situated in the Anglo-American legal system.

[79] Richard A. Posner, Law and Literature 286 (1988). John H. Langbein notes that a jury verdict requires "not certainty, but only persuasion," in Torture and the Law of Proof 80 (1977).

[80] Observers who have studied the lawyer's crucial transforming and contextualizing function at this stage include A. M. Honore, *Real Laws*, *in* Law, Morality and Society 99–118 (P. M. S. Hacker & J. Raz eds., 1977); Lynn Mather & Barbara Yngvesson, *Language, Audience, and the Transformation of Disputes*, 15 Law and Soc. Rev. 775 (1981); A. Sarat & W. Felstiner, *Law and Strategy in the Divorce Lawyer's Office*, 20 Law and Soc. Rev. 108 (1986).

[81] *Regents of the University of California v. Bakke*, 438 U.S. 265, 366–67 (1978) (Brennan, White, and Blackmun, J.J., concurring in part and dissenting in part).

that one, accepting this, rejecting that. There is little attempt at arriving rationally, inexorably, at a single and inescapable truth.[82] Rather, a supreme court opinion arrives, so to speak, at the best decision it could, given the opposing arguments before it. The court finds "not *the* answer to the problem, but the one that fits best the particular case."[83] What Rudden says about English opinions applies here: they are candid about addressing various arguments and there being "a choice as to the result," frankly defending the court's choices.[84] This is dramatically explicit in the American appellate courts' striking individualism, expressed in the practice of separate dissenting and concurring opinions, often criticizing or even attacking each other. This contentious individualism is sometimes rampant. Justices not only may concur or dissent; they may concur in part and dissent in part; may join with one or more colleagues in one or the other; or concur with colleagues in part and dissent in part; may join one group of colleagues to concur and another to dissent; may concur with one group of colleagues in part and concur with another group in part; and so on.

All this contentiousness "works" because it both acknowledges and reifies an adversarial system of justice, and so imparts to the court's decision a central element of legitimacy. But this adversarial ethos creates a problem. The open-ended arguing by itself need not arrive at a conclusion in the logical sense. The strict logic of the Continental opinion, with its tightly connected linearity and aura of objectivity, affirms the decision's legitimacy because it locates the decision "beyond the wills of the holders of power."[85] American supreme court opinions, their loose, contentious style and structure notwithstanding, reach both conclusions of law and, usually at the opinion's end, an actual decision, what linguists call a speech act. ("Reversed and remanded"; "We affirm the judgment of the Court of Appeals.") The problem is that the conclusions and the decision statements are sudden "conversion[s] of dialogue into monologue."[86]

---

[82] On this contrast between common law and inquisitorial writing of opinions, see HENRY J. ABRAHAM, THE JUDICIAL PROCESS 101 (3d ed. 1975); STEPHAN LANDSMAN, THE ADVERSARY SYSTEM, 3; J. B. WHITE, HERACLES' BOW 32 (1985).

[83] J. G. WETTER, THE STYLES OF APPELLATE JUDICIAL OPINIONS 50–51 (1960).

[84] B. Rudden, *Courts and Codes in England, France, and the Soviet Union*, 48 TULANE L. REV. 1010, 1015, 1021 (1974). *See* Rudden and also WETTER, STYLES OF APPELLATE JUDICIAL OPINIONS, for analyses of styles of Continental opinions in contrast to Anglo-American. Among the contrasts they note are that in Continental opinions indications of opposing arguments are sunk without a trace. "An impression is given that all is an easy deduction from the principles of the enacted law." Rudden, *Courts and Codes*, 1022. The Continental opinion includes only "those reasons alone which support the decision, excluding such as may be advanced in support of a different opinion." WETTER, STYLES OF APPELLATE JUDICIAL DECISIONS, 16–17. The language is of assertion, not argument. Rudden, 'Courts and Codes,' 1022. The Continental opinion is "an expression of volition" (WETTER, STYLES OF APPELLATE JUDICIAL DECISIONS, 17) that leaves "no trace of dialogue between bench and bar, or among the justices." Rudden, *Courts and Codes*, 1018. Rudden offers a typical complete—one sentence—opinion from the *Cour de Cassation* in France. *Id.* at 1021. *See also* Jean Louis Goutal, *Characteristics of Judicial Style in France, England and the U.S.A.*, 24 AM. J. COMPAR. L. 43 (1976) (discussing the relation of style to legal reasoning in the three countries).

[85] J. H. Schaar, *Legitimacy and the Modern State*, *in* LEGITIMACY AND THE STATE 111 (W. Connelly ed., 1982).

[86] W. J. Witteveen, "The Rhetorical Labors of Hercules." Paper presented at the International Association of Law and Semiotics, Pennsylvania State University, May 1988. Copy in author's file.

The opinion itself is in danger of appearing to be no more than a discussion of arguments with its conclusions of law and decisions arbitrarily tacked on. That does not, however, become a problem because appellate decisions join their adversarial character with the rhetoric of discovery discussed in Chapter 5. The court's decision legitimizes itself in good part by discovering precedent, that is, showing that its conclusions of law already exist, lying in previously decided cases, and not the product of the judges' personal biases or predilections.

The selection from *Bakke* given above ends with the Court rejecting the "the petitioner's view" that racial classification, for a purportedly acceptable purpose like affirmative action, should not be subject to strict scrutiny. The opinion's next several paragraphs serve to demonstrate that each of the reasons the Court offers for this rejection may be found in the Court's holdings in prior cases. For example: "Second, race, like gender and illegitimacy, see *Weber v. Aetna Casualty Co.*, 406 U.S. 164 (1972), is an immutable characteristic which its possessors are powerless to escape or set aside."[87] That this characteristic of race, gender, or illegitimacy may be self-evident matters no more than syntactical decencies. It must be found, in prior cases, and the opinion must be written so that this is asserted. This may be difficult to do persuasively,[88] but appellate courts write their opinions to show that the decision really was always, already there, in past cases, beyond the wills and personal predilections of the present members of the court. This traditional core concept of legitimacy in the exercise of power was first challenged by the Enlightenment notion of institutions as man-made and therefore properly subject to criticism and attacks on the one hand and change or destruction (the Declaration of Independence's "to alter or to abolish") on the other.[89] When Justice Holmes caustically commented that the "common law is not a brooding omnipresence in the sky," it reflected his Legal Realist rejection of the principle that the law was "out there" and that judges should think of themselves, as Milsom said medieval common law judges did, "as making law explicit rather than making it, as finding answers rather than choosing them."[90] In some respects this is akin to formalism, which makes a similar claim to legitimacy. Formalism, Richard Posner writes, "signifies the denial of the policy-political-ideological component of law. . . . Formalism responds to the legal profession's deeply felt need to represent judicial decisions as the

---

[87] *Bakke*, 438 U.S. at 360.

[88] *See, e.g.*, RUPERT CROSS, PRECEDENT IN ENGLISH LAW 60 (3d ed. 1977).

[89] What Jonathan Powis said about European aristocracy applies to the Enlightenment view of any institution exercising power. "Eighteenth century theorists placed aristocracy squarely in the context of man-made social institutions, and so exposed it to the possibility of criticism in quite unprecedented terms." JONATHAN POWIS, ARISTOCRACY 93 (1984). The Enlightenment idea that we understand and accept reality to the extent that we see it as made is a modern one and derives from the scientific revolution. *See* HANNAH ARENDT, THE HUMAN CONDITION 269–71 (Anchor ed. 1959) (on the modern "conviction that one can only know what he has made himself," and on its relation to scientific experiment, which "repeats the natural process as though man himself were about to make nature's objects").

[90] *So. Pacific Co. v. Jensen*, 244 U.S. 205, 222 (1917) (Holmes, J., dissenting); S. F. C. MILSOM, HISTORICAL FOUNDATIONS OF THE COMMON LAW 81 (2d ed. 1981).

product of an objective process of distinctively legal reasoning, a process that operates independently of the judge's personality."[91]

Partly to achieve this, the courts' opinions communicate a balance between the polarity of its agonistic grammar and the synchronic stasis of case law. In other words, they communicate their legitimacy by affirming their relational continuity with the adversarial legal system which is their pragmatic and communal context. Through an opinion's referencing of the norms of the adversarial system, it asserts its legitimacy. Whether or not opinions are seen as policymaking in legal dress, covert expressions of ideology, instruments of the ruling classes, or part of the continuing if imperfect search for justice; whether or not justices can avoid projecting their personal values into their opinions, the opinions themselves remain emblems of the legitimacy of the judicial process because these norms constrain "the justices' available alternatives. . . . The justices have significant discretion in shaping constitutional law, but all of their available paths are formed by institutionally embedded legal categories."[92]

The advising justices' longstanding and constant concern over the legitimacy of their advisory opinion jurisdiction accounts substantially for the way the advisory process and advisory opinions have grown more and more like appellate adjudications and appellate opinions. The fact that the venue of the advisory opinion process is otherwise powerfully associated with appeals contributes strongly to the aura of legitimacy, appeals by nature having always "engaged the litigant in the acceptance of superior authority."[93] Hence the expanding use of briefs and oral argument, lending "an increasingly judicial flavor to the advisory process, further blurring the already imprecise distinction between decisions of the court and opinions of the justices."[94] The forms of reasoning in advisory opinions "are indistinguishable from those in adjudicated opinions."[95] Some observers attribute the similarities to mere force of habit, the "judicial propensity for exactness and dependence on precedent,"[96] and to the justices assuming, apparently without reflection, that advising is somehow normal judicial work.[97]

---

[91] RICHARD A. POSNER, LAW, PRAGMATISM, AND DEMOCRACY 19 (2003). On the relation of formalism to the increase in judicial stature and authority in the mid-nineteenth century, see HAROLD M. HYMAN & WILLIAM M. WIECEK, EQUAL JUSTICE UNDER LAW: CONSTITUTIONAL DEVELOPMENT, 1835–1875 at 348 (1982). ("Formalism enhanced the status of the appellate judiciary, deified judge-made law as in equity, and applauded high judges' refusals to consult legislative documents when seeking lawmakers' intentions. A process was underway by 1865 . . . whereby "statutes are ordinarily regarded as isolated or sporadic encrustations upon the rational body of judge-made common law."" The internal quote is from E. Dumbauld, *Legal Records in English and American Courts*, 36 AMERICAN ARCHIVIST 30 (1976).)

[92] THOMAS M. KECK, THE MOST ACTIVIST SUPREME COURT IN HISTORY: THE ROAD TO MODERN JUDICIAL CONSERVATISM 277 (2004).

[93] Mary Sarah Bilder, *The Origins of Appeal in America*, 48 HASTINGS L.J. 913, 955 (1997). Bilder, tracing the origins of appeal in Massachusetts and Rhode Island, argues against Julius Goebel's and Roscoe Pound's view that appeal arose in America out of confusion about common law procedure.

[94] Charles M. Carberry, *The State Advisory Opinion in Perspective*, 14 FORDHAM L. REV. 81, 105 (1975).

[95] C. Dallas Sands, *Government by Judiciary—Advisory Opinions in Alabama*, 4 ALA. L. REV. 1, 26 (1951).

[96] ALBERT R. ELLINGWOOD, DEPARTMENTAL COOPERATION IN STATE GOVERNMENT 147 (1918).

[97] Oliver P. Field, *Advisory Opinions—An Analysis*, 24 INDIANA L.J. 203, 215 (1949).

But in light of the challenges to the legitimacy of advisory opinions, of which the advisory justices are certainly aware, the fact is that the adopted similarities are responses to those challenges. The justices, after all, are not supposed to be advisors anyway. Their authority to render nonjudicial advisory opinions in reality arises out of their authority to hand down adjudicated opinions. "The judge does not sit in the seat of justice in order to be consulted, but in order to decide an issue. . . . There seems to be no cogent motive for extracting opinions from the Bench except to give them an authority which cannot belong to any lesser opinion."[98] The advising process is not made "safe" by the justices' restrictions or by their insistence that their advisory opinions are nonbinding, since, we have seen, the former is easily cast aside by the public importance exception and the latter simply fails as a doctrine.

Advisory Opinions and Judicial Supremacy

Advisory opinion practice . . . allows simply too much judicial supremacy.[99]

Consequently, advisory opinions have taken on the character of adjudicated appellate process and along with it de facto judicial review, since the justices are generally requested to advise on constitutional questions, and to do so in a venue closely associated with appeals. Advisory opinions as de facto judicial review implicate avoidance and abstention doctrines, two principles of judicial restraint obviously at odds with the advisory process. As to abstention, it was already the U.S. Supreme Court's position in the 1880s that the Court is "bound by two rules, to which it has rigidly adhered, one never to anticipate a question of constitutional law in advance of the necessity of deciding it; the other never to formulate a rule of constitutional law broader than is required by the precise facts to which it is to be applied."[100] As to avoidance, Brandeis's articulation of it in *Ashwander* firmly established it on the federal level, likely owing to the opinion's prestige as much as anything, and it has been generally accepted in the states.[101] Regarding advisory opinions, however, the advising justices are free to disregard avoidance since advisory opinions are not adjudicated cases. And, having developed

---

[98] Carleton K. Allen, *Administrative Consultation of the Judiciary*, 47 LAW Q. REV. 43, 48 (1931).

[99] Sands, *Government by Judicary*, 37.

[100] *Liverpool, N.Y. & Phila. SS Co. v. Comm'rs of Emigration*, 113 U.S. 33, 39 (1885). Quoted in Neal Kumar Katyal, *Judges as Advicegivers*, 50 STANFORD L. REV. 1709, 1710 (1998).

[101] *Ashwander v. TVA*, 297 U.S. 288, 347 (1936) (Brandeis, J., concurring). ("The Court will not pass upon a constitutional question although properly presented by the record, if there is also presented some other ground upon which it may be disposed of.") Regarding the prestige of Brandeis's opinion, see, e.g., Justice Stevens' dissent in *Delaware v. Van Ardell*, 475 U.S. 673, 693 (1986) (Stevens, J., dissenting) (calling Brandeis' opinion "one of the most respected opinions ever written by a member of this Court"). Thomas Healy refers to its "long and distinguished pedigree." Thomas Healy, *The Rise of Unnecessary Constitutional Rulings*, 83 N.C. L. REV. 847, 857 (2005). On avoidance doctrine in the states, see, e.g., *In re Brown,* 903 A.2d 147, 157 (R.I. 2006) ("Neither this Court nor the Superior Court should decide constitutional issues unless it is absolutely necessary to do so.").

advisory opinions with all the characteristics of adjudicated opinions exercising judicial review, and with nonbinding doctrine a failure as a credible rationale for distinguishing advisory opinions from adjudicated opinions, the advising justices are implicated in the vexed matter of judicial supremacy.

Whether or not judicial supremacy may be tracked back to *Marbury v. Madison*, it was firmly established, if contested, by mid-nineteenth century.[102] By then we see "the rise in the [Supreme] Court's position relative to the other branches of government, and to the states."[103] By the mid-twentieth century the Supreme Court was able plausibly if controversially to declare judicial supremacy one of the "basic constitutional propositions which are among settled doctrines."[104] The Court asserted outright and unanimously that "the federal judiciary is supreme in the exposition of the law of the Constitution" and further claimed not only that judicial supremacy can be traced to *Marbury* but that it is the "basic principle" declared in *Marbury*.[105] Judicial supremacy, however, is a substantially later doctrine at least to the extent that it involves a basic reconceiving of the Constitution as ordinary law and as "a set of legal restraints rather than an instrument enabling self-government, and as such subject to judicial oversight."[106] The Court's

---

[102] *See, e.g.*, Larry Kramer, *The Supreme Court 2000 Term: We the Court*, 115 HARV. L. REV. 4, 86 (2001) (arguing that *Marbury v. Madison*, 5 U.S. 137 (1803), asserts only that the judiciary has a place in constitutional interpretation at the most equal to the other two branches, and that the predominant source of constitutional interpretation should be the legislature). Kramer expands on his thesis concerning popular constitutionalism in THE PEOPLE THEMSELVES: POPULAR CONSTITUTIONALISM AND JUDICIAL REVIEW (2004). Michael Stokes Paulson, also rejecting *Marbury* as the source of judicial supremacy, traces it to Joseph Story, whose COMMENTARIES ON THE CONSTITUTION OF THE UNITED STATES (1833) was the "first systematic argument for judicial supremacy, and the most important ever." Michael Stokes Paulson, *The Most Dangerous Branch: Executive Power to Say What the Law Does*, 83 GEO. L.J. 217, 311–12 (1994). Story's hostility toward advisory opinions as a threat to judicial independence and to his theory of judicial supremacy is reviewed in Chapter 2. Robert McCloskey sees a connection between the inchoate nature of judicial review in the nation's early years and the expansion of judicial power. "The very fact that the concept of judicial review was, at the outset, imperfectly understood was a point in its favor, for it enabled judges to build up the [Supreme] Court's power gradually and almost imperceptibly." ROBERT G. MCCLOSKEY, THE AMERICAN SUPREME COURT 11 (1960).

[103] HYMAN & WIECEK, EQUAL JUSTICE UNDER LAW: CONSTITUTIONAL DEVELOPMENT, 1835–1875 at 336. Chapter 10 is devoted to the expansion of judicial power. Other treatments of the rise of judicial supremacy in the nineteenth century and after include RANDY BARNETT, RESTORING THE LOST CONSTITUTION (2004); LARRY KRAMER, THE PEOPLE THEMSELVES; HOWARD GILLMAN, THE CONSTITUTION BESIEGED: THE RISE AND DEMISE OF LOCHNER ERA POLICE POWERS JURISPRUDENCE (1993).

[104] *Cooper v. Aaron*, 358 U.S. 1, 17 (1958). Judicial supremacy is not inconsistent with judicial restraint. Felix Frankfurter, for example, though always a strong proponent of judicial restraint was a "firm supporter of judicial supremacy" even if "only in its proper sphere." KECK, THE MOST ACTIVIST SUPREME COURT IN HISTORY, 295. Similarly, it is not tied to a court's ideological posture, conservatives as well as liberals asserting judicial supremacy. Justices O'Conner and Kennedy frequently adopted moderate positions in their opinions but nevertheless "authored some of the Court's most sweeping declarations of judicial supremacy" and "forcefully reaffirmed the Court's role as the supreme and final interpreter of the Constitution." *Id.* at 293, 294. Keck notes that the conservative Rehnquist Court showed "an utter lack of deference to Congress" and "brook[ed] no disagreement from the coordinate branches of the federal government." *Id.* at 283.

[105] *Cooper v. Aaron*, 358 U.S. at 17.

[106] Christopher L. Eisgruber, *Judicial Supremacy and Constitutional Distortion*, *in* CONSTITUTIONAL POLITICS: ESSAYS ON CONSTITUTION MAKING, MAINTENANCE, AND CHANGE 71 (S. A. Barber & R. P. George eds., 2001). On the argument that the Supreme Court has mistreated the Constitution as ordinary law, see generally

"aggrandizement" at the expense of the political branches, affirming an essentially hierarchical rather than coordinate relation among the three branches, is by now virtually taken for granted.[107] "The prevailing view, generally embraced by the public, by lawyers, and entrenched in basic civics lessons, is that the Supreme Court . . . interprets the Constitution and decides its meaning. Embedded in this view is the idea that the Court is the final arbiter of what the Constitution means."[108]

Judiciaries in the states have lockstepped the federal courts' assertions of judicial supremacy. Before 1850, writes Lawrence Friedman, state judicial review of statutes was "a rare, extraordinary event." By 1900 "it was a common occurrence. . . . What happened in the state courts paralleled what happened in the federal courts. The taste for power was even more intoxicating to the state tribunals." Indeed, the "wordy, excessive texts of the state constitutions were made to order for an aggressive judiciary."[109] By the early twentieth century, state constitutional conventions were debating placing controls on judicial power, complaining, as a delegate to the Ohio convention of 1912 did, that

> [t]he courts have by a series of interpretations managed to write into the laws . . . interpretations which materially and in some cases absolutely, ignore and reverse the will of the people as expressed by their legislative branch. In short, the judicial branch of the government has gradually overshadowed until it has well-nigh overturned the function of the other branches of the government and made these two

---

Larry Kramer, The People Themselves. For a review of cases that include the Supreme Court's defenses of its judicial supremacy assertions, see Larry Kramer, *The Supreme Court 2000 Term: We the Court*, 52–60.

[107] Rachel E. Barkow, *More Supreme Than Court? The Fall of the Political Question Doctrine and the Rise of Judicial Supremacy*, 102 Col. L. Rev. 237, 336, 341 (2002). By 2010 even so liberal a voice as President Obama's spoke "disparagingly" about the liberal decisions of the Supreme Court in the 1960s and 1970s, commenting in April 2010 that the Court made the "error" of overstepping bounds and "trampling on the role of elected officials." Liberals in the 1960s, he said, were "guilty" of being activist judges "who ignored the will of Congress, ignored democratic processes, and tried to impose judicial solutions on problems instead of letting the process work itself through politically." Charles Savage & Sheryl Gay Stolberg, *Obama Says Liberal Courts May Have Overreached*, New York Times, Apr. 30, 2010, at A15.

[108] Scott E. Gant, *Judicial Supremacy and Nonjudicial Interpretation of the Constitution*, 24 Hastings Const. L.Q. 359, 362–63 (1997). J. Mitchell Pickerell believes that coordinate review still lives in the way Congress responds to Supreme Court decisions. "Congress engages in coordinate review when it amends legislation that addresses the Court's judicial review decisions. . . . Members of Congress often modify legislation in response to the Court's judicial review decisions." J. Mitchell Pickerell, Congress and the Constitution 153 (2004). This sort of "review" by Congress, however, is not truly coordinate. With Congress limited to passively reacting to Supreme Court rulings, the Court maintains the initiative on the one hand and retains power to review (that is, to declare void) any amended statutes on the other, so that its supremacy stands.

[109] Lawrence M. Friedman, A History of American Law 311, 312 (1973). For examples of state judicial assertions of supremacy, *see id.* at 311–18. *See also* Kermit L. Hall, The Magic Mirror 230–31 (1989) (on the "surge in judicial review" in state courts in the late nineteenth and early twentieth centuries); G. Alan Tarr, Understanding State Constitutions, ch. 6 (1998) (discussing concerns about the legitimacy of judicial authority to interpret constitutions, and noting the extent to which state courts are in lockstep, and also noting the general rise in stature and power of state judiciaries).

> coordinate departments of government entirely subordinate and beneath and within the power and control of the judiciary.[110]

It is within this universe of judicial supremacy, where the chief instrument is judicial review,[111] that advisory opinions, unhindered by the restraints of adjudication, operate to expand supremacy through their unrestrained de facto judicial review. No surprise, therefore, that advising justices declare acts unconstitutional in advisory opinions more frequently than they do in adjudicated cases. This is "a striking contrast," one result of which is that the advisory opinion "restricts the legislature more than the regular operation of judicial review does."[112] In an earlier era of coordinate, departmental, review, advisory opinions may have been understood simply as innocent advice since the judiciary was not yet seen—and did not yet demand to be seen—as the final and exclusive arbiter of a constitution. Judicial review in this era was "a successful bid by the judges to an equal place in the scheme—to status as members of a coordinate branch, capable of making and acting upon independent judgments about the meaning of the Constitution."[113]

But in an era of judicial supremacy the advising justices, engaging in their de facto judicial review and capable of waiving all restrictions on advising by applying a public importance exception at will and without limit, enable and expand the supremacy. The advisory opinion process, unrestrained by justiciability standards, or by case or controversy requirements, or by the other threshold limitations on litigated appeals, together with its hypothetical and abstract analysis, permits the justices to expand judicial power substantively as well as procedurally. Further, the advising justices' use of hypothetical facts contributes greatly to this. "Insofar as advisory opinions are resolved on hypothetical facts, there is a . . . sense in which the court's power can be considered enlarged. A court that can ground a decision on a factual matrix of its own construction is an unfettered court. The *intentional* creation of facts for use in arriving at a predetermined result would, of course, be a parody of the judicial process." [114]

---

[110] Quoted in JOHN J. DINAN, THE AMERICAN STATE CONSTITUTIONAL TRADITION 125–26 (2006). *See* 123–30 on the proposals at state constitutional conventions to limit judicial power, especially that of judicial review. Proposals included requiring a supermajority or unanimous vote to void a statute (at 127–28), recall of judges (at 129), and recall of judicial decisions (at 129–130). The influence of the Progressive movement on proposals to limit judicial power during this period is discussed in Chapter 4 in this book.

[111] *See, e.g.*, Gant, *Judicial Supremacy*, 4. (Judicial review "is often taken as synonymous with judicial supremacy.")

[112] Field, *The Advisory Opinion—An Analysis*, 212–13.

[113] Larry Kramer, *The Supreme Court 2000 Term: We the Court*, 115 HARV. L. REV. 4, 86 (2001). *See generally*, Kramer on coordinate review and its relation to a "popular" constitution seen as the document of the people as a "corporate body capable of acting independently from within the political system" (at 86). From the large body of scholarship on coordinate review, useful in our context is Robert A. Schapiro, *Judicial Deference and Interpretive Cooordinacy in State and Federal Constitutional Law*, 85 CORNELL L. REV. 656, 661–69 (2000); Scott E. Gant, *Judicial Supremacy*, 359; Larry Alexander & Frederick Schauer, *On Extralegal Constitutional Interpretation*, 110 HARV. L. REV. 1359 (1997) (defending judicial supremacy and triggering a debate on the issue); Paulson, *The Most Dangerous Branch*, 217.

[114] Kennedy, *Advisory Opinions: Cautions About Non-Judicial Undertakings*, 178

In Colorado, it was through an advisory opinion that the supreme court asserted a major reconfiguration of separation of powers while addressing a politically charged issue. In 2003 the state received some $146 million from the federal government under a recently passed act to increase jobs. The only material requirement on the states accepting funds was that the funds be used only to "provide essential government services" or to cover the costs of unfunded federal mandates.[115] The question arose about whether these funds were "state moneys," which required state legislative appropriation before the governor could spend them, or whether they were "custodial moneys," given to the state for a particular purpose and which were under the direct control of the governor and not subject to legislative appropriation.[116]

The legislature and governor openly disagreed over whether the federal funds granted to the state were "custodial." The legislature argued that the funds were granted with no "particular purpose," to be used so flexibly and within such broad limits as not to constitute "custodial" funds. The governor disagreed, and the legislature asked the court to render an advisory opinion on whether or not the funds were "custodial" under Colorado law. (In Colorado the "supreme court," not the "justices," renders advice.) The court, applying a totality-of-circumstances standard, advised that the federal funds, disbursed with minimal guidance on how they were to be allocated or on the purpose for which they may be spent, "cannot fairly be described as 'custodial' in nature."[117]

What the court in fact did, as the lone dissenting justice pointed out, was to effect a judicial expropriation of power over spending.[118] The advisory opinion's adoption of a totality-of-circumstances standard for deciding when federal funds are custodial had the effect of leaving it to the judiciary to decide on whether the legislature or the executive has spending authority in any given instance. This lends to the judiciary "an unlimited discretion to decide, in each individual case," whether federal funds are under the control of the governor or must be appropriated by the legislature.[119] In an unequivocal assertion of judicial supremacy, the justices stated that their advisory opinion made the Colorado supreme court the "sole arbiter" of when federal funds are custodial and when they are not. The court granted itself, as the dissenting justice complained, "increased power over federal grants," and did so in a way that has created a "shift of power among the three branches of state government," a creation that the dissenting justice called, perhaps with some understatement, "unwise."[120]

The Colorado opinion exemplifies an insidious aspect of the advisory opinion process, in which a dispute between the political branches is "resolved" judicially by the nonpolitical branch co-opting the power over which the other two branches were in conflict.

---

[115] *In re Interrogatories Submitted by the General Assembly on House Bill 04-1098*, 88 P.3d 1196, 1198 (Colo. 2004). The federal jobs act is encoded at 42 U.S.C. sec. 801. The quoted text is from sec. 801(d)(1).

[116] *Id.* at 1198. The Colorado supreme court's definition of "custodial funds" is in *MacManus v. Love*, 499 P.2d 609, 610 (Colo. 1972).

[117] *In re Interrogatories Submitted by the General Assembly on House Bill 04-1098*, at 1203.

[118] *Id.* at 1206–07 (Coates, J., dissenting).

[119] *Id.*

[120] *Id.* at 1207.

The opinion set forth no principle by which the political branches could resolve their own disputes about the distinction between "custodial" and "state" funds, that is, over which branch has power over the funds. It cited no precedent for the justices' "advising"—in fact a binding precedent—that the judiciary will decide this whenever necessary, case by case, and depending on the totality of the circumstances; that is, depending on what facts it chooses to construct as the basis for its "advice." What is insidious is the effective contraction, indeed outright cancellation, of public or political deliberation on what is properly a political issue. This advisory opinion testifies to advisory opinions amounting for all practical purposes to "ex parte interpretations of the constitution by a majority of that small group of government officials which is the least subject . . . to democratic political controls."[121] This is the civic contraction that Frankfurter complained about,[122] and many commentators have agreed. One of them, for example, noted in 1937 that legislatures relying on advisory opinions lose opportunities inherent in the "beneficent ordeal" of debate and negotiation, reducing the sense of responsibility and "ownership" of public issues.[123] The very availability of the advisory process invites legislative surrender of any obligation to assess the constitutionality of a bill.[124] Further, because "the proposed legislation will only satisfy the courts if it falls into a preconceived pigeonhole of constitutionality based on judicial review of prior enactments, the boldness [of the legislation] is lost and the result is a dulled, cautious bill that tries too hard to be constitutional."[125] Similarly, it invites the executive to evade assessing the constitutionality of its own acts.[126] One result is that advisory opinions simply amount to "too much government by judiciary."[127]

It was not by chance that this argument against advisory opinions surfaced with James Bradley Thayer, nor for that matter that it was Thayer who in 1885 wrote the first law review article on advisory opinions. Thayer was responding to a request from his cousin in Rhode Island who was disturbed by a recent and controversial Rhode Island advisory opinion. In 1883 the Rhode Island senate requested the justices' advice on whether the state constitution permits the legislature to submit to the voters a ballot question asking voters if they wish to call a state constitutional convention.[128]

---

[121] Sands, *Government by Judiciary*, 38.

[122] Felix Frankfurter, *A Note on Advisory Opinions*, 37 Harv. L. Rev. 1002, 1007 (1924). The issue of advisory opinions' effects on diminishing civic participation in general is discussed in Chapter 2. Here we focus specifically on the relation to judicial supremacy. For an opposing view, see Katyal, *Judges as Advicegivers*, 53 Stanford L. Rev. 1709, 1713 (1998). Katyal argues that the U.S. Supreme Court's de facto advice giving allows it to avoid "broad rules and abstract theories" and so is "democracy enhancing" in allowing opportunities for public and political debate.

[123] F. R. Aumann, *The Supreme Court and the Advisory Opinion*, 4 Ohio St. L.J. 21, 48 (1937).

[124] *See, e.g.*, Pascal F. Calogero, *Advisory Opinions: A Wise Change for Louisiana and Its Judiciary?*, 38 Loyola L. Rev. 329 (1992). Calogero, then chief justice of the Louisiana supreme court, was writing to oppose creation of advisory opinion authority in Louisiana.

[125] Persky, *Ghosts That Slay*, 1179.

[126] *See, e.g.*, Kennedy, *Advisory Opinions: Cautions About Non-Judicial Undertakings*, 190.

[127] Sands, *Government by Judiciary*, 38.

[128] *In re The Constitutional Convention*, 14 R.I. 649, 650 (1883).

The underlying issue and call for a convention reflect the dynamics of nineteenth-century state constitutionalism, including the differing views on whether a constitution is a people's document, outside control of the government, or a legal document, subject to judicial interpretation. Under Rhode Island's 1842 constitution, foreign-born citizens could not vote, and several attempts in the 1870s to amend the constitution to permit them the franchise failed.[129] While a simple majority of voters favored the amendment, the ballot measures did not receive the three-fifths majority then required to amend the constitution. A group supporting broadening the franchise petitioned Congress under the Fourteenth Amendment's privileges or immunities clause, but the response was that if Congress recognized voting as one of the privileges or immunities of U.S. citizens, then all citizens, including men, women, and infants, would have the vote.[130]

Supporters of the amendment then called for a constitutional convention, which voters could presumably approve by a simple majority vote rather than the three-fifths required for amendments. The constitution was silent on conventions, but supporters "contended that the right and power of framing a constitution was, in every state, a right and power inherent in the people, and that it was not limited in the mode of its exercise by provisions of the existing constitution with regard to mere amendments." All that the supporters believed was required was for the legislature to submit to voters the question on calling a convention. Several such proposals were introduced in the legislature. All were defeated, but the issue apparently created enough public controversy that the senate, passing off this political hot potato to the nonpolitical branch, sought an advisory opinion from the justices.[131] The justices advised that the constitution may be amended only by means provided for by the constitution itself, and since the constitution was silent on calling conventions, Rhode Island may never again call a constitutional convention.[132]

This advice, apparently dooming the people of Rhode Island forever to be prohibited from calling another constitutional convention, triggered sharp reactions, including this lampoon.

> Alas! what a pity our fathers [the constitution's framers] didn't mention,
> That we boys, if very good, could hold a convention.
> They never said we shouldn't but didn't say we might,
> "Ergo," cry the sages, "you haven't got the right."
> 'Twas very bad, indeed, their permission to deny,
> But infinitely worse at once to up and die;

---

[129] This was part of a broader movement in the latter half of the nineteenth century to give immigrants the vote. "At least at some point from mid-century to the 1890s, nineteen states provided immigrants the franchise if they declared their intent to become citizens." But all these states revoked it "in the wake of the anti-immigrant agitation" from the 1870s to the 1920s. Michael Schudson, The Good Citizen: A History of American Civic Life 183 (1998).

[130] Irving B. Richman, Rhode Island: A Study in Separatism 319–20 (1918; 1st ed. 1905).

[131] Richman, Rhode Island: A Study in Separatism, 319–23.

[132] *In re* The Constitutional Convention, 14 R.I. at 652–53.

For thus they turned the lock and flung away the key,
And Rhode Island's "in a box" for all eternitee.[133]

A former Rhode Island chief justice, Charles S. Bradley, was among those disturbed by the advisory opinion, and he published a pamphlet inquiring into the authority of the justices to give such advice, and conceded that the opinion "must be . . . taken as it is."[134] The pamphlet, which may be the first publication devoted to the nature of the advisory opinion jurisdiction, raised such questions as advisory opinions' nonbinding nature and their relation to separation of powers.[135] Perhaps in order to obtain the support of a prominent legal scholar, Bradley asked his cousin at Harvard Law School to undertake a study of advisory opinions.

In the resulting article, Thayer reviewed advisory opinion practices in the advisory states as well as its history in England and colonial America. The article is neutral in tone, an academic analysis of the history and practice of advisory opinions even to an abundance of footnotes (comprising a third of the article's text). Thayer, however, repeatedly affirmed that advisory opinions are not and never have been binding, implying of course that the Rhode Island legislature need not feel bound to the supreme court's recent advisory opinion. "It needs no argument," he says, "to show that [advisory] opinions are not binding upon any body, and should not be."[136] Thayer's concern that advisory opinions be understood as nonbinding led him to write a piece for *The Nation* in 1889, soon after Colorado ratified a constitution with an advisory opinion provision. The provision seemed to attract Thayer's attention because of what he called a "peculiarity." The provision referred to the "Supreme Court" as the advice-giver, not the

---

[133] Quoted in Frankfurter, *A Note on Advisory Opinions*, 1009. The source of the poem, which Frankfurter cites only as "Richman, *Rhode Island*, 322," is IRVING B. RICHMAN, RHODE ISLAND: A STUDY IN SEPARATISM 322 (1918; 1st ed. 1905). Richman, a historian from Iowa, apparently did not compose the poem, just cited it from an unidentified source.

[134] CHARLES SMITH BRADLEY, THE METHODS OF CHANGING THE CONSTITUTIONS OF THE STATES, ESPECIALLY THAT OF RHODE ISLAND 13 (Boston 1885). Such pamphlets, like poems, as forms of civic participation seem to have largely disappeared.

[135] *Id.* at 13–15. *See also* AMASA M. EATON, CONSTITUTION-MAKING IN RHODE ISLAND (1899). Published by the Rhode Island Constitutional League, this pamphlet was devoted to overcoming the effects of the 1883 advisory opinion. Stressing that the opinion was not binding, Eaton called on the legislature to ignore the advisory opinion and proceed to call a convention. To treat the advisory opinion as if it were binding is "to ignore the recognized distinction between an *advisory opinion* and an *actual decision* of a litigated case by the court." (*Id.* at xxii) The legislature, however, would never reject or even ignore the "nonbinding" advisory opinion even in such a controversial instance. This confirms, in the face of strong public arguments against the opinion, the de facto binding nature of advisory opinions discussed in Chapter 5. The opinion would remain in force until the justices themselves reversed it in 1935.

[136] James B. Thayer, *Advisory Opinions*, *in* LEGAL ESSAYS 48 (1885, 1908). A half-century after the 1883 advisory opinion, the Rhode Island justices reversed themselves, advising that it could not have been the intention to construe the constitution so as to make constitutional conventions "an impossibility in Rhode Island." *Opinion of the Court to the Governor in the Matter of the Constitutional Convention*, 178 A. 433, 436 (1935). Criticism of the 1883 advisory opinion continued at least to 1927, when F. R. Aumann commented that it "has been an effective obstruction to the modernization of the Rhode Island constitution." Aumann, *The Supreme Court and the Advisory Opinion*, 46. On a similar issue in Massachusetts, see *Opinion of the Justices of the Supreme Judicial Court*, 60 Mass. 573 (1833).

"justices," in contrast to "everywhere else." The result was an opinion by the Colorado supreme court in which they declared that their advisory opinions have the force of precedent since the opinions were rendered by the court and not by the individual justices.[137] Thayer's prompt challenge to an advising court's unprecedented rejection of nonbinding doctrine reflects the depth of his concern about its effects on the legislative and political process.

> Here, then, . . . we have a State [which in its new constitution is] getting in trouble by tying up its Legislature with many petty restrictions, and then trying to get out of its trouble by giving the judges the portentous power of settling by an authoritative manifesto, unaided by argument, the question whether the Legislature has conformed to those requirements. And the consequences of this construction [of the advisory opinion provision as binding] are so serious that the Court restricts the natural meaning of the language of the new [advisory opinion] amendment so as to limit it to particular classes of questions [by the justices' limiting questions to those of "public," not private matters].[138]

The criticisms of advisory opinions' debilitating effects on civic discourse and the democratic process echo closely the familiar criticisms of judicial supremacy. Critics have attacked the extent to which the U.S. Supreme Court has eliminated other interpretive spaces in the public realm and protected "its own exclusive custody of the Constitution."[139] The general acceptance of judicial supremacy in our time has "fundamentally altered the meaning of Republican citizenship."[140] It treats "ordinary politics [as] too dangerous to permit without some independent body to control its excesses and injustices."[141] Another critic similarly argues that "judicial enforcement of the Constitution truncates . . . democratic choice." He accuses the Court of "snuffing out . . . democratic experimentation."[142] Another describes as a failing of judicial supremacy its tendency "to discourage serious deliberations outside the judiciary about the meaning of

---

[137] James B. Thayer, Letter, 49 The Nation 476 (Dec. 12, 1889). Thayer was an advisor to the North Dakota and South Dakota constitutional conventions.

[138] *Id.* Frankfurter's 1924 critique of advisory opinions, stressing their capacity to inhibit the political process, offers the Rhode Island 1883 opinion as an example of "ill-considered advisory opinions" that may become "millstones around the necks of succeeding generations." Frankfurter, *A Note on Advisory Opinions*, 1008.

[139] Larry Kramer, *The Supreme Court 2000 Term: We the Court*, 115 Harv. L. Rev. 4, 14 (2001). *See also* Healy, The Rise of Unnecessary Constitutional Rulings, 854 (arguing that the U.S. Supreme Court's "embrace of unnecessary constitutional rulings is part of a larger trend in which the Court has gradually squeezed the other branches of government out of the business of constitutional interpretation").

[140] Kramer, The People Themselves, 233. Kramer is especially disturbed by the extraordinarily widespread toleration of judicial supremacy. "Public acceptance of judicial supremacy pervades constitutional law and politics. . . . It changes how politicians, the press, and other affected actors internalize the Court's rulings." *Id.*

[141] *Id.* at 243.

[142] Posner, Law, Pragmatism, and Democracy, 232, 122.

the constitution," and its "exclusion of citizen interpretation."[143] Another explains that under judicial supremacy theory espoused by the modern Supreme Court, "the political branches lose their sense of responsibility to analyze independently the constitutionality of a particular course of action. . . . When the courts make the decisions, the people cannot hold the political branches accountable."[144]

This chorus on judicial supremacy echoes critics of advisory opinions because, as we have seen, advisory opinions are accepted as de facto judicial review in an era of judicial supremacy. Advisory opinion jurisdiction is so broad that advising justices may accept any questions relating to their respective state constitutions. The public importance exception provides a conceptually and practically convenient means of sliding past all established restrictions on advising. Justices seem to feel themselves free even on occasion to ignore the threshold matter of their jurisdiction altogether as they insert themselves into politically contentious controversies. A 2007 Michigan advisory opinion is a striking example, especially since Michigan has one of the most restrictive of advisory opinion provisions.

In April 2006 the Michigan legislature passed a bill requiring voters to present photo identification in order to vote, or failing that to sign an affidavit affirming the voter's identity before being allowed to vote.[145] The state's house of representatives asked the supreme court for an advisory opinion on the question—novel in Michigan's courts—of whether these identification requirements violated either the Michigan or the U.S. constitution. The request raised a sizable number of major constitutional issues affecting the right to vote. These included the correct applicable constitutional standard (rational basis or strict scrutiny), the relation of state to federal constitutional standards, the extent to which the right to vote may be burdened by regulations intended to prevent voter fraud, whether purchase of a photo ID card, if required, constitutes a poll tax, and whether the requirements unduly burden minorities, among other questions.[146]

The court, in an awkward position typical of the advisory opinion process, was being asked to advise on a major controversy but without adversarial parties (or, judicially speaking, any parties at all) before them. The court requested that the attorney general submit two separate briefs, one supporting the constitutionality of the statute, one opposing. This was likely an attempt to lend an advisory opinion proceeding an artificial aura of an adversarial proceeding. (If the court wanted both sides of the controversy to be presented, a single brief could easily have done that, though the appearance of a litigated appeal would not have been kept up.) That request also had the effect of suggesting an

---

[143] Gant, *Judicial Supremacy*, 400, 407. *See also* Stephen M. Griffin, *Judicial Supremacy and Equal Protection in a Democracy of Rights*, 4 U. Pa. J. Const. L. 281, 282, 300 (2002) (on countering judicial supremacy in the face of the Supreme Court's "relatively new interest in destroying civil rights created through democratic deliberation").

[144] Barkow, *More Supreme Than Court?*, 327–28. *See also, generally*, Jeremy Waldron, Law and Disagreement (1999).

[145] 2005 PA 71, sec. 523.

[146] *In re Request for Advisory Opinion Regarding Constitutionality of 2005 PA 71*, 740 N.W.2d 444 (Mich. 2007).

abstract intellectual exercise.[147] The court also seemed to acknowledge the political sensitivities involved by inviting briefs from the state's Democratic and Republican parties.[148] The court invited a brief from the state's elections bureau, and accepted briefs from the governor, a former attorney general, and, reflecting the racial and civil rights implications, several public interest groups including a joint brief from the NAACP, ACLU, American-Arab Anti-Discrimination Committee, and Detroit Urban League, among others. Other briefs included those from the Michigan Civil Rights Commission, the Lawyers' Committee for Civil Rights, the American Center for Voting Rights, and from the state's county clerks. In all, the justices received a total of twenty briefs or reply briefs.

The court's twenty-five-page advisory opinion addressed all issues raised both by the "opposing Attorney General" and by the "supporting Attorney General." The court concluded, with two of the seven justices dissenting, that the photo ID requirements of the statute in question were facially constitutional. But the advisory opinion was neither proper nor permissible. For one thing, Michigan's advisory opinion provision is uniquely restrictive in allowing advisory opinions only on the constitutionality of legislation "after it has been enacted into law but before its effective date."[149] The part of the photo ID law at issue became effective in 1997, some eight years before the request for an advisory opinion on its constitutionality. The court passed this off as what it called a "preliminary matter," doing so under the pretext that the 1997 statute had been reenacted without change in 2005, whose effective date was January 1, 2007, and the request for the advisory opinion was made before that. The court took this position despite Michigan's statute requiring that reenactments be construed as uninterrupted continuations of the original acts.[150] The court did not address this difficulty.

Second, neither the court nor the "opposing" or "supporting" attorney general's briefs addressed another defect in the advisory opinion process: the question presented was overly broad. Most states, including Michigan, do not accept requests for advice that are simply blanket requests on whether or not a statute is generally constitutional. The requesting authority must put specific questions of law to the advising justices.[151] In 1975, for example, the Michigan House of Representatives simply sent to the justices

[147] The Michigan court did this at least once before, some twenty years earlier, but in that instance the court also invited briefs "on the question of whether the Court should grant requests for an advisory opinion." *Order*, 401 N.W.2d 613 (Mich. 1987). The 2006 proceedings included no such request.

[148] *In re Request for Advisory Opinion Regarding Constitutionality of 2005 PA 71*, 712 N.W.2d 450 (Mich. 2006).

[149] Mich. Const. art. III, sec. 8. The provision is reviewed in Chapter 1. Its full text is in Appendix A.

[150] *In re Request for Advisory Opinion Regarding Constitutionality of 2005 PA 71*, 740 N.W.2d at 450–51 (Mich. 2006). The Michigan provision on reenactments is in Mich. Comp. Laws, sec. 8.3.u. Contrast this with the Alabama justices, who have refused to advise "on the constitutionality of pending legislation which is similar to legislation already enacted into law." This is because "the constitutionality of statutes should be tested by appropriate adversary proceedings when available or when at all possible." *Opinion of the Justices*, 405 So.2d 362, 364 (Ala. 1981), citing *Opinion of the Justices*, 394 So.2d 957 (Ala. 1981) and *Opinion of the Justices*, 96 So.2d 752 (Ala. 1957).

[151] This restriction is discussed in Chapter 3.

copies of a bill. The court refused to advise since requests must "particularize any claims of unconstitutionality. . . . A request stated too broadly cannot be considered."[152] The Michigan court has several times refused to advise on this ground.[153] In the photo ID advisory opinion, the court simply ignored this restriction even though one justice raised this in the original order seeking briefs from the attorney general and others.[154] The court did note that when a court is "considering a challenge to a state election law," each inquiry into the law must be fact and circumstance specific because "[n]o bright line separates permissible election-related regulation from unconstitutional infringement."[155] But here of course there was no "challenge" before the Michigan court, only an abstract and general question, and the court's answer, with no case or controversy before it, could hardly have been based on a fact and circumstance specific inquiry.

Third, as one of the amici briefs complained, the court "inserted itself into the issue" by taking it upon itself to change the question that the Michigan House of Representatives had submitted.[156] The question submitted asked if the photo identification requirements of the statute in question "violate either the Michigan constitution or the United States constitution."[157] The court changed this to a question which asked if the statute's requirements "on their face" violate either the Michigan or U.S. constitution.[158] This not only "materially change[d] the legal analysis" required,[159] but, as a dissenting justice sharply objected, it was questionable "whether the Court has the authority to alter a question presented. . . . By modifying the question, this Court effectively usurps the authority of the House to pose the question. Alternatively, the Court is acting, with no

---

[152] *Request for Advisory Opinion on Constitutionality of 1975 PA 227*, 235 N.W.2d 321, 322 (Mich. 1975). The court also refused to advise because the request was made before enactment, not after as constitutionally required.

[153] *E.g.*, *Request for Advisory Opinion on the Constitutionality of 1979 PA 57*, 281 N.W.2d 322, 324 (Mich. 1979) (Advisory opinion refused because the "questions are stated only in general terms; the request fails to particularize claims of constitutionality."). *See also Advisory Opinion on Constitutionality of 1974 PA 242*, 228 N.W.2d 772, 776 (Mich. 1975) (Levin, J. dissenting in part) (dissenting justice complaining about advising absent particularized claims of unconstitutionality).

[154] *In re Request for Advisory Opinion Regarding Constitutionality of 2005 PA 71*, 712 N.W.2d 450, 450 (Mich. 2006) (Cavanagh, J., dissenting to issuing an advisory opinion). Cavanagh was one of the two dissenters to the advisory opinion that found the Photo ID law constitutional, writing a seventeen-page dissent that brought up no questions regarding the propriety of the court rendering advice, despite his argument dissenting to the initial acceptance of the request for advice. *In re Request for Advisory Opinion*, 740 N.W.2d 444, 469–86 (Mich. 2006) (Cavanagh, J., dissenting). The other dissenting justice also raised no such objections. *Id.* at 486–503 (Kelley, J., dissenting). Another restriction that may have been infringed here is that the advice was on private rights, in this case of voters. *See, e.g.*, *Request for Advisory Opinion on the Constitutionality of 1979 PA 57*, 281 N.W.2d 322 (Mich. 1979) (refusing to advise in part because it may prematurely preempt taxpayers from bringing suit). The private rights restriction on advisory opinions is discussed in Chapter 3.

[155] *In re Request for Advisory Opinion*, 740 N.W.2d at 456, citing the U.S. Supreme Court holding in *Timmons v. Twin Cities Area New Party*, 520 U.S. 351, 359 (1997).

[156] *Brief of Amici Curiae National Association for the Advancement of Colored People*, et al., July 18, 2006, at 10.

[157] *Id.*

[158] *In re Request for Advisory Opinion Regarding Constitutionality of 2005 PA 71*, 712 N.W.2d 450, 450 (Mich. 2006) (order granting request for the advisory opinion).

[159] *Brief* of NAACP at 10.

case or controversy before it, to create an issue that it chooses to address." Either way, he said, the court "unwisely ventures onto infirm constitutional terrain."[160] The court, then, in finding the statute valid, chose to inquire into whether the photo identification requirements were valid facially. Even though this distorted the question from the house of representatives, it is usually the only kind of question an advisory opinion can address, since no "as applied" set of circumstances could plausibly be presented without an actual case or controversy. A challenge to facial constitutionality must show that "no set of circumstances exists" under which the statute in question would be valid.[161] Since no set of circumstances was argued before the court, the court responded to an abstract question with an abstract answer.

In a remarkable assertion of judicial supremacy through the advisory opinion process, the Michigan supreme court proceeded to answer its own question, superseding the actual question presented without explanation or defense.[162] The question implicated a sizable number of the most vexing and complex social and political issues of our time. The issues addressed in the advisory opinion included whether a statute requiring photo identification to vote violated the equal protection and due process clauses of the Fourteenth Amendment and the parallel clauses of the Michigan constitution, including the difficult question of whether the statute is subject to strict scrutiny. This relates to whether the identification requirements would have a disparate impact on minorities and whether it violates the 1965 Voting Rights Act or the Civil Rights Act of 1964. The court's question also directly involved questions of racial discrimination, immigration, voter fraud, and voter intimidation, among others. The depth of concern about these social and political issues is reflected in the large number of briefs amici curiae that were filed. A single one of those briefs was submitted by: the Detroit branch and the state conference of the National Association for the Advancement of Colored People; National Bar Association; American Civil Liberties Union of Michigan; League of Women Voters of Detroit; American-Arab Anti-Discrimination Committee; Project Vote; Association of Communities for Reform Now; Latin Americans for Social and Economic Development, Inc.; City of Detroit; Detroit Urban League; and National Conference for Community and Justice—Michigan.

The Michigan supreme court effectively withdrew an imposing set of pressing social and political issues from public and legislative debate sparked by a proposed statute requiring photo identification to vote. It "settled" the issues by a proceeding involving no case below, that is, no litigation by private parties who were actually affected by the statute and who presented an actual case or controversy before a jury of private citizens,

---

[160] *In re Request for Advisory Opinion*, 712 N.W.2d at 451 (Kelly, J., dissenting to order granting request for an advisory opinion) (citations omitted).

[161] *In re Request for Advisory Opinion*, 740 N.W.2d at 450.

[162] This facet of judicial supremacy as exercised by the U.S. Supreme Court was the target of a November 2010 *New York Times* editorial, decrying the recent tendency of the Court to decide "much broader questions than those presented to it." Recent cases show "that the current court is using its power with more latitude than any in memory, . . . [r]edefining itself as a constitutional court . . . limited only by limits it opts to recognize." *Our Constitutional Court*, NEW YORK TIMES, Nov. 23, 2010, at A26 (editorial).

concerning a challenged statute enacted after public and political debate. Rather, the court, comprising seven lawyers, based on other lawyers' briefs and oral arguments, "advised" the whole thing away.

Advisory Opinions and the Quality of Conflict

The advisory opinions' contribution in this way to the diminution of public debate affects the legal process as well as the political. The posture of the advisory opinion jurisdiction in an era of judicial supremacy raises the question of its relation to the adversarial nature of the judicial system. We have reviewed, in Chapter 2, the criticism of advisory opinions because they tend to be rendered in a factual void owing to the absence of litigation presenting opposing views. Advisory opinions, as Frankfurter expressed it, in the absence of facts are responses to sterile legal questions "bound to result in sterile conclusions unrelated to actualities."[163] This often noted factual vacuum, however, is not only, or even mainly, a matter of insufficient information on which the justices may base their advice. It is, rather, as well a matter of the effect of advisory opinions on the character of the conflict inherent in litigation in an adversarial legal system.

The very reality of the judicial space in which legal questions are resolved relies on "the simultaneous presence of innumerable perspectives and aspects."[164] Advisory opinions have exacerbated contraction of this space by aggravating two opposing but widely accepted if doubtful perceptions regarding legally relevant facts. One is the assumption of semantic immanence, that constitutional language has a single and correct meaning that is already "in" the language regardless of contingent facts, and that the high court justices, like some temple priesthood, alone have the capacity to divine the true meaning.[165] A second, developed by the legal realists of the 1920s and 1930s, is the primacy of the personal character of the judge over the perpetually indeterminate quality of facts in any legal context. One such realist, writing in 1930, believed that the "facts of any case were . . . necessarily elusive and essentially subjective. Not legal rules or precedents, but the judge's concept of justice and his social and political prejudices decided cases."[166] Both perceptions, though, sought to do what advisory opinions seek to do: to "settle once and forever a disputed point of constitutional law."[167] While one purports that the meaning of a statute or constitution lies in the prejudices and predilections of the judges, and the other that the meaning lies in the text and is

---

[163] Frankfurter, *A Note on Advisory Opinions*, 1005.

[164] HANNAH ARENDT, HUMAN CONDITION, 57 (describing public spaces in general).

[165] *See* RICHARD H. FALLON, JR., IMPLEMENTING THE CONSTITUTION, 7 (2001) (arguing for "rejecting the mesmerizing notion that the Court's only purpose is identifying the Constitution's true meaning").

[166] EDWARD A. PURCELL, JR., THE CRISIS OF DEMOCRATIC THEORY: SCIENTIFIC NATURALISM AND THE PROBLEM OF VALUE 83 (1973) (summarizing JEROME FRANK, LAW AND THE MODERN MIND 136 (1930, 1963)).

[167] J. E. Rhodes, *Advisory Opinions*, 6 ME. L. REV. 28, 35 (1912).

"discoverable by rational analysis,"[168] both have in common with the advisory opinion process that they downplay the role of fact, relegating it to providing mere informational background. Facts, however, play a more significant role in an adversarial system. They provide the element of a narrative that supports the construction of a pattern of conflict. In law, no story, no trouble; no trouble, no case or controversy.

What is so crucially missing from advisory opinion proceedings is narrative and its inherent depiction of conflict. An advisory opinion may attempt to hypothesize facts, but it cannot credibly hypothesize the legally relevant narrative that is central to the adversarial process. The contingent nature of narrative allows, in fact requires, the legal actors to assert conflicting structures and meanings in their narratives.[169] In the course of the telling, as the judge or jury hears the opposing narratives nothing seems predetermined. This is why advisory opinions constitute a kind of legal vacuum. This, when Frankfurter and many others complain about advisory opinion proceedings' lack of fact, is what is missing.

The vacuum is apparent in the Massachusetts advisory opinion on same-sex civil unions that we looked at earlier. The majority justices argued that the senate's bill was unconstitutional since it discriminated against couples in civil unions in contrast with couples who are married, despite the bill providing that civil unions would have all the "benefits, protections, rights and responsibilities of marriage."[170] A minority opinion argued that if persons in two separate groups have the same rights, there can be no "invidious discrimination,"[171] but the majority opinion passed this off by asserting that "[t]he history of this nation has demonstrated that separate is seldom, if ever, equal."[172] The opinion cites no American history other than *Brown v. Board of Education*, which held that segregated public schools that were purportedly separate but equal violated the equal protection of the laws guaranteed by the Fourteenth Amendment.[173] The *Brown* plaintiffs, however, introduced factual evidence of the harmful effects of separate but equal education, including, controversially, social science research findings, evidence that was central to the decision. The majority advisory opinion in Massachusetts could of course offer no such facts supporting a claim that the separate groups here (those in civil unions and those in marriage) cannot be equal, since there was no adjudicated proceeding whereby such facts could be introduced and be subject to challenge.

---

[168] The quoted phrase is from Purcell's discussion of legal realism in EDWARD A. PURCELL, JR., CRISIS OF DEMOCRATIC THEORY, 80.

[169] On the ancient role of narrative in the common law process, see MILSOM, HISTORICAL FOUNDATIONS OF THE COMMON LAW, 39–42 (on the development of the *narratio* during the thirteenth through sixteenth centuries as "the very centre of the legal process"). Milsom suggests that the modern barrister may have begun as one who could speak the *narratio* for another. (Since the litigants themselves were required to speak their claims and denials correctly—errors could be fatal—if litigants permitted another to speak for them they could disavow a defective *narratio*. Milsom notes that "[w]e do not know how it came about that the litigant was allowed to speak through the mouth of another," but it may be that the barrister "began as one who could harmlessly blunder." *Id.* at 39-40.).

[170] Senate Bill No. 2175, quoted in *In re Opinion of the Justices to the Senate*, 2004 WL 202184, at 1.

[171] *Id.* at 6–8 (Sosman, J., separate opinion).

[172] *Id.* at 4.

[173] Brown v. Board of Education, 347 U.S. 483, 495 (1954).

The best the majority could do was to assert that regarding the two groups here, separate but equal is somehow not really equal, that the bill at issue would maintain and foster "a stigma of exclusion."[174] A minority opinion suggested that it would make "eminent sense to obtain some direct experience with this first in the nation proposed program of 'civil unions,' . . . experience [that] will both identify where the theoretically identical treatment is not identical in reality and simultaneously inform those seeking genuine equality what remedies might best be fashioned to close the gap."[175] Such experience, however, is excluded by the advisory opinion process, which does not rely on the adjudicative process that would necessarily introduce such experience. That is, excluded initially were the contested issues that would have been debated in the legislature, and in the public arena, were the bill not to have been sent to the justices. Excluded in due course was the litigation that would have brought the contest into the arena of the trial court. But the advisory opinion process shut it all out.

The operation of the legal system's adversarial sector has been contracting generally, undermining the capacity of the system to address legal disputes through "the sharp clash of proofs presented by litigants."[176] This is partly owing to accusations (echoing those made in defense of advisory opinions) that the system is rife with inefficiency and delay.[177] But it reflects as well an uneasiness with the adversarial system's quality of conflict in itself, the uneasiness reflected in "the tendency [of liberal theorists] to theorize away conflicts—or, put otherwise, to remove politics from their theories of politics."[178] The decline is evidenced in the use of—and the pressure to use—such devices as settlements, plea bargains, mediation, declaratory judgments, summary judgment, administrative law procedures, and nonjury trials.[179] And advisory opinions.

The price may be high. A historic role of the adversary system has been "a rampart against tyranny," or at least a "legitimate means of challenging government actions."[180] Further, the "adversarial system grew as a consequence of the steady narrowing of

---

[174] *In re* Opinion of the Justices to the Senate, at 4.

[175] *Id.* at 10 (Sosman, J., separate opinion).

[176] Stephan Landsman, *The Rise of the Contentious Spirit: Adversary Procedure in Eighteenth Century England*, 75 CORNELL L. REV. 497, 500 (1990).

[177] *See, e.g.*, Stephan Landsman, *The Decline of the Adversary System: How the Rhetoric of Swift and Certain Justice Has Affected Adjudication in American Courts*, 29 BUFFALO L. REV. 487, 502–03 (1980) ("[R]eliance on the adversary process is declining . . . [partly owing to] judicial and scholarly criticism that various facets of the adversary process are delay ridden and inefficient . . . [which has] greatly facilitated the adoption of nonadversary methods.").

[178] KEN I. KERSCH, CONSTRUCTING CIVIL LIBERTIES 283 (2004).

[179] *See* Stephan Landsman, *The Decline of the Adversary System*, 504–10 (discussing all these except summary judgments and declaratory judgment, and noting that the "chief justification for change has been the claimed need for greater speed and efficiency").

[180] STEPHAN LANDSMAN, THE ADVERSARY SYSTEM 44–45 (1984). "For centuries adversarial courts have served as a counterbalance to official tyranny and have worked to broaden the scope of individual rights. . . . When adversarial process has been ignored in the operation of the courts, . . . human rights diminished and governmental repression increased." *Id.* at 46. *See also* Mirjan Damaska, *Evidentiary Barriers to Conviction and Two Models of Criminal Procedure: A Comparative Study*, 121 U. PA. L. REV. 506, 574 (1973) ("[T]he [adversarial] Due Process model is prepared to sacrifice efficiency in the interest of minimizing error. . . . Due Process ideology . . . consists of the belief that individual values are paramount and that official power must be limited.").

judicial authority" as rules of evidence and cross-examination pushed aside inquisitorial, judge-centered methods of truth seeking. This "reflected the belief that a neutral and essentially passive judiciary would be the most effective defender of what Blackstone called 'liberty.'"[181] In our time, however, the "political and policy influence of American courts and judges is unparalleled; no judiciary in the world wields greater influence in the governing of a nation and the fashioning of its policies."[182] Advisory opinions reinforce in practice and affirm in theory this posture of the judiciary and its concomitant removal of opportunity for members of the public to challenge authorities. Moving contentious questions directly to the advising justices and thereby resolving political controversies, and doing so in an era of widely accepted judicial supremacy in which the penchant for judicial lawmaking is unrestrained by the limitations of a case or controversy, puts an end to matters that should, in a republic, be subject to civic debate. The advisory opinion process withdraws conflict from the civic realm into the judicial realm and then withdraws it yet again from the adversarial arena to the attenuated, abstract region of advisory opinions. The twofold withdrawal is especially damaging when it involves matters—race, say, or same-sex marriage—that are at bottom moral issues that, as such, are inescapably subjects of debate. Moral argument "dominates both the beginning and the end of the democratic process."[183] The debate is inescapable because "the deepest source of our moral disagreement in politics may reside in the human condition itself."[184] It should not be for the advisory opinion process to diminish the capacity for moral, much less political, disagreement.

* * *

"The public," wrote Ann Althouse in a *New York Times* op-ed article, "may have become so used to the notion that a judge's word is what counts that it forgets why this is true. The judges have this constitutional power only because they operate by a judicial method that restricts them to resolving concrete controversies."[185] With that crucial limit completely absent in the advisory opinion process, the advising judges are untrammeled in their assertion of judicial power. This is not at all inconsistent with the dangers (which so disturbed Joseph Story) of advisory opinions risking judicial subjugation to the legislature. "[W]here high court justices do not adhere to commanding principles upon which judicial discretion may be exercised, and have no principled basis for declining to respond, the justices may lose their independence and become subservient to the requesting branch."[186]

---

[181] Stephan Landsman, *The Rise of the Contentious Spirit*, 604.

[182] Michael L. Buenger, *Friction by Design: The Necessary Contest of State Judicial Power and Legislative Policymaking*, 43 U. Richmond L. Rev. 571, 571 (2009).

[183] Amy Gutmann & Dennis Thompson, Democracy and Disagreement 41 (1996). *See also* Michael J. Sandel, Democracy's Discontents 328 (1996) (on restoring the "civic spaces [as] sites of deliberation about the common good" and increasing the prominence of the "distinctive moral language of civil society").

[184] Gutmann & Thompson, Democracy and Disagreement, 21.

[185] Ann Althouse, *A Law Unto Herself*, New York Times, Aug. 23, 2006, at A23 (op-ed article).

[186] Kennedy, *Advisory Opinions, Cautions About Non-Judicial Undertakings*, 195–96.

The dynamics of unconstrained judicial power may tilt either way owing to the tension, which we looked at in Chapter 1, between advice-giving as guidance and as assertion of power which inheres in advising within the corridors of power. Today, though, in dramatic distinction to Story's time, the expansion of judicial power has usually put all the aces in the judiciary's hand. A commentator notes that in recent years the advising justices have been increasingly judicious in their use of advisory opinions, rendering substantially fewer than previously.[187] He believes that "many attacks on the advisory process are unsupported by the contemporary data . . . [which show that] judicious use of the modern advisory opinion has strengthened, not weakened, representative government by preventing both public reliance on facially unconstitutional legislation and governmental expenditure on programs and initiatives likely to face a successful challenge."[188] But neither the lower numbers nor the purported pragmatic advantages can "save" advisory opinions. Lower numbers and pragmatic advantages do not compensate for the doctrinal and other flaws of the advisory opinion jurisdiction, nor for the expansion of judicial supremacy that it permits, nor, ultimately, for its challenge to the legitimacy and prestige of judicial lawmaking.

To the extent that constitutional interpretation by the judiciary is such lawmaking—few would deny it nowadays—advisory opinions are flawed interpretive discourse. The discourse carries the force of the law, claims of advisory opinions' purported nonbinding nature notwithstanding, and it is a force whose exercise is at odds with the values of state constitutionalism. "American constitutionalism is not simply an aggregate of distinct bodies of state and federal doctrine. Rather, American constitutionalism is the interpretive enterprise that seeks to understand the appropriate role for the rule of law in a democratic order."[189] Advisory opinions risk undermining the search for that understanding, an understanding central to the people's faith in and acceptance of the law. "When you are writing laws," the narrator says in Hilary Mantel's novel *Wolf Hall*, "you are testing words to find their utmost power. Like spells, they have to make things happen in the real world, and like spells, they only work if people believe in them."[190]

In forty states the supreme courts have no advisory opinions jurisdiction, and the large and real fact is that these states suffer little if any disadvantage. They seem to resolve constitutional questions as well, or as imperfectly, as do the ten advisory opinion states. Advisory opinions are an interesting but doubtful and perilous experiment in state constitutionalism. They do not seem to be worth the price.

---

[187] Persky, *Ghosts That Slay*, 1161, 1183 (noting a "sharp drop-off in advisory opinion activity" during 2000–2004, compared to the previous ten years, and that "in a span of thirty years [1974–2004] the acceptance rate of advisory opinion requests has fallen from 89% to 81%, the answer rate of advisory questions has fallen from 84% to 61%, and the number of requests submitted to the justices has plummeted by more than half.").

[188] *Id.* at 1161.

[189] Paul W. Kahn, *Interpretation and Authority in State Constitutionalism*, 106 Harv. L. Rev. 1147, 1156 (1993).

[190] Hilary Mantel, Wolf Hall 470 (2009).

APPENDIX } A

Advisory Opinion Provisions

Alabama

The Governor, by a request in writing, or either house of the Legislature, by a resolution of such house, may obtain a written opinion of the justices of the Supreme Court of Alabama or a majority thereof on important constitutional questions.

The justices of the Supreme Court may request briefs from the Attorney General, and may receive briefs from other attorneys as amici curiae as to such questions as may be propounded to them for their answers.

The opinion of the justices of the Supreme Court or a majority of them shall be a protection to the officers and departments of the state acting in accordance therewith in the same manner and to the same extent as opinions of the Attorney General of the state; and, in the event of a conflict between the opinions of the Attorney General and the opinion of the justices of the Supreme Court rendered in accordance with this article, the opinion of the justices of the Supreme Court shall take precedence and prevail. All opinions of the justices of the Supreme Court heretofore rendered in accordance with this article shall have the protective force and effect provided for in this article.

Ala. Code sec. 12-2-10, 11, and 12 (1995)

Colorado

The supreme court shall give its opinion on important questions upon solemn occasions when required by the governor, the senate, or the house of representatives; and all such opinions shall be published in connection with the reported decision of said court.

Colo. Const. art. VI, sec. 3

Delaware

(a) The Justices of the Supreme Court, whenever the Governor of this State or a majority of the members elected to each House may by resolution require it for public information, or to enable them to discharge their duties, may give them their opinion in writing touching the proper construction of any provision in the Constitution of this State, or of the United States, or the constitutionality of any law or legislation passed by the General Assembly, or the constitutionality of any proposed constitutional amendment which shall have been first agreed to by two-thirds of all members elected to each House.

(b) The Justices of the Supreme Court may appoint 1 or more members of the Delaware Bar, duly qualified to practice before said Court, for the purpose of briefing or arguing the legal issue submitted by the Governor or General Assembly.

(c) If the Governor should request an advisory opinion from the Court, he shall, within 5 days, notify the leadership of both Houses by sending them a copy of such request. If the General Assembly should request an advisory opinion from the Court, The Speaker of the House and the President Pro Tempore of the Senate shall within 5 days notify the Governor by sending him a copy of such request.

(d) Upon receipt of such advisory opinion from the Supreme Court the Governor or General Assembly shall, within 5 days, notify the opposite party by sending a copy of such advisory opinion.

Del. Code Ann. tit. 10, sec. 141(a), (b), (c)

Florida

The governor may request in writing the opinion of the justices of the supreme court as to the interpretation of any portion of this constitution upon any question affecting his executive powers and duties. The justices shall, subject to their rules of procedure, permit interested persons to be heard on the questions presented and shall render their written opinion not earlier than ten days from the filing and docketing of the request, unless in their judgment the delay would cause public injury.

Fla. Const. art. IV, sec. 1(c)

Maine

The Justices of the Supreme Judicial Court shall be obliged to give their opinion upon important questions of law, and upon solemn occasions, when required by the Governor, Senate, or House of Representatives.

Me. Const. art VI, sec. 3

Massachusetts

Each branch of the legislature, as well as the governor or the council, shall have the authority to require the opinions of the justices of the supreme judicial court, upon important questions of law, and upon solemn occasions.

Mass. Const. pt. II, ch. 3, art. 2

Michigan

Either house of the legislature or the governor may request the opinion of the supreme court on important questions of law upon solemn occasions as to the constitutionality of legislation after it has been enacted into law but before its effective date.

Mich. Const. art. III, sec. 8

New Hampshire

Each branch of the legislature as well as the governor and the council shall have the authority to require the opinions of the justices of the supreme court upon important questions of law and upon solemn occasions.

N. H. Const. pt. II, art. 74

Rhode Island

The judges of the supreme court shall give their written opinion upon any question of law whenever requested by the governor or by either house of the general assembly.

R. I. Const. art. X, sec. 3

South Dakota

The Governor has authority to require opinions of the Supreme Court upon important questions of law involved in the exercise of his executive power and upon solemn occasions.

S. D. Const. art. V, sec. 5

APPENDIX } B

A Note on Advisory Opinions Outside the United States

Many foreign jurisdictions permit advisory opinions, and many others prohibit them. There is no consistent pattern. Among common law nations, for example, Canada permits them and Australia does not. Given the manifold and complex differences among the many foreign jurisdictions with advisory opinions, it necessarily remains beyond the scope of this book to attempt a comparative study. In Canada, to take that as a brief example, the Supreme Court has "reference" jurisdiction, under which the federal government (the executive) may refer questions to the Court for advice. The reference authority is statutory, originally provided for in the Constitution Act of 1867, Section 101, enacted the year the Dominion of Canada was created, but now incorporated in the Supreme Court Act, section 53. References may be made to the Court on the constitutionality of federal or provincial legislation, and on the powers of Parliament or of the provincial legislatures or executives. The provincial legislatures may similarly enact laws permitting references to their respective Courts of Appeal, and all have done so.[1]

The references of the Canadian Supreme Court are binding judgments of the Court. The Court has interpreted its advisory duty narrowly. The constitutionality of the duty has still been debated but never successfully challenged.[2] References are relatively infrequent, averaging one every few years. The Court is obliged to answer any properly

---

[1] Discussion of the Canadian reference system is based on the Supreme Court Act, R.S.C. 1985, c. S-26, sec. 53; and on Department of Justice [of Canada], BACKGROUNDER ON REFERENCES TO THE SUPREME COURT OF CANADA (2003). (Retrieved from the website of the Canadian Department of Justice, June 1, 2004). On Canadian advisory opinions, see generally James L. Huffman & Mardi Lyn Saathoff, *Advisory Opinions and Canadian Constitutional Development: The Supreme Court's Reference Jurisdiction*, 14 MINN. L. REV. 1251 (1990). For a comparative, if dated, review of Canadian and American advisory opinions, see J. F. Davidson, *The Constitutionality and Utility of Advisory Opinions*, 2 U. TORONTO L.J. 254 (1937).

[2] *See* Huffman & Saathoff, *Advisory Opinions*, 1257, 1261–64.

presented reference in an opinion giving "the reasons for each answer, and the opinion shall be pronounced in like manner as in the case of a judgment on an appeal to the Court, and any judges who differ from the opinion of the majority shall in like manner certify their opinion and their reasons."[3] Briefs and oral argument are routine, though at the Court's discretion. In exceptional circumstances the Court may hear witnesses.

A prominent example of a reference concerned whether Quebec Province had the constitutional right, on the basis of its own referendum, to secede unilaterally from Canada. Quebec's Governor in Council (the provincial government) referred to the Supreme Court several related questions in 1996. The Court advised that Quebec may not secede solely on its own determination. In Canada's federal system, the Court said, secession of a province requires that the province engage in negotiations with the other provinces, whose rights and obligations must be taken into account. On the other hand, the other provinces of the Canadian federation may not "deny the right of the government of Quebec to pursue secession should a clear majority of the people of Quebec choose that goal," presuming the interests of the other provinces were adequately addressed.[4]

An amicus curiae in this reference proceeding challenged the constitutionality of the Supreme Court's authority to give advice, but the Court held that a court of appeal may "properly undertake other legal functions, such as the rendering of advisory opinions. There is no constitutional bar to this Court's receipt of jurisdiction to undertake an advisory role."[5]

The major international courts, playing an increasingly prominent role in international affairs, have always had "an extensive advisory competence."[6] Jaconelli suggests two reasons for the pervasiveness of advisory opinions in international courts. First, litigation is less frequent than in municipal law, "and the opportunities for thereby clarifying the law are correspondingly reduced." Second, the parties in international courts are states, so that the "difficulties of enforcing coercive decrees against such subjects" give advisory opinions "a peculiar importance."[7]

---

[3] Supreme Court Act, sec. 53 (4).

[4] *In the Matter of Section 53 of the Supreme Court Act, R.S.C., 1985, c. S-26; And in The Matter of a Reference by the Governor in Council Concerning Certain Questions Relating to the Secession of Quebec from Canada, as Set Out in Order in Council P.C. 1996-1497, dated the 30th day of September, 1996* [1998] 2 S.C.R. 217. (Retrieved from the website of the Supreme Court of Canada, Aug. 16, 2010.)

[5] *Id.*

[6] Joseph Jaconelli, *Hypothetical Disputes, Moot Points of Law, and Advisory Opinions*, 10 Law Q. Rev. 587, 603 (1985) (including citations to charters and treaties referring to advisory opinion jurisdiction of international courts). Article 47 of the European Convention on Human Rights gives the European Court of Human Rights an advisory opinion jurisdiction. The United Nation's highest court, the International Court of Justice, has the jurisdiction as well. In 2010, for example, the court advised that Kosovo's unilateral declaration of independence from Serbia did not violate international law. *See* Dan Bilefsky, *Kosovo's Declaration of Independence Is Within Law, U.N. Rules*, New York Times, July 22, 2010. (Retrieved from the website of the New York Times, Aug. 16, 2010.)

[7] Jaconelli, *Hypothetical Disputes*, 603.

APPENDIX } C

Annotated Bibliography

This bibliography offers a complete annotated listing of law journal articles appearing from 1885 through 2010 on state supreme court advisory opinions. Included also is a selection of articles on purported advising by federal courts and on advisory opinions in foreign jurisdictions.

Albertsworth, E. F. *Advisory Functions in the Federal Supreme Court*, 23 GEORGETOWN LAW JOURNAL 643 (1935).

This New Deal–era article supports an amendment to the U. S. Constitution to require the Supreme Court Justices to advise the other branches. Albertsworth points up the problems with retrospective judicial review, and argues that dissents and dicta are in fact advisory in nature, so that a distinct advisory duty is not a radical change.

Allen, C. K. *Administrative Consultation of the Judiciary*, 47 LAW QUARTERLY REVIEW (1931).

In this reply to Wade's article favoring English judges advising the executive in order to increase executive efficiency in an age of bureaucracy, Allen argues that it "is exactly from the executive officer's efficiency and zeal that we must save ourselves." An advisory opinion for Allen is "judgment disguised as opinion," and "it is not easy to see the advantage of imposing this additional [advisory] duty on judges."

Anonymous. Note, 3 HARVARD LAW REVIEW 228 (1889).

A discussion of the Massachusetts Supreme Judicial Court's recent (1889) refusal to answer a request for an advisory opinion. The author raises the question of whether the justices have the right to refuse in light of the mandatory language of the state constitution's advisory opinion clause. The author concludes that the justices may refuse only if the inquiry "is not within the terms of the constitution" (which refers to rendering advice on "important questions" and on "solemn occasions"), but it is for the legislature, not the justices, to decide when the question is important or the occasion solemn.

Anonymous. Note, 4 Harvard Law Review 437 (1890).

This two-paragraph note argues that the New York legislature's refusal to take the governor's suggestion to seek advice from the state's high court on a ballot reform bill was correct. Such advice would be improper absent constitutional authority.

Anonymous. Note, *Extrajudicial Opinions*, 10 Harvard Law Review 50 (1896).

Noting that advisory opinions "have been given only with extreme reluctance," the author is critical of them, given as they are without either a hearing or the assistance of counsel, and which "can hardly fail to be prejudicial to parties adversely interested, and to influence officials of lower tribunals, as well as to bias the subsequent opinions of the judges." If, though, advisory opinions are treated as personal and not official, and kept out of the official record, then the objections disappear.

Anonymous. Comment, *Advisory Opinions*, 21 Yale Law Journal 83 (1911).

A note showing that the early English judges gave advisory opinions reluctantly, more "from reverence, respect and subordination to the King than from a sense of duty as judges." The writer reviews several instances of requests from the king or House of Lords for advisory opinions.

Anonymous. Note, *Constitutional Law—Powers of the Judiciary—Obligation of the Courts to Give Advisory Opinions*, 26 Harvard Law Review 655 (1912).

Noting that advisory opinions are typically given without hearing and often with imperfect knowledge of the facts, the author argues that "[t]hese considerations, together with a feeling of jealousy for the independence of the judiciary, have often caused the judges . . . to be reluctant to give such opinions."

Anonymous. Note, *Duty of the Court to Give Advisory Opinions*, 2 Massachusetts Law Quarterly 542 (1917). (Author is cited as Frederick Grinnell in Aumann (1937), at 33.)

The note reviews the early history of advisory opinions, including the justices' reluctance to advise, and argues for the use of the "solemn occasion" requirement as a standard for acceptable advisory opinion requests.

Anonymous. Note, *Constitutional Law—Powers of the Judiciary—Advisory Opinions—Obligation of Courts to Give Same*, 34 Harvard Law Review 673 (1921).

Citing a South Dakota refusal to render an advisory opinion, this note argues that the court there is bound to answer advisory opinions. "In refusing to answer, the court flies in the face of the state constitution." The justices may refuse, however, if a request for advice is "patently unreasonable, frivolous, or in excess of the scope of the constitutional provision."

Anonymous. Note, *The Advisory Opinion and the United States Supreme Court*, 5 Fordham Law Review 94 (1936).

This New Deal–era note discusses proposals in Congress to amend the U.S. Constitution to permit or require the Supreme Court to give advisory opinions, the proposals appearing after the Court declared the National Industrial Recovery Act of 1933 (NIRA) unconstitutional in *Schechter v. United States*, with the resulting "waste and confusion." The author supports such proposals and argues that Supreme Court advisory opinions should be binding and so have "the dignity of a decision."

Anonymous. Note, *Advisory Opinions and the Constitutionality of Statutes*, 69 Harvard Law Review 1302 (1956).

The author reviews some criticisms and defenses of advisory opinions, concluding that "careful use" of the opinions may avoid the harm "frequently caused by unconstitutional statutes."

Anonymous. Note, *The Validity of the Restrictions on the Modern Advisory Opinion*, 29 Maine Law Review 305 (1978).

A study of the history and jurisprudence of the advisory opinion in Maine, arguing that the Maine justices, despite the mandatory language of Maine's advisory opinion provision, have restricted the scope of their advising by narrow construction of the phrase "solemn occasion." The note offers several defenses of the Maine justices' assertion of a right not to advise.

Anstead, H. L., et al. *The Operation and Jurisdiction of the Supreme Court of Florida*, 29 Nova Law Review 431 (2005).

This overview of the Florida supreme court (one of whose four authors was then the present chief justice and another a former chief justice) includes a section on advisory opinions, which is limited to a brief review of advisory opinion jurisprudence in Florida.

Aumann, F. R. *The Supreme Court and the Advisory Opinion*, 4 Ohio State Law Journal 21 (1937).

This New Deal–era study of proposals to require the U. S. Supreme Court to give advisory opinions focuses on the long delay between the passage of a law and the Court's declaring it unconstitutional, an issue raised by the then-recent rulings on the unconstitutionality of New Deal legislation. Aumann reviews examples of the long delays but concludes that the harm of advisory opinions outweighs the good: "the disadvantages of advisory opinions are numerous."

Bamberger, M. A. Reckless Legislation: How Lawmakers Ignore the Constitution (Rutgers University 2000).

This book has a section on advisory opinions (169–83), in which the author argues that the use of advisory opinions supports his view that legislatures knowingly pass unconstitutional legislation for political reasons. Further, "the benefits of the advisory opinion practice are generally outweighed by its practical problems."

Barry, J. T. *The Council of Revision and the Limits of Judicial Power*, 56 University of Chicago Law Review 235 (1989).

A study of the history of proposals for a council of revision made at the 1787 convention and in New York, to serve as an initial reviewer of a statute's constitutionality. The convention in Philadelphia rejected the proposal "because of the dangers of involving judges in the lawmaking process."

Bender, T. R. *Rhode Island's Public Importance Exception for Advisory Opinions: The Unconstitutional Exercise of a Non-Judicial Power*, 10 Roger Williams University Law Review 123 (2004).

The author is critical of the Rhode Island justices for too freely waiving, or simply ignoring, their established restrictions on the ground of purported public importance. He argues that "on every occasion the justices issue an advisory opinion pursuant to that [public importance] exception, they act outside their constitutional authority; that is, they engage in an unconstitutional exercise."

Bledsoe, M. M. *The Advisory Opinion in North Carolina: 1947 to 1991* at 70 North Carolina Law Review 1853 (1992).

North Carolina's justices are unusual in that they have rendered advisory opinions with neither statutory nor constitutional authority. This study of the state's advisory opinions concludes that they should be discontinued. (The justices have not given advisory opinions since 1985, stating that the opinions violate the state constitution's separation of powers clause.)

Burden, K. "State Constitutional Law – Separation of Powers – A "Judicial Trigger Provision" violates the Kansas Constitution's Separation of Powers Doctrine by Requiring Courts to Issue an Advisory Opinion," 40 *Rutgers Law Journal* 825 (2009).

An analysis and criticism of *State ex rel. Morrison v. Sebelius*, which ruled that a Kansas statute's "judicial trigger" provision was unconstitutional since it required the state supreme court to give an advisory opinion, a violation of separation of powers. The article argues that the opinion did not adequately rely on state case law, but merely adopted "the federal case or controversy requirement, without any searching analysis of state constitutional pedigree on the issue."

Calogero, P. F. *Advisory Opinions: A Wise Change for Louisiana and Its Judiciary?*, 38 Loyola Law Review 329 (1992).

Calogero opposes giving the Louisiana supreme court justices advisory authority. The article, whose author was then chief justice in Louisiana, was prompted by a bill introduced in 1990 that would require the justices to render advice on request of a majority of either house of the legislature, on constitutional questions of legislative powers regarding revenue and finance. The article reviews arguments for and against advisory opinions.

Carberry, C. M. *The State Advisory Opinion in Perspective*, 14 FORDHAM LAW REVIEW 81 (1975).

An extensive analysis of the role advisory opinions have played in the advisory states from 1960 to 1973. While finding advisory opinions reasonably acceptable, the author concludes that it is not likely that other states will adopt supreme court advisory opinions.

Clovis, P. C. and C. M. Updegraff. *Advisory Opinions*, 13 IOWA LAW REVIEW 188 (1927).

Arguing that "a large percentage" of laws passed each year is unconstitutional and that such laws adversely affect "important social and economic interests," the authors favor the advisory opinion as preventative justice—a logical means "of minimizing unconstitutional acts through the expertise of the justices."

Dahlquist, R. P. *Advisory Opinions as Extrajudicial Activity and Judicial Advocacy: A Historical Perspective*, 14 SOUTHWESTERN UNIVERSITY LAW REVIEW 46 (1983).

A history of the U. S. Supreme Court's relation to advisory opinions, with focus on *Hayburn's Case* and on the Court's 1793 refusal to advise the president. It discusses purported instances of the Court's informal advising and looks at the proposed New Deal legislation to give the Court advisory authority.

Davidson, J. F. *The Constitutionality and Utility of Advisory Opinions*, 2 UNIVERSITY OF TORONTO LAW JOURNAL 254 (1937).

A comparative review of the advisory opinion in Canada and the United States, especially of its utility with respect to issues regarding trade and commerce. The author's focus is on the need for factual details in court opinions on these issues, arguing that the advisory function is "seriously handicapped" by the lack of such facts in a court's review of legislation on trade and commerce.

Dubuque, H. A. *The Duty of Judges as Constitutional Advisors*, 24 AMERICAN LAW REVIEW 369 (1890).

This early article on advisory opinions argues that the Massachusetts justices have no right to refuse to render advice in light of the mandatory language of the Massachusetts constitution's advisory opinion provision. The justices' sudden first refusal to advise in 1877 (122 Mass. 160), ninety-seven years after adoption of the provision in Massachusetts, was not permissible: "The obligation to answer is absolute."

Edsall, P. W. *The Advisory Opinion in North Carolina*, 27 NORTH CAROLINA LAW REVIEW 297 (1949).

A comprehensive study of advisory opinions in North Carolina, where the justices have rendered advice without either statutory or constitutional authority, but rather as a "duty of courtesy and respect." Edsall observes that "the advisory function has become a powerful factor in legislation and administration" and concludes that "advisory opinions are certainly entitled to such weight as their intrinsic merit warrants."

Ellingwood, A. R. DEPARTMENTAL COOPERATION IN STATE GOVERNMENT (Macmillan 1918).

This book, the only book (before the present one) devoted to state supreme court advisory opinions, is a full and comprehensive treatment of the advisory opinion, even to inclusion of a list of all state advisory opinions rendered to 1917. Ellingwood, an enthusiastic proponent of the advisory opinion, viewed it as a "useful instrument" of government that supported interbranch cooperation. A contemporary reviewer, however, opined in the *American Political Science Review* (vol. 13, p. 155) that Ellingwood attached "too great an importance to the influence of advisory opinions in promoting cooperation."

Emery, L. A. *Advisory Opinions from Justices*, 2 MAINE LAW REVIEW 1 (1908).

In the first of two articles on the Maine constitution's advisory opinion clause, then chief justice Emery called for the sparing use of "an undesirable provision, . . . if indeed it must be used at all." He agreed that, at best, the provision should be seen as "an extraordinary power to be exercised only in extreme cases, in grave crises."

________. *Advisory Opinions of the Justices. No. II*, 11 MAINE LAW REVIEW 15 (1917).

In his second article on advisory opinions, Emery, now former chief justice, still "deprecates" Maine's advisory opinion provision. The article discusses the extent to which the justices may refuse to advise in view of the mandatory language of Maine's provision, by which advising is "required" of the justices. Noting that the requesting authority must ask only "important questions" and only on "solemn occasions," Emery argues that the requesting authority, not the justices, have the "right to determine both the importance and the occasion."

Entman, J. F. *Flawed Activism: The Tennessee Supreme Court's Advisory Opinions on Joint Tort Liability and Summary Judgment*, 24 MEMPHIS STATE UNIVERSITY LAW REVIEW 193 (1994).

The Tennessee supreme court has no authority to render advisory opinions, but Entman argues that the court's activism, while itself commendable, "is flawed" by the court's "penchant for issuing advisory opinions. At times the court's enthusiasm for lawmaking seems to eclipse its duty to resolve the dispute before it," resulting in decisions unsatisfactory either as law or as dispute resolution. Entman call for the court to "honor one of the first principles of judicial restraint—the rule against advisory opinions."

Farina, C. R. *Supreme Judicial Court Advisory Opinions: Two Centuries of Interbranch Dialog*, in THE HISTORY OF THE LAW IN MASSACHUSETTS: THE SUPREME JUDICIAL COURT 1692–1992 at 353–92 (R. K. Osgood ed., Supreme Judicial Court Historical Society 1992).

In this historical analysis of advisory opinions in Massachusetts, Farina observes that Massachusetts has undertaken a "a two-century experiment in what many have said to be impossible: a constitutional commitment to *both* a government of separated powers *and* a judiciary that renders advisory opinions to the legislature and executive." Advisory opinions serve to resolve disputes about constitutional rights and obligations that the "political process is not very good at resolving."

Field, O. P. *The Advisory Opinion—An Analysis*, 24 Indiana Law Journal 203 (1949).

A study of advisory opinions in five states (Colorado, Maine, Massachusetts, New Hampshire, South Dakota) that looks into the extent to which the advisory opinion remedies purported defects of judicial review of legislation after enactment into law. All advisory opinions rendered in these states are analyzed by such criteria as time, subjects of the requests, dissents, and lengths of the opinions. Field concludes that the ordinary process of judicial review is "seriously inadequate." The advisory opinion is a "supplement to" but not a substitute for judicial review.

Frankfurter, F. *A Note on Advisory Opinions*, 37 Harvard Law Review 1002 (1924).

This response to Manley Hudson's favorable view of advisory opinions attacks them as "ghosts that slay." It is, for Frankfurter, "extremely dangerous to encourage extension of the device of advisory opinions to constitutional controversies." Denying that "constitutionality is a fixed quantity," Frankfurter asserts that concepts like liberty and due process derive meaning "only if referred to adequate human facts. Facts and facts again are decisive."

Grinnell, F. W. Letter, 10 American Bar Association Journal 522 (1924).

In this brief letter Grinnell opposes proposals to give the U. S. Supreme Court advisory opinion duties. The Court "would be overwhelmed with a constant stream of questions on every conceivable subject." The legislative tendency "to 'pass the buck' to the Court and then abuse it for its decisions would be enormously increased." While advisory opinions may have value in some states, they would be "a serious mistake for the nation." Published the same year as Hudson's article supporting advisory opinions and as Frankfurter's attack on them, the letter may be a response to Progressive movement calls for making the Court a "cooperative body."

Hagemann, J. F. *The Advisory Opinion in South Dakota*, 16 South Dakota Law Review 291 (1971).

An analysis and evaluation of the South Dakota justices' sparing use of the advisory opinion. The justices express the "standard objections" to advisories and base their limitations on advising on those objections, despite South Dakota's constitution requiring the justices to render advisory opinions to the governor. Hagemann concludes that as long as the justices continue to respect the advisory opinion process, the process can be "a useful device in the scheme of South Dakota government."

Healy, T. *The Rise of Unnecessary Constitutional Rulings*, 83 North Carolina Law Review 847 (2005).

Healy undertakes an extensive review of the U. S. Supreme Court's rendering of unnecessary constitutional rulings, especially in cases of qualified immunity, habeas corpus, Fourth Amendment good faith searches, and harmless error. He argues that this is "part of a larger trend toward judicial supremacy." Addressing the question of whether such rulings violates Article III's ban on advisory opinions, he concludes that they do.

Hoffman, R. K. *Why Not Advisory Opinions for Illinois?*, 31 Chicago-Kent Law Review 141 (1952).

No reason, Hoffman replies. In Illinois "there is ample justification for the use of the advisory opinion." This includes efficiency in Illinois government, "a quality most conspicuously absent in our present system," and the expense and burden of unconstitutional legislation.

Hudson, M. O. *Advisory Opinions of National and International Courts*, 37 Harvard Law Review 970 (1924).

This discussion of advisory opinions at home and abroad favors their use in international controversies. Hudson raises the pragmatic question that, if a ruling on a statute's unconstitutionality applies to the statute in general (and not just to the parties' case from which the ruling arose), then why is the case itself necessary? Allowing American courts to rule on constitutionality of legislation before it is passed could help prevent "legislative stultification."

________. *The Effect of Advisory Opinions of the World Court*, 42 American Journal of International Law 630 (1948).

This 1948 "editorial comment" complains that even informed lawyers claim that advisory opinions of the World Court are seen by all, including the public, as binding judgments. This mistaken view may have developed because some parties, which are usually national governments, have themselves agreed to be bound by the Court's advisory opinions. But this is at their discretion. Hudson insists that the status of advisory opinions of the World Court (under the United Nations in 1948) had not changed since the Court's creation under the League of Nations (dissolved in 1946). The court's advisory opinions are nonbinding, intended only as guidance to the parties seeking advice.

Huffman, J. L. and M. L. Saathoff. *Advisory Opinions and Canadian Constitutional Development: The Supreme Court's Reference Jurisdiction*, 74 Minnesota Law Review 1251 (1990).

An extensive study of the advisory opinion in Canada, where courts have advisory jurisdiction on both national and provincial levels. By one estimate, the authors note, over 25 percent of leading decisions were made in advisory opinion proceedings.

The authors argue that the "Canadian experience . . . suggests that advisory opinions can prove beneficial" and that their dangers are "far fewer than American lawyers and judges generally assume."

Jaconelli, J. *Hypothetical Disputes, Moot Points of Law, and Advisory Opinions*, 10 Law Quarterly Review 587 (1985).

With focus on England and international courts, Jaconelli studies the "theoretical and practical problems posed by an activity which diverges markedly from the judicial role as it is traditionally conceived." He notes that advisory opinions have special value in international courts, where there is less frequent litigation and so less opportunity to clarify law thereby, and where the parties are sovereign states against whom enforcing coercive decrees is difficult. The advising powers of international courts, however, tend to be "severely limited."

Jay, S. Most Humble Servants: The Advisory Role of Early Judges (Yale University 1997).

This book offers a comprehensive study of the U. S. Supreme Court's precedent-setting refusal to offer an advisory opinion to the first president. Jay argues that the Court's 1793 refusal was based less on constitutional principles it cites (mainly separation of powers) and more on political considerations, including preventing the Court from becoming embroiled in a major conflict between Congress and the executive over control of foreign affairs. Jay believes that advisory opinions were not incompatible with separation of powers as understood in both England and America in the late eighteenth century, as evidenced by the several states whose early constitutions both mandated separation and provided for advisory opinions. (But see Topf (2001), arguing that the earliest advisory opinion clause, in the 1780 Massachusetts constitution, was included in order to constitutionalize it since advising was likely seen as offending the separation provision.)

Jay, S. *Servants of Monarchs and Lords: The Advisory Role of Early English Judges*, 38 American Journal of Legal History 118 (1994).

In light of England's acceptance of advisory opinions, and its rejection of separation of powers as grounds for banning them, Jay's article presents "a historical picture of a different way of conceptualizing the role of courts in society," where there has been a "long tradition of requiring judges to serve as advisors to the executive and the House of Lords." Jay looks into the origins of the English judges' advising role, stemming in part from judges originally being surrogates and servants of the king. Rendering advice nonetheless declined after 1760, for historical rather than doctrinal reasons.

Kannon, P. M. *Advisory Opinions in Federal Courts*, 32 Richmond Law Review 769 (1998).

Kannon argues that the claim that federal courts are barred from rendering advisory opinions is not accurate. While federal courts may not be compelled to advise, "under circumstances they themselves define, these courts may elect to give advice."

The device by which federal courts may advise include the practice of "assuming without deciding" and dicta, because statements "not necessary to support the decision amount to an advisory opinion." Advisory dicta, Kannon says, may be useful as "guidelines" but risk weakening the judicial process.

Katyal, N. K. *Judges as Advicegivers*, 50 Stanford Law Review 1709 (1998).

The federal judiciary "has used, and should continue to use, a range of interpretive and decision-making techniques to give advice to the political branches and state governments." Despite judicial declarations against advisory opinions "the Justices [of the U. S. Supreme Court] often act to provide advice in their published opinions," typically as dicta, and thereby providing "federal and state governments with ways to avoid constitutional problems and sort out the constitutional issues politically instead of relegating such questions to the judiciary." Advice-giving is "a hidden fourth power for the Court." (The other three are striking down legislation, validating legislation, or doing neither.) See Mikva's response to this article, below.

Kennedy, R. H. *Advisory Opinions: Cautions About Non-Judicial Undertakings*, 23 University of Richmond Law Review 173 (1989).

Kennedy focuses on a 1987 Florida advisory opinion to show that advisory opinions "have the potential to hazard substantive error, to effect a redistribution of governmental authority, and to damage a court." The 1987 opinion was a response to the governor's request for advice on the constitutionality of an already enacted statute. The opinion was rendered despite the court's longstanding bar against advising on enacted statutes. Kennedy discusses the costs of such "largely unexplained" intrusions by the judicial branch.

Marcus, M. *Separation of Powers in the Early National Period*, 30 William and Mary Law Review 269 (1989).

Marcus argues that in the early years of the republic, as the government struggled to get separation of powers doctrine straight, the U. S. Supreme Court's Justices thought of themselves as "acting in two ways: as an institution and as individuals." This division appeared to work well regarding the Justices' relations with the other branches. Hence, as an institution the Court declined to give an advisory opinion to the president in 1793, but individual Justices felt free to give advice to members of the legislature or executive.

McKeever, P. C. and B. O. Perry. *The Case for an Advisory Function in the Federal Judiciary*, 50 Georgetown Law Journal 785 (1962).

This article supports advisory opinions from the federal judiciary because "a measure of preventative jurisprudence is needed in the area of judicial review" in order to minimize the danger of unconstitutional legislation. In light of this need and "the lack of any absolute constitutional prohibition of an advising function, the voluntary acceptance by the

Justices of the Supreme Court of this method of intergovernmental cooperation is justified and indicated." Historically, judicial power no more included judicial review than it did advisory opinions, the former's acceptance and the latter's rejection essentially products of political pressures. Both, the authors, say, are basically similar.

Mikva, A. J. *Why Judges Should Not Be Advicegivers: A Response to Professor Neal Katyal*, 50 STANFORD LAW REVIEW 1709 (1998).

A reply to Katyal's thesis that advice-giving by the federal judiciary would promote democratic values or effective policymaking. Mikva questions the accuracy of Katyal's assertion that judges use dicta to give advice. His "fatal flaw" is the "notion that there is something in judges' status or stature that qualifies them to give . . . advice to elected officials." Katyal's article is cited above.

Persky, J. D. *Ghosts That Slay: A Contemporary Look at State Advisory Opinions*, 37 CONNECTICUT LAW REVIEW 1155 (2005).

Persky's comprehensive study of state advisory opinions argues that "judicious use of the modern advisory opinion has strengthened, not weakened, representative government by preventing both public reliance on facially unconstitutional legislation and governmental expenditures on programs or initiatives likely to face a successful challenge." Attacks on advisory opinions "are unsupported by the contemporary data." Persky offers an extensive analysis of the problems related to the purportedly nonbinding nature of advisory opinions.

Rhodes, J. E. *Advisory Opinions*, 6 MAINE LAW REVIEW 28 (1912).

Critical of advisory opinions, Rhodes believes that the judiciary should not be required to "pass upon either public or private rights by ex parte proceedings." The objections to advisory opinions, chiefly separation of powers and due process, are evidence that requiring justices to advise "is undesirable in our fundamental law."

Robinson, W. H. *Limitations upon Legislative Inquiries under Colorado Advisory Opinion Clause*, 4 ROCKY MOUNTAIN LAW REVIEW 237 (1932).

An analysis of the nine restrictions on advisory opinions imposed by the Colorado supreme court, "in its reluctance to give advisory opinions." Robinson concludes that the restrictions are "tantamount to saying that the court will refuse to entertain a question whenever the judges in their discretion decide not to answer it," and will give advisory opinions "only when the court so desires."

Sands, C. D. *Government by Judiciary—Advisory Opinions in Alabama*, 4 ALABAMA LAW REVIEW 1 (1951).

Sands reviews advisory opinion practice in Alabama, one of the two states (with Delaware) that provide for them by statute rather than by constitution. The supreme courts in both states, Sands notes with some skepticism, have ruled the statutes constitutional because advisory opinions are not judicial functions, so that the justices, not acting judicially, are free to "go fishing, play golf, or advise the governor and legislature on matters on constitutional law." He reviews the justices' restrictions on rendering advisory opinions, established soon after the statute passed in 1923, and discusses the extent to which advisory opinion practice in Alabama adheres to the restrictions.

Sirvet, E. and R. B. Bernstein. *John Jay, Judicial Independence, and Advising Coordinate Branches*, 2 JOURNAL OF SUPREME COURT HISTORY 23 (1996).

Before the U. S. Supreme Court's 1793 refusal to advise the executive, the Justices frequently responded to requests for advice. This article reviews several instances of Chief Justice Jay advising President Washington, usually in an exchange of letters. Jay, however, declined to advise where he thought it inappropriate or unnecessary. The 1793 request for advice, regarding Washington's neutrality policy in the war between France and Britain, was more formal, and for reasons not entirely clear, the Justices responded by refusing to advise based on concerns about separation of powers, a position they have maintained ever since.

Smiljanich, T. A. *Advisory Opinions in Florida: An Experiment in Intergovernmental Cooperation*, 24 UNIVERSITY OF FLORIDA LAW REVIEW 328 (1972).

Smiljanich examines advisory opinion practice in Florida, concluding that the justices there "are expanding their power to render advisory opinions," mainly in order to "reach vital questions of governmental importance." The author favors the advisory opinion as an efficient solution regarding problems of executive relations with the judiciary and legislature.

Smith, A. K. *Advisory Opinions in North Carolina*, 7 NORTH CAROLINA LAW REVIEW 449 (1929).

This brief note discusses advisory opinions in North Carolina, where the justices have neither constitutional not statutory warrant to advise, but have occasionally done so anyway despite the state constitution's separation of powers provision, as an act of "courtesy and respect," as the justices put it in 1870. This view, Smith says, "has persisted." Smith was writing in 1929. A half-century later the justices would decline to continue rendering advice.

Stevens, G. N. *Advisory Opinions—Present Status and an Evaluation*, 34 WASHINGTON LAW REVIEW 1 (1959).

Stevens offers a general analysis of advisory opinions in all the advisory states together with an account of refusals to advise in ten nonadvisory states. He concludes that advisory opinions' "disadvantages far outweigh its actual and potential advantages."

Thayer, J. B. *Advisory Opinions*, in LEGAL ESSAYS 42–59 (1908; first published 1885).

In 1883 the Rhode Island justices advised the senate that the state constitution does not permit calling of a constitutional convention (14 R.I. 649). Former chief justice Charles Bradley, apparently concerned about the justices' authority to offer such advice, asked Thayer, then at Harvard Law School, to write on advisory opinions, and this piece first appeared in 1885 as an appendix in Bradley's pamphlet on constitutional amendments in the state. In this earliest article on the law of advisory opinions, Thayer reviews advisory opinion provisions and their English history, discussing especially the nonbinding nature of advisory opinions in both countries. This emphasis may have arisen from the skepticism about the Rhode Island justices' 1883 advisory opinion (which Frankfurter's article uses as an example of ill-advised advisory opinions). Thayer concludes that "it is of grave importance that the notion of their binding quality should be dispelled."

Topf, M. A. *The Advisory Opinion on Separation of Powers: The Uncertain Contours of Advisory Opinion Jurisprudence in Rhode Island*, 5 ROGER WILLIAMS UNIVERSITY LAW REVIEW 385 (2000).

This article is devoted to a single state supreme court advisory opinion. The opinion addresses the question of whether members of the Rhode Island legislature may, by statute, sit on executive branch boards and commissions or appoint others to do so. The focus is on the fact that rendering this advisory opinion violated the justices' restrictions on advisory opinions, which they evaded by declaring a public importance exception. The article argues that the justices overuse the exception (in the fifteen-year period studied, more than the other nine advisory states put together), impoverishing public discourse and confusing standards for rendering advisory opinions.

________. *The Jurisprudence of the Advisory Opinion Process in Rhode Island*, 2 ROGER WILLIAMS UNIVERSITY LAW REVIEW 207 (1997).

A study of advisory opinion theory and practice in Rhode Island, applying arguments of proponents and opponents of advisory opinions. The article concludes that the Rhode Island justices, like their colleagues in other advisory states, have had doubtful success in protecting the legitimacy of advisory opinions.

________. *The Origins and Early History of Supreme Judicial Court Advisory Opinions in Massachusetts*, 7 MASSACHUSETTS LEGAL HISTORY 21 (2001).

This article attempts to explain the appearance of the first advisory opinion provision in the 1780 Massachusetts constitution, still in effect, especially with respect to why this common and proper practice had to be constitutionalized. The record is very sparse, but the answer appears to be that its purpose was to make the justices, as advisors, exempt from the strict bans on plural office holding. The article also studies the early history of the advisory opinion, tracking how it became widely seen as violating such basic doctrines as separation of powers.

________. *State Supreme Court Advisory Opinions as Illegitimate Judicial Review*, 2001 LAW REVIEW OF MICHIGAN STATE UNIVERSITY—DETROIT COLLEGE OF LAW 101 (2001).

Topf argues that advisory opinions are de facto judicial review, owing in good part to their being binding in effect if not in theory. The justices' claims that their advisory opinions are nonbinding amount to "little more than a jurisprudential fig leaf." As such it is difficult to defend the legitimacy of the advisory opinion process.

Veeder, V. V. *Advisory Opinions of the Judges of England*, 13 Harvard Law Review 358 (1900).

Veeder studies the role of English judges as advisors to the House of Lords. (The Scottish judges rarely, and Irish judges never, have functioned as advisors.) Veeder comments that cases on which the judges advised show "plainly the haphazard way in which the law has been developed," especially given the "relative unimportance of most of these cases."

Wade, E. C. S. *Consultation of the Judiciary by the Executive*, 182 Law Quarterly Review 169 (1930).

Wade argues that the growth in quantity and complexity of law in Britain has in turn resulted in the growth of administrative law, which has created two problems. First is the difficulty of controlling delegated legislation, and second is "encroachment of administrators into the judicial sphere." Wade defends judicial advice to the executive on grounds of the expense and inefficiency of litigation. (C. K. Allen's "Administrative Consultation of the Judiciary" is a reply to Wade.)

Warren, B. W. "Memorial to Arthur Prentice Rugg," 302 Mass. 635 [Supplement] (1940).

A transcript of one of the speeches given in the Massachusetts Supreme Judicial Court as memorial to Chief Justice Rugg and recorded in the Massachusetts *Reports*. Over half the address, without explanation, is devoted to defending advisory opinions, pointing to several advantages. Among them is that advisory justices are not burdened with the presumption of a proposed statute's constitutionality, which provides a "flexibility" that prevents passage of doubtful legislation. Warren notes that during Chief Justice Rugg's tenure some thirty-seven advisory opinions, nearly half of those then given, held measures unconstitutional, a far higher proportion than in litigated cases challenging constitutionality.

Westling, R. W. *Advisory Opinions and the "Constitutionally Required" Adequate and Independent State Grounds Doctrine*, 63 Tulane Law Review 379 (1988).

This article, noting that the "revival of state constitutions" has given rise to debate over the limits of the U. S. Supreme Court's power to review state constitutional decisions, focuses on the doctrine of adequate and independent state grounds as one such limit. Westling argues that the doctrine is based on the advisory opinion ban, and that the advisory opinion rationale underlying the doctrine is a constitutionally required rule arising from Article III.

Wheeler, R. *Extrajudicial Activities of the Early Supreme Court*, 1973 SUPREME COURT REVIEW 123 (1973).

A study of the early (pre-Marshall) Supreme Court's rejection of demands for official but extrajudicial service, in the face of a Congress and a president anxious to adopt the English practice of obliging judges to engage in extrajudicial activity. Wheeler focuses on *Hayburn's Case* (131–39), on various positions of Chief Justice Jay (139–44), and on rendering advisory opinions (144–58). Wheeler concludes that before the Court's 1793 refusal to advise President Washington, the record "is ambiguous as to whether the early Justices looked favorably on advisory opinions," since ex officio extrajudicial activity "was generally accepted," but the role of official advisors to the executive and legislature was apparently seen as more doubtful.

Williams, W. C. *Constitutional Law: Premature Federal Adjudication Through the Plain Statement Rule*, 8 UNIVERSITY OF FLORIDA JOURNAL OF LAW AND PUBLIC POLICY 129 (1996).

Williams argues that the U. S. Supreme Court's decision in *Michigan v. Long*, regarding the doctrine of adequate and independent state grounds, allows the Court to reach issues already resolved on solid state grounds, in effect rendering advisory opinions. *Long* "will increase the propensity of the Court to give non-dispositive adjudications," and in fact "in Supreme Court cases reviewing ambiguous state decisions after *Long*, the frequency of advisory opinions has risen."

APPENDIX } D

A Checklist of Articles Devoted to Advisory Opinions in a Single State

Alabama

Sands, C. D. *Government by Judiciary—Advisory Opinions in Alabama*, 4 ALABAMA LAW REVIEW 1 (1951).

Colorado

Robinson, W. H. *Limitations upon Legislative Inquiries under Colorado Advisory Opinion Clause*, 4 ROCKY MOUNTAIN LAW REVIEW 237 (1932).

Florida

Anstead, H. L., et al. *The Operation and Jurisdiction of the Supreme Court of Florida*, 29 NOVA LAW REVIEW 431 (2005).

Kennedy, R. H. *Advisory Opinions: Cautions About Non-Judicial Undertakings*, 23 UNIVERSITY OF RICHMOND LAW REVIEW 173 (1989).

Smiljanich, T. A. *Advisory Opinions in Florida: An Experiment in Intergovernmental Cooperation*, 24 UNIVERSITY OF FLORIDA LAW REVIEW 328 (1972).

Illinois

Hoffman, R. K. *Why Not Advisory Opinions for Illinois?*, 31 CHICAGO-KENT LAW REVIEW 141 (1952).

Kansas

Burden, K. "State Constitutional Law – Separation of Powers – A "Judicial Trigger Provision" violates the Kansas Constitution's Separation of Powers Doctrine by Requiring Courts to Issue Advisory Opinions," 40 *Rutgers L.J.* 825 (2009).

Louisiana

Calogero, P. F. *Advisory Opinions: A Wise Change for Louisiana and Its Judiciary?*, 38 LOYOLA LAW REVIEW 329 (1992).

Maine

Anonymous. Note, *The Validity of the Restrictions on the Modern Advisory Opinion*, 29 MAINE LAW REVIEW 305 (1978).

Emery, L. A. *Advisory Opinions from Justices*, 2 MAINE LAW REVIEW 1 (1908).

________. *Advisory Opinions of the Justices. No. II*, 11 MAINE LAW REVIEW 15 (1917).

Massachusetts

Farina, C. R. *Supreme Judicial Court Advisory Opinions: Two Centuries of Interbranch Dialog*, in THE HISTORY OF THE LAW IN MASSACHUSETTS: THE SUPREME JUDICIAL COURT 1692–1992 at 353–92 (R. K. Osgood ed., Supreme Judicial Court Historical Society 1992).

Topf, M. A. *The Origins and Early History of Supreme Judicial Court Advisory Opinions in Massachusetts*, 7 MASSACHUSETTS LEGAL HISTORY 21 (2001).

Warren, B. W. *Memorial to Arthur Prentice Rugg*, 302 Mass. 635 [Supplement] (1940).

North Carolina

Bledsoe, M. M. *The Advisory Opinion in North Carolina: 1947 to 1991*, 70 NORTH CAROLINA LAW REVIEW 1853 (1992).

Edsall, P. W. *The Advisory Opinion in North Carolina*, 27 NORTH CAROLINA LAW REVIEW 297 (1949).

Smith, A.K. *Advisory Opinions in North Carolina*, 7 NORTH CAROLINA LAW REVIEW 449 (1929).

Rhode Island

Bender, T. R. *Rhode Island's Public Importance Exception for Advisory Opinions: The Unconstitutional Exercise of a Non-Judicial Power*, 10 ROGER WILLIAMS UNIVERSITY LAW REVIEW 123 (2004).

Topf, M. A. *The Advisory Opinion on Separation of Powers: The Uncertain Contours of Advisory Opinion Jurisprudence in Rhode Island*, 5 Roger Williams University Law Review 385 (2000).

________. *The Jurisprudence of the Advisory Opinion Process in Rhode Island*, 2 Roger Williams University Law Review 207 (1997).

South Dakota

Hagemann, J. F. *The Advisory Opinion in South Dakota*, 16 South Dakota Law Review 291 (1971).

Tennessee

Entman, J. F. *Flawed Activism: The Tennessee Supreme Court's Advisory Opinions on Joint Tort Liability and Summary Judgment*, 24 Memphis State University Law Review 193 (1994).

INDEX